THE COMPLETE PATTERN DIRECTORY

THE COMPLETE PATTERN DIRECTORY

1500 Designs from All Ages and Cultures

ELIZABETH WILHIDE

BLACK DOG
& LEVENTHAL
PUBLISHERS
NEW YORK

Previous Page
Poppy | Maija Isola (for Marimekko) | p.67

Copyright © 2018 by Quarto Publishing PLC

Cover design by Jenna McBride

Cover detail of William Morris's "Strawberry Thief" © Victoria & Albert Museum, London

Cover copyright © 2018 by Hachette Book Group, Inc.

Black Dog & Leventhal Publishers
Hachette Book Group
1290 Avenue of the Americas
New York, NY 10104
www.hachettebookgroup.com
www.blackdogandleventhal.com

Simultaneously published in the UK by Thames & Hudson, 2018

First U.S. Edition: November 2018

Black Dog & Leventhal Publishers is an imprint of Running Press, a division of Hachette Book Group. The Black Dog & Leventhal Publishers name and logo are trademarks of Hachette Book Group, Inc.

The publisher is not responsible for websites (or their content) that are not owned by the publisher.

The Hachette Speakers Bureau provides a wide range of authors for speaking events. To find out more, go to www.HachetteSpeakersBureau.com or call (866) 376-6591.

Print book interior design by Josse Pickard

Library of Congress Control Number: 2018936890

ISBNs: 978-0-316-41823-2 (hardcover); 978-0-316-41838-6 (ebook)

Printed in China

10 9 8 7 6 5 4 3 2 1

Contents

Introduction · 10

Chapter 1: Flora · 14

Garden Flowers · 16

Roses · 16
Chrysanthemums · 20
Daisies · 24
Lilies · 26
Tulips · 30
Pansies · 32
Sunflowers · 34
Lotuses · 36
Anthemia · 38
Anemones · 40
Irises · 42
Marigolds · 46
Peonies · 48
Blossoms · 52
Honeysuckles · 54
Assorted Garden Flowers · 56
Designer Profile: William Morris · 58

Wildflowers · 64

Poppies · 64
Designer Profile: Maija Isola · 66
Dandelions · 68
Daffodils · 70
Clovers · 72
Thistles · 74
Hedgerows · 76
Meadows · 78
Assorted Wildflowers · 80
Style Profile: Arts & Crafts · 82

Multifloral · 84

Designer Profile: C. F. A. Voysey · 86
Designer Profile: Marianne Straub · 94
Style Profile: Art Nouveau · 98

Stylized · 100

Designer Profile: Charles Rennie Mackintosh · 102
Designer Profile: Orla Kiely · 106
Designer Profile: Augustus Pugin · 110

Abstract Floral Motifs	**112**
Damasks	112
Designer Profile: Timorous Beasties	
Alistair McAuley & Paul Simmons	**114**
Specialty: Japanese Katagami & Katazome	118
Generic Floral Motifs	**120**
Rosettes	120
Gardens	122
Sprays	128
Bouquets	130
Designer Profile:	
Phyllis Barron & Dorothy Larcher	**132**
Garlands	134
Sprigs	136
Baskets	138
Flowerpots & Vases	140
Leaves	**144**
Designer Profile: Raoul Dufy	**148**
Designer Profile: William De Morgan	**152**
Designer Profile: Richard Riemerschmid	**158**
Acanthuses	164
Seeds	166
Paisley	**168**
Specialty: Indian Botehs	170
Trees	**172**
Forests	172
Species	176
Fruits	**178**
Orchards	184
Vegetables	**186**
Patterns of Growth	**188**
Branching Designs	188
Designer Profile: Neisha Crosland	**190**
Designer Profile: Tord Boontje	**196**
Vines	198
Designer Profile: Tricia Guild	**200**
Stems	202
Chapter 2: Fauna	**206**
Domestic/Farm Animals	**208**
Dogs	208
Designer Profile: Cath Kidston	**210**
Rabbits	212
Horses	214
Stags	216
Assorted Domestic/Farm Animals	218
Wild Animals	**220**
Elephants	220
Assorted Wild Animals	222
Birds	**224**
Swallows	224
Doves	226
Designer Profile: Marion Dorn	**228**
Cranes	230
Style Profile: Japonaiserie	**232**
Parrots	234
Designer Profile: Josef Frank	**238**
Chickens	240
Peacocks	242
Peacock Feathers	246
Feathers	248
Garden Birds	250
Assorted Birds	252
Reptiles & Amphibians	**258**
Designer Profile: M. C. Escher	**260**
Marine Life	**262**
Fish	262
Crustaceans	266
Shells	268
Assorted Marine Life	270
Insects	**272**
Bees	272
Butterflies	274
Moths	278
Assorted Insects	280
Menagerie	**282**
Zoo	282
Farm	284
Wild	286
Designer Profile:	
Zika Ascher & Lida Ascher	**288**
Assorted Menagerie	290
Stylized Animals	**292**
Specialty: Molas (South American)	292

Skins	294
Mythical Creatures	**298**
Dragons	298
Style Profile: Chinoiserie	**300**
Assorted Mythical Creatures	302

Chapter 3: Geometric	**304**
Linear	**306**
Squares & Rectangles	306
Designer Profile:	
Charles Eames & Ray Eames	**308**
Checkerboard	314
Specialty: Gingham	316
Houndstooth	318
Specialty: Plaid	320
Tumbling Blocks	322
Specialty: Marquetry	324
Specialty: Parquetry	326
Tessellations	328
Triangles	330
Diamonds	336
Designer Profile: Sonia Delaunay	**338**
Hexagons	342
Octagons	344
Stripes	346
Specialty: Neoclassical Stripes	354
Style Profile: Neoclassicism	**356**
Specialty: Mexican Serapes	358
Greek Key or Meander	360
Designer Profile: Anni Albers	**362**
Arrows	364
Chevrons	366
Herringbone	368
Zigzags	370
Designer Profile: Eley Kishimoto	
Mark Eley & Wakako Kishimoto	**372**
Specialty: Ikat	374
Curved	**376**
Circles	376
Designer Profile: Vavara Stepanova	**378**
Spots	384
Ovals & Ogees	388

Scrolls	392
Style Profile: Ancient Egypt	**394**
Spirals & Coils	396
Waves	400
Designer Profile:	
Jack Lenor Larsen	**402**
Lozenges & Cartouches	408
Style Profile: Art Deco	**410**
Scallops	412
Crescents	414
Arabesques	416
Medallions	418
Quatrefoils & Trefoils	420
Grids & Knots	**422**
Basketweave & Cane Work	422
Trellises & Lattices	424
Designer Profile: Josef Hoffmann	**430**
Crosses	432
Knots	434
Style Profile: Celtic	**436**
Composite	**440**
Diaper Designs	440
Designer Profile: Enid Marx	**442**
Moorish/Islamic Tiles	444
Style Profile: Islamic	**446**
Specialty: Iznik Tiles	450
Specialty: Azulejo	452
Specialty: Suzani	454
Specialty: Samoan Tapa Cloth	456
Specialty: Fair Isle	458
Specialty: Kente Cloth	460
Specialty: Quilts	462
Specialty: Victorian Military Quilts	464
Assorted Composite	466

Chapter 4: Pictorial	**468**
The Human Figure	**470**
Abstract	470
Feliks Topolski & Henry Moore Designs	472
Folk	474
Parts of the Body	476
Classical	478

Style Profile:

The Classical World (Greek & Roman) 480

Pop 482

Assorted Human Figure 484

Urban 486

Buildings 486

Cityscapes 490

Urban Toile 494

Seaside 496

Designer Profile: Collier Campbell

Susan Collier & Sarah Campbell 500

Rural 502

Designer Profile: Edward Bawden 506

Specialty: Delft 510

Toile de Jouy 512

Style Profile: Baroque & Rococo 514

Travel 516

Wheels 516

Boats 518

Air 520

Spaceships 522

Assorted Travel 524

Household 526

Kitchens 526

Domestic Items 528

Designer Profile: Stig Lindberg 530

Accessories 536

Fans 540

Assorted Household 542

Work 546

Soviet 546

Play 548

Games 548

Sport 550

Music 552

Assorted Play 554

Skies 558

Suns 558

Clouds 562

Snow 564

Signs & Symbols 566

Stars 566

Hearts 568

Typography 570

Designer Profile: Alexander Girard 572

Specialty: Arabic Calligraphy 574

Fleur-de-lis 576

Chapter 5: Abstract 578

Free-Form 580

Painterly Patterns 580

Style Profile: Modernism 582

Designer Profile:

Vanessa Bell & Duncan Grant 588

Specialty: Marbling 590

Specialty: Shibori 592

Specialty: Tie-dye 594

Specialty: Plangi 596

Mobiles 598

Designer Profile: Lucienne Day 602

Specialty: Memphis 604

Style Profile: Postmodernism 606

Scribbles 608

Doodles 612

Specialty: Camouflage 614

Psychedelic 618

Designer Profile: Shirley Craven 620

Assorted Free-Form 622

Designer Profile: Gunta Stölzl 626

Designer Profile: Jacqueline Groag 630

Optical 632

Op art 632

Designer Profile: Barbara Brown 638

Scientific 640

Microscopic Forms/Crystallography 640

Style Profile: Mid-century Modern 642

Cellular 646

Universe 648

Index by Date 650

Index by Designer 656

Index by Country of Pattern Origin 659

Picture Credits 668

Acknowledgments 672

Introduction

Lively or sedate, free-flowing or rigorously ordered, pattern is where color and texture meet and make music. From the first rhythmic marks pressed onto clay vessels and the multiple handprints stenciled onto the walls of caves, to the latest digital designs, a delight in pattern-making has been intrinsic to the decorative arts since time immemorial. Pattern is as present in the details of the built environment as it is in woven and printed textiles; it is as apparent in the original expression of individual artists and designers as in the reiteration of long-standing craft traditions the world over.

Pattern gives pleasure. This is not surprising. Evident in the arrangement of petals on a flower head, in the branching growth of stems and vines, and in the spirals of a seashell, pattern is inherent in the natural world and inextricably linked to our delight in it. At some deep level, it is also how our minds work. Humans are hard-wired to organize what they see and experience into some kind of coherent narrative. In this sense, pattern is expressive of the human need to forge connections, to arrange distinct and disparate elements into compositions that are much more than the sum of their parts.

Throughout history, patterns have come in countless permutations of motif, colorway, and scale. Yet what all have in common is the regularity of repetition, the insistent rhythm that animates a flat surface with a sense of movement and vitality, and gives it depth. A pattern's repeat may be as simple as a regular grid of evenly spaced dots, or as elaborate as a branching design whose diverse elements take time to tease out, where the play of foreground against background is as complicated as a visual dance.

Technology and Process

Pattern is also intimately bound up with technology and process. It is a way of doing things as much as an end in itself. Just as it is possible to sense the way a tool must have been pressed into the malleable surface of damp clay from the marks it left behind, the method of tie-dyeing fabric can be inferred from the concentric rings of color created by the rubber band or string used as a resist, and the origins of certain geometric designs owe much to weaving. Until the Industrial Revolution and the arrival of mechanization, pattern was often created with the application of a great deal of labor and time: hours of stitching, often communal, went into comforters, and the same would

< Grand Thistle | Timorous Beasties | p.75

have been true of a wide range of other printed, woven, or embroidered textiles, the finest and most accomplished of which would have been expensive.

With mechanization, wallpaper and textiles could be produced faster and in much greater quantities. These developments broadened the market and lowered prices, bringing such goods within the reach of many more households. From the late 18th century well into the 20th century, millions of yards of printed cotton calico were manufactured in Lancashire mills and exported around the world.

Another significant technological development was screen-printing, which emerged before World War II and came into widespread use after the conflict. In turn, digitalization has brought a new dimension into play, allowing patterns to be printed on a wide range of different materials and products.

Arts and Crafts Movement

Perhaps the quintessential pattern designer of all time is English textile designer, poet, novelist, translator, and socialist activist William Morris. As the founder of the Arts and Crafts movement, Morris left an enviable creative legacy and has influenced successive generations of designers around the world. Many of his patterns are still in production today, more than a century after his death in 1896; he is probably the one pattern designer with whom most people are familiar. Able to distill the natural world into designs that never stoop to a false realism but which instead retain a sense of flat surface, he had a unique awareness of how to arrange foreground and background elements so that the result was full of vitality.

To modern eyes, Morris patterns might seem elaborate, dense, and even busy, but he was in many ways a great simplifier. The Arts and Crafts movement was based on the honest expression of construction and materials. Morris's golden rule—"Have nothing in your houses that you do not know to be useful or believe to be beautiful"—was not an argument against decoration, but a call for it to be applied appropriately.

Appalled at the poor quality of what was coming out of Britain's factories, Morris consciously rejected mass production in favor of hand-making, which made his goods expensive. His wallpapers and fabrics were block-printed; some are still made the same way. Similarly, he rejected the harsh chemical aniline dyes, which first appeared in the mid-19th century. He used traditional vegetable dyes, which were softer and faded in synchronicity with each other. To this end, he consulted old herbals and conducted experiments with different recipes. In the 1920s, British designers Phyllis Barron and Dorothy Larcher followed in Morris's footsteps, and revived block-printing and vegetable dyeing.

Many architects also turned their hands to designing patterns. For British architects C. F. A. Voysey and Charles Rennie Mackintosh, textile and wallpaper design represented an important supplement to their incomes when opportunities to build were scarce. For artists, too, pattern design could provide an alternative way of making their livings. French painter Raoul Dufy created many designs for dress and furnishing fabrics, often in collaboration with Bianchini-Férier, a leading silk manufacturer in Lyon, France. Ukrainian-born artist Sonia Delaunay designed fabrics for her own revolutionary clothing. In Britain during the 1920s and 1930s, screen-printing fostered such associations because it made short runs of adventurous designs more viable for manufacturers.

One of the finest postwar screen-printers was Czech-born designer Zika Ascher. Together with his wife Lida, he forged alliances with leading artists of the period, persuading Henri Matisse, Henry Moore, Ben Nicholson, and Feliks Topolski to create patterns for dress materials and furnishing fabrics, art that people could both wear and live alongside.

Women's Influence

Pattern design, particularly textile design, is a field in which women have excelled. While women have traditionally been associated with the crafts of sewing, textile printing, and embroidery, their pre-eminence in pattern design may perhaps reflect the fact that they were often excluded from other creative disciplines. Even the Bauhaus, the progressive modernist German art school, banned women from most of its departments, with the notable exception of the weaving workshop. There, Gunta Stölzl and Anni Albers revolutionized textile design with their woven geometrics. Other early pioneers and significant practitioners included Enid Marx, Marianne Straub, Marion Dorn, and Jacqueline Groag. In the postwar period, designers such as Lucienne Day, Barbara Brown, Maija Isola, Shirley Craven, and sisters Susan Collier and Sarah Campbell were hugely influential.

Among the curious aspects of the history of design and decoration are those periods during which pattern has been shunned. Over the centuries, fashions in interior decoration and dress have swung between the heavily ornate and the comparatively simple. The prevailing taste in the 18th century was for interiors that, while they could be richly decorated, were generally lighter and sparer than those of the mid- to late 19th century, a time when patterns ran riot over every surface. Until the 20th century, most households above a certain level of income lived among pattern to some degree.

The rejection of pattern in interior decor on aesthetic grounds rather than religious ones (as was the case for certain

< Ascension | Eley Kishimoto | p.253

faith groups) or as a consequence of financial hardship can be associated with the rise of the Modern Movement. *Ornament and Crime*, a 1913 essay by Czech modernist architect Adolf Loos, influenced successive generations of architects and designers who were eager to shrug off what they saw as the excessive elaboration of the previous generation and who wanted to embrace the pared-back functionalism of the Machine Age. Less became more. The same impulse resurfaced toward the end of the century with the vogue for minimalism, a related approach being expressed more mundanely in Swedish home-accessories company IKEA's advertising slogan: "Chuck out the chintz." For a while, pattern was seen as dated and something to avoid.

Yet pattern was not gone from people's homes for long, and in clothing it never really left the scene. Its re-emergence coincided with a fashion for mid-century modern style. Arguably, the most fruitful period for pattern design in the 20th century was during the immediate postwar years, particularly in the United States, Britain, and Scandinavia. It was as if creative energies pent up by the shortages and adversities of the war suddenly burst into action. New motifs drawn from advances in science and the work of contemporary artists expressed a forward-looking spirit of optimism and faith in the future.

Responding to Fashion

When pattern reappeared around the end of the 20th century, another shift took place. Designers such as Cath Kidston and Orla Kiely applied their designs not simply to clothes, wallpaper, or furnishing fabrics, but across a wide range of products, from changing mats to iPhone covers. Responding to the fashion cycle, patterns began to appear on a seasonal basis.

No book could contain all the patterns that have ever been created: it would have no end. Nevertheless, this directory of pattern, with more than 1,500 images, provides a considerable visual feast. With some exceptions, notably tiles, this book focuses chiefly on textiles, both furnishing and dress fabrics, and on wallpaper, the forms in which most people encounter pattern in their everyday lives.

The directory's thematic rather than chronological arrangement allows comparisons to be made between 18th-century *toiles de Jouy* and Scottish design firm Timorous Beasties' 21st-century subversion of the same genre, as well as revealing the centuries-long persistence of traditional motifs such as the Persian *boteh*, or the way certain types of patterning such as *ikat* crop up in various versions the world over. Supplementary features highlight the work of key pattern designers and describe the characteristics of distinct decorative styles throughout history. Powerful and transformative, pattern has an irrepressible *joie de vivre*.

Pirouette | Tord Boontje | p.406 >

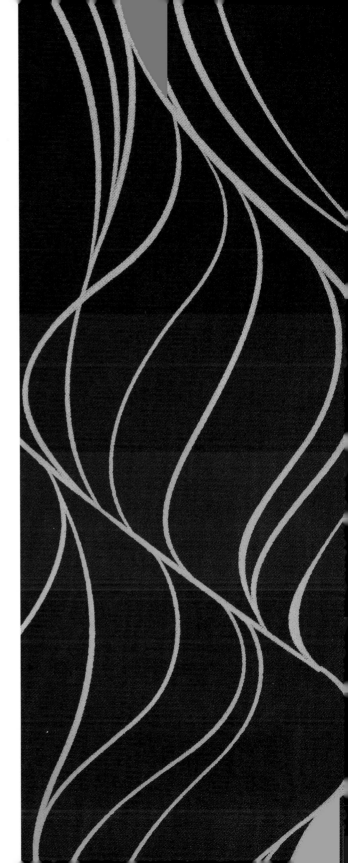

FLORA

01 | Rose | UK | 2014 | Neisha Crosland
This Surflex-printed wallpaper preserves the fine detailing and delicate lines of the original design, with its graphic leaf veining and thorny stems.

02 | Trellis | UK | 1868–70 | William Morris
This early Morris wallpaper pattern, which took twelve blocks to print, was inspired by the rose trellis in the garden of the Red House. Philip Webb drew the birds.

03 | **Happy** | UK | 2005 | Tord Boontje
Boontje's textile designs, produced for the Danish company Kvadrat, give traditional
motifs a contemporary twist, such as this updated rose pattern bristling with thorns.

04 | **Rosetta Glory** | UK | 2009 | Sam Pickard
Devon-based designer Pickard takes inspiration from the natural world. This
upholstery fabric is digitally printed linen.

05 | Rose and Teardrop | UK | 1915–28 | Charles Rennie Mackintosh
The rose was a favorite Mackintosh motif and featured in many of his interiors. Each of the twenty roses in this repeat is different.

06 | Secret Garden | UK | c.1990 | English Eccentrics
Helen and Colin David, the design duo behind English Eccentrics, now practice mainly as artists. This rose-patterned textile was produced in various colorways.

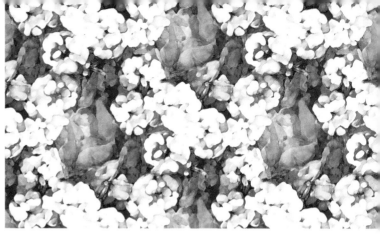

07 | Rosa | UK | 2013 | Imogen Heath
Blowsy and unashamedly pretty, this furnishing fabric by British designer Heath has a nostalgic quality that evokes old-fashioned chintz.

08 | Briar | UK | 1924 | C. F. A. Voysey
Arts and Crafts architect Voysey was a noted designer of pattern. This symmetrical wallpaper design with its light ground is typical of his later work.

09 | Ramblas | UK | 2010 | Designers Guild
This plain weave cotton furnishing fabric features boldly drawn rose blossoms in vibrant colors, strongly contrasted with charcoal outlines.

11 | Mini Mean Roses | UK | 2012 | Eley Kishimoto
This fashion fabric with its angular rose motif, reminiscent of early video games, has the quirky graphic quality characteristic of the design work of Eley Kishimoto.

10 | Dandy (Lemony) | UK | 2011 | Jocelyn Warner
Warner is one of the designers who pioneered the contemporary revival of wallpaper. This rose pattern features overscaled motifs.

12 | Rose | UK | c.1926 | Constance Irving
Produced for William Foxton, this gridded rose pattern, with flower heads studded on a latticed framework, shows the influence of Art Nouveau.

01 | Chrysanthemums papercut | Japan | 19th century

From the collection of British diplomat Sir Rutherford Alcock, this Japanese
cut-paper design dates from when Japanese goods began to reach the West.

02 | Kimono detail | Japan | 19th century
This Japanese patterned fabric is woven from bast fiber using the *kasuri* technique,
a resist-dyeing method similar to *ikat*. The blurriness is a typical feature.

03 | Futon fabric | Japan | 19th century
Chrysanthemums are very prevalent motifs in Japanese floral designs and
symbolize the emperor and the imperial family.

04 | Krysantemer (Chrysanthemums) | Sweden | 1940s | Josef Frank
Produced for the Swedish design firm Svenskt Tenn, this wallpaper design was
created by Austrian-born Frank during World War II, which he spent in New York.

05 | Wallpaper | UK | late 19th century | Charlotte Horne Spiers
Clearly influenced by Japanese patterns, with their fluidity and asymmetry, this airy
design for wallpaper was executed in watercolor.

06 | **Chrysanthemums & Snow Circles** | Japan | 20th century | Teruyo Shinohara
This detail is taken from a *bingata* panel. *Bingata* is a traditional Okinawan
resist dyeing method in which the patterns are typically created using cut stencils.

07 | **Chrysanthemum Blossoms** | Japan | 1882
Among the influential Japanese art and artifacts that began reaching Europe and the
United States during the 19th century were colored woodblock prints.

08 | Chrysanthemum | UK | 1877 | William Morris
In a trade brochure for the Boston Foreign Fair, Morris recommended choosing "Chrysanthemum" as a wallpaper in rooms where "decided patterning" was required.

09 | Wallpaper | USA | 1870–80
Characteristic of the dense patterning of High Victoriana, this machine-printed wallpaper was produced by Imperial Wallcoverings.

01 | Daisy | UK | 1871 | Harrison William Weir

Weir was a well-known Victorian animal artist. He also had a keen interest in gardening, reflected in this wallpaper design for Jeffrey & Co.

02 | Daisy | UK | 1868–70 | William Morris

The daisy was a favorite Morris motif and featured in embroidery produced by the firm and also in printed patterns. This wallpaper was a bestseller for fifty years.

03 | Buttercup and Daisy | UK | 1924 | C. F. A. Voysey
This lighthearted pastel wallpaper, designed by Voysey, was produced by Lightbown, Aspinall & Co. in England.

05 | Furnishing fabric | France | 1936 | François Ducharne
This dense, daisy printed silk crêpe, with its bright saturated colors singing out of a dark ground, has a painterly quality. Ducharne was a top producer of luxury silks.

04 | Dress fabric | UK | 1934
This design was printed on rayon georgette by Tootal, Broadhurst, Lee & Co. In the 1930s, rayon—a synthetic fiber that handles much like silk—was new on the market.

06 | Dress fabric | UK | 1935 | Calico Printers' Association
A printed rayon georgette from the Manchester-based Calico Printers' Association. Founded in the 19th century, the association was an amalgamation of textile firms.

02 | **Dress fabric** | France | **1937** | François Ducharne
Ducharne sold his printed silks throughout France and in the United States. During World War II, when silk was unavailable, the studio's production switched to rayon.

01 | **Water Lily** | UK | **2010** | Cole & Son
This bold large-scale wallpaper pattern reflects the 21st-century vogue for oversized motifs. The neutral colorway tempers the insistence of the design.

03 | **Water lily wallpaper and tiles** | France | **1897** | Eugène Grasset
This lithograph has stencil handcoloring. French-Swiss Grasset was a decorative artist, influential design teacher, and pioneer of Art Nouveau.

04 | **Day Lily** | UK | 1897 | Walter Crane
Crane is best known as an artist and illustrator of children's books, but he also
created many designs for wallpaper in the Arts and Crafts style.

05 | **Dress fabric** | UK | *c.* 1734–35
This 18th-century silk dress fabric, produced in London's Spitalfields, reflects
a growing fashion for patterns inspired by botanical illustrations.

06 | **Golden Lily** | UK | 1897 | John Henry Dearle
Dearle trained under William Morris and became chief designer of Morris & Co. in 1890. This wallpaper pattern was one of many he designed for the company.

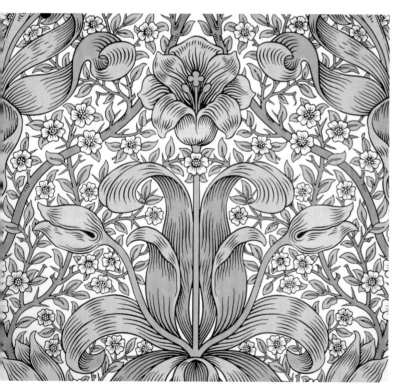

07 | **Lily** | UK | 1873 | William Morris
Morris's Lily wallpaper pattern demonstrates his unparalleled ability to create an intricate design with a finely judged balance of liveliness and repose.

08 | **Summer Lily** | UK | 2012 | Cole & Son
This original wallpaper pattern has been reissued on a smaller scale, with the prints available in a number of colorways suggestive of botanical prints.

09 | The Lily | UK | 1886–90 | Arthur Wilcock
The design of this printed cotton fabric has a sense of depth, with the light-toned
flower heads advancing against a dense background infilled with dots and tendrils.

10 | Les Arums (The Arum Lilies) | France | *c.*1920 | Raoul Dufy
An artist, Dufy was also a textile designer. His association with silk manufacturer
Bianchini-Férier lasted twenty years. This pattern was for furnishing fabric.

11 | Lily (Blue) | UK | 1999 | Jocelyn Warner
Printed in soft, pearly neutrals, this overscale wallpaper pattern evokes the habit
of natural growth as it twines up the wall.

01 | Tulip | UK | 1875 | William Morris

Half of the forty patterns that Morris created for printed cotton date from the 1870s
to 1880s, including this beautifully flowing naturalistic design.

02 | Printed cotton/rayon | UK | 1933 | Calico Printers' Association
With its bold splotches of bright primary colors and loose gestural marks, this fabric pattern has the cheerful vitality of spring tulips.

05 | Furnishing fabric | UK | 1924 | Minnie McLeish
McLeish was a freelance designer who created patterns for the leading British textile firm William Foxton. Strong outlines and jewel-like colors are typical.

03 | Comforter | USA | c.1850–80
Possibly made in either Pennsylvania or New Jersey, this 19th-century cotton quilt features surprisingly contemporary-looking stylized flowers.

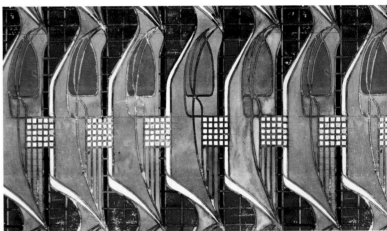

06 | Tulip and Lattice | UK | 1915–23 | Charles Rennie Mackintosh
Mackintosh created more than 120 textile designs toward the end of his career, although it is not known how many of these were put into production.

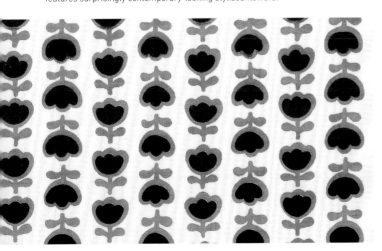

04 | Queuing Tulips | UK | 2001 | Eley Kishimoto
Dating from the year the studio made its first products for interiors, this pattern has bands of tulips in alternating directions. Kishimoto draws all her designs by hand.

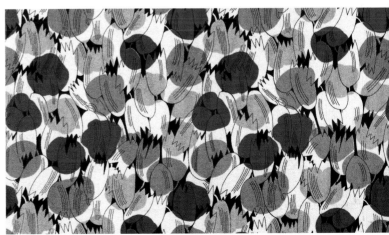

07 | Dress fabric | UK | 1933 | Calico Printers' Association
A painterly approach to pattern design was one of the hallmarks of British textiles between the two world wars. The inky black lines have a calligraphic quality.

01 | **Pansy Stripe** | UK | 2012 | Designers Guild
This demure and pretty cotton furnishing fabric, evocative of wild gardens, is from the Country Fabrics collection of 2012.

02 | **Furnishing fabric** | UK | 1922 | Sidney Haward
This pattern on printed linen was designed for the British textile company Story & Co. British textile producers were prominent during the interwar period.

03 | **Wallpaper** | France | 1930s | André Groult
Groult was a noted French decorator and designer, who is best known for his Art Deco furniture.

04 | **Pansy** | UK | 1945 | Enid Marx
Marx's woven cotton furnishing fabric was designed for the Utility Design Panel and manufactured by Morton Sundour Fabrics, Carlisle.

05 | **Printed cotton** | India | late 18th century to early 19th century
India, the second-largest producer of fiber in the world, has a long tradition of block-printing on cotton.

06 | Wallpaper | USA | 1968 | William Justema
US pattern designer Justema published a number of books on the subject of pattern.
The large pansy motif is typical of overscaled 1960s designs.

32
33

01 | Sunflower Stalks | USA | *c.*1885 | Carrie Carpenter
Pieced and appliquéd cotton comforter by Carpenter of Northfield, Vermont. Quilting
has been called a "democratic art" by folk art expert Robert Shaw.

02 | Sunflower | UK | 1898 | William De Morgan
De Morgan made ceramics and stained glass for Morris & Co., and later had his own
studio. His tiles often made a pattern when placed together.

03 | **Color lithograph** | France | 1902 | Alphonse Mucha
Plate 40 from *Documents Décoratifs* (1902). Czech-born Mucha was an Art Nouveau decorative artist who worked in Paris and was famous for poster designs.

05 | **Kennet** | UK | 1881 | William Morris
One of Morris's "river" chintzes, this pattern is diagonally structured to take account of the fact that the fabric is gathered in folds, unlike wallpaper, which is displayed flat.

04 | **Sunflower** | UK | 1879 | William Morris
This wallpaper pattern displays a characteristic feature of many Morris designs, known as the turnover structure, in which the repeat is mirrored.

06 | **The Cestrefeld** | UK | 1895 | C. F. A. Voysey
This block-printed wallpaper is typical of Voysey's pattern designs, with its natural motif and flowing repeat.

01 | Fleur de Lotus | UK | 2016 | Designers Guild

A delicate, painterly design, recalling botanical illustration, this cotton furnishing
fabric is available in a number of subtle colorways.

02 | **Ceramic tile** | UK | *c.*1880–1900
This tile was made by Minton, a leading British ceramics manufacturer founded in Stoke-upon-Trent in the late 18th century. It shows an Art Nouveau influence.

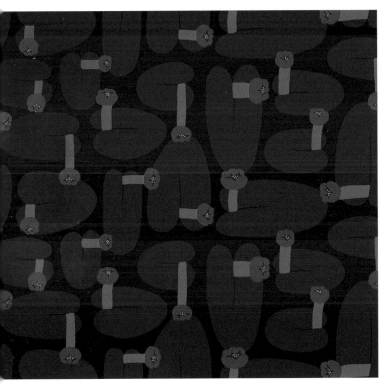

03 | **Mizukusa** | Japan | 2017 | Yuki Tsutsumi of Nuno for Steteco.com
A graphic contemporary interpretation of a water-plant motif, this fabric is supervised by innovative Japanese textile company Nuno for Steteco.com.

04 | **Baudard** | UK | 2010 | Designers Guild
Lotus blossoms and leaves float on a colored ground. The pattern is available as a rug and as a furnishing fabric.

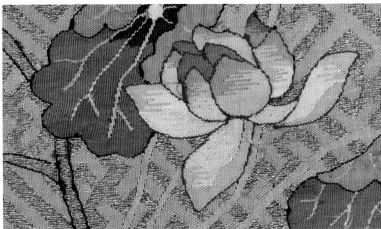

05 | **Textile** | China | 19th century
The detail of lotus flowers over a Chinese meander is from a woven silk tapestry marriage robe dating from the Qing Dynasty.

06 | **Lotus** | UK | 1858 | Owen Jones
This wallpaper pattern is by Jones, a key figure of 19th-century British design. His decorative compendium *The Grammar of Ornament* (1856) was hugely influential.

01 | Wallpaper border | France | 1800–20
This French block-printed lower wallpaper border features the palmette or
anthemion motif, a common feature of architectural and decorative ornament.

03 | Textile fragment | 18th century
This silk fragment of unknown origin is interwoven with metallic thread.
The anthemion motif is one of the most prevalent in decorative art.

02 | Palampore | India | mid-18th century
Palampores or chintz bedcovers were widely made in India for export during the
18th century. This example was produced on the Coromandel Coast.

04 | Wall stencil | UK | 1857–58 | Alexander "Greek" Thomson
Thomson was a leading Scottish Greek Revival architect who worked in a pure Ionic
style. This is a stencil for dining room decoration.

05 | Furnishing fabric | Turkey | 16th to 17th century
This velvet furnishing fabric with gold, silver, and silk pile dates from the Ottoman period. The palmette motif was employed in ancient Egypt.

06 | Textile | India | 18th century
Originating from the Coromandel Coast, this printed cotton chintz bedcover features an anthemion motif.

07 | Wallpaper | 1906–08
There is a distinctly Art Nouveau quality to this wallpaper pattern, with its crisply delineated flowing outlines.

01 | Stjärnmattan (Star Canvas) | Sweden | 1947 | Josef Frank

Frank designed this wallpaper for Svenskt Tenn. Anemones, violets, and flower
tendrils are arranged in a simple pattern in shades of green, blue, and bluish-gray.

02 | Anemone | UK | late 19th century | William Morris
Morris's beautifully observed patterns celebrated common English garden flowers and wildflowers, as seen in this block-printed wallpaper.

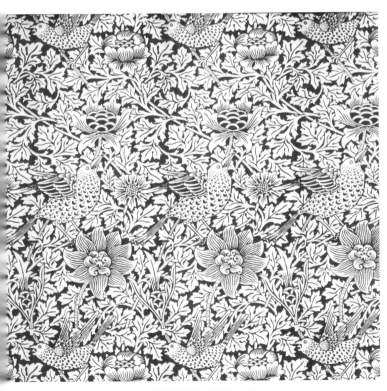

03 | Bird and Anemone | UK | 1881 | William Morris
Like many of Morris's designs for furnishing fabric, this pattern has a turnover structure in which the motif is mirrored.

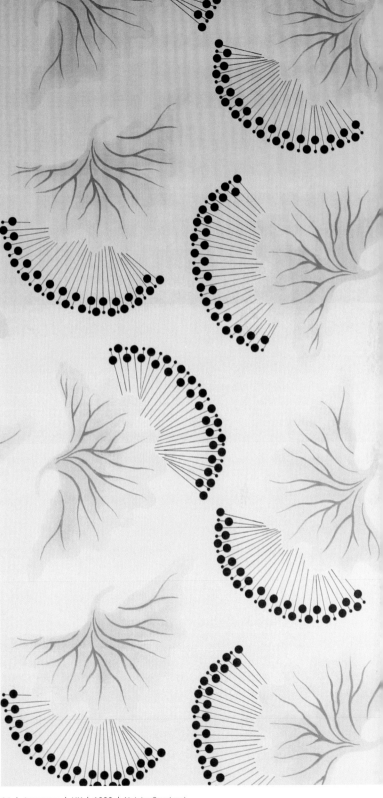

04 | Anemone | UK | 1999 | Neisha Crosland
This flex-printed wallpaper in a neutral colorway has a calligraphic quality to the pattern that recalls Japanese designs.

01 | **Iris** | UK | *c.*1887 | John Henry Dearle
While Dearle's patterns clearly share the characteristic Morris & Co. aesthetic, he developed his own design signature.

03 | **Wallpaper** | USA | 1906–07
This sample of machine-printed wallpaper shows a highly naturalistic design with the flower heads studded against a dense foliate background.

02 | **Wallpaper** | USA | 1906–07
This sample of machine-printed wallpaper was manufactured by the Gledhill Wall Paper Co., which was based in Bristol, Pennsylvania.

04 | **Scarf** | France | mid-19th century
The French silk industry, principally based in Lyon, originally grew out of a demand for cheaper and lighter silks than those produced in Italy.

05 | Antoinette | UK | 2016 | Designers Guild
This cotton satin furnishing fabric was digitally printed. The delicate design features
elegant iris flowers combined with fern fronds.

06 | Irises | UK | 1897 | Eugène Grasset
Grasset was a Franco-Swiss decorative artist. This chromo-lithograph of irises
appeared in his design book *Plants and Their Application to Ornament* (1897).

08 | Iris and Kingfisher | UK | 1877 | Walter Crane
This wallpaper design shows Crane's great skill as an illustrator. The stylized
fish-scale background adds visual texture and reflects a clear Japanese influence.

07 | Color lithograph | France | 1902 | Alphonse Mucha
Plate 36 from *Documents Décoratifs* (1902). Many of Mucha's best-known designs
were promotional posters for plays starring French actress Sarah Bernhardt.

09 | Pallida | UK | 1958 | Mary A. Harper
A screen-printed, glazed cotton furnishing fabric manufactured by leading British
textile company Edinburgh Weavers.

10 | Irises | France | 1897 | Eugène Grasset
A pioneer of Art Nouveau, Grasset was best known for his posters. This color lithograph is from his compendium *Plants and Their Application to Ornament* (1897).

11 | Wallpaper | USA | 1890–1920
The ribbons entwining the iris leaves and stems give the pattern a flowing quality on this block-printed wallpaper sample.

01 | Marigold | UK | 1875 | William Morris
Originally a design for wallpaper, this Morris pattern was subsequently available
in silk, cotton, and linen union furnishing fabrics.

02 | Textile | UK | 1903
F. Steiner & Co., the printing firm that manufactured this furnishing fabric, produced many Art Nouveau designs.

04 | Tiles | Spain | 1880s | Antoni Gaudí
With their marigold and dianthus motifs, these ceramic tiles form part of the decoration of the facade of Casa Vicens in Barcelona.

03 | African Marigold | UK | 1876 | William Morris
The soft subtle colors of Morris & Co. patterns on fabrics such as this printed cotton chintz were derived from Morris's experiments with vegetable dyeing.

05 | Printed cotton | India | 1772
This block-printed floral pattern from Rajasthan treats individual marigold flowers rather like sprigs, sparsely arranged on the ground.

01 | Peony | UK | late 19th century | Charlotte Horne Spiers
A wallpaper design created using watercolor and pencil on paper. Spiers worked as
a freelance artist in the Minton workshops and was a noted watercolorist.

02 | The Oswin | UK | *c.*1895 | C. F. A. Voysey
Produced for Essex & Co., this pattern for a machine-printed paper features diagonally running foliage interspersed with large flower heads.

03 | Temple altar cloth | Japan | 19th century
An exquisite altar cloth made from brocaded silk. In Japanese flower symbolism, peonies represent good fortune, honor, and bravery.

04 | Wallpaper | USA | *c.*1880
A machine-printed wallpaper, manufactured by Howell & Brothers of Baltimore, Maryland. The decorative arts showed a Japanese influence in the late 19th century.

06 | **Shanghai Garden** | 2015 | Designers Guild
Part of a collection inspired by Chinese landscape painting, this vibrant peony and rose patterned wallpaper captures the blowsy nature of the peony.

05 | **Wallpaper** | France | 1832–33
Zuber & Cie is a leading French producer of block-printed wallpapers and fabrics. It was founded in the late 18th century.

07 | **Peony tile** | UK | c. 1877 | Kate Faulkner
Faulkner was an Arts and Crafts designer who worked in different media. Like this ceramic tile pattern, many of her designs were produced for Morris & Co.

08 | **Peony** | **UK** | **1877** | Kate Faulkner
This printed cotton furnishing fabric (originally in pastels) was designed by Faulkner,
who contributed a number of pattern designs to Morris & Co.

01 | **Blue and Gold Cherry Blossom on a Pond** | Japan | 19th century

Cherry blossom is the most popular Japanese flower symbol. This cut-paper design features undulating lines representing water and characteristic asymmetry.

02 | Silk fragment | *c.*1900
Naturalistic shading makes a particular feature of the cup-shaped blossoms while
the repeat is thrown into relief by the dark background.

04 | Sakura Flower | UK | 2014 | Jenny Frean
Frean is the founder of First Eleven Studio, a creative team making printed,
embroidered, and woven designs. This pattern was produced for Sanderson.

03 | Bamboo and Cherry Blossoms | Japan | 1882
This highly stylized color woodblock print, one of the many that began to arrive
in the West in the 19th century, is surprisingly contemporary looking.

05 | Stafford | UK | *c.*1875 | Bruce J. Talbert
This pattern for furnishing fabric was created by Scottish architect Talbert, who was
a well-known designer of Gothic-style furniture.

02 | Pillow cover | UK | 16th to early 17th century
Household goods such as bed linen were often decorated with needlework, like this linen pillow cover with silk embroidery. Designs were taken from pattern books.

01 | Honeysuckle | UK | 1876 | William Morris
This pattern was Mary "May" Morris's favorite, and she called it "the very symbol of a garden tangle." May was William Morris's daughter and a noted designer herself.

03 | Honeysuckle | UK | 1883
A later honeysuckle design produced by Morris & Co. features a more open and airier structure than the pattern of 1876, but still conveys the twining nature of the plant.

04 | Fabric sample | UK | 1889–90 | Arthur Wilcock
Wilcock began his career designing textiles and wallpapers for Liberty in London.
This Morris-inspired design, imbued with movement, has large clusters of flowers.

01 | Furnishing fabric | UK | late 19th century | Lindsay P. Butterfield
A fabric made from woven silk and wool double cloth. Butterfield was strongly influenced by William Morris and C. F. A. Voysey.

03 | Wrapping paper design | 1937
This charming illustration for a wrapping paper design features motifs of small bunches of violets arranged in alternating directions.

02 | Hydrangea | UK | 1960s | John Drummond
Drummond designed this screen-printed cotton satin furnishing fabric for Hull Traders. He produced designs for several British firms, including Sanderson.

04 | Wallflower | UK | 1890 | William Morris
Morris's wallpaper design appeared in a book of samples published by Morris & Co. and printed by Jeffrey & Co. of London.

05 | Crocus | UK | 1903 | George Haité
Haité was an artist, writer, illustrator, and prolific designer in a range of media. This furnishing fabric was printed by G. P. & J. Baker.

06 | Fabric sample | UK | 1890 | Arthur Wilcock
In this Art Nouveau–inspired design with a horizontal emphasis, the flowers appear to grow across the width of the repeat, with thin, stemlike lines providing structure.

07 | Wallflower Stripe | UK | 2009 | Sam Pickard
This digitally printed linen furnishing fabric places scratchy stylized flower heads against a background of attenuated lines suggesting an upward pattern of growth.

William Morris (1834–96)

SEE PAGES > 16, 23, 24, 28, 30, 35, 41, 46, 47, 54, 56, 62, 64, 75, 80, 82, 92, 97, 116, 117, 134, 136, 140, 164, 165, 178, 185, 194, 199, 212, 226, 299

Poet, painter, weaver, typographer, illuminator, a designer of fabric, wallpaper, stained glass, tiles, furniture, tapestries, and carpets, and a socialist campaigner and activist, William Morris transformed the status of decorative art in the 19th century. His revival of block-printing and vegetable dyeing in an age of increasing industrialization, his deep love of nature, and his insistence on truth to materials and hand-crafted work laid the foundations of the Arts and Crafts movement.

Born in Walthamstow, England, Morris was sent to Marlborough College in 1848. From there he went to Oxford in 1853 to study theology. Influenced by the ideas of the Pre-Raphaelite Brotherhood and the writings of art critic and theorist John Ruskin, Morris resolved to devote his life to art.

After his degree, while working on murals at the Oxford Union, Morris met Jane Burden. They married in 1859 and set up home a year later at Red House in Kent, whose medieval-style design Morris had commissioned from his friend Philip Webb (1831–1915). The Red House became the center of a communal artistic life. Pre-Raphaelites Dante Gabriel Rossetti (1828–82) and Edward Burne-Jones (1833–98), and their wives, joined Morris and Jane in decorating and furnishing it, which led to the establishment of a cooperative workshop, Morris, Marshall, Faulkner

and Co., based in London. After a financial reorganization of the business, the Red House was abandoned, and the "Firm" as it became known moved to London premises. By 1875, Morris & Co. was producing distinctive hand-crafted work. Commercial success followed, along with commissions to decorate houses, churches, and public institutions.

The 1870s and 1880s were the most fruitful period for Morris's pattern designs. Many of his best-known fabrics and wallpapers date from this time, including "Tulip" (1875) and "Honeysuckle" (1876). When the workshop moved to Merton Abbey in Surrey, Morris immersed himself in old herbals and experimented with vegetable dyeing, particularly the indigo discharge process. The resulting colors were much softer than those produced by the harsh new aniline chemical dyes. Printing was done by hand, with the designs cut into pearwood blocks, which meant that, despite Morris's insistence on creating "art for all," his products remained expensive. Morris's designs evoke the natural world in such a way as to never abandon a sense of surface or give a false sense of depth. He observed nature intently; his patterns immortalize the wildflowers and garden plants of southern England. They are also imbued with rhythm, with dark foreground elements crossing over and under light background ones; later designs display a turnover structure common in weaving.

Far Left A designer, writer, and social activist, William Morris inspired the Arts and Crafts movement.

Left "Snakeshead" (1876), reputedly Morris's favorite of his own designs, portrays the snakeshead fritillary native to Oxford's water meadows.

Opposite Morris named his popular "Strawberry Thief" (1883) pattern after the thrushes that stole the strawberries in the kitchen garden of his countryside home, Kelmscott Manor, in Oxfordshire, England.

08 | Hyacinth | UK | late 19th century | John Henry Dearle

This wallpaper is characteristic of Morris & Co. designs with its equal emphasis on the twining patterns created by stems and leaves and on individual flower heads.

09 | Hyasintti (Hyacinth) | Finland | 1968 | Anneli Qveflander
Qveflander is a Finnish sculptor and designer noted for her use of strong color.
This fabric was created for Marimekko.

11 | Clematis | UK | 1960 | Mary A. Harper
This pattern for a furnishing fabric, produced by Edinburgh Weavers, overlays light
shapes with dark to create a shimmering sense of movement and translucency.

10 | Clematis | UK | 2007 | Neisha Crosland
The asymmetry of the repeat and the careful placing of the individual elements give
this elegant hand-painted silk wallpaper a Japanese quality.

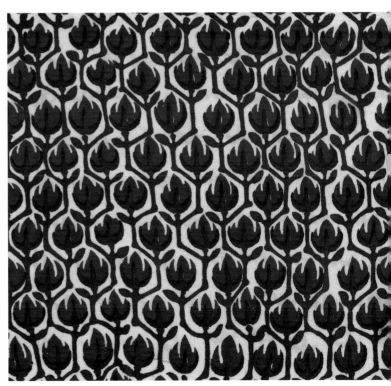

12 | Textile | Germany | 1910 | Richard Riemerschmid
Riemerschmid was a leading figure in the Deutsche Werkstätten and a proponent
of Jugendstil, the German version of Art Nouveau.

13 | **Bachelor's Button** | UK | 1892 | William Morris

This hand block-printed wallpaper features the type of pattern that Morris believed
worked well on flat surfaces.

14 | **The Iolanthe** | UK | *c.* 1897 | C. F. A. Voysey
Designed for Essex & Co., this wallpaper pattern displays Voysey's typically crisp
outlines and balance of dark and light areas.

15 | **Larkspur** | UK | 1874 | William Morris
The "Larkspur" wallpaper pattern dates from one of Morris's most fruitful periods;
it is one of his best-loved designs.

16 | **Textile design** | UK | 1915 | C. F. A. Voysey
Executed in pencil and watercolor, this textile design displays Voysey's skill
at creating stylized, restful patterns.

01 | **Poppy** | UK | 1885 | May Morris
May Morris designed for her father's firm as well as for other companies.
This wallpaper design was produced for Jeffrey & Co.

02 | **Poppies** | UK | 1901 | Lindsay P. Butterfield
A designer in the Arts and Crafts idiom, Butterfield brought a simplicity to patterns, as
seen in this fabric that is reminiscent of C. F. A. Voysey's work.

03 | **Poppy** | UK | 1880 | William Morris
Poppy was one of the wallpapers that Morris recommended for "keeping the wall very
quiet," because it had no "pronounced lines."

04 | **Frieze** | USA | 1900–20
This frieze was machine-printed on oatmeal paper and manufactured by William H. Mairs
and Co. of New York. Borders and friezes introduced contrasting patterns to the wall plane.

05 | **Wallpaper** | USA | 1906–08
The all-over floral pattern of this machine-printed wallpaper on ingrain paper gains
intensity from its range of saturated red tones.

06 | Fabric sample | UK | 1933 | Calico Printers' Association
A printed rayon georgette dress fabric produced by the Calico Printers' Association.
Strong contrasts of red and green, with black and white, add punch to a graphic print.

Maija Isola (1927–2001)

SEE PAGES > 173, 205, 613

Throughout her career, Maija Isola was almost exclusively associated with the Finnish fashion and furnishings company Marimekko, which was virtually unknown outside Finland until 1958, when it exhibited at the World's Fair in Brussels. Then, in 1960, Jackie Kennedy chose several Marimekko dresses to project the youthful style of her husband's presidential campaign. Four years later, Isola's "Unikko" (Poppy, 1964) textile design became one of the most recognizable prints of the Pop era.

Isola was born in Riihimäki, Finland, and studied at the Central School of Industrial Arts in Helsinki. After graduating in 1949, she designed a number of screen-printed cotton fabrics for Printex, a newly founded Helsinki-based textile company. When Marimekko was set up as a subsidiary to promote Printex fabrics through its clothing and furnishings collections, Isola began working directly for them, eventually becoming the company's principal textile designer.

Like many Scandinavian designers, Isola was influenced by nature; folk art was another inspiration. Some of her early work included prints made with the photogram process, using real plants to create the patterns. Most of her best-known designs date from the late 1950s and 1960s and display a strong graphic style, with crisp outlines, flat patterning, and overscale repeats. Her bold sense of color was well in tune with the dynamic spirit of Pop art. Typical Isola designs of the period include "Lokki" (Seagull, 1961), with its dramatic wave forms, and "Kaivo" (Well, 1964), which reveals Isola's fascination with African tribal art.

"Poppy" came about as Isola's response to an assertion by Armi Ratia, Marimekko's founder, that the company did not produce floral patterns, a statement presumably made as a way of dissociating the firm's products from the conservative floral prints of the day. The asymmetric design, clashing colors, and use of graphic contrast made it a success. Since then, "Poppy" has appeared in many different colorways and in countless applications, from household goods to accessories.

Isola, who was something of a free spirit, traveled widely around the world, absorbing cultural influences that enriched her work. As a consequence, her daughter, Kristina (b.1946), was raised largely by her grandmother. In 1964, when Kristina was eighteen years old, she, too, joined Marimekko and collaborated with her mother. In more recent years, Kristina devised a "Mini-Unikko" (Mini-Poppy, 1964) range for children and introduced new colorways for her mother's prints, some fifty of which remain in production. The patterns gained a new lease of life toward the end of the 20th century, with the revival of interest in decorative design. In later life, Isola retired from print design to concentrate on painting.

Top Finnish textile designer Maija Isola photographed at work in 1966.

Above Textile designs by Isola are on display at the Design Museum in Helsinki, Finland. She designed more than 500 fabric patterns.

Opposite Isola's design "Poppy" (1964) was created for Marimekko, the Finnish fashion and furnishings company for which she worked for nearly forty years. Its bright colors, overscaled repeat, and graphic simplicity are characteristic of her work. As soon as it was launched, "Poppy" was an immediate success and became emblematic of the youthful optimism of the Pop era.

01 | Dandelion Two | UK | 2005 | Angie Lewin for St. Jude's

A furnishing fabric created for St. Jude's Prints. Lewin is a British printmaker whose
skeletal plant forms reflect her interest in local landscapes and horticulture.

02 | Dandelion One | UK | 2005 | Angie Lewin for St. Jude's

Lewin designed this furnishing fabric for St. Jude's Prints, which she co-founded
with her husband. The animated dandelion design has a mid-century modern quality.

03 | Dandelions | France | 1897 | Eugène Grasset
Grasset was a leading light of Art Nouveau. This is a chromo-lithograph from his design primer *Plants and Their Application to Ornament* (1897).

04 | Dandelion Clocks | UK | 1953 | Lucienne Day
This design for a furnishing fabric, with its spindly rendition of seed heads, reflects Day's interest in gardening and plant structure.

05 | Wallpaper | USA | 1906–08
The dandelion motif, with its stems and jagged leaves, is arranged across the pale background like a floral spray on this sample of machine-printed wallpaper.

01 | **Osterlocken (Narcissus)** | Austria | 1910–12 | Franz von Zülow
Zülow was an artist who also designed fabrics and ceramics, such as this graphic
pattern with Secessionist overtones for a linen furnishing fabric.

02 | Fabric sample | USA | 1883–1900
The darker vertical bands on this sample of printed and woven cotton velvet made by Associated Artists give structure to the thicket of leaves dotted with flower heads.

03 | Fabric sample | USA | 1883–1900 | Candace Wheeler
In 1883 Wheeler, one of the first US female interior and textile designers, founded Associated Artists, which made this printed and woven cotton velvet sample.

04 | Daffodil | UK | 1891 | John Henry Dearle
This pattern for cotton furnishing fabric, produced by Morris & Co., has an undulating, flowing structure. The small background leaves provide graphic contrast.

01 | **Clover** | UK | *c.*1906–09
Liberty, founded in the 19th century, marketed progressive "art" textiles such as this.
The airiness of this clover print reflects the general lightening of Edwardian interiors.

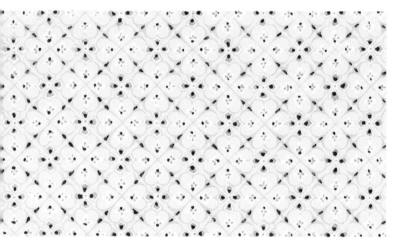

02 | **Wallpaper** | UK | 19th century | Owen Jones
Jones's wallpaper, with its clover and floral pattern, was produced in rectangular
sheets framed by two borders.

03 | **Arlette** | Austria | 1901 | Koloman Moser
This color lithograph is Plate 16 from *Die Quelle: Flächen Schmuck* (*The Source:
Ornament for Flat Surfaces*, 1901), showing Moser's design for woven silk.

04 | **Clover** | UK | late 19th century
This wallpaper pattern from Morris & Co. shows a finely judged balance of movement
and repose, with the curves of the stems interspersed with flower heads and leaves.

05 | Klöverblad (Cloverleaf) | Sweden | 1940s | Josef Frank
Produced for Svenskt Tenn, this fresh simple design for wallpaper, with its green
meandering stems, conceals four-leafed clovers amid the repeat.

01 | **Obi** | Japan | late 19th century
Brocaded silk with metallic thread. An *obi* is the sash that forms part of traditional Japanese dress and it is a feature of both men's and women's kimonos.

02 | **Thistle** | UK | 1897 | Eugène Grasset
This chromo-lithograph appeared in Grasset's book on design, *Plants and Their Application to Ornament*, published in London.

03 | **Teazle** | UK | 1894 | Walter Crane
The pattern of natural growth is evoked in this design for wallpaper, contrasting large flower heads and leaves with tiny sprigs and stems infilling the background.

04 | Thistle | UK | late 19th century | William Morris
A greeny-yellow color was fashionable in artistic circles in the late 19th century. This design for wallpaper achieves depth through variations in tone not color.

05 | Tile design | UK | late 19th century | William De Morgan
In his ceramic work, De Morgan adopted what he termed a "Persian" palette of reds, blues, lemon yellows, purples, and greens.

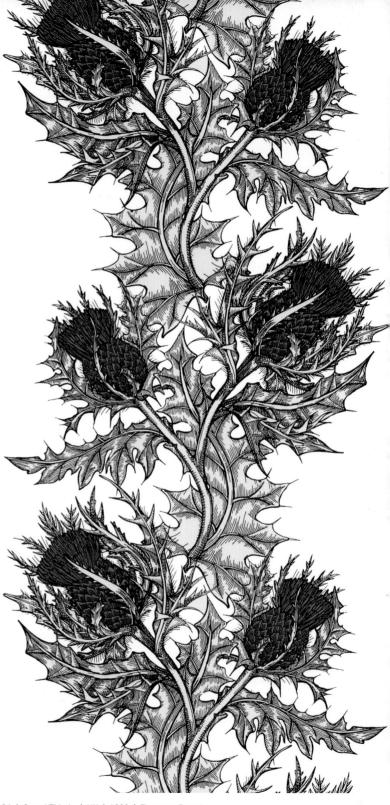

06 | Grand Thistle | UK | 1993 | Timorous Beasties
This design for wallpaper and furnishing fabric is no sanitized view of nature but a closely observed depiction of wildness.

01 | **Winter Berry** | **France** | **19th century**
A design on paper from *L'ornement des tissus*. For centuries, pattern books have been a common means of disseminating designs.

03 | **Hedgerow** | **UK** | **2009** | Angie Lewin for St. Jude's
This furnishing fabric was printed by St. Jude's Prints. Native British flora, especially wild plants, are of particular interest to Lewin, who studied horticulture.

02 | **Blackberry** | **UK** | **late 19th century** | John Henry Dearle
Designed by Dearle, who took on the running of Morris & Co. on Morris's death, this wallpaper pattern is much airier than typical Morris prints.

04 | **Fool's Parsley** | **UK** | *c.*1907 | C. F. A. Voysey
Arts and Crafts architect Voysey was a noted designer of pattern. This symmetrical wallpaper design with its light background is typical of his later work.

05 | **Cow Parsley** | **UK** | **2003** | Cole & Son
The skeletal stems and dotted flower heads of cow parsley are stylized in this
large-scale wallpaper pattern, with the repeat reversed out of a soft colored ground.

01 | **Dress fabric** | UK | 1937 | Calico Printers' Association
The adoption of screen-printing in interwar Britain made adventurous designs more
viable to produce. like this lively. painterly pattern for rayon crêpe dress fabric.

03 | **Field** | UK | 2016 | Tord Boontje
Furnishing fabric designed for Christopher Farr. With individual motifs sparsely arranged across a white ground, this pattern recalls botanical prints.

02 | **French Meadow** | UK | 2015 | Imogen Heath
Digital printing preserves the calligraphic strokes and brushmarks of this fluid, stylized furnishing fabric design with its alternating bands of color.

04 | **Meadow Flowers** | UK | 1896 | Walter Crane
Crane's wallpaper design, with its naturalistic rendering of a wildflower meadow, was printed by Jeffrey & Co.

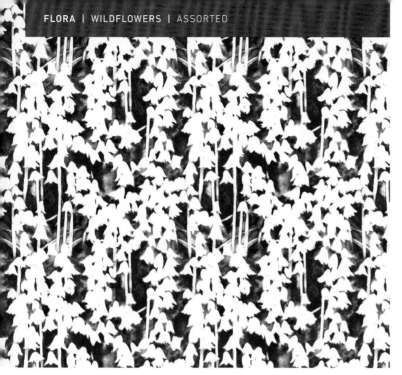

01 | Bluebell | UK | 2014 | Imogen Heath
By reversing the pattern out of a dark ground, attention is drawn to the bell-like shape of the flowers of this furnishing fabric rather than their defining blue color.

03 | Corncockle | UK | 1883 | William Morris
Glowing with rich colors, this design for cotton chintz contrasts tone and scale to create a rhythmic all-over composition.

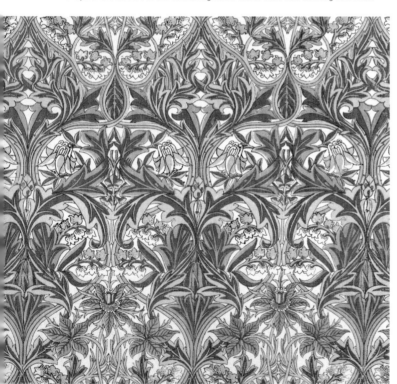

02 | Bluebell | UK | 1876 | William Morris
Sometimes also known as "Columbine," this design for a printed linen union furnishing fabric features dense entangled symmetries.

04 | Fritillaria | UK | 2017 | Designers Guild
Digitally printed satin cotton. This beautifully drawn and closely detailed pattern of fall flowers gains drama from its dark background.

05 | **The Nure** | UK | 1924 | C. F. A. Voysey
With its flowing vertical structure, outlined forms, and dotted shading, this wallpaper design shows Voysey's characteristic lightness and simplicity.

06 | **Snowdrops** | UK | 2017 | Jenny Frean
This printed design, produced for Crate & Barrel, preserves the loose, fluid brushmarks of the original artwork.

07 | **Söndagsmorgon** | Sweden | 1940s | Josef Frank
A light, airy wallpaper pattern featuring flowers, grasses, and leaves interspersed with pink wood anemone. Frank made a close study of flora and fauna.

08 | **Pimpernel** | UK | 1876 | William Morris
Morris chose this wallpaper to decorate the dining room of his London home, Kelmscott House, situated on the Thames at Hammersmith.

09 | **Woodland Weeds** | UK | 1905 | John Henry Dearle
Around the turn of the 19th century, interiors became much lighter and brighter, a trend reflected in the pale tones and comparative simplicity of this wallpaper design.

Arts and Crafts (1880s–1920s)

The Arts and Crafts movement grew out of the social and economic context of the Industrial Revolution, which originated in late 18th-century Britain. In 1851, the Great Exhibition at the Crystal Palace in London's Hyde Park was organized to showcase the mass-produced goods that were appearing. While the intention was to celebrate progress, many of these products were cheaply made and excessively decorated.

William Morris (1834–96; see p. 58) played a leading role in the Arts and Crafts movement that emerged in subsequent decades, and which challenged the impact that industrial production was having on design and society. Influenced by the writings of John Ruskin, who believed that art had a moral purpose and who revered nature, and by Augustus Pugin's (1812–52; see p. 110) championing of a Gothic Revival, what reformers such as Morris proposed instead was a return to the traditions of the medieval guilds, in which workers were not cogs in a machine that relied on a separation of labor, and in which traditional crafts were revived. "Honesty of construction" was a central belief, and superfluous decoration was rejected in favor of the truthful expression of materials. Morris's company, which produced handmade furniture, textiles, ceramics, and wallpaper, was influential in Britain, Europe, and the United States, and his

reforming ideals were adopted by successive generations of designers. Morris wanted "art for all." The irony was that his goods were too expensive for ordinary households.

Arts and Crafts designers had a radical impact on 19th-century pattern-making. Many contemporary mass-produced textiles and wallpapers were highly representational, using three-dimensional shading to create so-called "naturalistic" or scenic effects. Morris rejected such a false sense of depth, restoring a sense of surface. However, his designs were never static compositions, but displayed an inherent natural rhythm.

Nature was the touchstone. Motifs were drawn from the flowers and foliage of the British countryside, and from animals and birds. Nature was also evoked in the use of vegetable dyes—soft colors derived from plant sources such as madder and indigo, which faded in synchronicity with each other, unlike the garish aniline dyes that were used in commercial production.

Other sources of inspiration included Gothic Revival motifs, Islamic tiles, and illuminated manuscripts. In the later decades of the 19th century, the impact of Japanese prints could also be seen in airier patterns with a stronger graphic quality.

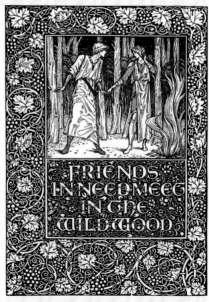

Far Left A sample of "Marigold" (c. 1875) block-printed wallpaper by William Morris.

Left A woodcut illustration for *The Well at the World's End : A Tale* (1896) by Morris.

Opposite A Persian-style plate (c. 1890–1907) by British ceramicist William De Morgan (1839–1917).

01 | **Cray** | **UK** | **1884** | William Morris
The diagonal structure of this design, one of four "river" patterns for chintz, was inspired by an historic Italian cut velvet Morris saw in the Victoria & Albert Museum.

03 | **Textile design** | **France** | **19th century**
Design on paper taken from *L'ornement des tissus* (1877). Once dubbed "the French Manchester," Mulhouse was a noted textile center.

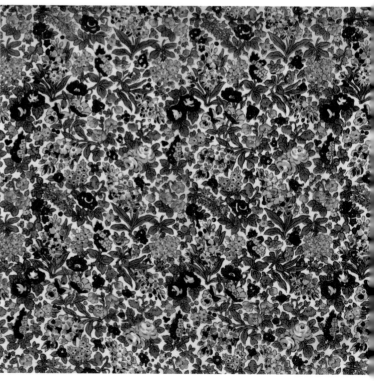

02 | **Arcadia** | **UK** | **1886** | May Morris
In addition to being a designer of textiles, jewelry, and wallpaper such as this sample, May Morris helped to elevate needlework into an applied art form.

04 | **Textile** | **UK** | **1920s**
Liberty's silk and lawn handkerchiefs have long been a popular product line. Many of these patterns were designed in-house.

05 | Furnishing fabric | UK | 1930
Art Moderne or Art Deco was a popular interwar decorative style. This pattern for furnishing fabric for Arthur Sanderson & Sons features childlike floral forms.

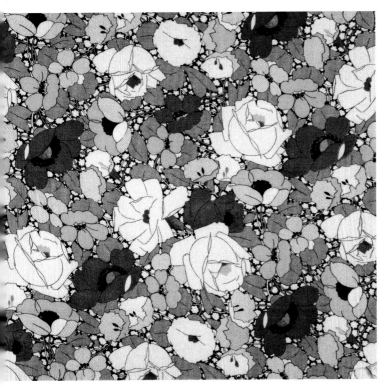

06 | Dress fabric | UK | 1933 | Calico Printers' Association
The orange and green of this fabric in printed crêpe is a classic Art Deco color combination, found in textiles and wallpaper patterns as well as ceramic decoration.

07 | Kentish Rose | UK | 2012 | Cath Kidston
Pretty floral motifs are a cornerstone of Cath Kidston designs, and Kentish Rose is a modern take on vintage florals with a softer, darker palette.

C. F. A. Voysey (1857–1941)

SEE PAGES > 18, 25, 35, 49, 63, 76, 81, 105, 108, 113, 123, 136, 175, 189, 217, 226, 250, 257

British Arts and Crafts architect Charles Francis Annesley Voysey is as well known for the textile and wallpaper patterns he created throughout his career as for his buildings. Fittingly, he was also the designer of the Sanderson wallpaper factory (1901) in Chiswick, west London.

Voysey was born in Hessle, Yorkshire, and educated by his father, a clergyman. He attended Dulwich College after the family moved to London. In 1874, he became articled to the Gothic architect John Pollard Seddon (1827–1906), for whom he later worked as an assistant. After gaining further experience in other architectural firms, he set up his own practice in London in 1881 to 1882.

Influenced by William Morris (1834–96; see p. 58) and the Arts and Crafts movement (see p. 82), Voysey developed a characteristic style of his own, both in his buildings and in his furniture and pattern design, focusing on honesty of construction, simplicity, and truth to materials. Modest private houses formed the bulk of his architectural work and their plain vernacular appearance, along with their bright green exterior woodwork and trim, had a significant impact on English suburban development as it emerged during the interwar period. However, by 1910, the Arts and Crafts style was falling out of fashion and Voysey built nothing after 1918.

For many of his own houses, Voysey designed every interior fitting, including fireplaces, architectural details, and furniture. His furniture was produced mainly in oak and left unstained and unvarnished in Arts and Crafts style. "Simplicity in decoration is one of the essential qualities without which no true richness is possible," he wrote.

Voysey began designing patterns for fabric and wallpaper in the early 1880s and carried on until 1930, more than a decade after his architectural work dried up. His early designs were produced for Jeffrey & Co.; later his wallpapers were produced by Essex & Co. By the 1890s, he was well regarded as a pattern designer and had developed his own distinctive approach: gentle colorways in pastel colors, stylized natural motifs arranged in flowing repeats, and a contrast of light-toned, crisply outlined foreground elements with darker backgrounds. Particularly characteristic was the recurrence of birds in his designs. Other creatures, from fish to seahorses, also crop up in his patterns, along with English cottage garden flora. The heart is another recurrent symbol in his work.

Later patterns are more sparsely detailed, with elements often arranged on a light ground. They also took on a narrative quality and many were intended to be used in nurseries. A large number of his wallpaper designs were also produced as furnishing fabrics and carpets.

Far Left A portrait of English architect and designer C. F. A. Voysey created in 1901.

Left "The Furrow" (1902–03) is a wallpaper pattern that Voysey designed for Essex & Co. Motifs drawn from nature were common in his work.

Opposite "Galahad" (1899) is a stately symmetrical machine-printed wallpaper design in characteristically soft Voysey colors.

08 | Seaweed | UK | 1901 | John Henry Dearle

Dearle joined Morris & Co. as an apprentice. While this pattern adheres to the firm's style, like much of Dearle's later work, it also shows Persian and Turkish influences.

09 | Wallpaper | USA | 1879–87

This was produced by the American Wall Paper Manufacturers' Association. Mid-to late 19th-century interiors featured dense combinations of patterns in rich colors.

10 | **Wilderness** | 2005 | Tord Boontje
Birds, butterflies, and hares nestle among twining flowers and foliage in this
screen-printed polyester curtain fabric designed for Kvadrat.

11 | **Seaflower** | UK | 2008 | Sam Pickard
This digitally printed pattern, with its branching Tree of Life structure, gains depth
by overlaying tones. Small touches of color are dotted across the repeat.

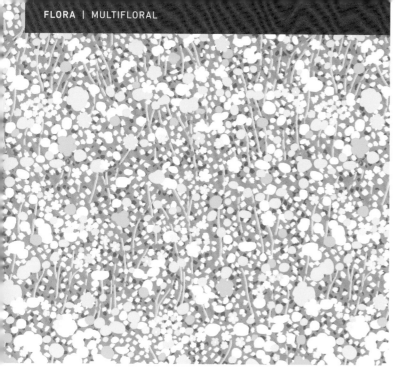

12 | Meadow Day | UK | 2012 | Imogen Heath
An even scattering of white circular shapes across the ground of this pattern simulates the effect of dappled light on grassland on this furnishing fabric.

14 | Masson | UK | 2016 | Designers Guild
Evocative of a cottage garden in summer, this large-scaled repeat furnishing fabric is printed on cotton.

13 | Domino paper | France | c. 1760–70
Domino papers were produced in single sheets for lining trunks and dressers. This Rococo example was printed by Les Associés of Paris, France.

15 | Wallpaper | USA | 1900–20
This machine-printed wallpaper features a pattern of lilies of the valley, tulips, and other flowers. Foliage is striped and dotted.

16 | Elizabeth | UK | 2016 | Claire de Quénetain
This pattern of flowers and leaves in a predominantly blue palette preserves the
fluidity of the original artwork.

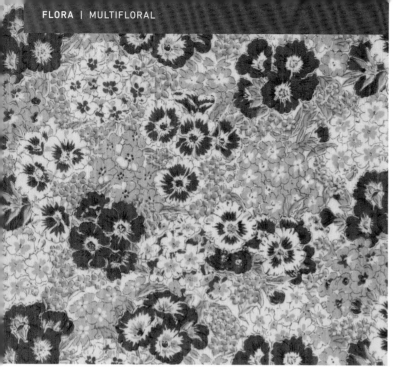

17 | **Dress fabric** | UK | 1936
This bright and cheerful Liberty print dress fabric is an all-over pattern that conveys a mood of general floweriness.

19 | **Pink and Rose** | UK | 1890 | William Morris
A late wallpaper pattern by Morris, who suffered a breakdown in health the year after he created it. Like all Morris papers, it was hand-printed using fruitwood blocks.

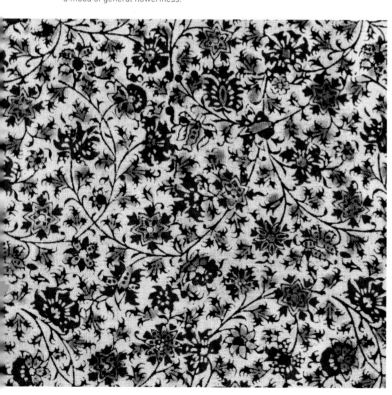

18 | **Textile** | Iran | 1800–70
This cotton and silk floral textile is typical of the Middle Eastern patterns that influenced Western art and design in the late 19th century.

20 | **Textile** | UK | mid-19th century
This mid-19th-century cotton fabric, of English origin, displays the rather garish colors of the new aniline dyes.

21 | **Primavera** | Sweden | 1920s | Josef Frank
An early floral textile design for Svenskt Tenn, this pattern displays various spring flowers popping up across the ground as if they had just emerged from the earth.

23 | **Dress fabric** | UK | 1934
Dress fabric in printed rayon georgette manufactured by Tootal, Broadhurst, Lee & Co., a Manchester-based textile company founded in the late 18th century.

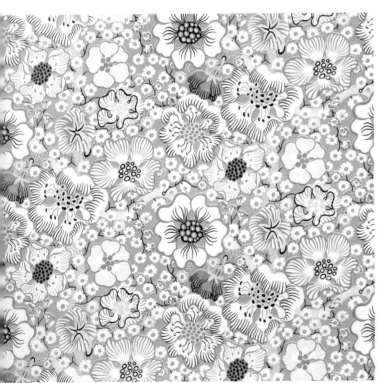

22 | **Eldblomman** | Sweden | 1940s | Josef Frank
In this wallpaper design, stems twist their way up the repeat, while thin spiraling lines and small flowers contrast with the larger elements.

24 | **Wallpaper** | UK | 1770–80
Block-printed wallpaper, possibly of English origin. The design, based on natural, organic forms, expresses the spirit of enquiry of the Age of Enlightenment.

Marianne Straub (1909–94)

SEE PAGES > 315, 337, 348, 380, 424

A leading figure in the British commercial textile industry, Marianne Straub applied her thorough knowledge of hand-weaving to the manufacture of woven materials. Her approach resulted in patterns that have a strong visual and textural appeal. Many designers of fabric conceive their work rather as artists conceive paintings. Straub's method was grounded in the physicality of the material itself: its feel, drape, and weight, along with the use or uses to which it would eventually be put.

Straub was born in a Swiss village, the daughter of a cloth merchant. She spent four years of her childhood hospitalized with tuberculosis. Her art studies at the *Kunstgewerbeschule* (School of Applied Arts) in Zurich, which centered around hand-weaving, exposed her to Bauhaus principles. In 1932, she moved to Bradford, home of the British wool manufacturing industry, and enrolled at Bradford Technical College, where she spent a year extending her weaving skills into the sphere of mechanization.

After a period working with the influential weaver and dyer Ethel Mairet (1872–1952) at her workshop in Ditchling, East Sussex, in 1934, Straub became a consultant designer for the Rural Industries Bureau, working in conjunction with Welsh mills. The post gave her experience and expertise in mass production, and reinforced her ambition to create designs that ordinary people could afford. Three years later, she took up the position of head designer at the Bolton-based textile manufacturer Helios, becoming the firm's managing director in 1947. "Crofton" (1938), a stylized leaf pattern, is typical of her work of this period.

When Helios was taken over by Warner & Sons in 1950, Straub carried on working with the company, an association that lasted until 1970. Warner was based in Braintree, Essex, and in 1953, Straub moved to Great Bardfield, a nearby village. In the mid-1930s, Eric Ravilious (1903–42) and Edward Bawden (1903–89; see p. 506) had been instrumental in establishing Great Bardfield as an artists' colony, where they were soon joined by Kenneth (1915–97) and Diana Rowntree (1915–2008), Michael Rothenstein (1908–93), and painter and wallpaper designer John Aldridge (1905–83). The group was defined by a figurative approach to image-making; while Straub's patterns gradually became more abstract, they never moved away from a naturalistic starting point.

During the 1960s, Straub created designs for Tamesa Fabrics. One of her fabrics was used as upholstery on British European Airways' Trident aircraft. Another design, "Straub," was utilized on buses, tube trains, and British rail carriages between 1969 and 1978. She was made a Royal Designer for Industry in 1972.

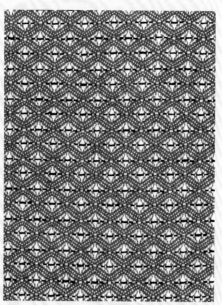

Far Left Swiss-born Marianne Straub had a background in weaving.

Left "Millom" (1949) is a furnishing fabric designed by Straub for Helios, a company with which she had a long association.

Opposite "Adelaide" (1949) was designed for Helios.

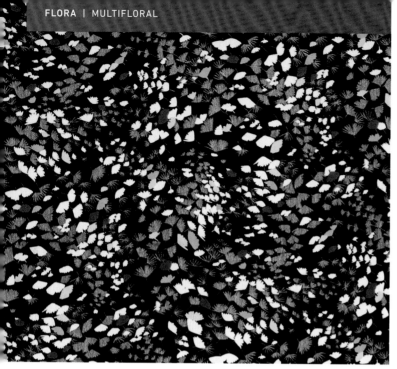

25 | Dress fabric | UK | 1937 | Calico Printers' Association
A dress fabric in printed cotton crêpe made by the Calico Printers' Association. The swirling design features almost abstract shapes reminiscent of leaves and petals.

27 | Columbine | UK | 1900–32 | Allan Vigers
Trained as an architect, Vigers designed many wallpapers for Jeffrey & Co. Rhythmic patterns featuring wild and garden flowers were typical of his work.

26 | Multifloral | UK | 1934–36 | Vanessa Bell
Produced for Allan Walton Textiles, this multifloral design for furnishing fabric by British artist and designer Bell shows the influence of Postimpressionism.

28 | Austria | UK | 1922 | Sidney Haward
This is a wallpaper pattern designed for Jeffrey & Co. Haward's work carried the Arts and Crafts aesthetic into the early 20th century.

29 | **Pattern design** | UK | *c.* 1830–40
Executed in pencil and watercolor, this full color "cartoon" is a design for tapestry, wallpaper, or silk fabric.

31 | **Botanica** | Sweden | 1998 | Maria Åström
A furnishing fabric produced by Ljungbergs. For Åström, the essence of pattern-making is finding the rhythm and flow in the repeat.

30 | **Delft Flower** | UK | 2017 | Designers Guild
The multicolored blooms on a rich dark background of this digitally printed linen furnishing fabric recall the sumptuous quality of 17th-century Dutch flower paintings.

32 | **Lodden** | UK | 1883 | William Morris
This design for cotton chintz furnishing fabric shows Morris's immense skill at interweaving elements of the pattern, so that the eye travels across the surface.

Art Nouveau (*c.* 1880–1910)

Art Nouveau was a *fin de siècle* movement in art and design that occurred throughout Europe and the United States. Known by various names in different locations—"Jugendstil" in Germany and "Stile Liberty" in Italy—the term "Art Nouveau" caught on after the Exposition Universelle in Paris in 1900.

The movement grew out of the rejection of what 19th-century reformers saw as a false distinction between fine art and applied art, with fine art historically deemed the superior. Its architectural practitioners, such as Charles Rennie Mackintosh (1868–1928; see p. 102), Josef Hoffmann (1870–1956; see p. 430), and Victor Horta (1861–1947), sought to create "total works of art"—buildings in which every aspect conformed to the same creative vision. Other leading lights included painter and graphic artist Alphonse Mucha (1860–1939), glass designer and jeweler Réné Lalique (1860–1945), architect Hector Guimard (1867–1942), glass designer Émile Gallé (1846–1904), and glass designer and manufacturer Louis Comfort Tiffany (1848–1933).

While Art Nouveau had its roots in the Arts and Crafts (see p. 82) movement, it was not backward-looking, and instead embraced modernity and technological progress. In common with Aestheticism, Art Nouveau showed the influence of Japanese *ukiyo-e* (pictures of the floating world) prints, which reached the West in the middle of the century, particularly their asymmetry, areas of flat color, and organic motifs. Some of the earliest examples of Art Nouveau were posters designed by Mucha. Advertising everything from stage shows to bicycles, they employed the language of the new style to sell the products of an industrial age.

There were two versions of the style: one where the emphasis was on curves and one which was linear. Sinuous, curving shapes, entwining tendril-like or whiplash lines, and natural motifs characterized the designs produced in the first category, whether they were chairs, posters, pieces of jewelry, Paris Metro entrances, or Tiffany lamps. In the second, elongated verticals and gridded geometric elements were more typical. In each case there was an absence of overt historical reference or quotation.

Pattern-making played an important role in this supremely decorative style. In both wallpaper and printed and woven textiles, natural motifs dominated: flowers, leaves, buds, seedpods, and roots. These were often highly stylized and flattened, reduced to near abstraction. Mackintosh's characteristic rose motif, which began as stenciled decoration in his interiors, is one example. Gridded patterns were also produced and were a notable feature of the work of Hoffmann across different disciplines.

Far Left From Alphonse Mucha's *Documents décoratifs* (*Decorative Documents*; 1901–02).

Center Left The outlines in Mucha's *The Precious Stones: Topaz* (1900) recall Japanese prints.

Left Mucha used flat color in his poster *The Precious Stones: Amethyst* (1900).

Opposite "Cherry Blossom" glass and bronze Tiffany table lamp from the early 20th century.

01 | A New Language | UK | 2016 | Claire de Quénetain
The abstract shapes and squiggles of this screen-printed linen furnishing fabric
were inspired by nature and create a lively and spontaneous effect.

02 | Checkered Flower | UK | 1997 | Neisha Crosland
Crosland's early designs, such as this graphic floral star, were printed on velvet
scarves, stationery, and accessories.

03 | **Angolese Starflower** | Japan | 2005 | Ryoko Sugiura
This contemporary design of printed angora, wool, and nylon blend fabric for Nuno
has an angular starburst quality.

04 | **Les Cornets** | France | *c.*1924 | Raoul Dufy
A woodblock-printed linen and cotton furnishing fabric for Bianchini-Férier. The
large-scale motifs show the influence of the Wiener Werkstätte (Vienna Workshops).

05 | **Bloomsbury** | UK | 2010 | Eley Kishimoto
This graphic floral print has a retro feel. Eley Kishimoto have created patterns for
Hussein Chalayan and Alexander McQueen, among other fashion designers.

Charles Rennie Mackintosh (1868–1928)

SEE PAGES > 18, 31, 400

Charles Rennie Mackintosh, arguably Scotland's greatest architect and designer, concerned himself with every aspect of his buildings from furniture to light fittings to wall decoration. He had a relatively brief career, which coincided with the flowering of a northern version of Art Nouveau. Toward the later part of his life, unable to secure architectural commissions, he produced many textile designs.

Mackintosh was born in Glasgow. At the age of sixteen, he was apprenticed to an architectural firm, taking evening classes in painting and drawing at Glasgow School of Art at the same time. In 1899, he became a junior draftsman at Honeyman and Keppie. There, he formed a friendship with Herbert MacNair (1868–1955) and with two other art students, sisters Frances (1873–1921) and Margaret Macdonald (1864–1933). "The Four," as they styled themselves, began experimenting in different media, creating artworks in a nascent Art Nouveau style. Mackintosh married Margaret in 1900, thus beginning an intense creative partnership.

Charles's architectural approach evolved during early projects. In 1896, after winning a competition, he began work on a new building to house the Glasgow School of Art, and met Catherine Cranston (1849–1934), who commissioned him to design the interiors and furnishings for a number of fashionable Glasgow tea rooms, including the Willow Tea Rooms (1903). Other notable designs were two private houses, Windyhill (1900–01) and Hill House (1902–04), for which he designed many pieces of furniture, lighting, and other details in collaboration with his wife.

By the turn of the century, Charles's unique vision was attracting attention in Europe and both he and his wife were invited to participate in the "8th Exhibition of the Secession" in Vienna in 1900, where the furnished room they exhibited won much critical acclaim. No such recognition came on home turf, however, and after 1910 his architectural work began to dwindle and eventually he resigned from the firm.

In 1915, the Mackintoshes moved to Chelsea in London, following some months spent at Walberswick on the Suffolk coast. Charles began to design textile patterns to supplement his income. In the period up to 1923, he produced more than 120 designs, principally for two firms, Foxton's and Sefton's, both for furnishing and dress fabrics. Many were based on simple stylized flowers and organic forms, such as tulips, roses, and chrysanthemums; others feature bold, abstract geometric shapes or gridded elements. In 1923, the Mackintoshes left for the south of France, where they spent the next four years. During that time, Charles abandoned design and devoted himself to watercolor painting.

Far Left Scottish architect and designer Charles Rennie Mackintosh, photographed in 1893.

Left Mackintosh's Japanese-inspired Hill House chairs (1903) with their attenuated ladder backs.

Opposite A printed cretonne furnishing fabric designed by Mackintosh in c. 1922.

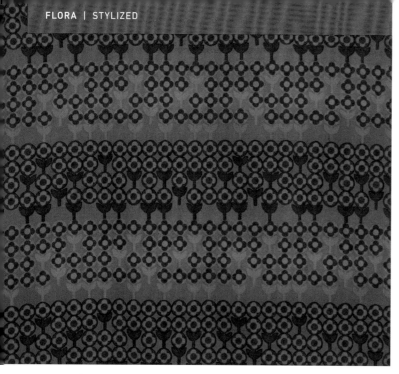

06 | Verdure | UK | 1965 | Peter Hall
Created for Heal's by one of its leading designers, this fabric pattern, machine screen-printed on cotton, notched up sales of more than 11,000 yards (10,000 m).

08 | Furnishing fabric | UK | 1928 | Minnie McLeish
Scottish artist McLeish's design for this roller-printed cotton, manufactured by William Foxton, shows the influence of Cubism.

07 | Textile | France | 1919
Designed by the Atelier Martine, the design studio of French couturier Paul Poiret, this block-printed satin dress fabric features vivid stylized flowers.

09 | Majella | UK | 2016 | Designers Guild
This lustrous silk jacquard weave furnishing fabric comes in a number of vibrant colors. The pattern is based on a stylized interpretation of scrolling plant forms.

10 | **Requena** | UK | 2012 | Designers Guild
A floral stripe with a twist: this pattern alternates vivid bands of flowers drawn in a free-flowing style.

12 | **Wallpaper design** | UK | *c.* 1900 | C. F. A. Voysey
Executed in ink and watercolor, this design reflects Voysey's preference for outlined forms and soft pastel colors.

11 | **Dress fabric** | France | 1936 | François Ducharne
A luxury silk dress fabric from leading French designer and maker Ducharne. The vivid stains of color and loose gestural outlines give the pattern a painterly quality.

13 | **Happy Flowers** | UK | 2012 | Javier Mariscal
Produced for Christopher Farr, this linen furnishing fabric was created by Mariscal, one of contemporary Spain's leading artists and designers.

Orla Kiely (b.1963)

SEE PAGES > 137, 157, 203, 608

Fashion designer Orla Kiely is well known for her crisp graphic patterns, which present a fresh contemporary take on mid-century modern style. Her trademark print "Stem" (2001), which has featured in countless variations, has been applied to a diverse range of products, including clothing, bags, umbrellas, and home accessories.

Kiely was born and spent her childhood in a Dublin suburb, attending a convent school. She cites nature as a particular source of creative inspiration and was strongly influenced by her grandmother, who enjoyed making things. By the age of twelve, she had developed an interest in fashion, textiles, sewing, and knitting. After school, she studied at the National College of Art and Design in Dublin, eventually specializing in Print for Fashion. After a year in New York gaining technical design experience, she moved to London, where she was employed by the US fashion company Esprit, working on print and clothing designs, a position that took her to the Düsseldorf head office for a couple of years. She followed this by studying for a Master of Arts at the Royal College of Art in London, where she specialized in knitwear. A hint of future commercial success came when a Harrods buyer bought a range of hats she designed for her final show.

Kiely's design business began as a home-based enterprise that she and her husband, Dermott Rowan, conducted in their spare time. Gradually, her designs began to attract wider attention. A key shift was away from hats, into bags. When the British department store chain Debenhams asked her to launch a diffusion range at the end of 1997, she and her husband moved the company's office out of their home into premises in Battersea, London. Another leap forward occurred when Kiely started using patterns in her designs, rather than solid colors.

The following years saw the company grow and the range expand, first into clothing, then into biannual collections of womenswear, and eventually into accessories, home furnishings, luggage, stationery, umbrellas, and jewelry. With the business' headquarters now based in Clapham, London, there are also Orla Kiely shops all over the world.

Pattern remains central to her look. Along with stylized leaf, fruit, vegetable, and floral prints, there are playful designs featuring glassware, cutlery, cars, and even Martians, all executed with strong lines and bold, clear colors reminiscent of vintage 1960s and 1970s palettes. Her fascination with endless permutations offered by the repeat is evident in designs that play with scale and proportion. Kiely is Visiting Professor of Textiles at the Royal College of Art.

Far Left Irish designer Orla Kiely photographed in London in June 2005.

Left "Tulip" (2006) is a characteristically crisp graphic floral pattern that has appeared on a variety of products.

Opposite Kiely's patterns, such as "Striped Petal" (2012), have a strong mid-century modern aesthetic.

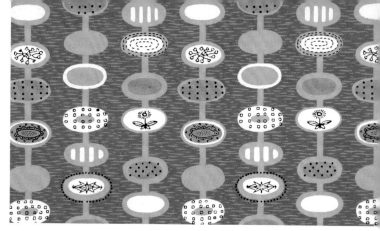

15 | Provence | UK | 1951 | Lucienne Day
This hand screen-printed wallpaper, manufactured by John Line & Sons for the Festival of Britain, features vertical bands of flattened ovoid shapes.

16 | Cockpen | UK | 1918 | C. F. A. Voysey
This pattern for roller-printed cotton furnishing fabric combines stylized plant and bird forms. Many of Voysey's designs were sold through Liberty of London.

14 | Shadow | UK | 2005 | Tord Boontje
This screen-printed polyester curtain was created for Kvadrat. Its asymmetric pattern creates the illusion of light falling through a window and casting shadows.

17 | Furnishing fabric | UK | 1912
This fabric, with its design of poppies and seedpods, was duplex-printed for Liberty & Co., Ltd. Duplex-printing means the fabric is fully reversible.

18 | Wallpaper | UK | 19th century | Owen Jones
In this floral wallpaper design, the stylized flower and leaf forms are tightly
organized in a symmetric structure.

Augustus Pugin (1812–52)

SEE PAGES > 417, 441, 576, 577

A leading 19th-century design reformer, Augustus Pugin played an important role in helping to bring about the Gothic Revival, a shift in architectural style that took inspiration not from classicism but from the medieval period. As an architect, he designed many churches and ecclesiastical institutions. He is best known for his interior designs for the Palace of Westminster, schemes for which he produced more than 100 wallpapers, along with floor tiles, stained glass, carvings, and metalwork.

Augustus Welby Northmore Pugin was born in London, the son of Auguste Pugin, a French-born draftsman and refugee from the French Revolution. As a young man, Augustus attended Christ's Hospital school in London and learned drawing from his father, for whose practice he went to work after he left school. For a time, he also ran a business supplying Gothic furniture and detailing. In 1835, he converted to Catholicism, a step that had a significant effect on his design thinking: the following year, he published *Contrasts*, a manifesto arguing for a Gothic revival in both the structure of society and in buildings.

During this time, Pugin built up a considerable architectural practice, designing many churches in England, and some in Ireland and Australia, along with colleges, schools, monasteries, convents, and private houses.

He also worked for Charles Barry (1795–1860) and James Gillespie Graham (1776–1855), supplying drawings for their entries into the architectural competition for a design for a new Palace of Westminster, to replace the one destroyed by fire in 1834. Barry, who eventually won the competition, asked Pugin to assist him on the interior schemes.

At the Palace of Westminster, Pugin put his radical design ideas into practice. He believed that there was a moral aspect to design: that good design had innate integrity and that bad design celebrated what was false and deceitful. In his view, wallpaper, for example, which was intended to be displayed on a flat surface, should only be decorated with flat patterns and not give a false illusion of depth. His patterns were formal geometric and based around medieval motifs, including heraldic symbols, and stylized floral forms such as the fleur-de-lis. From 1844 onward, Pugin supplied wallpaper designs to the manufacturer Crace & Son. In 1851, he designed the Medieval Court for the Great Exhibition in London, along with Gothic-style furnishings.

One of the last designs that Pugin created for the Palace of Westminster was for the bell tower, now colloquially known as "Big Ben." Soon after, in 1852, he suffered a mental breakdown and was committed to Bedlam, dying shortly after.

Far Left Augustus Pugin, the great champion of the Gothic Revival style.

Left Pugin's bedroom at The Grange, Ramsgate, England, is papered with one of his own designs.

Opposite This wallpaper, designed for the Royal Gallery of the Houses of Parliament, was manufactured by Scott & Co., *c*.1850.

01 | Marble Damask | UK | 2015 | Timorous Beasties

The impact of Timorous Beasties' designs rests on its subversion of pattern structures and motifs.

02 | The Lerena | UK | 1897 | C. F. A. Voysey

A color machine-printed wallpaper manufactured by Essex & Co. A closer inspection of the damask-like design reveals birds perched in holly trees.

04 | Cellini | UK | 2013 | Designers Guild

This digitally printed linen furnishing fabric is a contemporary take on the classic damask pattern with a blurred softness.

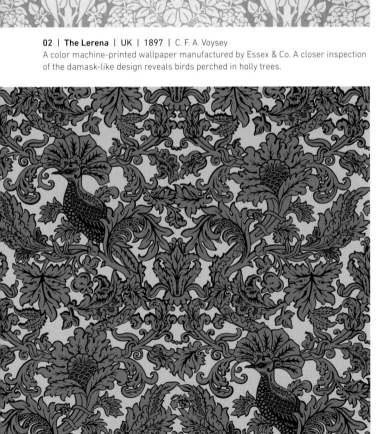

03 | Balabina | UK | 2016 | Cole & Son

A sample of screen-printed wallpaper. The original archive block-printed wallpaper was reworked to include a hoopoe bird.

05 | Damask sample | late 17th to early 18th century

A fabric sample of unknown origin, woven with silk and metallic yarns. Damask takes its name from the city of Damascus where early silks were made.

Timorous Beasties

Alistair McAuley (b.1967) & Paul Simmons (b.1967)

SEE PAGES > 75, 112, 116, 124, 172, 177, 189, 195, 204, 251, 258, 272, 273, 278, 279, 287, 346, 375, 491, 494, 495, 512, 563, 564, 584, 617

Joint partners of Glasgow-based design company Timorous Beasties, Alistair McAuley and Paul Simmons originally met while both were studying textile design at Glasgow School of Art in the 1980s. Their work, described by one critic as "William Morris on acid," subverts traditional textile and wallpaper patterns in wayward and often experimental ways.

The pair were initially drawn together by their shared dislike of the safe, predictable wallpaper and fabric designs that constituted much of what was on the market in the late 1980s. Timorous Beasties, which is named after a line in Robert Burns's poem "To a Mouse" (1785), was founded in 1990, the start of a decade that saw minimalism emerge as the dominant trend in interiors. Their critical breakthrough came in 2004 with the launch of "Glasgow Toile," a contemporary updating of the 18th-century pastoral *toile de Jouy*. On close inspection, rather than the expected rural idyll, the design reveals a tough inner-city urban-scape of crumbling tower blocks with drug addicts, prostitutes, and homeless people.

While classic traditional forms are often points of departure, the visceral impact of these designs comes from their shocking, often tongue-in-cheek quality. Patterns featuring birds, butterflies, and flowers, which have been common motifs in print design for centuries, are rendered in such a highly realistic way, with scales, claws, thorns, and so on, that what is celebrated is the beauty of wildness, not a twee or sanitized version of nature. "Napoleon Bee" features the type of closely observed drawing that might have come from the pages of an entomologist's journal or a 19th-century copperplate engraving.

The work of Timorous Beasties serves as an ongoing conversation with design history, the sting in the tail being the double-take. The "Hotch Blotch" fabric range injects a chaotic disorder of drips and splatters into the stately structure of a damask pattern. In other designs, chinoiserie, Rococo, and Victorian paper-cut silhouettes feature as layered influences. In 2005, McAuley and Simmons decorated lampshades with images of syringes, bacteria, fetuses, and tsetse flies, composed in traditional patterns such as paisley and argyle, for a window installation at the London headquarters of the Wellcome Trust, a medical research institution.

With growing commercial success, the company is now able to manufacture its own products directly. While textile and pattern design remain at the heart of what it does, there have been other commissions and collaborations with clients such as Nike, Famous Grouse, Penguin Books, and Fortnum & Mason, and on a range of products, including packaging, book designs, and furnishings.

Top Paul Simmons (left) and Alistair McAuley (right) of Timorous Beasties, pictured at the Designer of the Year award at the Design Museum, London, in 2005.

Above Timorous Beasties' studio is located in Hillhead, Glasgow.

Opposite "Damsel Damask" (2015), which is available as a velvet furnishing fabric and wallpaper, is a surreal, provocative, and intensely hued pattern. Like many of Timorous Beasties' designs, it subverts a traditional pattern in a way that causes vague unease. Like their *toiles* that play up gritty urban scenes, or their damasks that feature psychedelic paint smears and spatters, or their patterns composed of moth bodies, these contemporary Baroque patterns invite a double take.

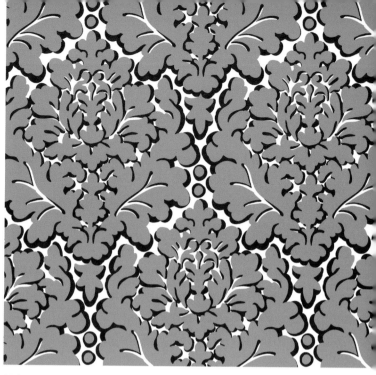

07 | **La La Lyon** | UK | 2013–14 | Eley Kishimoto
The shaded contours of this hand screen-printed wallpaper give the illusion
of a raised surface. The same pattern is applied to a range of accessories.

06 | **Autumn Flowers** | UK | 1888 | William Morris
This wallpaper design, which recalls traditional damask patterns, arranges flowers,
foliage, and fruit forms around a central vertical axis.

08 | **Birdcage** | UK | 2007 | Timorous Beasties
Available as both wallpaper and furnishing fabric, this pattern features damask-like
scrolls suggesting an antique birdcage, with birds perched within.

09 | **Furnishing fabric** | UK | *c.*1888 | William Morris or John Henry Dearle
This silk and wool textile is a brocatel, a type of brocade woven in high relief. It is not always possible to attribute Morris & Co. patterns definitively to Morris or Dearle.

10 | **Aldwych** | UK | 2012 | Cole & Son
An updated, Rococo-style damask wallpaper pattern, taken from the Cole & Son archive, that features highlights of textured glitter.

11 | **Noailles Nuit** | France | 2017 | Christian Lacroix for Designers Guild
Furnishing fabric and wallpaper by the French fashion house Christian Lacroix.
A classic damask pattern on a grand scale, with extravagant scrolls and flourishes.

Katagami is the traditional Japanese art of creating finely cut paper stencils, which are subsequently used to print on paper, or in the production of resist-dyed textiles (an art known as *katazome*). To create the stencils, layers of *washi* paper made from fibers of the mulberry bush are bound together with a high-tannin glue. These robust sheets are then cut, punched, or drilled into various shapes and patterns. Stylized floral, stem, and leaf forms are common designs.

    Katazome, a traditional Japanese dyeing technique, is often employed to produce patterned cotton or silk for kimonos, with indigo being one of the dyes traditionally used. In *katazome*, a resist, typically made of rice paste, is forced through the stencil onto the textile, masking the cut-out areas in the paper stencil. Once the paste has dried, the fabric is then coated with a sizing solution made of soy beans and left to dry again, before the coloring dye is brushed on. Finally, the resist paste is washed off the fabric, leaving behind a pattern in the original fabric color. The technique can be used to create highly sophisticated patterns.

01 | **Sarasa** | India | 18th century
Cotton textile, resist- and mordant-dyed, produced on India's Coromandel Coast, for the Japanese market. *Sarasa* is the Japanese term given to these sought-after fabrics.

02 | **Mikado** | USA | 1954 | Alexander Girard
Cotton and polyester furnishing fabric manufactured by Maharam. Designed for Knoll, this pattern was inspired by folk art and Girard's travels in India and Mexico.

03 | **Briar** | UK | 2000–01 | Eley Kishimoto
A contemporary take on the traditional rosette or bud pattern, this graphic design shows rosebuds nestled against each other.

04 | Cotton textile | France | *c.*1835
Produced in France, this cotton textile features a regular repeat of rosettes on a background subtly enlivened by small-scale scalloped patterning.

05 | Whig Rose comforter | USA | *c.*1850
A cotton appliqué comforter of the American school. "Whig Rose" was a popular 19th-century quilting pattern that took its name from a political party.

06 | Cotton textile | 1800–50
In this printed fabric of unknown origin, rosettes of spiraling petals that alternate in direction are surrounded by linked pairs of rings.

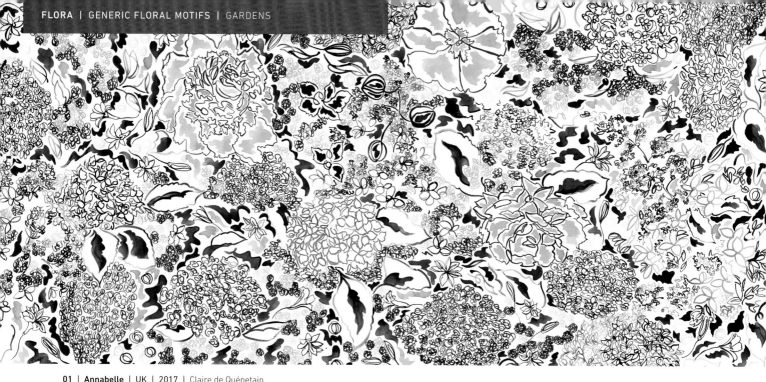

01 | Annabelle | UK | 2017 | Claire de Quénetain
This is a linen union furnishing fabric. The soft-colored pattern, with its twisting lines and squiggles, is animated with life.

02 | Cottage Garden | UK | 1974–77 | Collier Campbell
Screen-printed cotton furnishing fabric, manufactured by Liberty. This dense floral print encapsulates the nostalgic quality of 1970s decoration.

03 | The Rainbow | UK | 2017 | Claire de Quénetain
Emphatically drawn lines and patches of vibrant color on this linen union furnishing fabric give the energetic composition a great sense of movement.

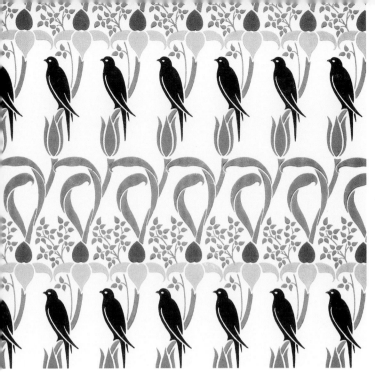

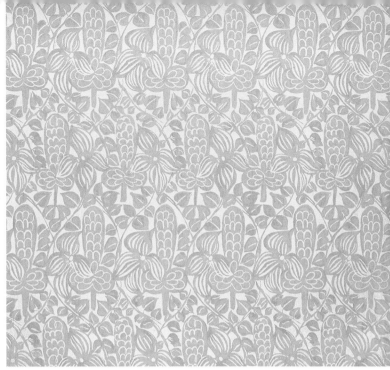

04 | **Minto** | UK | 1901 | C. F. A. Voysey
The basic structure of the pattern on this color machine-printed wallpaper is alternating rows of birds and flowers, yet there is a strong diagonal emphasis.

05 | **Arabesque** | 2017 | Raoul Dufy
Revived by Christopher Farr, this Dufy wallpaper design, taken from the artist's archive, is a dense pattern of floral and leaf motifs.

06 | **Royal Garden** | UK | 2013 | Cole & Son
Part of Cole & Son's Historic Royal Palaces collection, this large-scale wallpaper pattern features the shady leaves of the bird cherry tree.

07 | Furnishing fabric | UK | 1920s
A roller-printed cotton manufactured by F. Steiner & Co. of Lancashire. The pattern shows an exotic landscape with onion-domed buildings.

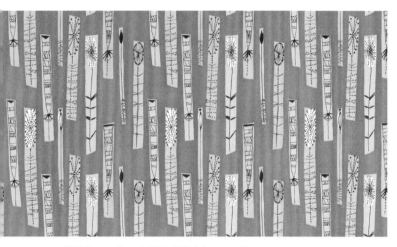

08 | Flower Show | UK | 1954 | Lucienne Day
A printed cotton furnishing fabric designed for Heal's. This pattern is an abstract impression of the flower show, a perennial feature of English life.

09 | Furnishing fabric | UK | c.1923
A cotton and satin furnishing fabric manufactured by Joshua Smith. The garden pattern includes potted trees, paths, and trellises.

10 | Bloomsbury Garden | UK | 2016 | Timorous Beasties
Lush and rather eerie, the pattern for this wallpaper and furnishing fabric features loose serpentines festooned with fruit and flowers, and dotted with butterflies.

11 | Paradiset (Paradise) | Sweden | 1940s | Josef Frank
The wallpaper designs that Frank produced during his wartime exile in New York
represent a hope for a better world during a time of immense upheaval and conflict.

12 | Embroidered textile | UK | 2011 | Tony Trickey
One of the designers working with First Eleven Studio, Trickey has a humorous
illustrative style that translates into embroidery or flat pattern.

13 | **Mughal Garden** | UK | 2016 | Matthew Williamson at Osborne & Little
Wallpaper in which a hummingbird and tiger are concealed among the lush foliage
of an exotic Mughal garden.

14 | **Culpeper** | UK | 2015 | Neisha Crosland
The botanical-style drawing and sparse placement of the motifs across the ground
of this Surflex-printed wallpaper suggest the illustrations in an old herbal.

15 | **Garden** | UK | 2016 | Tord Boontje
A wallpaper created for Christopher Farr. The cascade of floral motifs recalls
Boontje's best-selling hanging light fixture, "Garland," released in 2002.

01 | **Textile design** | **UK** | **late 19th century** | William Kilburn

This watercolor design was painted by Kilburn, who was a leading British botanical illustrator, as well as a designer and printer of calico fabrics.

02 | Corsage | UK | 2016 | Designers Guild
This is a digitally printed cotton satin furnishing fabric. Its fresh and pretty floral pattern features sprays of orchid blossom.

03 | Dress fabric | UK | 1935 | Calico Printers' Association
The floral spray has a long history as a decorative motif, both in embroidery and printed patterns such as this rayon crêpe dress fabric.

04 | Trailing Rose | UK | 2014 | Cath Kidston
Cath Kidston is known for vintage-inspired prints. This floral pattern has appeared on a diverse range of products from homeware to iPhone cases and backpacks.

01 | **Textile design** | UK | *late 18th century* | William Kilburn
This watercolor is by Kilburn, who was a successful calico printer and designer, and also a campaigner for copyright in textile design.

03 | **Furnishing fabric** | UK | *c.* 1921
This pattern, manufactured by F. W. Grafton & Co. of Manchester, places tightly clustered bouquets against a gridded background.

02 | **Galaxy Bouquet** | UK | 2001 | Eley Kishimoto
This exuberant pattern, available as wallpaper and applied to a range of other products, shows bouquets tied with candy-striped ribbon against a starry background.

04 | **Wallpaper** | UK | 1927
The epitome of floral wallpaper, this 1920s design displays strongly colored blooms against a reticent, recessive background.

05 | Windflower Bunch | UK | 2016 | Cath Kidston
This pattern features four different bouquets arranged in rows of alternating pairs—
an undulating structure that gives a gentle sense of rotation.

Phyllis Barron (1890–1964) | Dorothy Larcher (1884–1952)

SEE PAGES > 349, 350, 368, 502

Phyllis Barron and Dorothy Larcher, who lived and worked together for thirty years, were leading exponents of block-printing during the interwar period, when there was a revival of interest in textiles as an applied art form. Their designs were hand-printed using wood or lino blocks and subtle vegetable dyes, and sold through specialist shops.

Barron and Larcher originally trained as painters, Larcher at Hornsey College of Art and Barron at the Slade School of Fine Art. Before the two women met, both had become intrigued by block-printing: Barron had discovered wood blocks in 1905 when on a painting holiday in France as a teenager, while Larcher came across the technique in India when she was working as a paid companion. At the time, textile design was not considered a serious field of study at art schools and much of what Barron learned before setting up the workshop with Larcher in 1923 came from independent research and trial and error.

The first Barron and Larcher workshop was in Hampstead, London. Soon they were selling their work to interior decorators and fashion designers. In 1926, when some of their textiles were displayed at Heal's Mansard Gallery in the "Handmade Textiles and Pots" exhibition, they won critical acclaim. The same year, textile artist Elspeth Anne Little opened

Modern Textiles, a shop in London's Beauchamp Place, which became an important outlet for Barron and Larcher fabric. A significant commission came about in the late 1920s when Barron was asked to supply fabric samples suitable for drapes for Hugh Grosvenor, 2nd Duke of Westminster's hunting lodge in Bordeaux. Living with the duke at the time was the Parisian couturier Gabrielle "Coco" Chanel (1883–1971), who was entranced by the fabrics and ordered cushions for her garden in Paris.

In 1930, Barron and Larcher moved to Hambutts House in Painswick, Gloucestershire, setting up a studio in the stables of the grounds. A particular feature was a large indigo dyeing vat; indigo, along with other rich dark shades such as walnut and iron black, featured often in their patterns. There, for the next decade, they produced furnishing and dress fabrics, controlling every stage of design, from cutting the blocks to growing the plants to create the vegetable dyes. Barron's patterns tended to be abstract or geometric, whereas Larcher's were more naturalistic.

In 1932, they were asked to provide the interior furnishings for a new wing at Girton College, Cambridge. Subsequently, they created drapes for the choir stalls at Winchester Cathedral. In 1940, when wartime shortages began to bite, they closed the workshop. In later life, Barron taught at Dartington Hall in Devon and Larcher returned to painting.

Far Left Phyllis Barron and Dorothy Larcher at a French market in the 1930s.

Left "Feather Pattern," a Barron and Larcher textile design dating to 1930.

Opposite "Bouquet" (2016) is one of a number of Barron and Larcher patterns produced by Christopher Farr Cloth in association with the Crafts Study Centre.

01 | Wreath | UK | 1876 | William Morris

Also known as "Poppy," this wallpaper design with its scrolling foliage bears
a similarity to another Morris design, "Acanthus."

02 | Textile design | UK | late 18th century | William Kilburn
A watercolor by Kilburn. He contributed botanical illustrations to *Flora Londinensis* published in six volumes between 1777 and 1798.

03 | Heaven Scent | UK | 2005 | Tord Boontje
The pattern of this furnishing fabric for Kvadrat forms a long serpentine shape so that however it is used on furniture, the effect will be asymmetrical and organic.

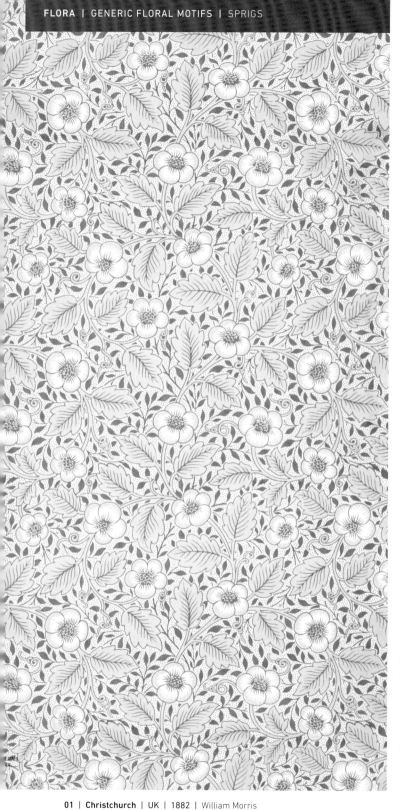

01 | **Christchurch** | UK | 1882 | William Morris
This wallpaper design displays Morris's mastery of intricate pattern repeats, where foreground and background are closely interlinked.

02 | **Furnishing fabric** | UK | *c.*1900 | C. F. A. Voysey
This was manufactured by Liberty and is attributed to Voysey. Thin dark green curling stems add definition to a light-tone print.

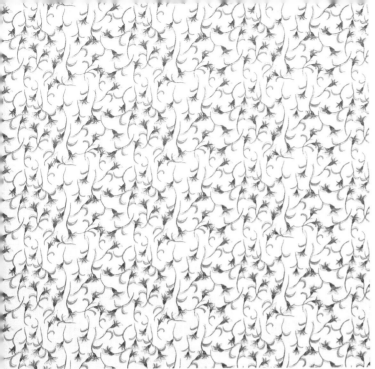

03 | Amapola | UK | 2012 | Javier Mariscal
Furnishing fabric manufactured by Christopher Farr Cloth. Small individual sprigs twisting this way and that give an overall textural quality to this design.

04 | Rhododendron | UK | 2012 | Orla Kiely
Kiely's patterns, typically applied across a range of products, have a strong graphic look and draw various sources of inspiration, from vintage textiles to nature.

05 | Itty Bitty | UK | 1999–2000 | Eley Kishimoto
In this contemporary reworking of the traditional floral sprig, the tiny scale of the flowers and the pink and acid-yellow color combination create a light all-over design.

01 | Textile | UK | 1835

Posies in woven wicker baskets are deflected at slight angles from the central columnar plant stand in this English printed cotton textile.

02 | Textile | UK | 1830s

This English printed textile is an essay of flowing curves, with the basket handles looped through with twining stems.

03 | Textile design | France | early 19th century
This textile design was produced in Jouy, a town in Île-de-France that gives its name to the eponymous *toile*. The motifs are arranged in diaper pattern.

04 | Comforter | USA | *c.*1849 | Mary Hergenroder Simon
Thought to be the work of Simon, this Baltimore Presentation comforter in cotton and silk velvet features appliquéd wreaths and baskets of fruit and flowers.

05 | Wallpaper | USA/France | 1920
A French floral-themed wallpaper distributed by Nancy McClelland, a leading interior decorator and specialist in historic wallpapers, from her store in New York.

01 | Furnishing fabric | UK | 1926–28
This woven and block-printed linen furnishing fabric, of tulips, lily-of-the-valley, and gladioli in a vase, was manufactured by Morton Sundour Fabrics of Carlisle, UK.

03 | Sudbury | UK | 2010 | Cole & Son
In this medium-scale classical-style damask wallpaper, urns draped with garlands are printed on a silk moiré-effect background.

02 | Attica | UK | 1949 | Marion Mahler
This horizontally structured pattern features an array of ancient Greek urns and vases. It was designed for Edinburgh Weavers.

04 | Flowerpot | UK | 1883 | William Morris
This dense, small, stylized pattern of flowerpots was designed specifically to be used as a lining fabric for drapes.

05 | **Furnishing fabric** | UK | *c.* 1870–80 | Owen Jones
This twill satin silk tissue furnishing fabric with an Etruscan design was probably
created by Owen Jones for Warner & Sons.

06 | **The Formal Garden** | UK | 1904 | Walter Crane
A printed furnishing fabric manufactured by Jeffrey & Co. The formal symmetry
of the design, with its large-scale central potted trees, is offset by twining stems.

07 | **Charleston Flowers** | UK | 1995 | Jenny Muncaster
This oil pastel design on paper incorporates decorative elements similar to those
found at Charleston, Vanessa Bell's home in Sussex.

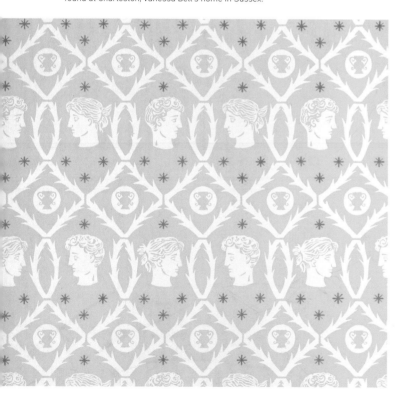

08 | **Tuscany** | UK | 1951 | John Minton
Minton was a noted British artist, designer, and illustrator. This screen-printed
wallpaper features circular motifs enclosing vases.

09 | **Fabric panel** | 18th century
This linen panel is of unknown origin. Its symmetrical design has Neoclassical vases
arranged in rows, separated by serpentine wreaths.

10 | Art Room | UK | 2017 | Mini Moderns
Mini Moderns, founded in 2006 by Keith Stephenson and Mark Hampshire, specializes
in applied pattern, much of which is inspired by vintage textiles and products.

01 | **Evergreen** | UK | 2017 | Imogen Heath
This mid-scale contemporary design for a furnishing fabric is a gentle all-over
pattern that evokes the sensation of looking up through a canopy of leaves.

02 | **Arbutus** | UK | 1913 | Kathleen Kersey
This wallpaper pattern of leaves and berries over a foliate background was designed
by Kersey and produced by Morris & Co.

03 | **Versailles Garden** | UK | 2016 | Designers Guild
A sumptuous silk satin furnishing fabric features a pattern of leaves embroidered
in black, white, and shades of gray.

05 | **Leaves** | 1967 | USA | Alexander Girard
A screen-printed linen furnishing fabric manufactured by Herman Miller. The simple
graphic pattern creates a textural effect.

04 | **Eden** | USA | 2014 | Hella Jongerius for Maharam
Produced for leading contemporary US textile company Maharam, this pattern
features high-contrast leaf silhouettes.

06 | **Bramble** | UK | *c.*1875 | Bruce James Talbert
Woven silk tissue manufactured by Warner & Ramin. A Scottish architect, interior
designer, and author, Talbert was noted for his Gothic furniture.

07 | Armature Feuille | UK/France | Contemp. Revival 2016 | Raoul Dufy
One of the Dufy designs revived by Christopher Farr Cloth, this delicate leaf pattern
has a soft, feathery quality.

08 | Stylized leaf and flower design | UK | 1930s
Design on paper. In this pattern, the foreground leaf motif is in white, while the
background is a strong ocher color.

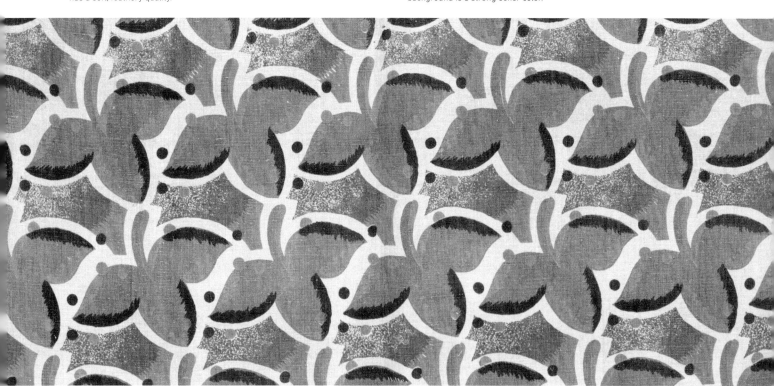

09 | Rustic | UK | 1938 | André Bicât

Furnishing fabric manufactured by Donald Brothers of Dundee. Bicât was an artist,
set designer, and printmaker who also taught at the Royal College of Art.

10 | Odhni | UK | 2014 | Designers Guild
This printed cotton furnishing fabric with metallic textural detail features a flowing, batik leaf pattern that overlays an ombré background.

11 | Eden | USA | 1966 | Alexander Girard
Girard, who designed some 300 patterns for Herman Miller, was heavily influenced by folk art, particularly that of Mexico.

12 | Palm Jungle | UK | 2012 | Cole & Son
This contemporary reworking of a design taken from the Cole & Son archive uses multilayering to achieve a sense of depth.

Raoul Dufy (1877–1953)

SEE PAGES > 29, 101, 123, 146, 150, 268, 287, 349, 479, 505, 513

French artist Raoul Dufy is best known for his Fauvist-style paintings, which feature strong outlines, bright colors, and lively optimistic subjects, such as horse races, regattas, and other fashionable social events. Yet, he was also a significant textile designer and the founder of a factory that produced printed fabrics.

Dufy was born in Le Havre, Normandy. In 1900, after military service, he won a scholarship to the École des Beaux-Arts in Paris. He exhibited for the first time at the Salon des Artistes Français in 1901. He also showed regularly at Berthe Weill's Montmartre gallery and took part in the Salon des Indépendants in 1903. Two years later, Dufy was greatly influenced by the Fauvist exhibition at the Salon des Indépendants, which included *Luxe, Calme et Volupté* (1904) by Henri Matisse (1869–1954).

In parallel to his career in fine art, Dufy pursued a serious interest in textiles, encouraged by his friendship with the Parisian couturier Paul Poiret (1879–1944). Dufy's designs were a radical departure from conventional printed silks and velvets of the day. His bold overscaled pattern "La Perse" (1911), with its exotic Persian floral motifs, was typical of the stunning designs Poiret fashioned into dramatic coats and capes. These fabrics soon came to the attention of leading French silk manufacturer Bianchini-Férier, based in Lyon, and Dufy began an association with the company that lasted nearly twenty years. Many of Dufy's designs display floral and leaf motifs; horses, buildings, and 18th-century features such as scrolls and arabesques also appear in his patterns. Initially, the fabrics were printed from woodblocks he carved himself. Their painterly quality and well-judged balance between positive and negative shapes, which was derived in part from Cubist influences, echoed the preoccupations shown in his works in watercolor and oil. By 1920, both in textile design and fine art, Dufy had developed his own subtler version of Fauvism, which was more obviously decorative, optimistic, and illustrative, mingling the representational with elements taken from mythology.

As well as textiles and fine art, Dufy worked in other media, including ceramics and book illustration, producing plates for writers such as Apollinaire and Gide. His enormous fresco, *La Fée Electricité* (*The Electricity Fairy*), celebrating electrical power, was created for the Exposition Internationale des Arts et Techniques dans la Vie Moderne in Paris in 1937 and was hugely popular. Vibrant with all the colors of the rainbow, combining allegorical subjects with portraits of scientists and inventors, it was donated to the Musée d'Art Moderne in Paris in 1964.

Far Left French artist Raoul Dufy painting in Caldes de Montbui, Spain, in 1949.

Left "Blue Roses" (1905), a Dufy fabric design for the Lyonnais firm Bianchini-Férier.

Opposite This woodblock-printed linen furnishing fabric was designed by Dufy for the French silk manufacturer Bianchini-Férier.

13 | Kolkata Fern | UK | 2018 | Sam Pickard
This cross between a fern and a paisley pattern by Pickard, was inspired by a journey from a Somerset village to Kolkata in eastern India.

15 | Sans Souci | UK | 1930–40
A cotton furnishing fabric made by leading British textile company Edinburgh Weavers. Blocks of color, along with gray, are overlaid on a tonal pattern of leaf shapes.

14 | Grands Feuillages (Large Leaves) | France | c.1920 | Raoul Dufy
Furnishing fabric produced by Bianchini-Férier. A striking combination of black, white, and red takes the place of more naturalistic colors.

16 | Leaf Pattern | UK | 1888 | Lewis Foreman Day
Day was a leading figure in the Arts and Crafts movement and wrote a number of books on pattern design and ornament.

17 | **Wallpaper** | UK | 1860 | Owen Jones
Jones painted this wallpaper design with a bodycolor and gouache on paper.
The pattern blends elements of naturalism with a symmetric structure.

18 | **Jardin Exo'chic** | UK | 2014 | Christian Lacroix for Designers Guild
This digitally printed cotton sateen furnishing fabric forms part of a collection created
for Designers Guild. Splashy washes of intense color overlay a jungle of ferns.

William De Morgan (1839–1917)

SEE PAGES > 34, 75, 83, 164, 242, 298

Designer, potter, inventor, and stained-glass artist William De Morgan is best known for his ceramics. His revival of lusterware, a glowing metallic finish typical of Moorish pottery and Italian majolica, echoed a late Victorian fascination with the decorative arts of the Middle East, and those of Turkey, Persia, and Syria in particular.

De Morgan was born into an intellectual family in London. In 1859, he enrolled at the Royal Academy Schools. Although he was discouraged by the school's approach to art education, while he was there he was introduced to William Morris (1834–96; see p. 58).

De Morgan began his long-lasting collaboration with Morris in 1863, when he started designing stained glass for the company, before moving on to take over the tile-making side of the business, which had not previously enjoyed much success. At first, he used commercially produced blank tiles, decorating them with his own designs; later, he developed a biscuit tile of his own, which he preferred for its appealing irregularities.

In 1872, De Morgan set up a studio of his own in Chelsea, although his association with Morris continued for many years. He also made hand-decorated vases, platters, and other dishes for Morris & Co. In 1879, a key commission came from the artist Frederic, Lord Leighton (1830–96), who asked De Morgan to work on the magnificent Arab Hall, which was the centerpiece of Leighton House in London, a purpose-built "studio-house." The Arab Hall, with its golden dome, was designed to showcase Leighton's vast collection of Islamic tiles. De Morgan's role was to arrange more than 1,000 tiles and to replace those missing or broken, which he did spectacularly successfully. He also produced luminous peacock-blue tiles for the adjacent Narcissus Hall.

De Morgan's experiments with glazing led him to perfect lusterware; he developed a type of pattern transfer that helped give a handmade product more consistency. In addition to what he termed a "Persian" palette of colors—rich reds, blues, lemon yellows, purples, and greens—his motifs reflect the influence of 16th-century Iznik ware. As well as geometric designs, fish, birds, and fantastical creatures were produced in panels, where the design was made by placing tiles together.

From 1882 to 1900, De Morgan produced tiled panels for the smoking rooms of twelve P&O liners; they depicted landscapes representing countries visited by the ships on their voyages to the Middle East. In 1888, financial difficulties forced him into partnership with architect Halsey Ricardo (1854–1928). The pottery moved to Fulham but it made little profit. In 1907, De Morgan left the pottery and devoted his time to writing fiction.

Far Left William De Morgan portrayed with one of his ceramics in 1909.

Left De Morgan is noted for his revival of lusterware, which is prized for its iridescent colors.

Opposite One of sixty-six earthenware tiles, created by De Morgan and William Morris in 1876, that formed a decorative panel.

20 | Foliage | UK | 19th century
The crossing and interlacing of foreground and background elements and the carefully juxtaposed tones are characteristic of Morris & Co. wallpaper designs.

19 | Kayin | UK | 2015 | Osborne & Little
This soft, dense all-over pattern features scattered leaf silhouettes, their smudged shapes seeming to emerge from shadows.

21 | Wallpaper (Hedera) | UK | c. 1920s
A block-printed wallpaper made by Arthur Sanderson & Sons. The firm was established in Islington in 1860 as an importer of French wallpapers.

22 | Ivy Block | UK | 2013 | Sam Pickard
This screen-printed linen furnishing fabric is by British designer Pickard. Its twisting
all-over pattern of ivy leaves and stems is given depth by its shadowed image.

23 | **Bramble** | **late 19th century** | Kate Faulkner

Still in production in the 21st century, like many Morris & Co. designs, this wallpaper
pattern features a dense tangle of bramble bushes evenly covering the ground.

24 | Banana Leaf | UK | 2005 | Neisha Crosland
This subtle vertically structured furnishing fabric in linen union features rows of scrolling banana leaf motifs in alternating directions.

25 | Multi Acorn Spot | UK | 2012 | Orla Kiely
A hallmark of Kiely's style is a strong mid-century modern look. This stylized acorn cup pattern has all the directness of a Pop art design.

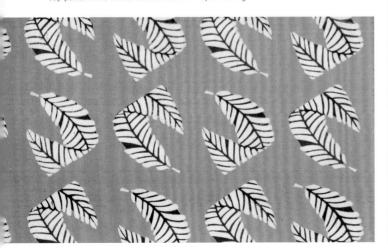

26 | Stenciled paper | Japan | 20th century
This is a sample of Japanese school, hand-stenciled and dyed paper. The use of stencils to pattern both fabric and paper is a long-standing Japanese tradition.

27 | Leaf (Black/Gold) | UK | 1999 | Jocelyn Warner
A scanned image of a young eucalyptus leaf is turned into a climbing branch, forming part of a classic ogee repeat in this wallpaper design.

Richard Riemerschmid (1868–1957)

SEE PAGES > 61, 174

German pattern designer Richard Riemerschmid was also a painter, architect, city planner, and designer of glass, furniture, and ceramics. He was active in the Deutsche Werkstätten (German Workshops), which not only promoted craftwork but also embraced the machine production of well-designed goods. The German Workshops organization was closely allied with the Deutsche Werkbund (German Association of Craftsmen), whose purpose was to make German goods more competitive.

Riemerschmid was born in Munich and studied painting at the city's Academy of Fine Arts between 1888 and 1890. He was a Symbolist painter, and at the beginning of his career he made his living producing artwork for advertising. By the late 1890s, he had turned his attention to design, specifically furniture, prompted by the fact that he could not find any to his liking when it came to furnishing his first marital home. A chair he produced in 1899 for a music room exhibit he created at the "Deutsche Kunstausstellung" (German Art Exhibition) in Dresden attracted attention.

He also began to design buildings, particularly private houses, including his own villa in Munich (1898–1906). Later, he designed a number of significant interiors, including luxury cabins for a passenger ship and the interior of the Munich Playhouse (1900–01).

Riemerschmid's involvement with the German Workshops included designing the plan for a "garden city" at Hellerau, some of the housing for the project and the factory (1909–10) where the Workshops eventually relocated. However, he became much better known and acclaimed for both his furniture and his pattern designs. Clarity, the use of simple materials, and a rejection of the flights of fancy of the German form of Art Nouveau, Jugendstil (Youth Style), typify his work. Some of his furniture designs are in the collections of major museums around the world.

Textiles were a significant part of the Workshops' output. Riemerschmid designed patterns for printed and woven fabrics; he also created designs for wallpaper. Most of his works feature small, highly simplified motifs drawn from nature, such as leaves and flowers. Arranged in dense repeats, they have a soothing rhythmic quality and serve as modest backgrounds. A similar pattern decorates the rim of a dinner and coffee service he designed for Meissen between 1903 and 1904, which has been reissued as "Blaue Rispe" (Blue Meadow-grass).

Riemerschmid also played an important role as an educator. He was the director of the Munich *Kunstgewerbeschule* (School of Applied Arts) from 1913 to 1924 and the director of an art and design college in Cologne from 1926 to 1931.

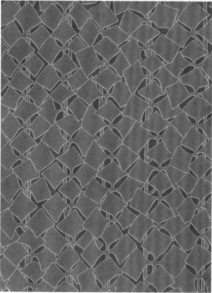

Far Left Richard Riemerschmid was a leading figure in the Deutsche Werkstätten in the early 20th century.

Left This wallpaper design with repeating leaves was produced by the German firm Erismann & Co., Breisach.

Opposite A wallpaper pattern by Riemerschmid from 1908 featuring heart-shaped leaves.

29 | Tribe | UK | 2014 | Kate Blee
A wallpaper and polyester furnishing fabric produced by Christopher Farr Cloth.
Blee, who founded her design studio in 1986, is well known for her rugs and textiles.

28 | Woodland | UK | 2017 | Osborne & Little
This wallpaper design features isolated, multicolored leaves of recognizable species
scattered across the ground.

30 | Jindai | UK | 2014 | Designers Guild
Precisely drawn oriental flowers and leaves are arranged in a loosely linear grid
in this cotton furnishing fabric.

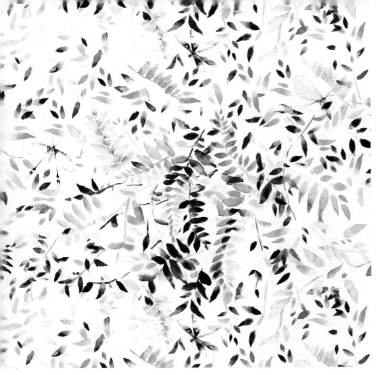

31 | Zaffera | UK | 2017 | Designers Guild
Brightly colored dragonflies dart through a painterly pattern of leaves in this linen union furnishing fabric.

32 | Athenian | UK | 19th century | Lewis Foreman Day
Day designed many textiles and wallpaper patterns such as this. His wallpaper designs were often manufactured by W. B. Simpson & Co.

33 | Hawthorn Rusts | UK | 2009 | Sam Pickard
Pickard prints her many designs in her own north Devon studio. In this pattern for furnishing fabric, finely ruled vertical lines anchor tumbling hawthorn leaves.

35 | Belladonna | Japan | 2004 | Reiko Sudo
A printed cotton fabric manufactured for Nuno. The leading Japanese textile company produces both traditional and contemporary fabrics.

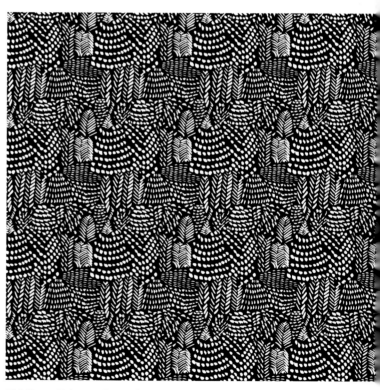

34 | Caterpillar Leaf | UK | 2005 | Neisha Crosland
This vertically structured pattern on flexo-printed wallpaper features a climbing leaf and stem motif, each leaf finely outlined with bristling hairs.

36 | Komorebi | Japan | 2012 | Yumi Yasui of Nuno for Steteco.com
This printed design by Nuno for the apparel company Steteco.com is for fabric to make *steteco*, which are short, loose trousers traditionally worn under kimonos.

38 | Tropicana | UK | 2015 | Matthew Williamson at Osborne & Little
The large-scale pattern of stylized palm leaves of this wallpaper and cotton
furnishing fabric has a loose, painterly quality.

37 | Chrysler | UK | 2016 Osborne & Little
This wallpaper's stylized pattern of Art Deco leaves recalls the architectural detailing
of New York's Chrysler Building.

39 | Comforter | USA | *c.*1860
This comforter was probably made in Rhinebeck, Dutchess County, New York. The twelve
oak-leaf blocks that comprise the pattern are made of appliquéd dark blue cotton.

01 | Granville | UK | 1896 | John Henry Dearle
Designed in the year of William Morris's death, this wallpaper pattern was one of
many that Dearle created as chief designer of Morris & Co.

02 | Wallpaper | UK | 1895 | Walter Crane
The scrolling acanthus leaf is one of the most prevalent vegetal motifs in the history
of decoration and ornament.

03 | Tile panel | UK | 1876 | William Morris and William De Morgan
Made at the Chelsea Pottery for Morris & Co., this earthenware tile panel reveals
how a complete pattern could be assembled from individual tiles.

04 | Acanthus | UK | 1875 | William Morris
Very popular with the public in its day, the subtle color gradations in this wallpaper
pattern were achieved by the use of thirty separate printing blocks.

02 | Kompotti | Finland | 2012 | Aino-Maija Metsola
This is a furnishing fabric produced by Marimekko. Metsola is a Helsinki-based designer who has been collaborating with Marimekko since 2006.

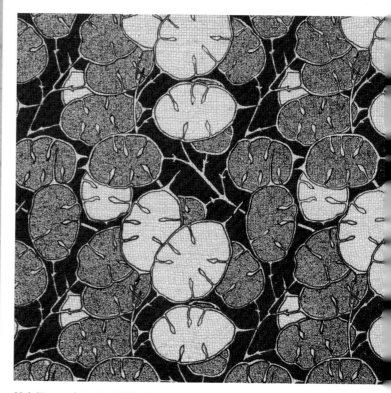

01 | Wallpaper | France | 1810–20
Possibly French, this wallpaper design features stately vertical rows of symmetrical plant forms with dependent seedpods.

03 | Silvanus | Austria | 1901 | Koloman Moser
This color lithograph is Plate 23 from *Die Quelle: Flächen Schmuck* (*The Source: Ornament for Flat Surfaces*, 1901). The wallpaper pattern features honesty seedheads.

04 | **Fabric design** | France | 19th century
This design on paper is taken from *L'ornement des tissus* (1877). The fabric pattern features podlike squiggles.

05 | **Dress fabric** | Netherlands | 1951
Printed using traditional Indonesian wax block batik, this fabric is manufactured by Dutch company Vlisco, which produces fashion designs for African consumers.

01 | Rajapur | UK | 2003 | Cole & Son

This wallpaper and furnishing fabric features an ornate all-over paisley pattern and
comes in a range of electric, vivid colorways.

02 | Textile pattern | UK | 19th century | George Haité
Haité designed many shawl patterns during the mid-19th century. Large repeats and brilliant color typified his designs.

03 | Shawl | France/UK | mid-19th century
This wool and silk shawl is of French or Scottish origin. The "four seasons" design features a different ground color in each quadrant.

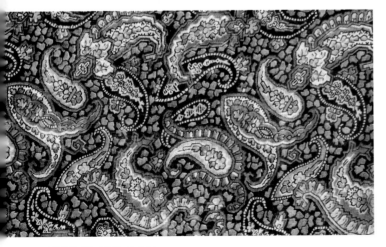

04 | Textile | 19th century
Paisley patterns were popular throughout the 19th century and particularly featured on women's shawls.

05 | Indian | UK | 1868 | George Gilbert Scott
This intricate paisley-like wallpaper, produced by Morris & Co., was designed by Scott, the Gothic Revival architect best known for the Albert Memorial.

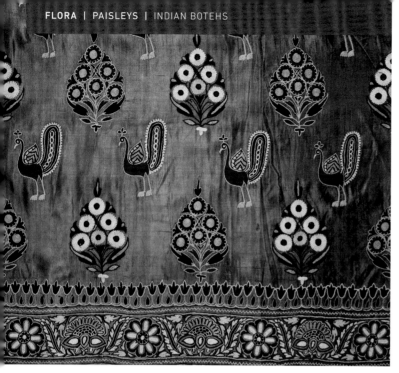

01 | Detail of a skirt | India | c.1880
Produced in Kutch, India, this embroidered silk satin skirt features vegetal and
animal motifs of the kind that were borrowed by Western designers.

03 | Textile | India | c.1880
This paisley or *boteh* motif is hand-embroidered onto a cotton handkerchief.
It was made in Lucknow.

02 | Detail of a skirt | India | 1850
This hand-printed cotton skirt was made in Kutch, a Gujarati district that is well
known for its textile art, particularly embroidery.

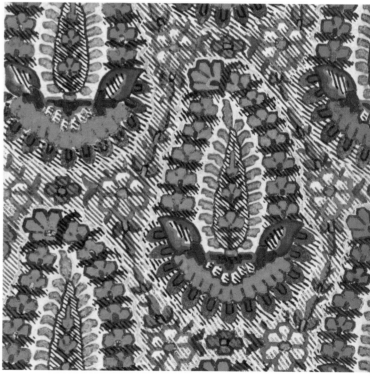

04 | Paisley design | UK | 19th century | George Haité
Paisley is named after Paisley, Scotland, where woven and printed paisley patterns
were produced from 1840. Elaborate designs were made possible by Jacquard looms.

05 | **Montracy** | UK | 2017 | Designers Guild
The paisley motif on this furnishing fabric is based on the *boteh* or *buta*, a pine cone
or teardrop-shaped motif, with a curved top, of Persian origin.

01 | Birch Wood | UK | 2016 | Timorous Beasties
When gathered into soft translucent folds, this delicate lace fabric is banded by the characteristic patterning of birch bark.

02 | Forest | UK | 1959 | Lucienne Day
Like many of Day's designs, this printed cotton furnishing fabric, with its graphic repeat of tree trunks, was produced for Heal's.

03 | **Mandara** | **UK** | **2008** | Matthew Williamson at Osborne & Little
This wallpaper design features an all-over pattern of silhouetted forest trees arranged across a light contrasting ground.

05 | **Wood's Edge** | **USA** | **1974**
This printed linen union furnishing fabric was produced by Elenhank, a US textile firm founded in 1946 by Eleanor and Henry Kluck.

04 | **Tuuli** | **Finland** | **1971** | Maija Isola
Isola's heavyweight cotton furnishing fabric, designed for Marimekko, differs in its realism from her pop designs of the 1960s. This design is based on a photograph.

06 | **Wallpaper** | *c.*1880
This machine-printed wallpaper sample is of unknown origin. Mass-market Victorian designs were often dense and naturalistic.

07 | Korpi | Finland | 2016 | Aino-Maija Metsola
This furnishing fabric is produced by Marimekko. Metsola creates original designs
in a range of media, including ink, watercolor, and gouache.

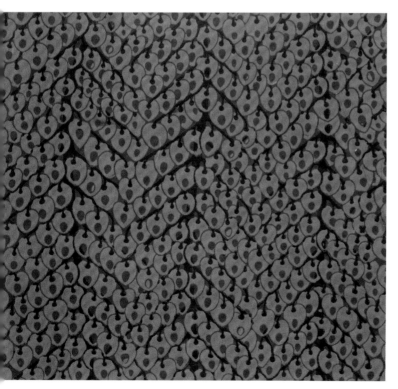

08 | Wallpaper | Germany | early 20th century | Richard Riemerschmid
This wallpaper, featuring a highly stylized pattern of flowering trees, was produced
by Erismann & Co. of Breisach, Baden-Wurttemberg in southern Germany.

09 | Lochwood | UK | 2013 | Nina Campbell, distributed by Osborne & Little
Campbell's wallpaper and furnishing fabric are distributed by Osborne & Little. The
forest pattern in Impressionist style is printed in soft, pretty colors.

10 | **Textile** | USA | 1919 | Herman A. Elsberg
US textile designer and collector Elsberg designed this silk and metallic thread furnishing fabric. He also owned a silk factory in Lyon, France.

11 | **The Fairyland** | UK | 1896 | C. F. A. Voysey
In this Voysey wallpaper design, stylized doves fly in an arc beneath the treetops, with the ground beneath blooming with hyacinths and carpeted by mushrooms.

01 | Papercut | Japan | 19th century
This Japanese gold fir trees paper features golden feathery leaves against a gridded
maze-like pattern. It is from the collection of British diplomat Rutherford Alcock.

02 | Oak Tree | UK | 1896 | John Henry Dearle
In this branching all-over wallpaper pattern, scrolls of oak branches interspersed
with acorns generate a sense of circular movement.

03 | Royal Oak and Ivy | UK | 1799
This printed cotton furnishing fabric was made for leading draper Richard Ovey.
In this naturalistic pattern, ivy clambers around the trunk and branches of an oak.

04 | Birch Tree Sun | UK | 2007 | Angie Lewin for St Jude's
A furnishing fabric produced by St Jude's. A wintry northern sun shines through the bare trunks of birch trees, with their banded bark patterning.

05 | Tulip Tree | UK | 1903 | Lewis Foreman Day
Day produced many designs for textiles such as this furnishing fabric for Turnbull & Stockdale of Lancashire. He helped to found the Arts and Crafts Exhibition Society.

06 | Tree of Life | UK | 1998 | Timorous Beasties
In this exotic wallpaper pattern, the traditional Tree of Life motif, commonly found in Indian and Persian textiles, is transformed into an exuberant climbing garland.

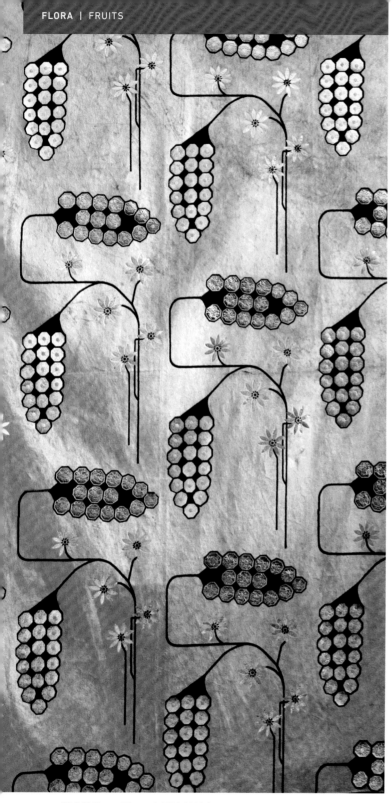

02 | **Apple** | UK | 1877 | William Morris
This wallpaper, dating from Morris's most prolific period, displays boldly contoured scrolling leaves and apples against a ground evenly covered with small-scale leaves.

01 | **Hollywood Grape** | UK | 2008 | Neisha Crosland
The stylized pattern of this pigment- and foil-printed velvet furnishing fabric has more than a touch of Hollywood glamour.

03 | **Still Life** | UK | 2003 | Eley Kishimoto
A charming and quirky fabric pattern combines stylized fruit shape motifs with patches of crosshatched shadow.

04 | Fruktlåda (Fruitbox) | Sweden | 1947 | Stig Lindberg
A furnishing fabric designed for NK Textile Design Studios and now made by
Ljungbergs. The fruit shapes contain seeds, branches, leaves, and even worms.

05 | Fiki (Fig) | Sweden | 1993 | Maria Åström
A furnishing fabric designed for Ljungbergs. Åström usually begins designing
by drawing from nature, often in pencil.

06 | Furnishing fabric | UK | 20th century | Pat Albeck
Albeck was a leading postwar British pattern designer, whose best-selling work
featured on textiles, wallpaper, and ceramics.

07 | Dress fabric | USA | 1927
A printed silk and crêpe de Chine fabric manufactured by Stehli Silks of New York. The textile company boasted that it "employed only first-rate artists."

09 | The Orange Tree | UK | 1902 | Walter Crane
Block-printed wallpaper designed for Morris & Co. All Morris papers were printed by hand using separate blocks for each color, which gave the colors great body.

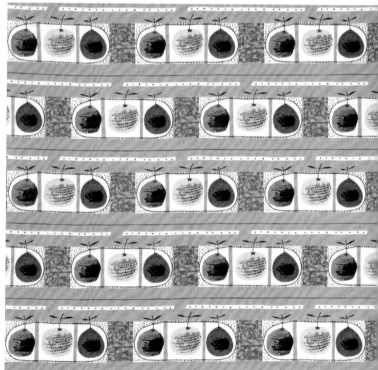

08 | Wild Strawberry | UK | 2012 | Cath Kidston
Inspired by memories of a pinafore dress printed with strawberries that Cath wore as a little girl, this print features a pattern of bright fruits and delicate white flowers.

10 | Kier | UK | 1954 | Robert Stewart
Stewart's screen-printed linen and cotton furnishing fabric is a typical mid-century modern design. Stewart designed contemporary patterns for Liberty.

11 | Bird and Pomegranate | UK | 1926 | John Henry Dearle
Dearle designed this wallpaper for Morris & Co. The "Firm," as it was called,
contracted out its wallpaper printing to Jeffrey & Co.

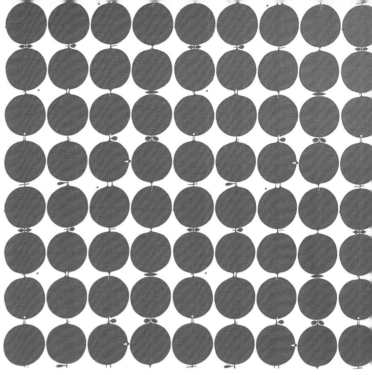

13 | Tallyho (orange) | Sweden | 1961 | Stig Lindberg
This furnishing fabric was designed for Ljungbergs. The minimalist design, with its stylized apple motif, was originally intended for use in public buildings.

12 | Parati | UK | 2015 | Christian Lacroix for Designers Guild
Part of a collection created by the House of Lacroix for Designers Guild, this wallpaper pattern features exotic tumbling fruit, graphically rendered.

14 | Pears and Cherries | UK | c.1880 | Bruce James Talbert
This all-over pattern for a furnishing fabric has a simple branched structure, with the red fruit standing out against the plain colored ground.

15 | **Pear** | **UK** | **2016** | Sarah Battle
Battle, a founder member of First Eleven Studio, takes her inspiration from nature and from quirky everyday objects.

16 | **Habanera** | **UK** | **2015** | Matthew Williamson at Osborne & Little
Williamson's first collection of fabrics and wallpapers launched in 2013. This pattern originated as hand-painted artwork.

01 | Dress fabric | Netherlands | 2017 | Sanne van Winden
The Dutch textile firm Vlisco was founded in 1846 and produces wax print designs
for consumers in Central and West African countries.

02 | Apple Tree | UK | 2006 | Ryoko Sugiura
Printed fabric produced for Nuno, one of Japan's leading textile companies.
The pattern transforms apple trees into cheerful, stylized lollipop shapes.

03 | Wallpaper | UK/USA | 1870–85
This wallpaper pattern, produced either in Britain or the United States, has an Arts
and Crafts feel to it, with its branching lines and relatively open repeat.

04 | Woods and Pears | UK | 2012 | Cole & Son
In this updating of a contemporary classic, what were originally bare trees have
borne fruit. The pears are printed in metallic gold.

05 | Vegetable Tree | Sweden | 1944 | Josef Frank
This vivid and playful pattern for Svenskt Tenn is a variation on Frank's favorite Tree
of Life motif, with stylized vegetables growing from tree branches.

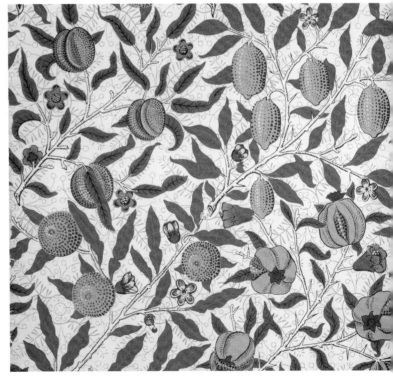

06 | Pomegranate | UK | 1865–66 | William Morris
An early Morris wallpaper design, also known as "Fruit," this pattern proved lastingly
popular and is still in production. Philip Webb may have drawn the pomegranates.

01 | Bavaria Stripe | Netherlands | 2013 | Studio Job for Maharam
Studio Job, founded in 2000 by Dutch designers Job Smeets and Nynke Tynagel,
creates work inspired by the everyday. This fabric was designed for Maharam.

02 | Puutarhurin Parhaat | Finland | 2009 | Maija Louekari
A heavyweight cotton furnishing fabric designed for Marimekko. Louekari
is a Helsinki-based designer and illustrator.

03 | Summer Stock | USA | 1956
A machine-printed wallpaper manufactured by Katzenbach and Warren. The bounty
of a summer garden is depicted in this cheerfully domestic pattern.

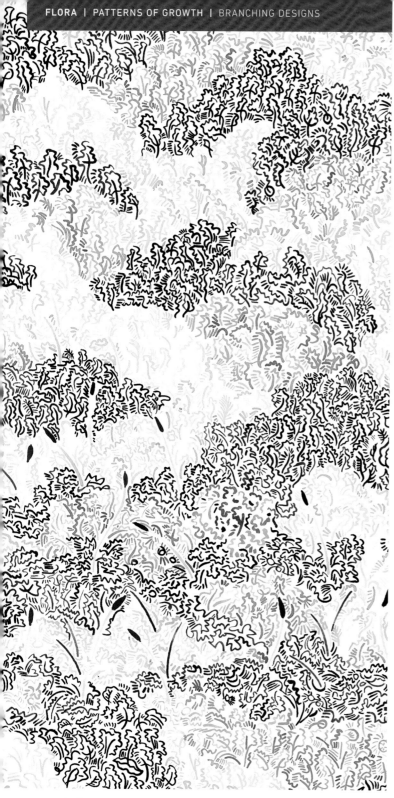

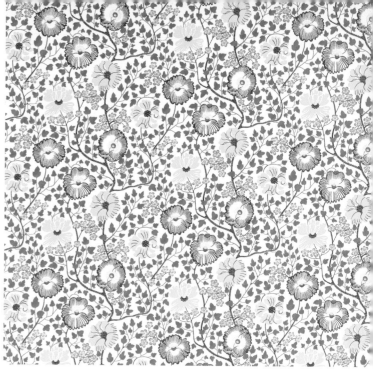

02 | Sagoträdet | Sweden | 1940s | Josef Frank
In this wallpaper pattern for Svenskt Tenn, small purple flowers and green leaves provide a contrast in scale with the foreground blooms and stems.

01 | A Discreet Revival | UK | 2016 | Claire de Quénetain
The soft colors and densely detailed twisting lines and squiggles of this linen furnishing fabric suggest the abundance of nature.

03 | Pepper Trail | UK | 2011 | Neisha Crosland
This bold contemporary wallpaper pattern, with its stylized floral trail motifs, curls and uncurls against the plain ground.

04 | Wild Olive | UK | early 20th century | C. F. A. Voysey
Wallpaper designs were Voysey's principal source of income after his architectural commissions dried up from 1910 onward.

05 | Bird Branch Stripe | UK | 2014 | Timorous Beasties
The Timorous Beasties' large-scale branching trail pattern on velvet furnishing fabric includes silhouetted birds and butterflies.

06 | Cascade (Ivory Black) | UK | 2009 | Jocelyn Warner
This freestyle flowing wallpaper pattern of climbing stems, tumbling leaves, and blossom contrasts highlighted and shadowed areas.

Neisha Crosland (b.1960)

SEE PAGES > 16, 41, 61, 100, 127, 157, 162, 178, 188, 326, 340, 367, 371, 377, 386, 388, 404, 408, 413, 426, 428, 441, 467, 558, 637, 648

Wallpaper, textile, flooring, and accessories designer Neisha Crosland is renowned for her elegant patterns, often executed in soft sophisticated neutrals, inspired by everything and anything from quail's eggs or the mottled texture of granite, to 17th-century French Huguenot silks, or a scrap of one of her grandmother's dresses. Her designs appear on a multitude of products, from scarves to espresso cups.

British-born Crosland was an avid collector as a child, picking up shells, pebbles, feathers, or whatever caught her eye, and then taking immense pleasure in arranging them. After boarding school, she went to study in London, first taking an art foundation course at Central School of Art and Design, followed by graphics at Camberwell College of Arts. During a visit to a William Morris (1834–96; see p. 58) exhibition at the Victoria and Albert Museum, she came across vivid 15th-century Ottoman Empire patterns, which inspired her to change to textile design.

Camberwell's textile course not only addressed Crosland's love of pattern-making, drawing, and painting, but also introduced her to a range of hands-on skills, such as crushing beetles to make red dyes and screen-making. At the Royal College of Art, where she subsequently took her Master of Arts, she continued to experiment.

A hint of success came early. At Crosland's Royal College degree show in 1986, the British firm Osborne & Little commissioned her to design a wallpaper collection. The "Star" collection became a bestseller and a feature of many fashionable British interiors at the time.

In 1994, Crosland started her own company, designing printed velvet scarves and accessories, which were stocked by leading retailers. She also sold her hand-painted designs to fashion houses and fabric companies. Five years later, she branched out into wallpaper and furnishing fabrics and began to build her brand name. Her first wallpaper collection featured patterns such as "Anemone" and "Hawthorn," whose motifs were drawn from the natural world. The wallpapers were distributed by the Paint & Paper Library in Chelsea, London.

Over the years, Crosland has ventured into other areas of surface decoration, designing patterns for embroidered fabric, tiles, vinyl flooring, rugs, fine china, and stationery. All her work is produced under license by companies such as Harvey Maria, The Rug Company, Crate & Barrel, and Fired Earth. She also designs home and fashion accessories for the Hankyu Department Store chain in Japan. Her designs are well balanced, and individually scaled and adapted to different media. She was made a Royal Designer for Industry in 2006 for her textile design.

Far Left Neisha Crosland launched her own textile company designing scarves and accessories in 1994.

Left Over the years, Crosland's patterns have appeared on a range of products. "Boomerang" (2008) features on painted terracotta tiles.

Opposite "Birdtree" (2003), a design for a furnishing fabric, is a characteristically elegant pattern of flowering branches.

07 | Ludlow | UK | 2010 | Cole & Son

This wallpaper pattern, with its graceful branching lines, was taken from an
18th-century fabric produced for Colonial Williamsburg, Virginia.

08 | **Wallpaper** | **UK** | **1789–91** | William Kilburn
This is a watercolor design for flowered fabric. Kilburn was a botanical illustrator as well as a designer of textile patterns.

09 | **Blossom** | **UK** | **late 19th century** | Kate Faulkner
Along with John Henry Dearle, who ran Morris & Co. after Morris's death, a number of other designers created patterns for wallpaper and fabric for "The Firm."

10 | **Tiara** | **Finland** | **2014** | Erja Hirvi
A furnishing fabric designed for Marimekko. Hirvi has been collaborating with the textile firm since 1995. This pattern was inspired by vintage Marimekko fabrics.

12 | A Forest | UK | 2017 | Mini Moderns
This large-scale graphic print wallpaper, by designers Keith Stephenson and Mark Hampshire, was inspired by the branch formation of oak trees.

11 | Until Dawn | UK | 2004 | Tord Boontje
A drape/interior panel designed for Artecnica. Like Boontje's best-selling "Garland" light, this panel made of die-cut Tyvek consists of intertwining floral and foliage forms.

13 | Willow | UK | 1874 | William Morris
One of Morris's best-loved and most popular designs, "Willow" was one of the few patterns he considered suitable for both wallpaper and fabric.

14 | **Ruskin Floral** | UK | 2016 | Timorous Beasties
In this wallpaper and fabric design, individual flowers are bright pops of color
standing out against a shadowy gray ground of leaves and twisting stems.

Tord Boontje (b.1968)

SEE PAGES > 17, 79, 89, 108, 127, 135, 194, 406, 613

Toward the end of the 20th century, austere minimalism gave way to a more decorative approach. In the vanguard of this new wave of design was Dutch industrial product designer Tord Boontje. His best-selling "Garland" (2002), produced for Habitat, was a romantic innovative lampshade consisting of thin photo-etched metal cut into tendrils, leaves, and flower shapes. Wound around a bare light bulb, it cast lacy patterns of light and shade.

Born in Enschede in the Netherlands, Boontje graduated from the Design Academy Eindhoven in 1991, and from the Royal College of Art, London, in 1994. Two years later, he established Studio Tord Boontje in south London, designing for mass production as well as creating one-off pieces. In 2003, after the success of "Garland," he was named Designer of the Year by *Elle Decoration*, which was the first of many awards.

Boontje's textile work demonstrates a fascination with romantic themes, natural growing forms, and the intriguing play of light and shade. Much of this output has been created for Kvadrat, one of Europe's leading manufacturers of design textiles. Founded in 1968 in Ebeltoft, Denmark, the company originally produced textiles by leading Danish designers, such as Nanna Ditzel (1923–2005) and Finn Juhl (1912–89).

A number of Boontje's textiles use a technique known as "burn-out" to create patches of transparency within the fabric. Burn-out involves applying chemicals to remove specific fibers within the weave, thus creating a voile-like translucency that contrasts with areas of greater opacity. "Nectar" (2005) features a cascade of swirling blossom and leaves; "Crystal" (2009) simulates the effect of cracked glass. In other designs, a kinetic effect is achieved by laser cutting. "Eternal Summer" (2005) and "100 Years" (2009), the latter with its theme of tree rings and wood grain, both allow glimpses of light through the fabric, animating a flat surface with great vitality. Other Boontje textiles give traditional patterns a contemporary twist. In the upholstery fabric "Heaven Scent" (2005), the pattern is not all-over, or arranged centrally on the ground, but forms a long serpentine shape so that, however it is positioned, the effect is always organic and asymmetrical, a reminder of natural growth.

After relocating his studio to rural France in 2005, Boontje returned to London in 2009 to take up the position of head of design products at the Royal College, a post he left in 2013. Textiles remain only one element of his London studio's output; others include lighting, graphics, ceramics, furniture, and site-specific installations.

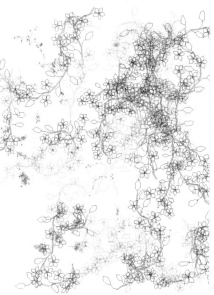

Far Left Dutch designer Tord Boontje at the Milan Furniture Fair in 2009.

Left "Nectar," a drape designed for Kvadrat in 2005.

Opposite The "Prince" (2005) furnishing fabric is an updated rose pattern bristling with thorns.

01 | **Twine** | **UK** | **2007** | Sam Pickard

This all-over printed pattern of tangled vine stems employs shadowed background
elements to achieve a sense of depth.

02 | Great Vine | UK | 2013 | Cole & Son
This wallpaper pattern of shady vine leaves was inspired by the Great Vine at
Hampton Court Palace, thought to be the oldest and largest vine in the world.

03 | Vine | UK | 1873 | William Morris
Hand-printed in distemper colors by Jeffrey & Co., Morris's printers. Morris referred
to this design as a "close vine trellis."

04 | Wisteria (Lilac Rose) | UK | 2011 | Jocelyn Warner
This vertically structured climbing wallpaper pattern captures the pendant habit
of growth of wisteria flowers.

Tricia Guild (b.1946)

SEE PAGES > 18, 32, 36, 37, 43, 50, 80, 90, 97, 104, 105, 113, 129, 145, 147, 160, 161, 171, 248, 274, 314, 336, 384

As founder of an international design empire, Tricia Guild's confident, dynamic handling of color and pattern brought originality to interior design and decoration when much of what was commercially available was bland and unadventurous. Her success is proof that the products of a highly individual creative approach can gain widespread appeal.

Born Patricia Kaye, Guild was an up-and-coming interior designer when she married her first husband, designer Robin Guild (1938–2006), in 1969. A year later, they bought a small decorating company on London's King's Road, which had sold Indian hand-blocked textiles, and founded Designers Guild, opening a showroom on the site. The Designers Guild London flagship store occupies the same premises.

Tricia, who up to that point had been frustrated by the lack of inspiring patterns and colors with which to decorate, was then able to design her own. Naturalistic patterns in soft, subtle colorways soon gave way to bolder painterly designs in vibrant colors. A trip to India influenced her trademark use of strong color, and nature, especially gardens, has remained a lifelong source of inspiration. With their fresh contemporary feel, her designs for both textiles and wallpaper reinvented florals and geometrics for a new generation.

In 1973, when she and Robin parted company, Guild continued to run the business, which then sold ceramics and furniture, and began a series of collaborations with artists. By the 1980s, Designers Guild was making a name for itself in the interiors world. Today, the company has offices and showrooms in Paris and Munich, as well as outlets worldwide.

Although floral and geometric prints remain an important part of the range, which numbers 9,000 fabrics and 2,000 wallpapers, other influences include Eastern decorative arts and Italian architecture, along with classical motifs. Fabrics include linen union, damask, silk, velvet, jacquard, and tapestry. In 2008, the company launched the "Royal Collection" of fabrics and wallcoverings on behalf of the British royal household, inspired by interiors at Buckingham Palace and Windsor Castle, among other royal houses. Designers Guild has developed many other products under licence, ranging from furniture to stationery.

However, it is Tricia's flair for color that has become her design signature: orange, lime, magenta, cerulean blue, fuchsia, and sharp yellow in invigorating combinations add verve to her patterns and interior schemes. She was awarded an Honorary Fellowship from the Royal College of Art in 1993 and was appointed an Officer of the Order of the British Empire for services to interior design in 2008.

Far Left Tricia Guild, founder of Designers Guild, in London in 1985.

Left "Cellini" is Designers Guild's contemporary take on a classic damask pattern.

Opposite Designers Guild's "Japoneries" is a jacquard two-tone oriental floral furnishing fabric.

01 | **Lumimarja** | Finland | 2004 | Erja Hirvi
Hirvi's fabric designs for Marimekko are inspired by nature. This pattern features branches in winter.

03 | **Isabella** | UK | 1951 | Jacqueline Groag
Czech-born Groag was one of the designers who brought a modernist aesthetic to British design in the postwar period. A wallpaper designed for John Line & Sons.

02 | **Blossom (Renaissance Gold)** | UK | 2009 | Jocelyn Warner
This delicate fashion-inspired wallpaper pattern has a 1950s vintage feel. The petals are built up from three layers of tone to give shape and form.

04 | **Floral Pattern** | Japan | 2004 | Yuka Taniguchi
A printed cotton fabric manufactured by Nuno. This minimalist linear design consists of a regular striped pattern of dots and leaf-shaped marks.

05 | **Multi Stem** | **UK** | **2012** | Orla Kiely
One of the most recognizable patterns of the 21st century, Kiely's trademark
"Stem" has appeared in various formats and on a wide range of products.

06 | Viper Grass | UK | *c.* 1890 | Arthur Wilcock
Wilcock designed wallpaper and textiles such as this furnishing fabric for British
manufacturers and producers before emigrating to the United States.

07 | Kimono detail | Japan | 1870–90
This stylized design of bamboo stems, overlaid by flattened wavelike swirls, reveals
the crisp, graphic quality of Japanese pattern-making.

08 | Bamboo | UK | 2011 | Timorous Beasties
Timorous Beasties' translucent printed lace fabric, patterned with bamboo stems,
makes a striking contemporary alternative to the traditional sheer drape.

09 | **Heinä** | **Finland** | **1957** | Maija Isola
Isola, who had a love of nature, based this Marimekko pattern on her observation of real grasses, collected and pressed by her daughter for a school project.

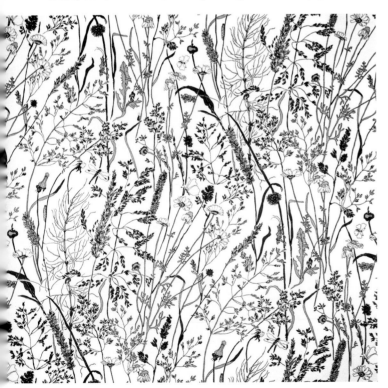

10 | **Gräs (Grass)** | **Sweden** | **1990s** | Birgitta Liedgren
The pattern for this furnishing fabric, designed for Ljungbergs, was inspired by Liedgren's walks in the countryside near Stockholm.

11 | **Bamboo** | **UK** | **2008** | Sam Pickard
Pickard's botanical patterns have been used to create large-framed wall panels to bring the freshness of natural growth to the interior.

FAUNA

01 | **Pedigree Entourage** | UK | 2012–13 | Eley Kishimoto

Many of Eley Kishimoto's patterns play tricks with perception. This corgi print is a "houndstooth" pattern with a twist.

02 | **Sausage Dogs** | UK | 2014 | Cath Kidston
Cath Kidston's novelty prints have a whimsical charm. This pattern, featuring jacketed dachshunds, appears on a range of products including children's plates.

03 | **George and Rufus** | UK | 1938 | Ben Nicholson
British artist Nicholson was also a noted designer of patterns. This whimsical furnishing fabric was produced for him by Edinburgh Weavers.

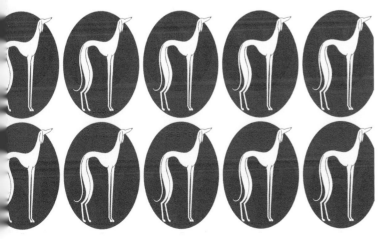

04 | **Saluki design** | UK
This saluki dog pattern is based on an original archived image depicting the elegant, exotic breed that is also known as a Persian greyhound.

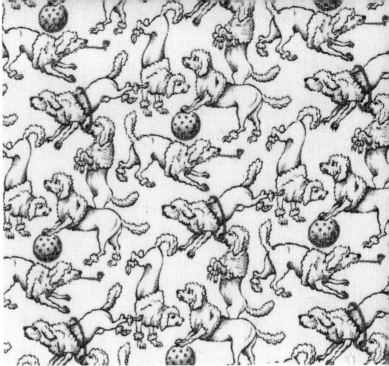

05 | **Fabric sample** | UK | late 19th century
Red, white, and blue printed cotton fabric of unknown origin. Clipped poodles frolic across the plain ground, jumping through hoops and balancing on balls.

06 | **Dogs** | UK | 2010 | Tony Trickey
Trickey's humorous sketches translate into flat patterns or embroidered textiles. This embroidered pattern was created for First Eleven Studio.

Cath Kidston (b.1958)

SEE PAGES > 85, 129, 131, 180, 209, 254, 486, 491, 495, 498, 503, 556, 562

Cath Kidston built a successful business out of a passion for nostalgic floral patterns. Unashamedly pretty, cheerful, and light-hearted, her designs, many of which are based on vintage fabrics, are a romantic take on British style and appear across a wide range of products—from fashion to homeware, bags, and accessories.

It all started with Cath's eye for color and design, so after trying her hand at various jobs (including dog walking, modeling, and interior design) she hit on an idea, and in 1993 opened a small shop in Holland Park, West London. Originally selling antique finds and vintage fabric, Cath soon began to design and produce her own prints and products, taking inspiration from vintage pieces and giving them a modern twist. The first offerings were a floral ironing board cover and rose wallpaper, and from there it began to grow.

Her first print, "Antique Rose Bouquet" (1993), was a reworking of a traditional rose-patterned wallpaper. The timing was perfect. With the country experiencing an economic downturn, the mood was nostalgic and wistful and Cath Kidston's cheerful, cozy prints became a key element in what would become known as modern vintage. They were also part of a growing trend for pattern to be applied across a wide range of household products.

Establishing the brand, however, took time. Going into wholesale, which enabled her designs to be sold through other stores, and exhibiting at trade fairs to increase distribution began to win her greater publicity. To the original floral designs, she added new prints—dots, stars, and a pattern featuring a cowboy on horseback that was inspired by her love of vintage Americana.

The quintessential British brand has now become synonymous with classic design and nostalgic style, and is renowned for floral prints and bright, playful patterns. Its unique range of everyday, practical products has brought modern vintage to fans all over the world. Cath no longer works for the brand, having stepped down as Creative Director in 2014. Today, as when the brand began, the design team seek inspiration from a treasure trove of quirky British vintage finds, creating pretty, colorful prints with a nod to nostalgia that turn modern products into something witty, fresh, and fun.

Today, Cath Kidston stores can be found across Britain, as well as in countries including Japan, Korea, Thailand, Saudi Arabia, and China.

Top Cath Kidston's "Pets Party" displays a host of guinea pigs, each decked out in its finest party attire.

Above Inspired by an old wallpaper found at a vintage market, "Antique Rose Bouquet" is the definitive Cath Kidston floral and has been a constant part of the range ever since the brand started in 1993.

Opposite The brand aims to create cheerful, practical products that bring a smile to your face and brighten up your day. Inspired by Cath's pet Sealyham Terrier, the "Billie" print was introduced in 2015.

02 | Rabbit | UK | 2016 | Aki Ueda Castellani
This printed design has the spare graphic quality of a stenciled pattern, with pink rabbits arranged in alternating rows amid sprigs of foliage.

01 | Brer Rabbit | UK | 1882 | William Morris

At the time this pattern was designed, Morris and his family were intrigued by the Uncle Remus stories published in 1881. Philip Webb drew the rabbit.

03 | Printed design | UK | 2013 | Liza Saunders
Saunders, one of the designers producing work for First Eleven Studio, has a background in fashion. Her textile patterns are printed digitally or by silkscreen.

04 | **Bunny Dance** | UK | 2008–09 | Eley Kishimoto
This exuberant bunny pattern has appeared on a range of clothing and has also been
used as a book jacket for the Virago edition of Molly Keane's *Good Behaviour* (1981).

02 | Horses | UK | 2008–09 | Eley Kishimoto
Horses in a number of different gaits animate the surface of the pattern with a great sense of movement and vitality.

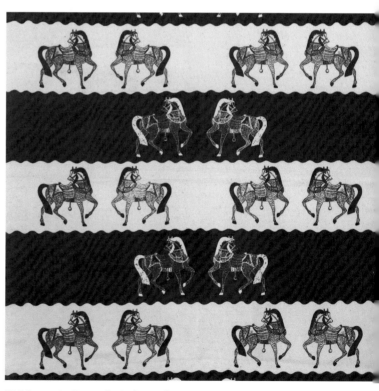

01 | Horses' Heads | UK | 1936
This interlocking positive and negative pattern appears on a printed cotton dress fabric produced by Dilkusha.

03 | Spencerian Horses | USA | 1939 | Marguerita Mergentime
Mergentime was a US textile designer who was noted for the patterns she created for household tablecloths and linen.

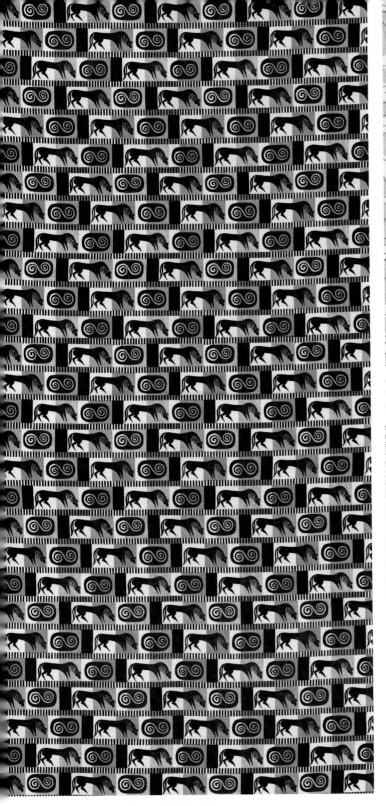

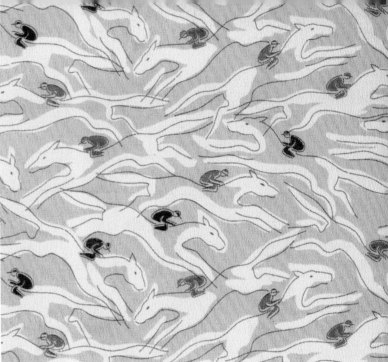

05 | **Jockeys** | UK | 1945 | Calico Printers' Association
Horses rendered in loose outlines race across the vivid yellow ground of this printed rayon crêpe dress fabric.

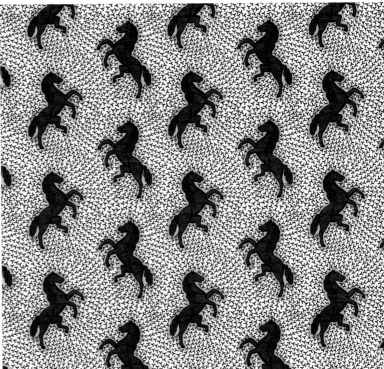

04 | **Altamira** | UK | 1952 | Christine Clegg
A printed cotton furnishing fabric, designed for Edinburgh Weavers. The pattern features rows of horses and spirals.

06 | **Jumping Horse** | Netherlands | 1930
This dress fabric manufactured by Vlisco is patterned using a wax block print. Vlisco produces fabric for the African market.

01 | **Falcon Hunt** | USA | 1920–30 | Herman A. Elsberg

Elsberg was inspired by marginal drawings on a Persian manuscript. This furnishing
fabric, handwoven on a jacquard loom, features golden gazelles and silver falcons.

02 | Enara | UK | 1951 | Karen Willinger
Cotton furnishing fabric, designed for Edinburgh Weavers. Willinger was one of
a number of textile designers who produced work for this progressive textile firm.

03 | Fabric design | USA | 1962 | Lilli Meissinger
The pattern of this screen-printed cotton furnishing fabric shows confronted stags
and birds in blocks of green.

04 | Fighting Stags | UK | c.1855
This furnishing fabric was roller-printed in Lancashire. Naturalistic or scenic
patterns were popular in the 19th century.

05 | The Duleek | UK | 1899 | C. F. A. Voysey
A woven wool wall hanging designed for the manufacturer Alexander Morton.
In addition to stags and swans, the central band includes Voysey's favorite doves.

01 | Rambo Blacks | UK | 2013 | Liza Saunders

This printed cotton furnishing fabric was designed for Habitat. Saunders is one
of the First Eleven Studio group of designers.

02 | Wallpaper | France | 1906–07
The naturalistic pattern on this machine-printed wallpaper features a cat playing with a ball of yarn, overlooked by a mouse.

03 | Printed endpaper | France | 1908 | Benjamin Rabier
Endpaper from *Les images en musique*. Rabier was an illustrator and cartoonist, best known for creating the *La vache qui rit* (The Laughing Cow) cheese logo.

04 | Pichhwai | India | late 19th century
Pichhwais are large painted cloths that hang in Hindu shrines or temples. This example, made of embroidered cotton and silk thread, was produced in Gujarat.

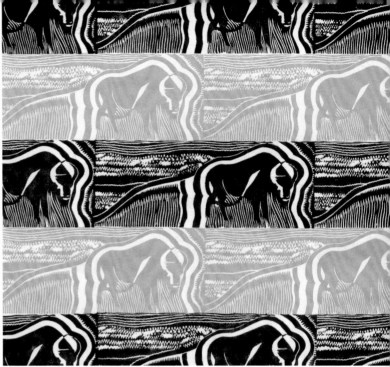

05 | Buffalo | UK | 1951 | Armfield Passano/Diana Armfield R.A.
Armfield started her career in partnership with Roy Passano; they contributed to the 1951 Festival of Britain and their work is in the permanent collection at the V&A.

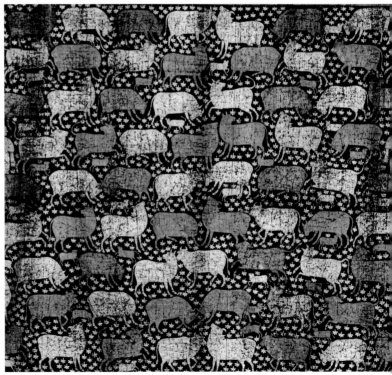

06 | Pichhwai | India | late 18th century
This *pichhwai* was produced for the Festival of Cows. The pattern of cows and calves on a flowery field features an extensive use of silver and gold thread.

01 | **Small Elephants** | UK | 1974 | Neil Bradburn
This cotton furnishing fabric was designed for Heal's. The graphic pattern was
a best selling textile in the 1970s.

02 | **Elefant (Elephant)** | Sweden | 1930s | Estrid Ericson
A linen furnishing fabric designed for Svenskt Tenn. Ericson, who enjoyed traveling,
based this pattern on a model from the Belgian Congo.

03 | Safari Dance | UK | 2017 | Cole & Son with Ardmore Ceramic Art
The dancing elephants in this wallpaper were taken from large urns painted by Zinhle
Nene, which are in the museum of Ardmore Ceramics in South Africa.

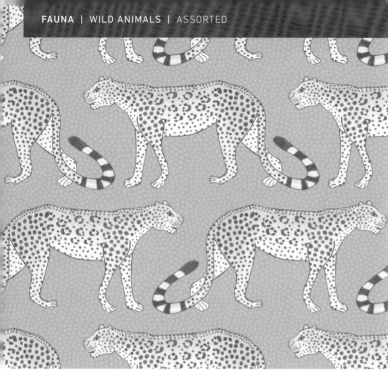

01 | **Leopard Walk** | UK | 2017| Cole & Son with Ardmore Ceramic Art
This wallpaper pattern was taken from a design painted by Punch Shabalala, an
artist working with Ardmore Ceramics in South Africa.

02 | **Leopards** | UK | 2016 | Varpu Kronholm
Kronholm is a London-based pattern designer and artist who works in digital media.
Her work has been licensed to appear as wallpaper and scarves.

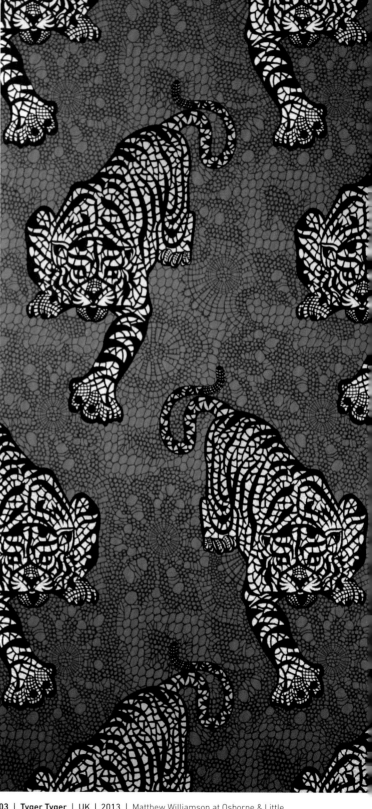

03 | **Tyger Tyger** | UK | 2013 | Matthew Williamson at Osborne & Little
This holographic-foiled wallpaper, with its stalking tiger motif, glows with rich,
jewel-like colors.

04 | Endpaper | France | 19th century
An endpaper from a book published by Firmin Didot of Paris. The pattern is similar
to damask and features highly stylized animals.

01 | Almond Blossom and Swallow | UK | late 19th century | Walter Crane

Swallows, with their characteristic forked tails, fly against flowering almond
blossom in a wallpaper pattern clearly influenced by Japanese design.

02 | Birds | UK | 2016 | Aki Ueda Castellani
The irregular marks left by the stencil or printing block on this printed design
contribute a great sense of movement to the swallow pattern.

03 | Wallpaper | France | 1921–22 | Paul Vera
This machine-printed wallpaper was designed by the French painter and designer
Vera, who was one of the pioneers of Art Deco.

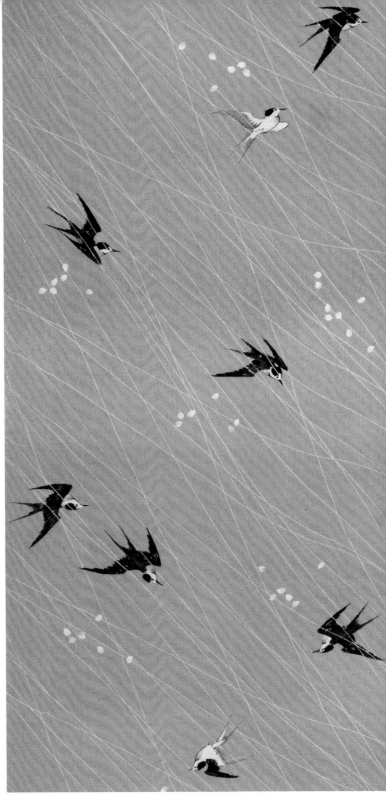

04 | Silk fabric | Japan | 19th century | Nampei
Attributed to Nampei, this painted silk was created using a stencil resist. Birds are
common motifs in Japanese patterns.

02 | Dove and Rose | UK | 1879 | William Morris
The drawing room walls at Wightwick Manor in Wolverhampton, West Midlands, are covered with this woven silk and wool double cloth furnishing fabric.

01 | Purple Bird | UK | c.1899 | C. F. A. Voysey
This silk and wool double cloth was made by Alexander Morton of Darvel, Ayrshire. The pattern features pale purple birds perched in diagonally slanting foliage.

03 | Doveflight | UK | 2005 | Mark Hearld for St Jude's
Perching and flying doves animate this furnishing fabric designed for St Jude's. Hearld studied natural history illustration at the Royal College of Art in London.

04 | Doves | UK | 1935 | Calico Printers' Association
The pattern of doves on this cotton furnishing fabric has a strong diagonal emphasis.
The bird motifs are arranged over slanting scalloped bands.

Marion Dorn (1896–1964)

SEE PAGE > 256

Painter, illustrator, and wallpaper and fabric designer Marion Dorn was well known in 1930s Britain as "the architect of floors," creating original carpeting for many luxury hotels and ocean liners. Influenced by Constructivism and other European avant-garde art movements, her work featured graphic geometric motifs and stylized naturalistic forms.

Born in Menlo Park, California, Dorn was educated at Stanford University, graduating in 1916 with a degree in graphic arts. In 1919, she moved to New York with her husband and former tutor Henry Varnum Poor, where she first gained attention as an illustrator and designer of batiks.

On a trip to Paris in 1923, Dorn met US-born poster designer Edward McKnight Kauffer (1890–1954), who was visiting from London. The two fell in love and Dorn moved to London to be with him later the same year. They married in 1950.

Throughout the 1920s, Dorn's reputation grew. In 1925, five of her batik designs were featured in *Vogue* and she began to focus on textiles. Many of her designs, block-printed on silk, linen, and velvet, were stocked by leading London stores; some were also put on display in museums and galleries. After she exhibited at the "International Exhibition of Arts and Crafts" at Leipzig in 1927, and published a book of rug designs the following year, she gained a number of commissions from leading architects and decorators, such as Syrie Maugham, for whom she created a textured white rug for the famous "white room," as well as from prestigious London hotels such as Claridge's, the Berkeley, and the Savoy. Cunard also commissioned Dorn rugs for their new liner, the *Queen Mary*. Typically, her rugs, essentially floor-level modern art, featured bold, calligraphic bands and waves, evocative of the Art Deco style.

By 1934, she had set up her own textile company, Marion Dorn. Her upholstery design for the London tube, "Colindale Moquette," a stylized leaf pattern, dates from this time. During the same period, Dorn began her fruitful association with the progressive firm Edinburgh Weavers, which had adopted the then-new technique of hand screen-printing. The process made short runs of cutting-edge designs commercially viable.

Another key association was with Warner & Sons, which printed twenty-two of Dorn's designs between 1934 and 1942, many of which were also screen-printed. These featured motifs drawn from nature, such as leaves, shells, and birds.

In 1940, Dorn and McKnight Kauffer moved to New York and she carried on designing for a number of US textile and wallpaper firms. Her last major commission, in 1960, was to create a carpet for the Diplomatic Reception Room at the White House.

Top Marion Dorn, seated among her textile designs, photographed for *House and Garden* in 1947.

Above "Three Poppies, Four Wheat Sheaves, and Hand" is a textile design dating from 1938. Many of Dorn's fabrics were stocked by leading London stores.

Opposite "Avis," a furnishing fabric Dorn designed for Edinburgh Weavers in *c.* 1939, is a graphic pattern depicting birds in flight.

02 | **Stenciled paper** | Japan | mid-20th century
A sample of Japanese hand-stencil-dyed paper. In Japan, the *tsuru* (crane) is revered as a symbol of good luck and longevity.

01 | **Wallpaper** | UK | 1930–50
This machine-printed English wallpaper, dating from the mid-20th century, has the delicacy of chinoiserie designs.

03 | **Wallpaper** | UK | *c.*1890 | Silver Studio
Silver Studio, founded in 1880 by Arthur Silver, was a leading British textile and wallpaper design studio, much associated with Art Nouveau.

04 | Yellow and Green Trees with Cranes | Japan | 1882
This is a color woodblock print from a Japanese pattern book for kimono design.
Cranes, which are monogamous, often appear on wedding kimonos.

05 | Cranes Flying in an Abstract Pattern | Japan | 1882
This unusual motif, featuring aerial views of cranes, is from another color woodblock
print reproduced in a Japanese pattern book for kimono design.

Japonaiserie (1850s–1920s)

Japonaiserie, or Japonisme, was a mid- to late 19th-century style of decoration that reflected a Western fascination with the Orient. Under the ruling Tokugawa Shogunate, Japan had pursued a policy of isolation since the 17th century. That changed in 1854 when the US Navy forced Japan to sign a treaty opening it to world trade.

Japanese art and artifacts poured into Europe and the United States. Some of the most influential of these were the least expensive: woodblock prints known as *ukiyo-e*, pictures of the floating world. Collected by artists including Vincent van Gogh and Henri Matisse (1869–1954), and exhibited at Siegfried "Samuel" Bing's influential Parisian gallery, the work of artists like Utagawa Hiroshige was a revelation for those schooled in the Western tradition. The flat areas of solid color, asymmetry, lack of shading and depth, and focus on decorative patterning influenced the development of Impressionism and Art Nouveau.

The simplicity and elegance of the Japanese products on display at the International Exhibition of 1862 in London and the Paris Exposition Universelle in 1878 were revelatory. Enthusiastically embraced by leading lights in the Aesthetic movement, Japanese-style motifs and artifacts were seen in fashionable interiors.

British designer Christopher Dresser (1834–1904) was a collector, importer, and distributor of Japanese objects. Simple Japanese-style geometries were a feature of his work, which included wallpaper, carpets, metalwork, and textiles. In a break from Arts and Crafts ideals, his designs elevated taste and modernity over the craft aesthetic. Similarly, British architect and designer Edward William Godwin (1833–86), created a style of Anglo-Japanese furniture inspired by the smooth surfaces of black Japanese lacquer. His rectilinear ebonized designs were imitated widely.

What brought Japonaiserie to a wider market was the commercial sense of retailer Arthur Lasenby Liberty. His shop, East India House, opened in London's Regent Street in 1875 and sold household goods, furniture, wallpapers, fabrics, and decorative objects. Imported Japanese objects and Japanese-inspired products, textiles, and wallpapers addressed a growing middle-class market for the artistic and exotic.

Japan had been exporting its silks since 1859. Soon after, Western textile and wallpaper design displayed Japanese influences. Motifs included cherry and plum blossom, chrysanthemums, grasses, irises, butterflies, and birds, with graphic elements such as fretwork, undulating lines representing flowing water, and tiny stylized repeats suggesting Japanese stencil-printed *komon*. Asymmetry was a feature of such patterning, with motifs placed to treat the entire surface as the field of design.

Top *Rapids at Naruto* (1857) by Utagawa Hiroshige, one of the finest masters of Japanese *ukiyo-e* prints. Japanese woodblock prints, sometimes used to wrap artifacts exported to Europe after the country opened to world trade, had an immense influence on Western artists and designers.

Above A pair of round, flat-bodied porcelain bottles (*c.* 1870–80) by Christopher Dresser. He first visited Japan in 1876, and admired Japanese designs and products.

Opposite An earthenware tile (*c.* 1875) by Dresser, featuring a Japanese-inspired design of cranes flying over waves. As well as collecting, importing, and distributing Japanese goods, his designs show a strong Japanese influence.

01 | Textile design | UK | 1922
Manufactured by Arthur Sanderson & Sons, this pattern appears as a plate in *Modern Decorative Art in England 1* by the artist and designer W. G. Paulson Townsend.

02 | Cockatoo | UK | 1891 | Walter Crane
A wallpaper design produced by Jeffrey & Co. It features the greeny-yellow colors associated with late 19th-century decor.

03 | Textile | UK | 1785–95
Exotic birds perch on the branches of a flowering tree in this English printed textile. Both flora and fauna are rendered in detail.

04 | Macaw | UK | 1908 | Walter Crane
This is a block-printed wallpaper. Crane is known for his illustrations for children's books, but he also designed tiles, textiles, pottery, wallpaper, and stained glass.

05 | Wallpaper | Russia | c.1910 | Natalia Goncharova
Goncharova was an avant-garde Russian artist, much influenced by folk art, who also designed costumes and stage sets for Sergei Diaghilev's Ballets Russes.

07 | Embroidered textile | UK | 2009 | Tony Trickey
Shadowed by their solid gray silhouettes, the multicolored parrots create
an animated embroidered pattern.

06 | Parrot with Pineapple | USA | 2015 | Yoko Honda
Honda's exotic tropical design, featuring parrots, pineapples, and banana leaves, has
appeared on limited edition deckchairs. Her work revives 1980s style patterns.

08 | Chinese Magpie | UK | 1913 | William Turner
This machine-printed wallpaper is thought to have been designed by Turner, an
English landscape artist.

09 | Arini | UK | 2015 | Matthew Williamson at Osborne & Little
This wallpaper typifies Williamson's bold use of color in all his designs for fashion
and patterns for homewares.

Josef Frank (1885–1967)

SEE PAGES > 21, 40, 73, 81, 93, 125, 185, 188, 276

Architect, painter, and furniture designer Josef Frank is best known for his textiles, particularly those he produced between 1941 and 1946. Vivid overgrown gardens of the imagination, bursting with life and color, his rich inventive patterns made a powerful statement about nature's essential goodness at a time when war ravaged continents.

Frank was born at Baden bei Wien near Vienna to Jewish parents. He trained as an architect at Vienna University of Technology and completed a doctorate in 1910. Between 1919 and 1925, he taught at the Vienna School of Arts and Crafts and established an architectural practice specializing in public housing and residential projects.

A founding member of the Vienna Werkbund, Frank was a modernist whose buildings eschewed superficial decoration in favor of functionalism. However, his interiors were noted for their emphasis on domestic comfort, color, and pattern. This approach is evident in the work he produced for Haus & Garten, a design and furnishings firm he co-founded in 1925. In 1932, Frank's furniture designs came to the attention of Estrid Ericson (1894–1981), the founder of Svenskt Tenn in Stockholm. After commissioning Frank to design for the firm, Ericson offered him the position of chief designer.

In 1933, as the political climate worsened in Europe, Frank and his Swedish wife Anna decided to leave Vienna and take up Ericson's offer. Frank's association with Svenskt Tenn lasted thirty years, during which time he produced more than 2,000 pieces of furniture for the company, as well as over 200 designs for carpets, wallpaper, and textiles.

Frank took Swedish citizenship in 1939. However, in 1941, as Nazism held most of Europe in its grip, he and his wife went into exile again, this time fleeing to New York. The subsequent five years, before their return to Stockholm in 1946, were a period of remarkable creativity. Technically at the height of his powers, Frank began to experiment with repeat, motif, and color. Birds and butterflies, trees and flowering plants, fruit and vegetables, the subject matter of his patterns evoked a paradise on earth, expressing a sustaining belief in the human spirit and hope for the future at a time of fear and despair. Not all of the designs that date from this period featured flora and fauna. Others, such as "Manhattan" (1943), with its motifs of New York street plans, were more architectural in character and reflect the influence of his new surroundings.

During the 1950s, commissions began to dwindle and Frank increasingly turned his attention to watercolor painting. In later years, he spent most of his summers painting in the south of France.

Far Left Josef Frank created many designs for Svenskt Tenn of Stockholm.

Left Frank designed the "Varklockor" wallpaper in the 1940s. The leaves and flowers are of the same scale as they would be in a bouquet.

Opposite "Gröna Fåglar" ("Green Birds") was designed between 1943 and 1945, while Frank was living in exile in New York.

01 | Chickens | UK | 2016 | Sarah Battle

A printed design produced by Battle, a First Eleven Studio founder member.
Her designs often feature cats, birds, and quirky objects.

03 | **Furnishing fabric** | UK | 1957 | Hans Tisdall
This woven cotton furnishing fabric with a cockerel pattern was manufactured by
Edinburgh Weavers. Tisdall was an artist and designer of book jackets and textiles.

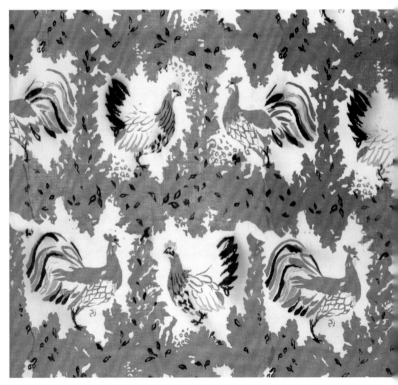

02 | **Happy Family** | Netherlands | 1952 | Ted van de Ven
A dress fabric manufactured by Vlisco using the wax block-printing technique,
a variant of Indonesian batik. Elements of the motif are arranged in a diaper pattern.

04 | **Furnishing fabric** | UK | 1950 | Margaret Cooper
Cooper designed and made this screen-printed fabric while she was a student
at Central Saint Martins College of Art and Design in London.

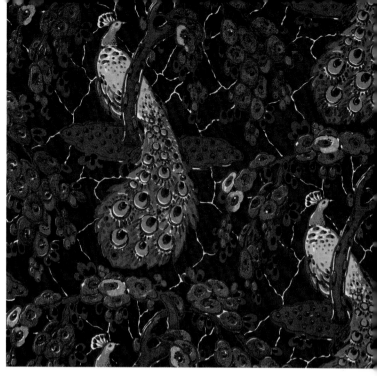

01 | Silk fragment | UK | late 19th century
This English silk textile glows with russet, pink, and ocher tones. The rich pattern of peacocks and exotic flowers and foliage is reminiscent of Middle Eastern design.

02 | Furnishing fabric | UK | c.1922
A printed cotton manufactured by F. Steiner & Co, a Lancashire-based calico dyers and printers. The design is vivid with bright pink and electric blue.

03 | Peacock, Grapevine, and Vases | UK | late 19th century | William De Morgan
De Morgan was fascinated by the decorative arts of Turkey, Persia, and Syria. This is one of his designs for a ceramic tile panel.

04 | Cedar Tree | UK | 1910 | Louis Stahl
A machine-printed wallpaper produced by Arthur Sanderson & Sons. Unlike many of Stahl's patterns, which show a strong Art Nouveau influence, this is more naturalistic.

05 | Byron | UK | 2012 | Cole & Son
This opulent damask wallpaper pattern, reminiscent of late Victorian designs, features gilded peacocks printed in rich mineral colors.

07 | Printed design | UK | 1922 | R. Silver
A plate from *Modern Decorative Art in England 1* (1922) by W. G. Paulson Townsend. An artist and teacher, he thought the study of museum artifacts was invaluable in art education.

06 | The Peacock | UK | c.1890
This is a machine-printed English wallpaper. In its vertically structured pattern, the sweep of the peacocks' tails echoes the serpentine curve of the branch.

08 | Textile | UK | c.1825
In this dense floral and peacock patterned fabric, the color of the "eyes" in the peacocks' tails is echoed by the large-scale blooms.

09 | The Peacock Garden | UK | 1889 | Walter Crane
Exotic birds such as peacocks held a special fascination for the Victorians.
This Crane wallpaper design is rich in detail and close observation.

01 | Peacock Feathers | UK | *c.*1887 | Arthur Silver
This roller-printed cotton fabric was manufactured by Rossendale Printing Co. for
Liberty. Silver was a designer and the founder of Silver Studio.

02 | Scarf | UK | 1930
Here entwined peacock feathers, which have often been used to trim hats, form a decorative border for a Liberty silk crêpe scarf.

03 | Wallpaper | France | 1810–20
Peacock feathers form part of this brightly colored block-printed handmade wallpaper, with Neoclassical elements.

04 | Leopardo | UK | 2015 | Matthew Williamson at Osborne & Little
With its large-scale motifs, this wallpaper pattern features leopards stalking between stylized peacock feathers.

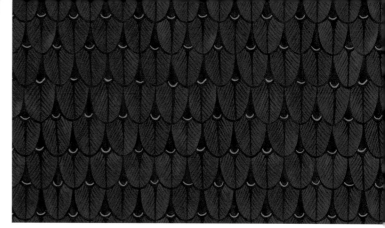

02 | Narina | UK | 2017 | Cole & Son with Ardmore Ceramic Art
Inspired by the detailed patterning on Ardmore pottery, this feather motif wallpaper takes its name from the South African Narina trogon bird.

03 | Feathers | USA | 1957 | Alexander Girard
This pattern for printed cotton is a play on translucency, with overlapping colored feather shapes arranged in a tight geometric grid.

01 | Quill | UK | 2017 | Designers Guild
This digitally printed cotton furnishing fabric is patterned with a richly detailed collection of feathers of different scales and tones.

04 | Woodblock print | Japan | 1882
This color woodblock print of feathers on a lavender background comes from a Japanese pattern book of designs for kimonos.

05 | Starling | UK | 2014 | Imogen Heath
This beautifully calligraphic pattern for a furnishing fabric suggests a starling's plumage in gestural strokes, lines, dots, triangles, and scallop shapes.

06 | Textile | France | *c.* 1870
Soft curling plumes of feathers are arranged in vertical bands against a vivid red ground on this silk textile.

07 | Feathers | USA | 1935–45 | Tirzah Dunn
A machine-printed wallpaper, with crossed feathers in shades of pink, red, and gray on a light gray ground. Dunn designed wallpaper in a wide range of styles.

08 | Feathers | UK | 2015 | Mini Moderns
This wallpaper design was a collaboration between Mini Moderns and the "Banksy of the bird world," artist Matt Sewell. The pattern is based on his feather collection.

01 | Brown Birds Perched on Holly | UK | 1902 | C. F. A. Voysey
This cotton furnishing fabric was manufactured by Wardle & Co., which printed textiles by many Arts and Crafts designers, including William Morris.

03 | Birds of America | UK | *c.*1830 | John James Audubon
A cotton furnishing fabric printed in Lancashire. The pattern is taken from an illustration by Audubon, the US ornithologist who published *The Birds of America* (1827–38).

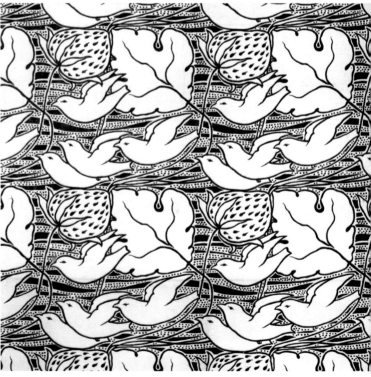

02 | Bird Garden | UK | 2009 | Mark Hearld for St Jude's
Produced for St Jude's, this intricate pattern features birds placed within roundels, against a detailed background of fruit, flowers, and foliage.

04 | Strawberries and Birds | UK | 1897 | C. F. A. Voysey
A cotton furnishing fabric printed by Newman, Smith & Newman. Voysey designed a number of patterns that featured both strawberries and birds.

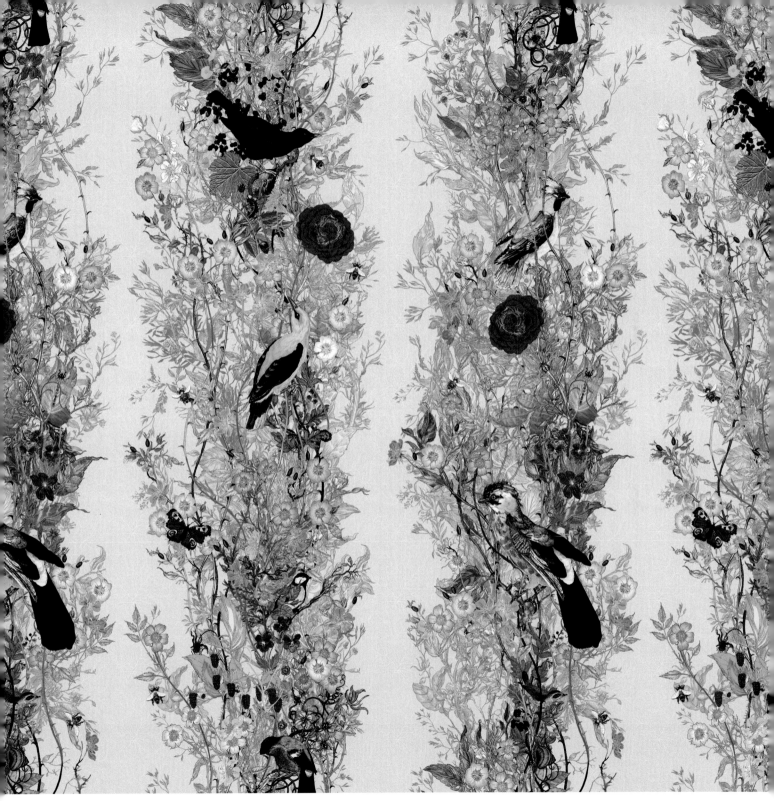

05 | The Fruit Looters | UK | 2015 | Timorous Beasties
Available both as a wallpaper and furnishing fabric, this vertically structured pattern
includes a variety of fruit and feathered fruit thieves within its dense design.

01 | **Tropical Birds** | UK | 2010 | Cole & Son
From an original design of the 1950s by Una Lindsey, this striking wallpaper pattern
shows tropical birds taking flight.

02 | Birds on Branch | UK | 2016 | Aki Ueda Castellani
In this crisply detailed printed design, the traditional sprig motif is transformed into a twig with a bird perched on it.

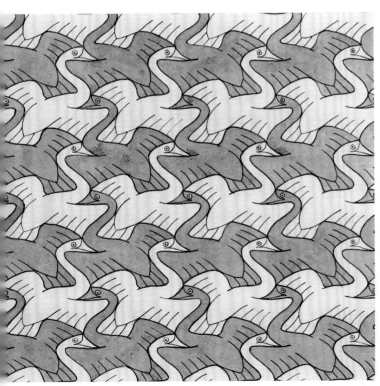

03 | Swan | Netherlands | 1955 | M. C. Escher
This ink and watercolor design is by the Dutch graphic artist Escher. He was a master of tessellated patterns, as these interlocking swans demonstrate.

04 | Ascension | UK | 2011–12 | Eley Kishimoto
A wool and silk hand-printed wrap scarf. In this design, motif and ground merge into one as a flock of birds ascends to blue sky.

252
253

05 | Flock | UK | 2015 | Jenny Frean, First Eleven Studio for Sanderson
A printed design for Indigo Bay. A sense of depth and distance is economically
achieved in this pattern by varying the tones of purple.

06 | Little Birds | UK | 2012 | Cath Kidston
Like most of Kidston's designs, this pattern decorates a range of products,
from handbags to iPhone cases.

07 | Star-ling | UK | 2017 | Mini Moderns
As the name suggests, this Mini Moderns wallpaper pattern combines
a murmuration of starlings flying across constellations of stars.

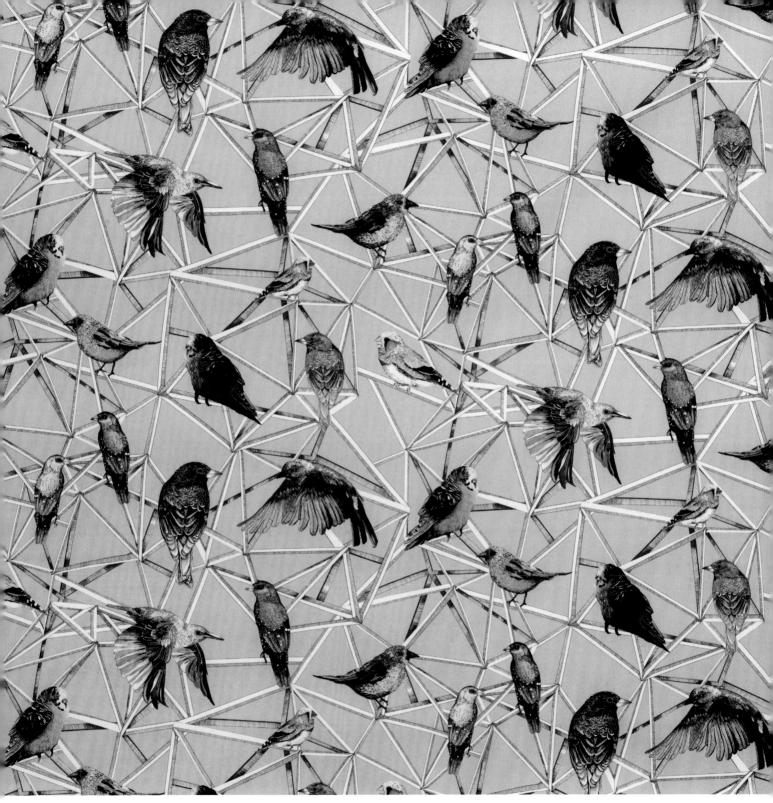

08 | **Aviary** | UK | 2017 | Osborne & Little
In this furnishing fabric, brightly colored birds perch on a geometric structure
reminiscent of the Snowdon Aviary at London Zoo.

10 | Gulls | UK | 2002 | Eley Kishimoto
This tessellated pattern of interlocking gulls is overlaid by wavy lines suggesting water. Eley Kishimoto produces both fashion collections and homeware.

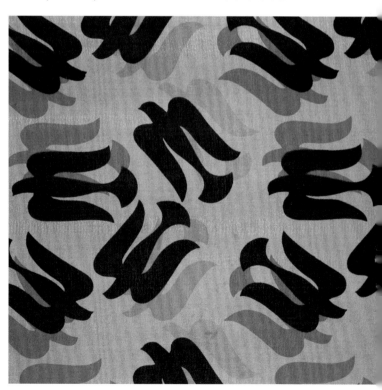

09 | Gulls | UK | 2015 | Mini Moderns
Inspired by the seascape at Dungeness in Kent, this Mini Moderns wallpaper pattern features a seagull motif that appears in the company's Whitby design.

11 | Aircraft | UK | 1958 | Marion Dorn
This is a screen-printed linen and rayon furnishing fabric. Dorn was a hugely successful and prolific pattern designer.

12 | The Owl | UK | 1898 | C. F. A. Voysey
A jacquard-woven wool furnishing fabric manufactured by the Scottish firm
Alexander Morton. This pattern shows pairs of owls perched over nests of chicks.

13 | Die Tausend Raben (A Thousand Ravens) | Austria | 1901 | Koloman Moser
This color lithograph of a tessellated raven pattern is taken from Moser's *Die Quelle:
Flächen Schmuck (The Source: Ornament for Flat Surfaces)*, 1901.

02 | Amazon | UK | 2015 | Jacqueline Colley
One of a series of drawn and digital prints inspired by the Amazon, this lush jungle pattern includes poison dart frogs.

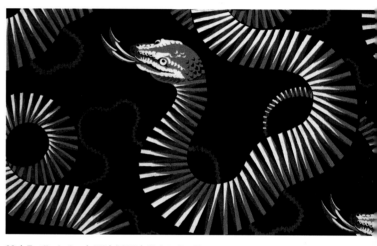

03 | Textile design | UK | 1887 | Christopher Dresser
Dresser was a prolific designer across a wide range of disciplines, as well as a noted design theorist. He was heavily influenced by Japanese art and design.

01 | Iguana | UK | 1990 | Timorous Beasties
Timorous Beasties has an unconventional approach to design. The iguana motif of this wallpaper pattern is drawn with unflinching honesty.

04 | Les Jardins Majorelle | UK | 2013 | Jacqueline Colley
Inspired by the Moroccan artist and botanical garden of the same name, this drawn and digital print features exotic fauna and flora.

06 | Lizard | Netherlands | 1959 | M. C. Escher
Escher's lizards are among his best-known tessellations. They are based on the simple geometric shape of the hexagon, rotated and flipped.

07 | Lizard | Netherlands | 1942 | M. C. Escher
Illustration in India ink, gold ink, colored pencil, and poster paint. Escher's fascination with tessellation was inspired by his studies of the Alhambra in Granada, Spain.

05 | Nicaragua | UK | 2015 | Jacqueline Colley
Colley is an award-winning illustrator and textile designer. This print has appeared on a number of products.

08 | Turtle | USA | 1950–70 | Tommi Parzinger
German-born furniture designer and painter Parzinger was based in New York. His furniture was collected by high-profile clients.

M. C. Escher (1898–1972)

SEE PAGES > 253, 259, 262, 264, 270, 280, 303

Maurits Cornelis Escher is best known for his lithographs and woodcuts that play with perspective and space, striking visual puzzles of perception. He was fascinated by tessellated patterns and arrangements of shapes in which what is foreground and what is background are interchangeable.

Escher was born in Leeuwarden, the Netherlands, and spent most of his childhood in Arnhem. He was unsuccessful at school but went on to technical college in Delft for a year. He then studied drawing and woodcuts at the School for Architecture and Decorative Arts in Haarlem from 1919 to 1922, and switched to graphics from architecture soon after his arrival. A key influence on his development as an artist was his trip to Italy and Spain in 1922. The intricate tilework at the Alhambra in Granada made an indelible impression, particularly during a repeat visit in 1936, and was the start of his interest in the mathematics of tessellation.

On his return to Italy the following year, he met Jetta Umiker; in 1924 they married and settled in Rome, where they remained until 1935. Extensive travels each year throughout Italy gave Escher material in the form of sketches of landscapes and architecture to later work up into prints. At first observation, his output began to reveal his obsession with mathematical analysis and geometry.

The worsening political climate in Italy prompted the family to move to Switzerland in 1935, where they stayed for two years. After a subsequent three-year stay in Brussels, they settled back in the Netherlands, at Baarn, in 1941. There, he created many of the works for which he is best known.

Throughout his lifetime, Escher was largely shunned by the art world; his first retrospective exhibition in the Netherlands did not take place until he was seventy years old. Although his work had Surrealist elements, and shared with Cubism a preoccupation with multiple points of view, it did not fit into any recognizable movement and was admired more by scientists and mathematicians than art critics, despite its demonstrative technical proficiency and virtuoso draftsmanship.

Escher found sudden global fame, however, when a dramatic change in popular culture was ushered in by the psychedelic experiments of the mid- to late 1960s. After his work was published in *Scientific American* in 1966, he found his prints in demand for posters, book jackets, and album covers, by a host of groups including Mott the Hoople. Escher's visionary world, which repeatedly investigated representations of infinity, such as the Möbius strip, or the continuous flights of steps depicted in the lithograph *Ascending and Descending* (1960), chimed powerfully with the hippy sensibility and explorations of multiple realities.

Far Left Dutch graphic artist M. C. Escher, photographed in November 1971.

Left "Lizard/Fish/Bat" is an Escher design dating from 1952.

Opposite "Bird/Fish" (1961) is one of Escher's many tessellated patterns. Escher became entranced by tessellation when visiting the Alhambra in Granada, Spain.

01 | **Fish** | Netherlands | 1955 | M. C. Escher
Escher was famous for the kind of tessellation seen in this watercolor illustration.
He said his obsession with tessellations amounted to "a real mania."

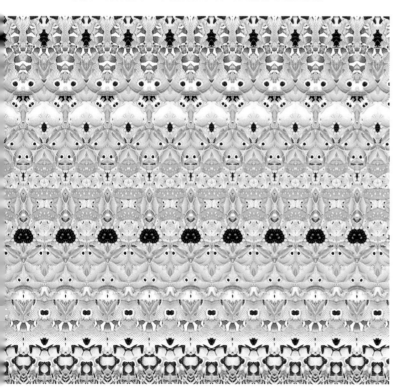

02 | **Tropical Fish Stripe** | UK | 2016 | Robyn Parker
Parker's vivid digital prints have been applied to a wide range of products, from tote
bags to smartphone covers.

03 | **A Fish Is a Fish** | USA | 1951 | Ken Scott
A printed cotton fabric produced by W. B. Quaintance & Co. of New York. Scott was
a US fashion and textile designer who worked mostly in Italy.

04 | **Block print** | UK | *c.*1925–30 | Doris Carter
A pattern that tells a story: the large foregrounded fish is being reeled in by the silhouetted figure of an angler standing by the water's edge.

05 | **Aquaria** | UK | 1952 | Vincent Malta and Richard Munsell
Printed textile created by Vincent Malta, designed by Richard Munsell, and produced by Associated American Artists.

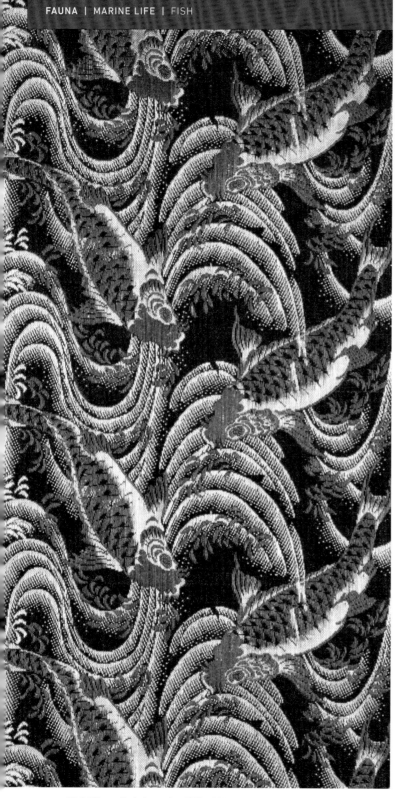

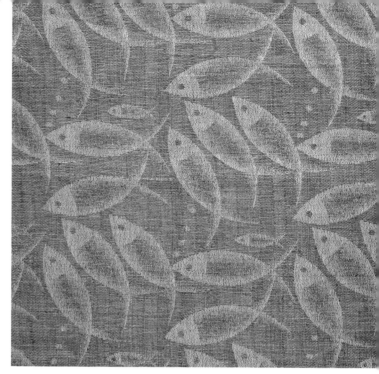

07 | Mandalay | Ireland | c. 1935 | Felix C. Gotto
Gotto's reversible linen furnishing fabric was designed for Old Bleach Linen, Ireland,
a large textile firm that produced fabrics for hotels and ocean liners.

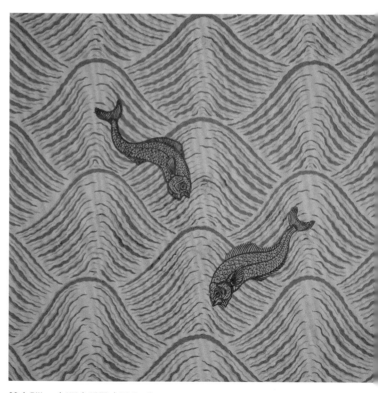

06 | Silk textile | Japan | c. 1880–1930
This Japanese polychrome-patterned silk has alternating rows of fish arranged
against an undulating watery background.

08 | Billow | UK | 1879 | Walter Crane
Displaying a Japanese influence, both in its motifs and stylization, this wallpaper
pattern was produced by Jeffrey & Co.

09 | Nautilus | UK | 2015 | Cole & Son
This wallpaper pattern features a pair of shimmering anglerfish swimming through a dreamlike landscape of underwater plants.

10 | Poisson (Fish) | USA | 1955 | Pablo Picasso
A cotton fabric manufactured by Fuller Fabrics. Dan Fuller worked with Picasso and other leading artists, selecting motifs from their work to make into patterns.

11 | Dress fabric | Netherlands | 1951
A Dutch wax block–printed fabric designed and produced by Vlisco for the African market. The horizontally structured pattern features alternating rows of fish.

02 | Sea Bed | UK | 2016 | Jacqueline Colley
Drawn and digital media. Colley's illustrations, often inspired by nature, have been applied to textiles and other products.

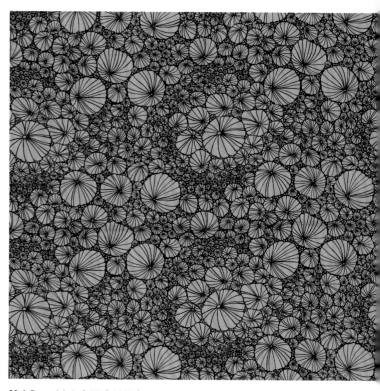

01 | Crabs | USA | 1925 | André Durenceau
This color lithograph is by the French-American artist and textile designer Durenceau, who worked in the Art Deco style.

03 | Dress fabric | UK | 1975 | Martin Battersby
A fabric designed for Liberty. Battersby was a *trompe-l'oeil* artist and expert on Art Nouveau who began his career designing for Liberty.

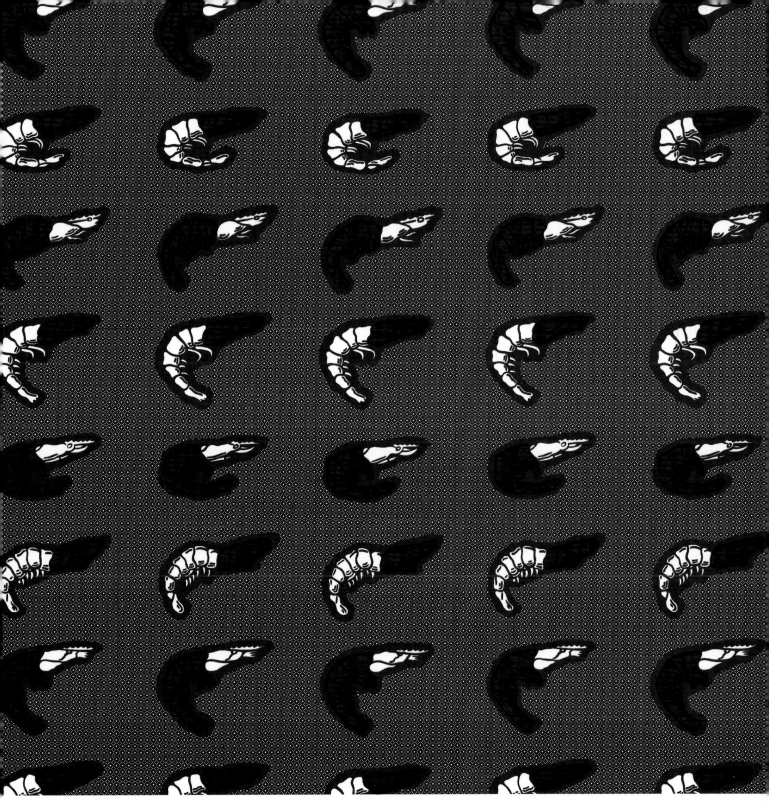

04 | Dress fabric | Netherlands | 1956
Vlisco's wax-resist printed fabrics have been used by various global brands and
by designers such as Stella McCartney and Comme des Garçons.

01 | Les Conques (The Conches) | France | 1925 | Raoul Dufy
Dufy's block-printed linen furnishing fabric was designed for French textile
manufacturer Bianchini-Férier.

02 | Sea Shells | USA | 1956
Printed cotton fabric made by the Apponaug Company. The three-dimensional
all-over pattern of sea shells and their shadows has a photographic quality.

03 | Dress fabric | Netherlands | 1982 | Jan Mollemans
Vlisco was founded in the mid-19th century and began printing fabric
in a mechanized version of batik wax-resist.

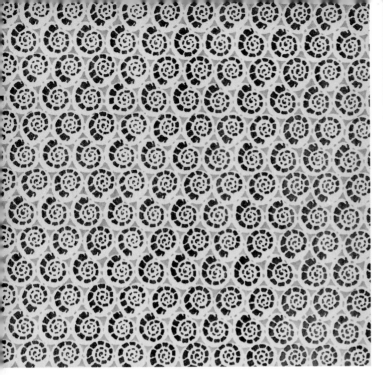

04 | Paper sample | France | 1920
A machine-printed paper from a sample book, *Patria Papiers de Fantaisie*, produced by Maison Maunoury et Cie. The pattern has alternating rows of stylized shells.

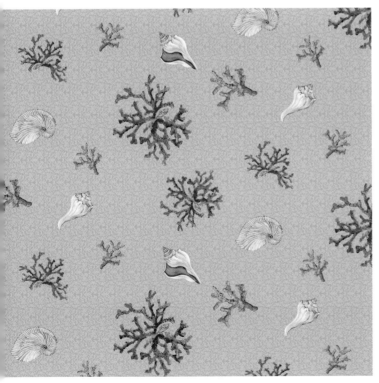

05 | Coral and Shells | USA | 2012 | Kimberly McSparran
McSparran is a US designer of patterns for homeware, wallpaper, and textiles as well as a pet portrait artist.

06 | Shells and Sand | USA | 1960 | William Justema
A wallpaper printed by James D. Gaffney. Rotating oversized scallop shell motifs appear on a background stippled with irregular gold dots.

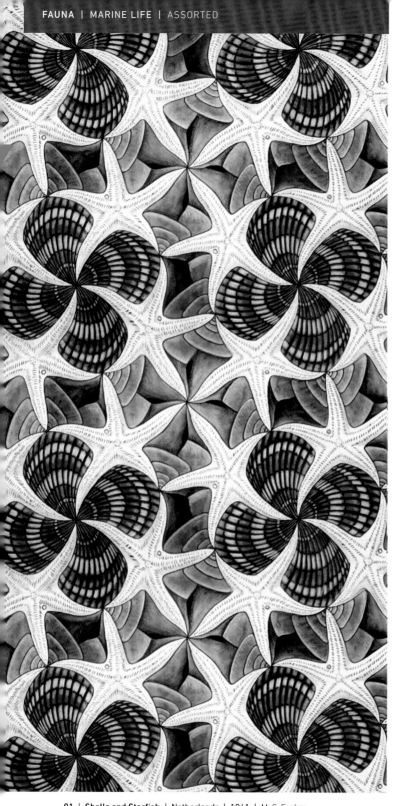

01 | **Shells and Starfish** | Netherlands | 1941 | M. C. Escher
Although his designs are now well known, Escher spent much of his career in
relative obscurity as his work did not fit into conventional artistic genres.

02 | **Sea Things** | USA | 1950 | Charles and Ray Eames
Although all the textile patterns produced by the Eames Office were credited to both
Eameses, they were all solely the work of Ray.

03 | Wallpaper | France | 1920–25
This French wallpaper was collected and distributed in the United States by decorator and wallpaper historian Nancy McClelland.

05 | L'Eau (Water) | France | 1925 | Yvonne Clarinval
A silk textile manufactured by Tassinari et Chatel. Various marine creatures, such as jellyfish, starfish, coral, and seahorses are arranged on a turquoise ground.

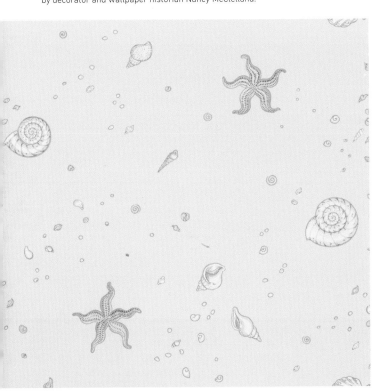

04 | Wallpaper | UK | 1879 | Walter Crane
Produced by Jeffrey & Co., this block-printed wallpaper features marine motifs of starfish and shells widely spaced on the ground.

06 | Sea Horses | UK | 1938 | Calico Printers' Association
The graphic black heads of the seahorses pull the motif further into the foreground of this printed dress fabric.

01 | Bees with Honeycomb | USA | 1881 | Candace Wheeler
Wheeler is often credited as the "mother" of interior design. She designed this wallpaper pattern for her own textile company, Associated Artists.

02 | Wild Honey Bee | UK | 2011 | Timorous Beasties
This all-over wallpaper design features an asymmetric pattern of swarming honey bees densely covering the ground.

03 | Damask | France | 19th century
This is the Bonaparte emblem and royal crest of Napoleon III. The bee, symbolizing immortality and resurrection, was an emblem of the First and Second Empires.

04 | Imperial Apiary | UK | 2014 | Timorous Beasties
In this wallpaper design, highly detailed bee motifs are regularly placed against
a glowing damask-patterned background.

01 | **Charonda** | **UK** | **2006** | Designers Guild
In this finely drawn and delicately colored pattern for a printed cotton furnishing
fabric, the butterflies are arranged like specimens.

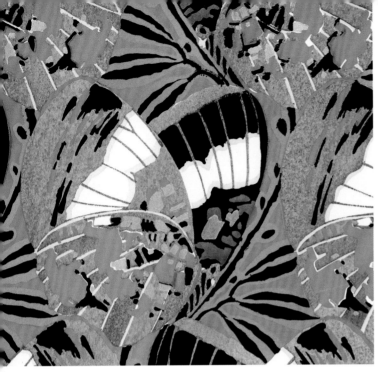

02 | Pochoir print | France | 1925 | E. A. Séguy
This is Plate 20, from *Papillons* (*Butterflies*, 1925). *Pochoir* printing, a technique similar to stenciling, was often used in Art Nouveau and Art Deco designs.

04 | Papillon | UK | 2008 | Sarah Hough
This digital artwork has been reproduced under licence on a range of products, from textiles to stationery.

03 | Furnishing fabric | UK | 1923 | Minnie McLeish
A fabric designed for the firm of William Foxton. This highly decorative pattern features stylized butterflies and flower heads.

05 | Hydrangeas and Butterflies | Japan | 1882
Japanese color woodblock prints took the West by storm in the late 19th century. This print comes from a pattern book for kimono design.

06 | Butterfly | Sweden | 1943–45 | Josef Frank
A furnishing fabric manufactured by Svenskt Tenn. Butterflies, dragonflies, and beetles are grouped around small pools of water.

08 | Camberwell Beauty | UK | 2014 | Mini Moderns
This calligraphic wallpaper, from Mini Moderns' "The Buddha of Suburbia" collection, features butterfly wings made up of lettering.

07 | Butterflies | UK | 2013 | John Dilnot
Dilnot's screen-printed design reflects his interest in natural history. He studied graphic design at Canterbury College of Art and fine art at Camberwell School of Art.

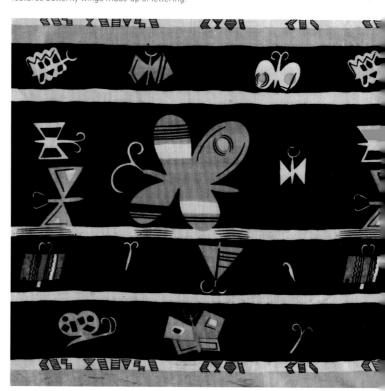

09 | Dress fabric | Austria | c.1925
A detail of silk dress fabric from the Wiener Werkstätte (Vienna Workshops). This highly graphic horizontally structured pattern gains impact from its black background.

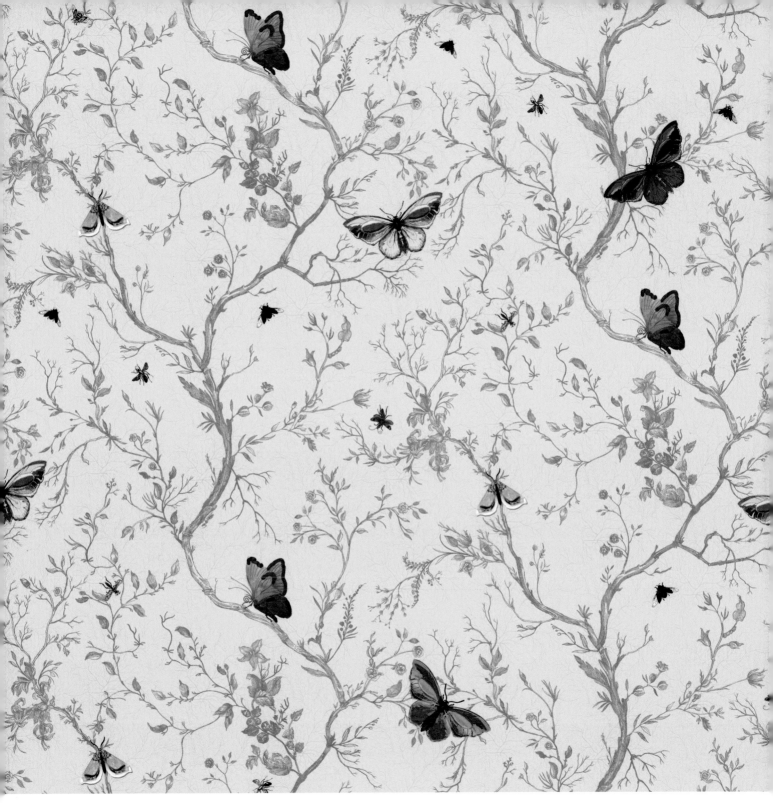

10 | Butterflies | UK | 2011 | Timorous Beasties
Brightly colored butterflies and insects are arranged across a background
of branches and wild flowers.

01 | **Zig Zag Moth** | UK | 2011 | Timorous Beasties
At first glance, this pattern appears to resemble a Missoni zigzag knitted fabric, but it
is actually made up of moth bodies.

02 | White Moth Circle | UK | 2011 | Timorous Beasties
This wallpaper and furnishing fabric pattern invites a double take. Superficially delicate and lacelike, it is composed of moth bodies.

03 | Inky Insects | UK | 2015 | Varpu Kronholm
Silhouetted insect shapes are infilled with inky splashes of color, thus creating a pattern within a pattern.

04 | Moths | UK | 2009 | John Dilnot
British artist, designer, and printmaker Dilnot has had a strong interest in natural history since childhood.

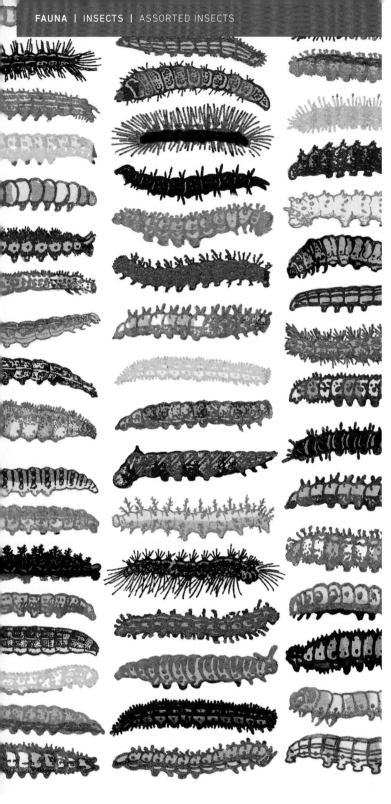

02 | **Beetle** | Netherlands | 1953 | M. C. Escher
Beetles, particularly scarab beetles, feature in a number of Escher artworks, including this tessellated pattern.

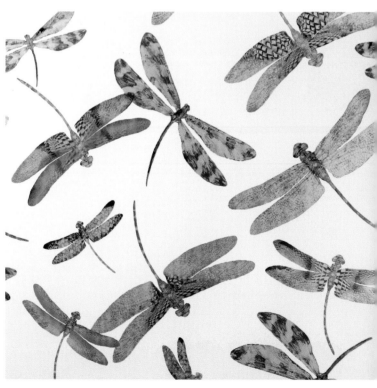

01 | **Caterpillars** | UK | 2009 | John Dilnot
This screen print on paper features multicolored vertical rows of caterpillars closely observed to make a strikingly graphic design.

03 | **Dragonfly Dance** | UK | 2014 | Matthew Williamson at Osborne & Little
The dragonfly motif in this wallpaper pattern first appeared on the shoulder of a cashmere cardigan worn by British model Kate Moss.

04 | **Tsunotombo (Owlfly)** | 2012 | Fumi Ito
A printed cotton fabric designed for Nuno. The individual motifs resemble cut-paper
stencils, a traditional element in Japanese printing.

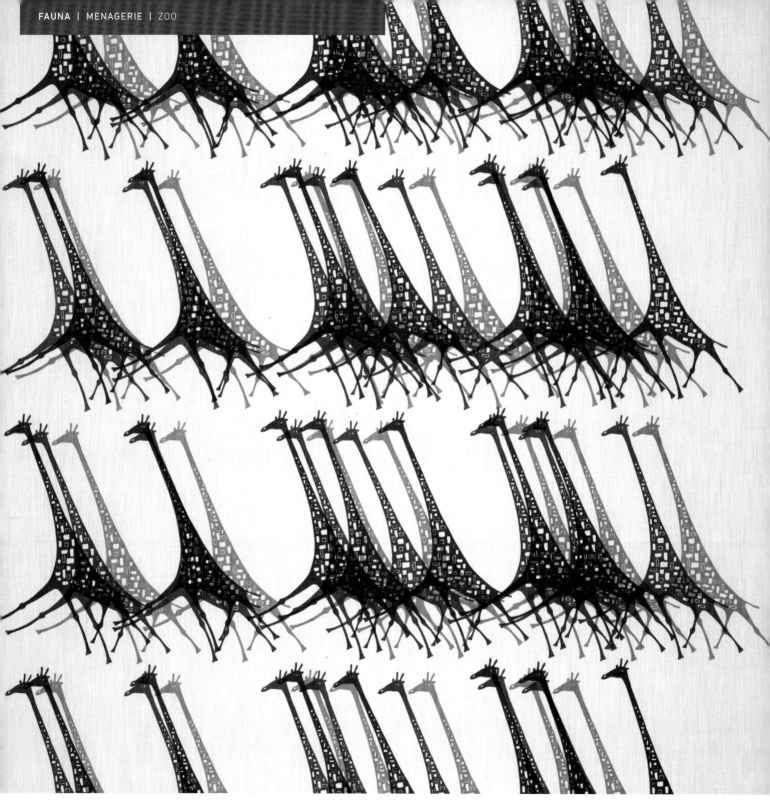

01 | Girafters | USA | 1949 | Ben Rose

A sample of modacrylic and rayon furnishing fabric, reprinted in 1988. Rose was
an artist turned award-winning designer. This witty pattern is a visual pun.

02 | **Bird Zoo** | UK | 1940–49 | Joe Martin
Printed cotton produced by F. Schumacher & Co. This vertically structured pattern features perching birds facing in alternating directions.

03 | **Zoo** | UK | 2012 | Tony Trickey
An embroidered textile designed for First Eleven Studio. Loosely drawn animals, executed in stitching, are overlaid by patches of bright color.

04 | **Animal Kingdom** | USA | 1950 | Edgar Miller
A wallpaper manufactured by Bassett & Vollum. Miller was a hugely versatile artist, craftsman, and designer, who excelled in the field of stained glass.

02 | Sheep | UK | *c.*1926–29 | Doris Scull
This lino block print on unbleached linen has a graphic quality, with the repeats arranged on the diagonal. Scull was a graduate of the Royal College of Art.

03 | Design on paper | 1928
Bright primary colors and a repeat featuring triangular shapes give additional impact to a winsome, childlike design.

01 | Moo! | UK | 2007 | Mini Moderns
This charming nursery wallpaper, with its farm scenes, is printed in water-based inks on paper from sustained forests.

04 | Bavaria | USA | 2013 | Studio Job for Maharam
Polyester and cotton furnishing fabric designed for Maharam. This dense all-over pattern, bursting with detail, features Bavarian farmyard scenes.

05 | Harvest Hare | UK | 2012 | Mark Hearld for St Jude's
A wallpaper and furnishing fabric designed for St Jude's. This design won the Elle
Decoration British Design Award in 2012.

02 | **Savuti** | UK | 2017 | Cole & Son collaboration with Ardmore Ceramic Art
Part of the Ardmore collection, inspired by African traditions and culture, this Cole & Son wallpaper celebrates one of Africa's best-known national parks.

01 | **Fantasque** | UK | 2016 | Osborne & Little

This metallic-toned jungle wallpaper, with its strong graphic shapes, was inspired by the artistic and cultural movements of the early 20th century.

03 | **Veljekset (Brothers)** | Finland | 2017 | Maija Louekari
A furnishing fabric designed for Marimekko. The pattern was inspired by Finnish folk tales and features bears, lynxes, and owls.

04 | La Jungle (The Jungle) | France | *c.*1914 **|** Raoul Dufy
This screen-printed cotton fabric features a flowing pattern of elephants and tigers on a background of twining stems and leaves.

05 | Zambezi | UK | 2017 | Cole & Son collaboration with Ardmore Ceramic Art
Inspired by the work of Sotho sculptor Benet Zondo, this wallpaper commemorates Operation Noah, when animals were saved from the flooded Zambezi in the 1960s.

06 | Merian Palm | UK | 2013 | Timorous Beasties
This lush, highly detailed wallpaper pattern, with its strong vertical emphasis, comes in an extremely wide repeat.

Zika Ascher (1910–92) | Lida Ascher (1910–83)

SEE PAGES > 313, 472, 504, 535, 553, 612

One of the most influential forces in postwar fashion, the work of Ascher Studio blurred the boundaries between art, industry, and craft. From the 1940s until the 1970s, it remained in the vanguard, its fabrics chosen by couturiers as much for their drape and handling as for their luminous colors and original patterns.

Born in Prague into a Jewish family, Zika Ascher grew up to be a champion skier. In 1939, he was on honeymoon skiing in Norway with his wife, Lida, when Germany annexed Czechoslovakia. Instead of returning home, the couple moved to England. During World War II, while Zika served in the British Army, Lida designed fabrics. After the war, they founded their own studio. With Lida designing and Zika experimenting with the new process of screen-printing, their collaboration resulted in innovative fabrics that proved popular on the catwalk.

Typical of their adventurous approach was Zika's decision to commission leading contemporary artists such as Feliks Topolski (1907–89) to produce designs for scarves in the immediate postwar years. Zika formed a creative association with Henri Matisse (1869–1954), in particular, which lasted until the artist's death, culminating in the "Océanie, le ciel" (Oceania, the Sky, 1946) fabric wall panels.

The Aschers' "Artist Squares" were hailed as a "revolution in industrial design" when they were first exhibited at the Lefevre Gallery in London in 1947. The "Artist Squares" were headscarves of a generous scale and addressed the demand for affordable fashion in the austere postwar era. Eventually featuring work by artists including Matisse, Henry Moore (1898–1986), and Ivon Hitchens (1893–1979), the scarves remain stunning examples of creative cross-fertilization. Zika's desire to match the texture and brushwork of the original artwork as closely as possible meant that some of the designs—such as Hitchens's "Summer Azure" (1947)—took as many as twenty screens to print. Many of the artists produced designs for fashion fabric too, and Moore's "Barbed Wire" (1943) was printed on rayon.

Central to the Aschers' design philosophy was a belief in the importance of hand-making. Lida's hand-drawn designs, both geometrics and calligraphic prints, displayed touches of irregularity that gave them vitality. Zika, a superb colorist and technical perfectionist, translated sketches into repeats, selected colors and fabrics, and oversaw production at the studio's printworks. His flair and inventiveness prompted the introduction of new types of fabric to the world of couture, from fine lightweight silk originally produced as an insulation material for electrical wiring, to shaggy mohairs in bright fluorescent colors.

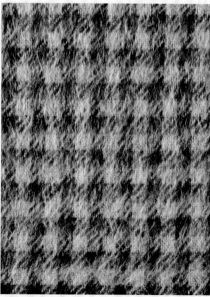

Far Left Zika Ascher judging a fabric design contest he organized to search for promising new designers.

Left Woven mohair, nylon, and wool dress fabric created by Zika in 1957.

Opposite "Jungle" (*c.*1946) is a screen-printed spun rayon, designed by Feliks Topolski.

01 | Embroidered silk textile | late 12th to 14th century
Originating in eastern Central Asia, this embroidered textile features flowers and animals evenly covering the plain ground.

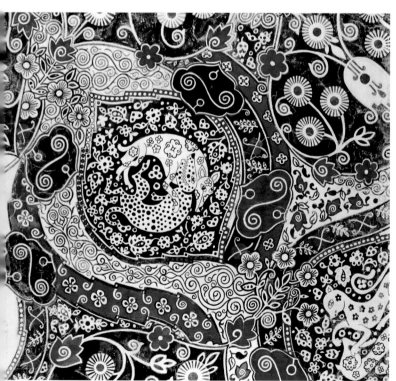

02 | Gouache on paper | Russia | 1971 | Nina Shirokova
Russian artist and designer Shirokova studied at the Moscow Textile Institute. She was responsible for designing the interior of Aeroflot planes in 1964.

03 | Wallpaper | UK | 1953
This Arthur Sanderson & Sons wallpaper was possibly intended for use in nurseries and children's rooms. It depicts stylized animals amid sprays of flowers and foliage.

04 | **Parade** | USA | 1957 | John Rombola
A wallpaper manufactured by Harben Papers. Another light-hearted whimsical pattern, this design includes a number of circus motifs.

05 | **Scarf** | UK | 2012 | Sarah Campbell Designs
A co-founder of Collier Campbell, Sarah Campbell now works independently. This hand-painted silk scarf is a joyous menagerie filled with spots and stripes.

06 | **Furnishing fabric** | UK | 1929 | Dorothy Hutton
Designed for the firm of William Foxton, this nursery pattern tells the story of Noah's Ark, complete with individual animals floating on the floodwaters.

Mola, or *molas*, are the distinctive patterned shirt panels created by the Guna, indigenous peoples of Panama and Colombia. Traditionally, Guna women decorated their bodies by painting them in geometric designs. After colonization by the Spanish and the arrival of Catholic missionaries, such designs were transferred to fabric and have since become a key element of the traditional costume of Guna women. *Mola* means "shirt" or "clothing."

Molas are usually handmade using a reverse appliqué technique. Originally produced in geometric designs that echoed body painting, they have evolved to include other motifs, such as stylized animals, birds, and fantastic creatures.

In reverse appliqué, a demanding and time-consuming technique that requires super-fine stitching, layers of up to seven different colored fabrics are sewn together. The pattern is subsequently created by cutting away parts of each fabric layer, typically working from the largest element of the pattern to the smallest. Occasionally *molas* are further embellished by embroidery.

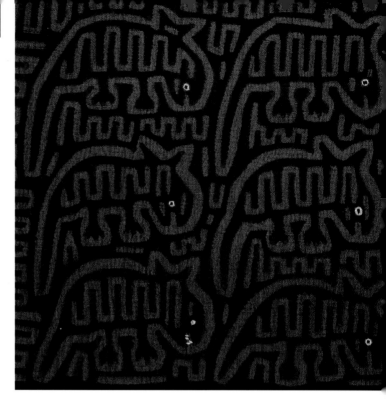

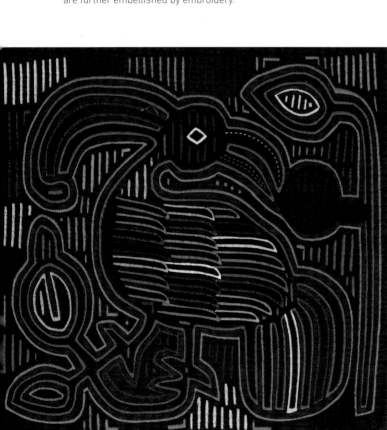

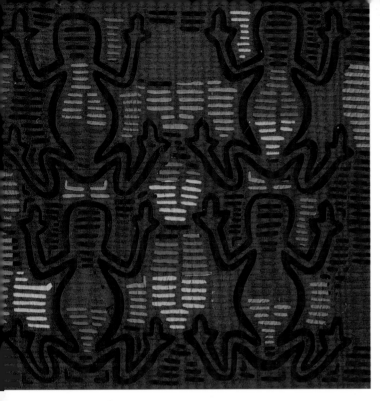

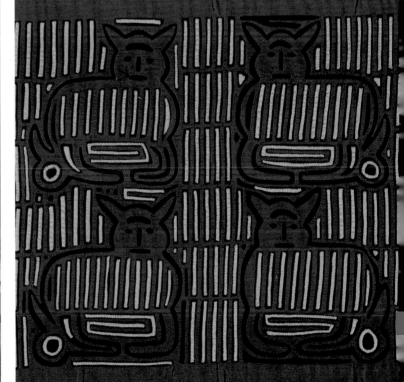

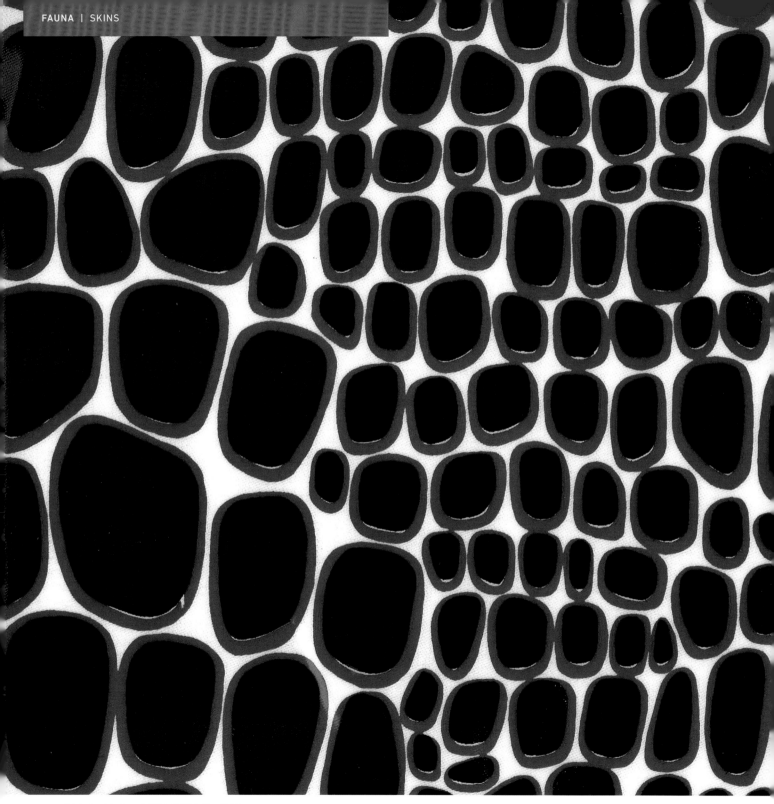

01 | Graphic Croc | UK | 2007 | Eley Kishimoto
The bold, contemporary take on crocodile skin pattern features black splodges
outlined in bright red for a graphic effect.

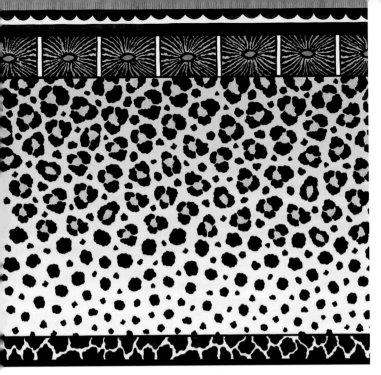

02 | Zulu Border | UK | 2017 | Cole & Son with Ardmore Ceramic Art
Inspired by the decorative pedestal of a ceramic vase, this wallpaper border is
patterned in leopard spots.

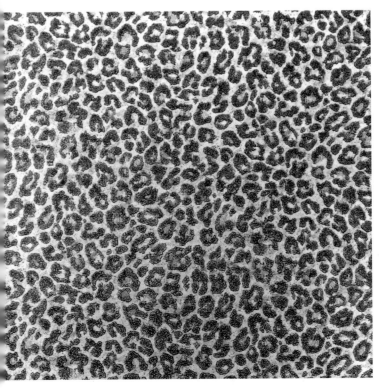

03 | Pardus (Leopard) | UK | 2015 | Osborne & Little
This glamorous leopard-print wallpaper pattern has a metallic effect for
added glitz and shimmer.

04 | Giraffe | UK | 2016 | Anna Hayman
British designer and printmaker Hayman uses linocuts to create her patterns, which
are then digitally printed onto fabric.

05 | Monster Skin | UK | 2009 | Eley Kishimoto
The slightly irregular loops on this hand screen-printed wallpaper are part of the pattern's quirky appeal.

06 | Dress fabric | Netherlands | 2016 | Francesca Franceschi
Designed for Vlisco, this dress fabric, with its simulated snakeskin pattern, is made using a wax-resistant printing method.

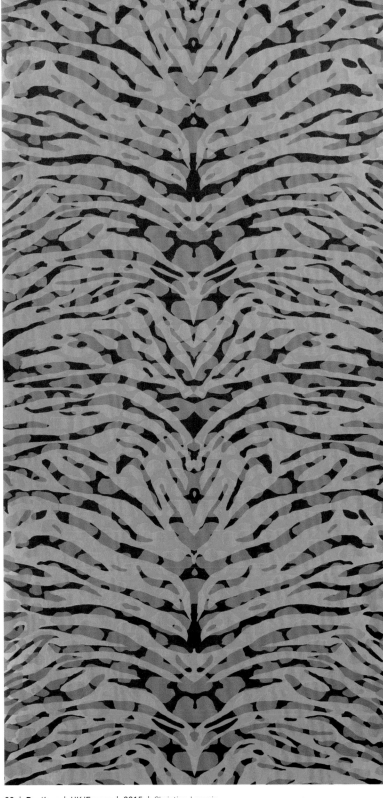

07 | Dress fabric | Netherlands | 1922
Mass-produced imitation batik fabric, manufactured in the Netherlands by Vlisco, has proved very popular in various African countries.

08 | Pantigre | UK/France | 2015 | Christian Lacroix
Part of the House of Lacroix collection created for Designers Guild, this furnishing fabric in cut velvet has a raised pattern of tiger stripes.

01 | **Chinese Dragon** | UK | 1968 | Anthony Little for Osborne & Little
The dragon is a very popular symbol in Chinese art and design, and stands for
power, luck, and nobility.

03 | **Celestial Dragon** | UK | 2013 | Matthew Williamson at Osborne & Little
The pattern of this wallpaper features an imperial Chinese dragon motif with beaded
scales on a metallic wave background.

02 | **Tile panel** | UK | *c.* 1882–88 | William De Morgan
De Morgan's tile panel, made of white earthenware with a luster glaze, depicts birds,
dragons, and foliage. The full-size panel includes a border with a serpentine pattern

04 | **Lithograph** | France | 1873 | Albert Charles Auguste Racinet
"Chinese and Japanese," Plate 13 from *Polychromatic Ornament* (1873). Chinese and
Japanese dragons are associated with water, not fire.

05 | Porcelain book cover | China | c.1730
In ancient China, emperors were believed to be the sons of dragons. Ordinary people were not allowed to own anything with a dragon motif.

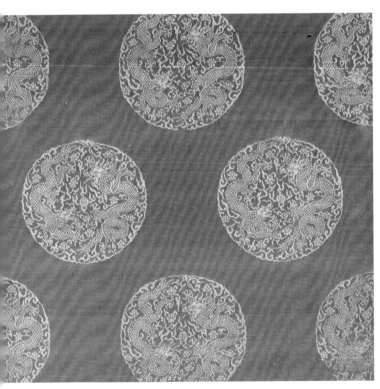

06 | Textile | China | 19th to 20th centuries
In this silk and twill weave fabric, the dragon symbols are contained in gold medallions regularly spaced across the ground.

07 | Peacock and Dragon | UK | c.1880 | William Morris
This woodblock print for a textile design is among the few Morris patterns that do not focus principally on flowers and foliage.

Chinoiserie (17th century–18th century)

Chinoiserie, the West's playful interpretation of Chinese art and artifacts was popular from the mid-17th century to the mid-18th, and was rooted in a European fascination with the Orient. The term is misleading: at the time "China" was in common use as a shorthand for Asia, including India.

From ancient times, goods from the Far East were transported along the Silk Road to India, Persia, and countries around the Mediterranean. Yet by the beginning of the 15th century, this route had collapsed. It was not until over a century later—when the Portuguese established toeholds in the region at Goa and Macau—that trade links reopened. In 1711, the British East India Company opened a trading post at Guangzhou, the only Chinese port where foreign trade was allowed. However, further regulations were soon imposed by the Chinese government. The result was that although Chinese silk, tea, and porcelain arrived in the West in greater quantities, they retained their status as luxury goods. With direct contact between East and West strictly limited, and reliable first-hand accounts rare, Oriental culture retained its pervasive mystique.

The vogue for chinoiserie arose out of this combination of exotic allure and misinformation. From the mid-17th century to the mid-18th, the style affected all branches of decorative arts, from ceramics to embroidery.

Closely associated with the Rococo style, chinoiserie was expressed in fretwork, asymmetric compositions featuring fantastical birds and dragons, and imaginary landscapes dotted with pagodas, bridges, stunted trees, and figures dressed in a supposedly Oriental manner. After the ponderous severity of the Baroque, such depictions of an idealized world brought light-heartedness and sensuality to interior schemes of decoration. Chinoiserie also spurred a demand for wallpaper, which was a luxurious product, being exclusively hand-painted.

Rooms were decked out in the style and filled with Chinese porcelain; many grand palaces featured Chinese-style pleasure pavilions in their formal grounds. One of the finest chinoiserie interiors was created by the Prince Regent at the Royal Pavilion in Brighton between 1802 and 1821.

For years, European manufacturers vied to discover the secret of porcelain production, which was solved early in the 18th century at the Meissen factory near Dresden under the patronage of August II, Elector of Saxony. Types of tin-glazed pottery, such as majolica, azulejo tiles, and Delftware, already well established, were direct attempts to replicate the blue and white decoration found on Ming porcelain. From this emerged the "Willow" pattern in the late 18th century, another manifestation of chinoiserie in its depictions of birds, pagodas, and willow trees.

Far Left These tin-glazed earthenware chinoiserie tiles (c. 1725–50) were probably made in Bristol.

Left Hand-painted 18th-century chinoiserie wallpaper from Marble Hill House, Twickenham, Middlesex.

Opposite Chinoiserie porcelain teapot (c. 1760) from the Doccia manufacture in Sesto Fiorentino, Tuscany.

01 | Wallpaper | France | 1850–55
This block-printed embossed wallpaper, possibly of French origin, features back-to-back griffins in an arabesque design.

02 | Reveries | UK/France | 2017 | Christian Lacroix for Designers Guild
This digitally printed cotton furnishing fabric features mythical creatures in an unusual version of a *toile* pattern.

03 | Silk hanging | China | 19th century
This Chinese silk hanging depicts a phoenix, traditionally regarded as a female symbol and often paired with a dragon, which is regarded as male.

04 | Unicorn | Netherlands | 1950 | M. C. Escher
The use of three different colors in this pencil and watercolor design on paper highlights the intricacies of the tessellation.

05 | Panpipes | UK | late 19th century | Harry Napper
This is a sample of woven silk, cotton, and wool furnishing fabric. Napper originally worked for Silver Studio, before branching out on his own as a textile designer.

GEOMETRIC

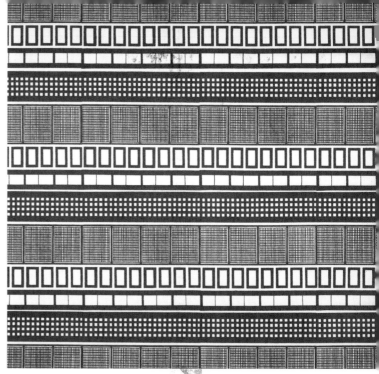

02 | Tenayuca | USA | 1954 | Ben Rose
This screen-printed furnishing fabric with horizontal rows of rectangles was designed by Rose and manufactured by his textile firm. It was reprinted in 1988.

01 | Woven hanging | Germany | 1926 | Anni Albers/Gunta Stölzl
When Albers joined the Bauhaus weaving workshop in 1923, it was run by Stölzl, who taught her how to weave using a hand loom.

03 | Dress fabric | France | 1929 | Chanel
This silk dress fabric, with its pattern of overlapping loosely drawn rectangles, displays a sober use of color.

04 | Vista | UK | 2017 | Imogen Heath
Heath's monochromatic furnishing fabric makes effective use of contrasting black and white rectangles and triangles, mediated with gray.

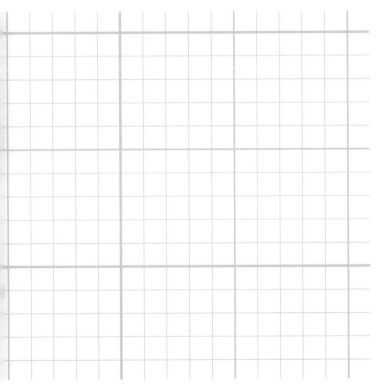

05 | Homework | UK | 2017 | Mini Moderns
This witty graph paper wallpaper design by Mini Moderns was inspired by the designers' maths and physics homework books.

06 | Zambezie | USA | 1965–69 | Ben Rose
This wallpaper, screen-printed on vinyl, was created for modern interiors. The vertically structured pattern features stacked linear squares.

Charles Eames (1907–78) | Ray Eames (1912–88)

SEE PAGES > 270, 382

Postwar designers Charles and Ray Eames brought a modernist sensibility to US furniture design, producing a range of innovative and commercially successful chairs and other products, many of which featured a groundbreaking use of new materials. Their own house, Case Study House #8 (1949) in Pacific Palisades, was a landmark of postwar domestic design. Hugely versatile, they also created textiles and films.

Charles Eames was born in St. Louis, Missouri; Ray in Sacramento, California. In the mid 1920s, Charles studied architecture at Washington University. After running his own practice in St. Louis, in 1938 he returned to further his architectural studies at Cranbrook Academy of Art in Michigan; he would later become the head of its industrial design department. There, Eames met Finnish designer Eero Saarinen (1910–61) and Bernice "Ray" Kaiser, who became his second wife. Ray was a graduate of Bennett College, New York, and had studied Abstract Expressionism in New York under the artist Hans Hofmann; at Cranbrook she was studying painting and other arts-related subjects. Charles and Ray married in 1941, a year after Charles and Eero won the Organic Design in Home Furnishings competition organized by the Museum of Modern Art (MoMA). Their design was a molded plywood chair.

During World War II, the Eameses, who had moved to Los Angeles in 1942, carried on experimenting with molded plywood. A splint, modeled on Charles's leg, was ordered in large numbers by the US Navy, and Ray produced a number of plywood sculptures. The results of these creative investigations were the DCM and LCW chairs (both 1946), which won great critical acclaim and were put into production by the cutting-edge US furniture company Herman Miller during the 1950s.

In 1950, the Eameses created a new chair design, La Chaise, for the International Competition of Low-cost Furniture Design, organized by MoMA. A striking organic form, it was made of molded fiberglass and was not upholstered. The Eameses went on to create many iconic pieces of furniture, working in association with Herman Miller.

Charles and Ray Eames had an intensely collaborative and playful approach to living and working. However, all of the graphics produced by the Eames Office, including textile design, can be attributed to Ray. In the late 1940s, she created a number of patterns, two of which, "Crosspatch" (1947) and "Sea Things" (1947), were produced by Schiffer Prints. Other notable designs from the same period include "Circles" (1947) and "Dot Pattern" (1947). These have been reissued by the US fabric company Maharam as part of a collection of 20th-century textiles.

Far Left Ray and Charles Eames on the floor of their living room at Eames House, Los Angeles, in 1959.

Left The iconic Eames DAR (1950) armchair is made of molded fiberglass and metal rods.

Opposite Ray created "Crosspatch" (1947) for a textile competition at the Museum of Modern Art, New York.

07 | Assembled Check | UK/USA | 2016 | Paul Smith for Maharam

This furnishing fabric, with its blocky pattern, was designed by British fashion
designer and retailer Smith for Maharam, a leading US textile company.

08 | Bar Line | UK | 2016 | Emma Jeffs
This furnishing fabric was produced by N & N Wares, the company established by
Jeffs in 2012. Jeffs combines digital design with craft.

10 | Fabric swatch
This is an unattributed sample of unknown date from a private archive. The simple
geometric design of rectangles on a dotted ground has an all-over textural effect.

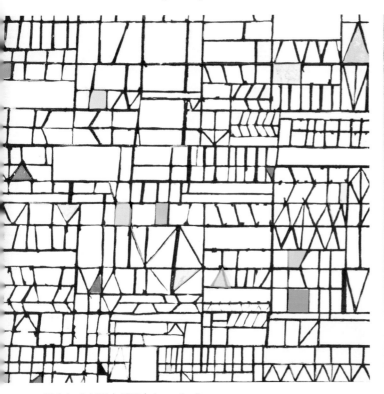

09 | April | UK | 1952 | Jacqueline Groag
This asymmetric geometric design, with its bright color accents, was produced
as a wallpaper in 1976 by Sandudd Vantaa of Finland.

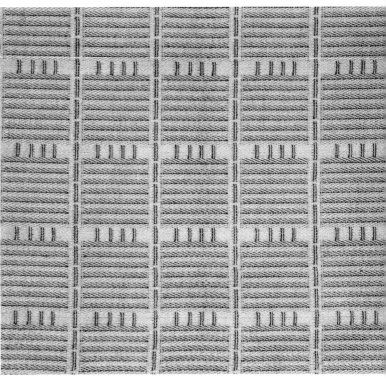

11 | Thisbe | UK | 1945 | Enid Marx
The product of wartime rationing, this cotton furnishing fabric was designed for the
Utility Design Panel and manufactured by the Board of Trade.

12 | Toccata | UK | c. 1952 | Peter Shuttleworth
This wallpaper was produced by the Lightbown Aspinall branch of Wallpaper
Manufacturers, a company that helped to pioneer the use of screen-printing.

13 | Textile | Russia | 20th century | Sergei Vashkov
Designed in the early 20th century by Vashkov, this half-silk satin fabric was
manufactured by the Ulovyanishnikov Manufactory in Moscow.

14 | Textile | UK | 1967 | Sonia Delaunay

Delaunay's design, created between 1925 and 1927, was later manufactured
by Ascher Studio as a screen-printed silk organza.

15 | Optical | UK | 2009 | Sam Pickard

Although Pickard is best known for her botanically inspired prints, she has also
created a number of geometric designs, such as this optical pattern.

02 | Frith Moss | UK | 2017 | Designers Guild
This refined velvet weave furnishing fabric has a raised pattern of nesting squares.
It is available in seventeen different colors.

01 | Checkerboard | UK | 2016 | Rebecca Hoyes
London-based Hoyes is a surface pattern designer specializing in textiles; her
approach fuses traditional and contemporary techniques.

03 | Checkerboard | UK | 2002–03 | Eley Kishimoto
Eley Kishimoto's painterly pattern, with its effective use of uneven white edges, has
been applied to a range of products, from clothing to bags.

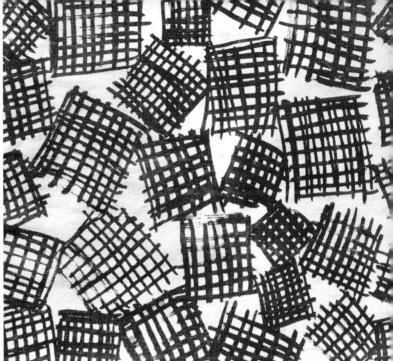

04 | Matrix | US | 1973 | Jack Lenor Larsen
The vibrancy of complementary colors gives this wool furnishing fabric, with its
simple pattern of squares, a particular intensity.

06 | Printed design | UK | 2014 | Sally Lloyd-Thomas
Lloyd-Thomas is a member of the design company First Eleven Studio.
This crosshatched pattern is a digital print on fabric.

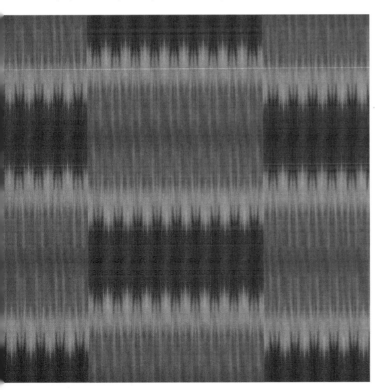

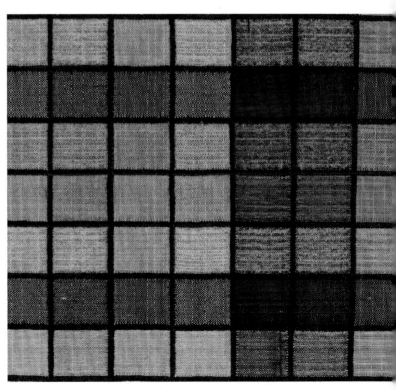

05 | Misty Ikat | UK | 2012 | Ptolemy Mann
Mann, who trained as a weaver, now produces a range of commercial *ikat* fabrics.
She is also an architectural color consultant.

07 | Reflections 1 | UK | 20th century | Marianne Straub
Trained as a weaver, Straub was acutely interested in the physical properties
of fabric, its weight and how it draped.

Thought to have originated some 500 years ago, the pattern known as "gingham" was first produced in the countries of Southeast Asia. The term itself comes from the Malay word *genggang*, which means "striped," and it was as a striped fabric that examples of gingham first made their way to the West, probably imported by the Dutch. Gingham's evolution into the characteristic pattern familiar today came about in the 18th century when factories in Manchester, England, opted to weave the fabric in checks or plaids, often in blue and white. Over time, this became more popular than the striped form.

While many contemporary versions of the checked pattern are surface-printed, in proper gingham the pattern is woven into the fabric. Yarns are dyed before weaving. The colored yarns form the warp, going against the uncolored weft yarns, thus producing a material that is lightly textured on both sides and reversible.

Gingham is often employed as a test fabric when designing fashion items. It is also used to make a cheap fitting shell before making items of clothing in an expensive fabric.

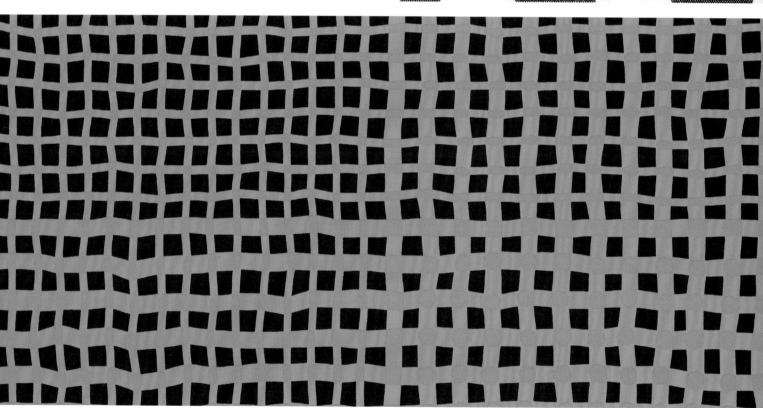

01 | **32:64** | **UK** | **2014** | Studio Houndstooth
Founded by Philippa Brock and Jo Pierce in 2012, Studio Houndstooth is a
multidisciplinary, experimental research studio specializing in textiles and materials.

02 | **Ashfield (Ripon Dark Navy)** | **UK** | **2016** | Ian Mankin
This wool furnishing fabric in a houndstooth pattern comes from Ian Mankin's
collection Ashfield. Ian Mankin is a noted designer and producer of natural fabrics.

03 | **Dogtooth** | **UK** | **2000** | Eley Kishimoto
A striking graphic pattern deconstructs traditional houndstooth. Patterning within
each shape gives a textural quality.

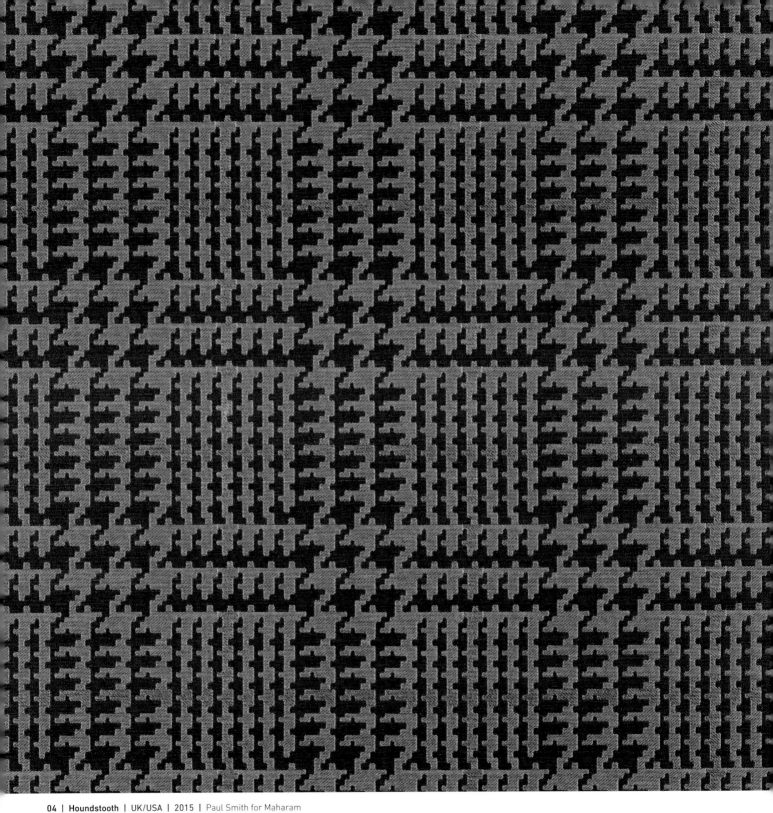

04 | Houndstooth | UK/USA | 2015 | Paul Smith for Maharam
Smith designed this furnishing fabric for Maharam. Houndstooth is a pattern with
origins in ancient woven textiles. The classic version is a tessellation.

Tartan and plaid (which strictly speaking are not interchangeable terms) are criss-crossed multicolored patterns that have become synonymous with Scottish dress and culture. Very early examples of such designs have been found in textiles dating to the 8th century BCE in areas of Central Europe where Celtic tribes settled. Other ancient examples have been found in China.

From the 16th century onward, tartan grew in popularity throughout Scotland, so much so that in 1746, when tartan had become a symbol of the Jacobite cause, the authorities banned it under the Dress Act (the law was later repealed in 1782). At that time, tartans featuring specific colors had yet to be associated with different clans. This came about more than a century later, when the new commercial aniline dyes allowed for more economic production. Coinciding with the popularity of the romantic novels of Walter Scott, and Queen Victoria and her husband Prince Albert's fascination with the Highlands, the fashion for tartan clothing, wallpaper, and fabric became a craze.

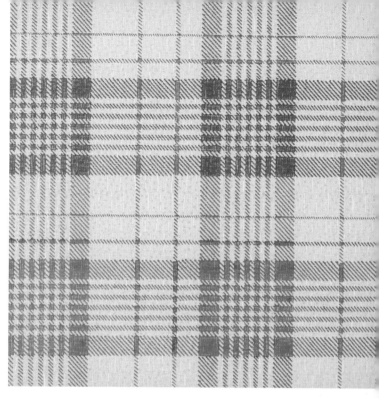

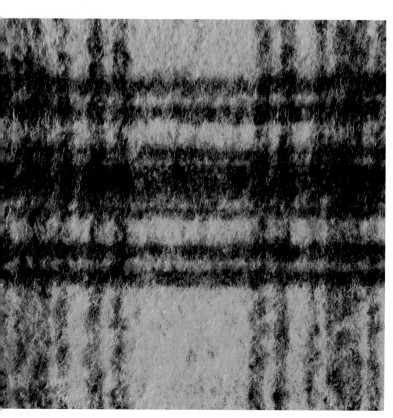

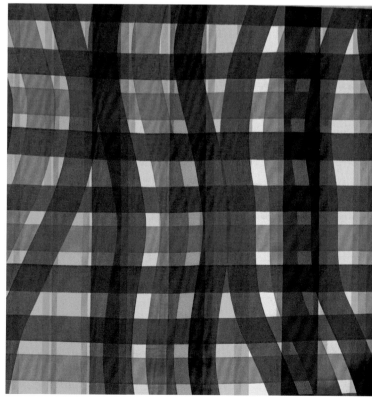

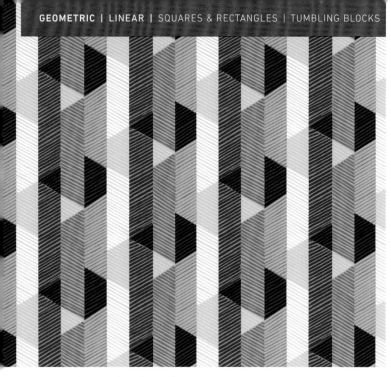

01 | Allegro | UK | 2012 | Imogen Heath
This furnishing fabric by British textile designer Heath is available in a number
of different colorways and features a geometric block pattern.

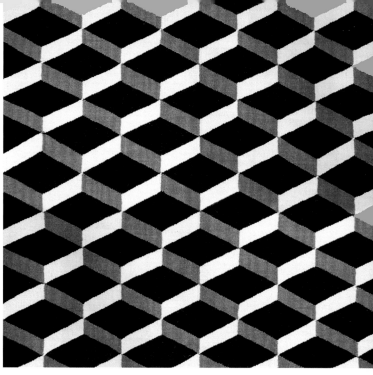

03 | Lorenzo | USA | 2015 | Jonathan Adler
A Peruvian llama reversible flat-weave rug. Adler opened his first store
in New York in 1998 and the company has since grown into a lifestyle brand.

02 | Puzzle | UK | 2015 | Cole & Son
This screen-printed wallpaper features a cascade of tumbling blocks.
In addition to this monochrome version, other brighter colorways are available.

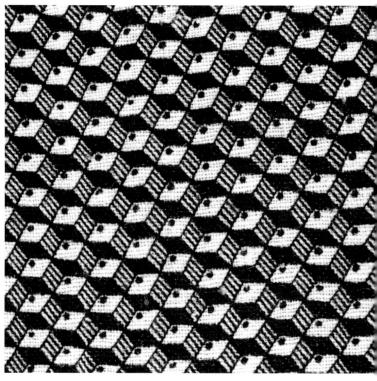

04 | Textile | UK | *c.* 1824
This printed cotton sample, taken from a Lancashire book of dye recipes, features
a geometric design that looks strikingly contemporary.

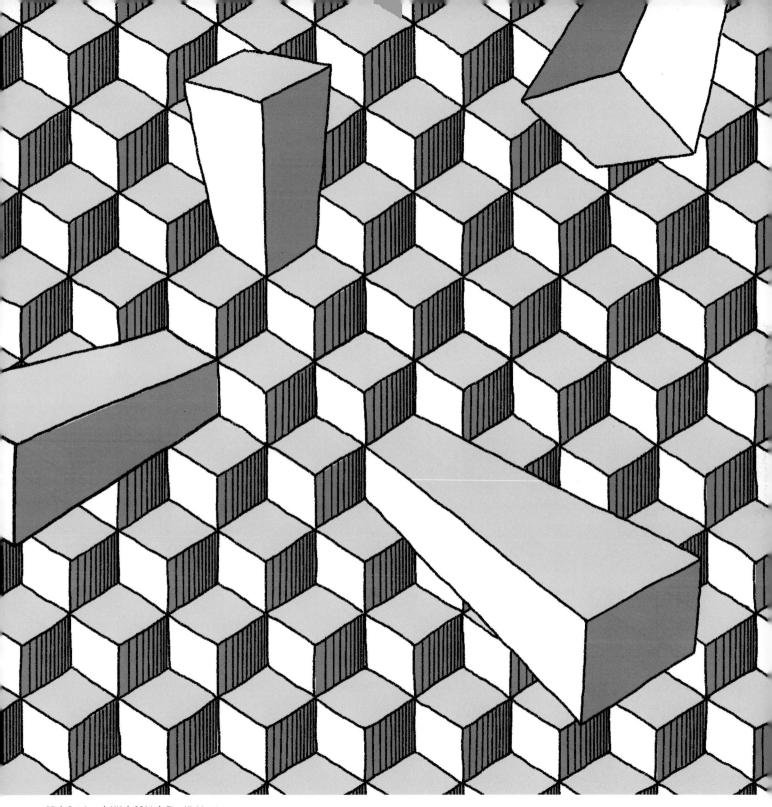

05 | Cuteboy | UK | 2014 | Eley Kishimoto
This is an updated version of the traditional quilting pattern, tumbling block, in which
a three-dimensional effect is generated by color placement.

Marquetry, a veneering technique dating from 16th-century Florence, is a way of creating decorative patterns or pictures out of shaped pieces of wood veneer and other materials, including bone, ivory, tortoiseshell, brass, and thin sections of semi-precious stones. Veneers might be taken from different colored woods, such as boxwood for the lightest tones and ebony for the darkest, or dyed to create non-natural shades.

Over the centuries, marquetry decoration has been applied to table tops, cabinets, chests, and other forms of furniture; it has also been used to create self-contained pictorial panels. Unlike inlay, in which patterns are created by cutting into a surface and filling these depressions with a contrasting material, marquetry is applied to the top of a smooth surface.

One of the best-known practitioners of marquetry was French cabinetmaker André-Charles Boulle. He created furniture for Versailles with marquetry decorations in tortoiseshell and gilt-bronze. Similar boulle-work decorations feature on the cases of instruments such as barometers.

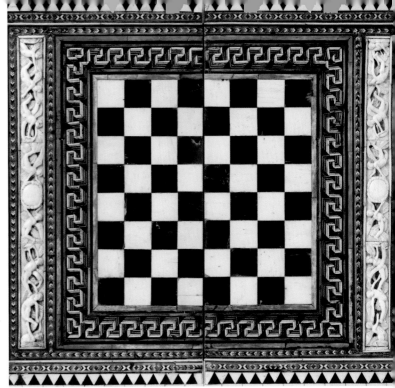

Parquetry differs from marquetry in that the patterning is exclusively geometric and is constructed by piecing together strips or solid blocks to form a type of mosaic overlaid on a subsurface. Parquetry patterns are almost always made of wood and are generally found as flooring, although some instances of parquetry decoration on furniture are known.

Parquetry evolved in France during the 17th century as a cheaper and lower maintenance alternative to marble flooring, which required frequent washing that sometimes rotted the joists beneath the floors. Early examples took the form of large diagonal squares, but over the years many different patterns emerged, including those based on triangles, lozenges, stars, and sunbursts. The most popular design is herringbone or chevron.

To further enhance a parquetry pattern, different types of timber may be combined in the same design. Contrasting colors and grains of woods such as oak, cherry, lime, mahogany, and maple bring depth and richness to the decorative interlocking geometries.

01 | Printed design | UK | 2014 | Rebecca Hoyes

Textile designer Hoyes, of First Eleven Studio, works closely with a number
of retailers. This bright. tessellated design was produced for Habitat.

02 | Cube Star (Coral) | UK | 2013 | Jocelyn Warner

In this large-scale repeat wallpaper pattern, stars appear at the intersections of cubes. The tessellated shapes create a kind of optical illusion.

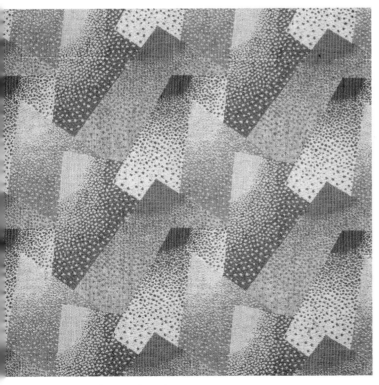

03 | Mosaic | France | *c.* 1931

This woven cotton furnishing fabric is patterned with interlocking shapes; variations of tone are achieved by dotted shading.

04 | Lithograph | UK | 1842 | Owen Jones

This is from *Plans, Elevations, Sections and Details of the Alhambra* (1836–45) by Jones. The tessellated tile patterns of the Alhambra greatly influenced M. C. Escher.

01 | Textile | UK | *c.* **1920s**
The triangular design and bold colors of this roller-printed cotton furnishing fabric by Arthur Sanderson & Sons show the influence of the Ballets Russes.

02 | Multi Triangles | USA | 1954 | Alexander Girard
Girard, who designed many patterns for Herman Miller, initially trained as an architect in London and Rome. His geometric designs display great economy.

03 | Prisma | Sweden | 1952 | Sven Markelius Ljungbergs
This furnishing fabric was manufactured by Ljungbergs. Markelius was a leading Swedish modernist architect, responsible for a number of civic projects.

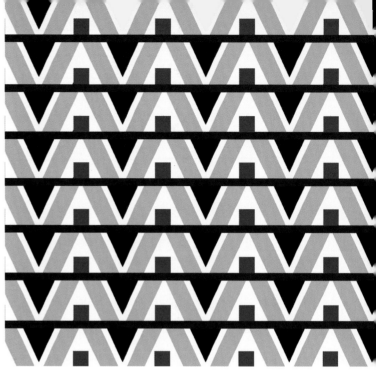

04 | Printed design | UK | 2016 | Rebecca Hoyes, First Eleven Studio
This well-balanced pattern by London-based Hoyes is reminiscent of Aztec design and features rows of truncated and inverted triangles.

05 | Trapeze | USA | 1950–54
A linen plain-weave screen-printed furnishing fabric made by Laverne of New York. Founded by two painters, Laverne was known for its geometric and abstract textiles.

06 | *Zirconia* | UK | 2015 | Osborne & Little
A wallpaper pattern featuring contrasting colored triangles arranged in a diamond
form. The name is taken from the synthetic cubic gemstone.

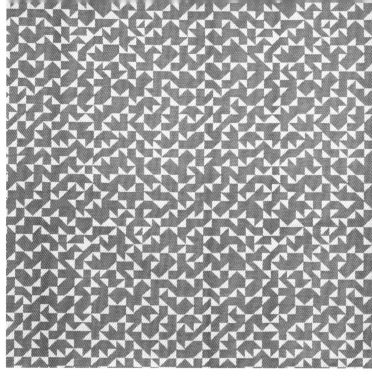

08 | **Intaglio** | Italy | Contemp. Revival 2014 | Anni Albers
A furnishing fabric manufactured by Christopher Farr Cloth. Albers, well known for her weaving work at the Bauhaus, later designed patterns for mass-produced fabric.

07 | **Oomph** | Sweden | 1952 | Viola Gråsten, Ljungbergs

A hand-printed furnishing fabric manufactured by Ljungbergs. This kaleidoscopic pattern features swirling colors and triangular shapes.

09 | **Printed design** | UK | 2008 | Sally Lloyd-Thomas
Produced by First Eleven Studio, this simple pattern of tilting triangles has a hand-drawn quality. Lloyd-Thomas's work often includes only two or three colors.

10 | Mera | UK | 2016 | Imogen Heath
The soft bleached-out colors on this furnishing fabric give its simple geometric
triangular pattern a nostalgic quality.

11 | Wallpaper | UK | 19th century | Owen Jones
Jones was a prolific designer and promoter of design reform. This pattern
is reminiscent of Gothic architectural detailing popular in the 19th century.

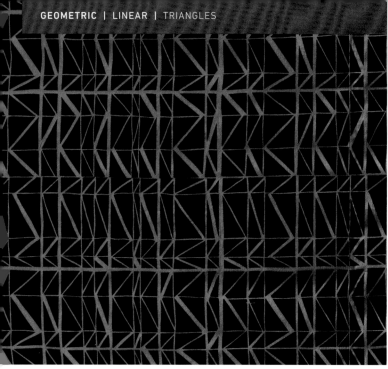

12 | Textile | USA | 1950–55 | Marianne Strengell
Strengell was an influential modernist Finnish-American textile designer and, for
a number of years, professor at the Cranbrook Academy of Art in Michigan.

13 | Pochoir print | France | 1928 | André Garcelon
This vibrant design, evocative of Art Deco, is taken from *Inspirations*, a pattern book
published by Charles Massin & Co in Paris.

14 | Folded Geometric | Australia | 2017 | Marni Stuart
In Stuart's bright digital print, triangles of varying sizes suggest a folded surface
akin to Japanese origami.

15 | **Design 706** | USA | 1956 | Frank Lloyd Wright
Produced by F. Schumacher & Co., this wallpaper is part of the Taliesin Line range.
Taliesin West in Scottsdale, Arizona, was Wright's winter home.

16 | **Geotaxis** | UK | 2007 | Sam Pickard
In this wallpaper design, slender triangular shapes have been arranged in organic
twisting fans of varying scales.

02 | Veren | UK | 2017 | Designers Guild
Reminiscent of Art Deco detailing, this small-scale repeat wallpaper pattern
comprises linear dashes arranged in stylized diamond shapes.

01 | Circus | UK | 2001, 2015 | Cole & Son
This striking wallpaper design is a large-scale repeat of vibrant, multicolored
overlapping harlequins.

03 | Kites | UK | 2012 | Kangan Arora
A screen-printed cushion design from Arora's Kites collection, inspired by the small
paper kites flown in Gujarat each January to celebrate the Uttarayan festival.

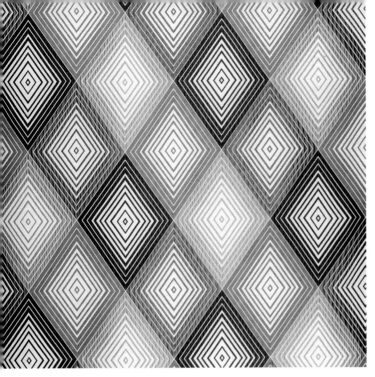

04 | Normandie | UK | 2016 | Osborne & Little
Named after the SS *Normandie*, a French ocean liner that launched in 1935, this
furnishing fabric has a pattern of large jacquard diamonds.

05 | Pochoir on paper | France | 1930 | Sonia Delaunay
Plate 24 from *Compositions, Couleurs, Idées* (*Compositions, Colors, Ideas*) by Delaunay.
The *pochoir* stenciling technique was popular in France in the 1920s and 1930s.

06 | Totley | UK | 1947 | Marianne Straub
A furnishing fabric manufactured by Helios of Bolton, Lancashire. Straub was chief
designer at the progressive firm Helios from 1937 to 1947.

Sonia Delaunay (1885–1979)

SEE PAGES > 313, 337, 341

Painter, sometimes shopkeeper, and designer of wall coverings, textiles, and clothing, Sonia Delaunay extended her art into the realms of dress design and everyday living, celebrating the new freedoms enjoyed by women in the early decades of the 20th century.

Born Sarah Stern to a Jewish family in Odessa, Ukraine, Delaunay was raised in St. Petersburg from the age of five by her wealthy aunt and uncle. Widespread travel throughout Europe gave Sonia (as she renamed herself) an informal art education. Her talent for drawing was spotted at secondary school and at eighteen years old she enrolled at the Academy of Fine Arts in Karlsruhe, Germany. In 1905, she moved to Paris, where she encountered the work of the Fauves. Her marriage of convenience to homosexual German art dealer and critic Wilhelm Uhde in 1908 enabled her to resist family pressure to return to Russia. Uhde put on the first exhibition of her work the same year.

In 1909, she met and fell in love with the avant-garde painter Robert Delaunay (1885–1941). They married the following year, after her divorce, and she had a son a few months later. Instead of domesticity subsuming her art, it transformed it. Her first abstract composition, which showed influences both of Cubism and Ukrainian folk art, was a comforter she pieced together out of scraps of fabric for her son's cradle. She soon extended the same approach to the design of clothing, creating what she called "simultaneous dresses" that followed the movement of the female body. Producing these at a time when there was a move away from couture in favor of ready-to-wear, she took the groundbreaking approach of designing fabric with the final garment and wearer in mind.

By 1913, Delaunay had returned to painting. Together with Robert, she came up with a version of Cubism, termed "Orphism," which featured concentric circles and bisecting planes. The couple spent World War I in Spain and Portugal, where Sonia opened shops and designed clothing. On their return to Paris in 1921, she carried on making clothes, designed fifty bold abstract textiles for a Lyon manufacturer, devised film and theatre sets and costumes, and opened a fashion studio. The Delaunay apartment was home to a circle that included Surrealist and Dadaist poets: she incorporated lines from their works into her fabric designs.

The economic depression of the 1930s caused a downturn in her business and she returned to painting. After the war, and the death of her husband in 1941, Sonia continued to work, developing a range of textiles in 1976 based on her designs in the 1920s. In 1964, she was the first living female artist to have a retrospective exhibition at the Louvre, Paris.

Far Left Ukrainian-born painter and designer Sonia Delaunay photographed in France in 1957.

Left Dress and fabric designed by Delaunay in 1926.

Opposite Fabric printed in the Orphic Cubist style pioneered by Delaunay.

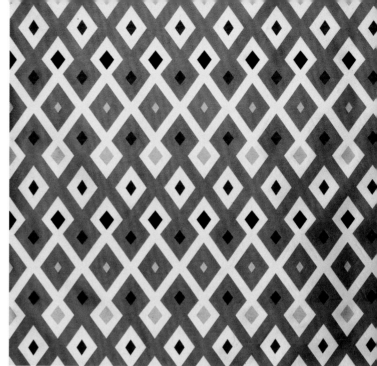

08 | Samoa | UK | 2012 | Lorca, distributed by Osborne & Little
This lustrous silk furnishing fabric has a geometric pattern of interlocking diamonds in rich, jewel-like colors inspired by the isles of Polynesia.

07 | Jali | UK | 2015 | Kangan Arora
Arora designed this hand-knotted rug for rug company FLOOR_STORY. Born in India, Arora uses a range of techniques, from quilting to embroidery to screen-printing.

09 | Fez | UK | 2008 | Neisha Crosland
Crosland takes inspiration for her patterns from a wide range of sources. This diamond design for flexo-printed wallpaper has a Moorish flavor.

11 | **Pochoir on paper** | **France** | *c.*1929 | Sonia Delaunay
This book illustration, showing Delaunay's characteristic geometric patterning, is from *Tapis et Tissus* (*Carpets and Fabrics*), published in 1929 by Éditions d'Art Charles Moreau.

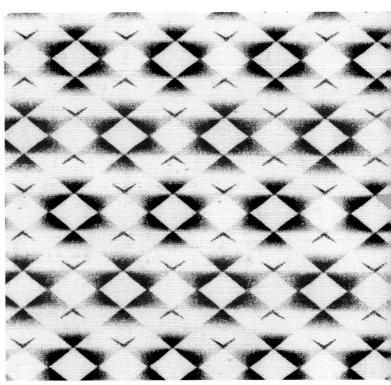

10 | **Textile** | **Japan** | **19th century**
The all-over pattern on this indigo printed fabric combines traditional Japanese stylized floral motifs with diamond shapes outlined in dotted lines.

12 | **Textile** | **USA** | **19th century**
This printed fabric, with its simple shaded diamond patterning, has a surprisingly contemporary appearance despite its age.

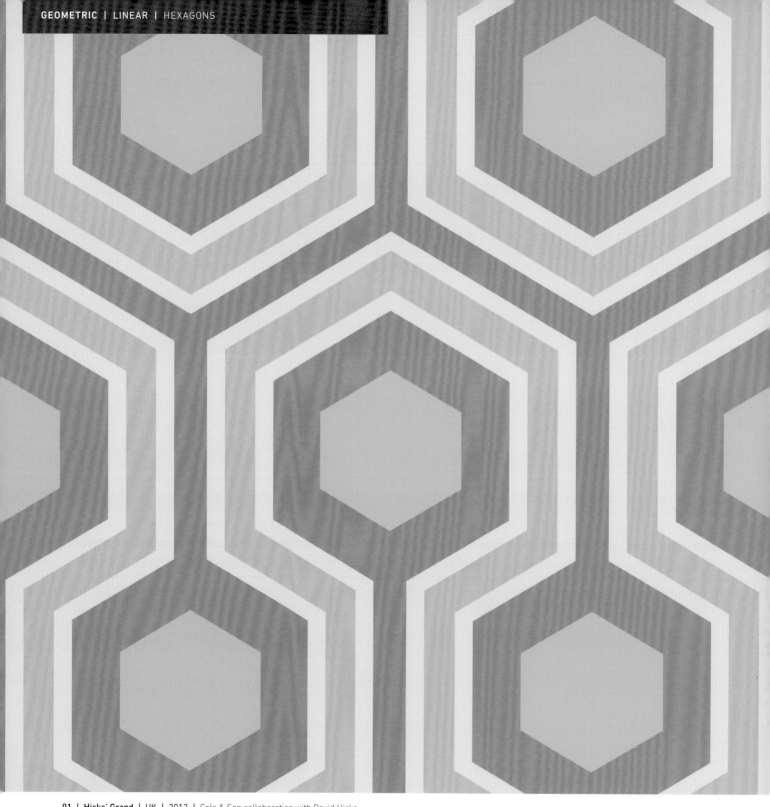

01 | Hicks' Grand | UK | 2012 | Cole & Son collaboration with David Hicks

This wallpaper was manufactured with the English decorator and designer known for bold color combinations and strong geometric prints.

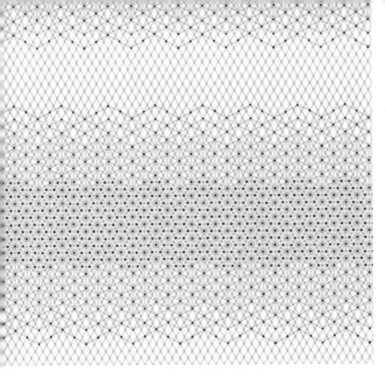

02 | Marker Hexagon | Japan | 2017 | Gaku Masui
One of several printed fabrics designed by Masui for Nuno. This hexagonal design resembles circuitry.

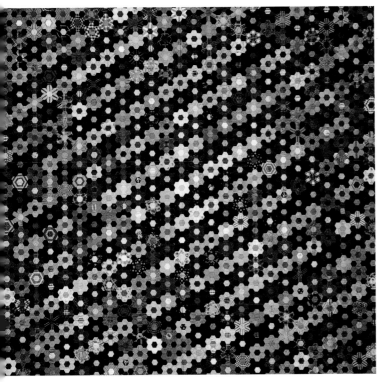

03 | Comforter | USA | 1864 | Anne Record
This brilliantly colored silk comforter, formed of pieced hexagonal shapes resembling rosettes, was made in New Bedford, Massachusetts.

04 | Wallpaper | UK | 1852–74 | Owen Jones
This wallpaper with a floral and geometric design may have been manufactured by a number of different firms, including William Morris's printers Jeffrey & Co.

02 | Color Dance | USA | 2016
Cloud9 Fabrics produced this cheerful cotton fabric for Joann, a leading US fabric and craft retailer based in Cleveland, Ohio.

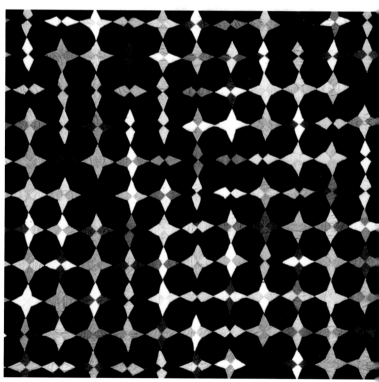

01 | Walpole | USA | 1946
This machine-printed wallpaper, manufactured by Thomas Strahan Company of Boston, Massachusetts, displays a traditional use of an octagonal motif.

03 | Comforter | USA | c.1925
This cotton patchwork comforter, with a black hummingbird design was made in Amish country, Pennsylvania.

04 | Nairobi | USA | 1965–69 | Ben Rose
This screen-printed vinyl wallpaper was created by Rose. He received many awards
during his career as a textile and wallpaper designer.

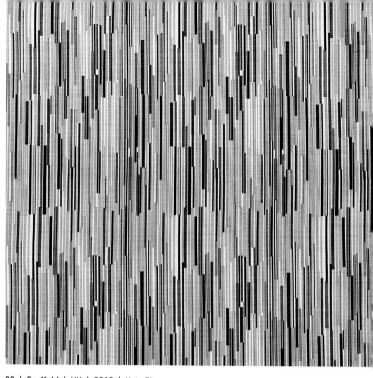

02 | Scaffold | UK | 2012 | Kate Blee
A furnishing fabric produced by Christopher Farr Cloth. Blee set up her design studio in London in 1986. She creates distinctive rugs and textiles for various designers.

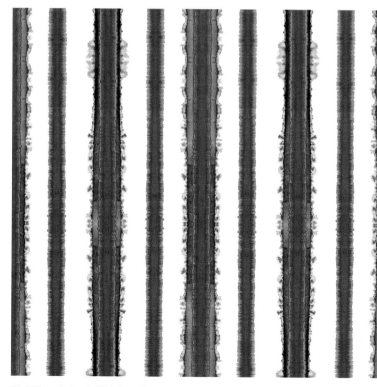

01 | Meteoric | USA | 1965–69 | Ben Rose
This wallpaper was screen-printed on vinyl. Rose originally trained as an artist. His patterns epitomize mid-century modernism.

03 | Blotch Stripe | UK | 2011 | Timorous Beasties
In this wallpaper pattern, a simple striped design has been subverted by the blotched edges, as if ink or paint has bled into the background.

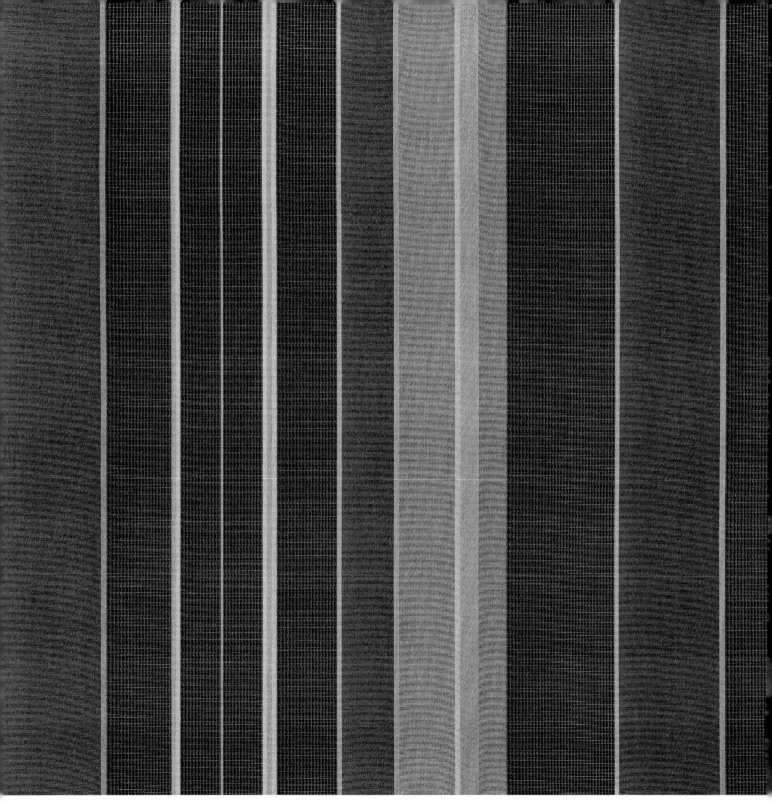

04 | Repeat Classic Stripe | USA | 2002 | Hella Jongerius for Maharam
A furnishing fabric designed for Maharam. Jongerius is a Dutch industrial designer
who has collaborated with Droog design company on a number of projects.

05 | Lindfield | UK | 1949 | Marianne Straub
Straub designed this furnishing fabric for Helios. She trained as a weaver and many
of her patterns have a textural appeal.

06 | Jodhpur Blue | UK | 2017 | Ptolemy Mann
India's "Blue City" of Jodhpur was the inspiration for this hand-dyed, woven wool rug. It
has a graphic striped central section bordered by richly colored horizontal banding.

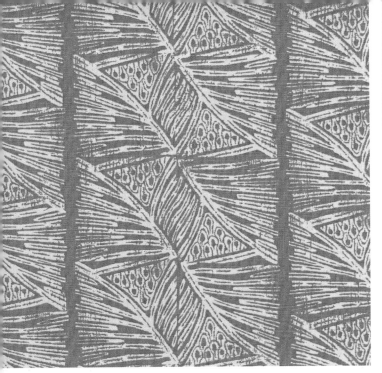

07 | Skate | UK | 2016 | Phyllis Barron and Dorothy Larcher
This furnishing fabric manufactured by Christopher Farr Cloth features broad stripes
of fan shapes reminiscent of cartilaginous skate wings.

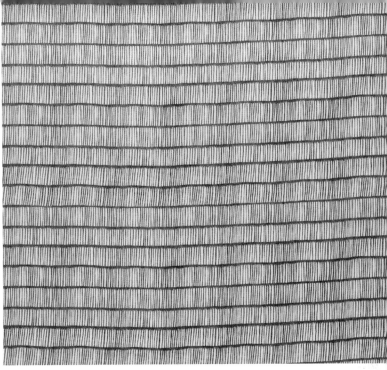

09 | Crochet | UK/France | 2016 | Raoul Dufy
Part of the Raoul Dufy Collection produced by Christopher Farr Cloth, this elegant
hand-printed linen furnishing fabric is a subtle horizontal stripe.

08 | Treads | USA | 1962 | Alexander Girard
Girard's pattern for a furnishing fabric displays a simple yet effective design
evocative of the tracks left by tires.

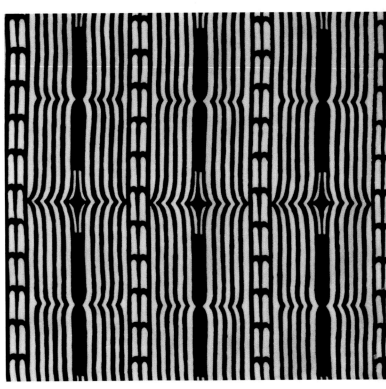

10 | Wasserfall | Austria | 1910–1912 | Josef Hoffmann
Wiener Werkstätte patterns from 1910 were available exclusively at Wertheim
department store in Berlin. Hoffmann's textiles were ideal for clothes and accessories.

11 | Ottoman Stripe | USA | 2012 | Paul Smith for Maharam
This is a furnishing fabric designed for Maharam. Stripes are a feature of the Paul Smith design brand.

12 | Pointed Pip | UK | 1938 | Phyllis Barron
The soft colors in Barron and Dorothy Larcher's textile designs were achieved using vegetable dyes, with which they experimented extensively.

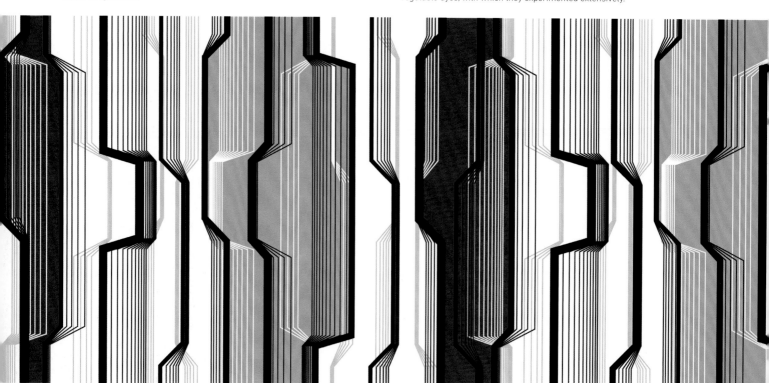

13 | V Stripe | UK | 2013 | Sam Pickard
Pickard set up her textile studio in 1996. This variation on the typical stripe pattern has a three-dimensional quality

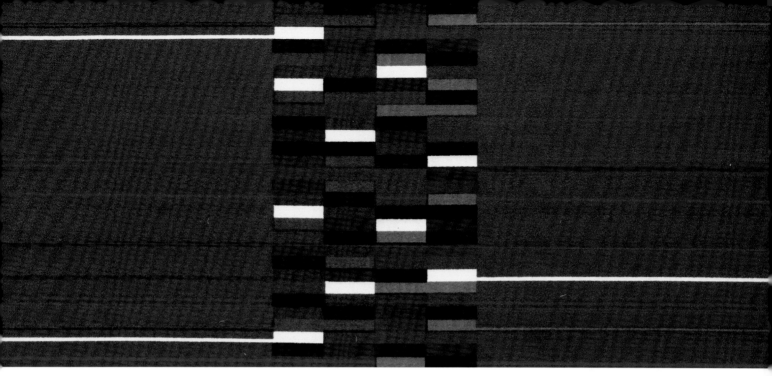

14 | Causeway | UK | 1967 | Lucienne Day
The design of this screen-printed cotton crêpe fabric, produced by Heal's, reflects
Day's move into bolder, more architectural patterns.

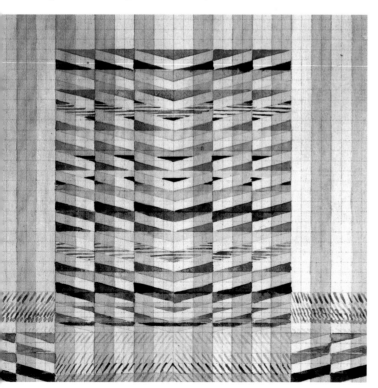

15 | Textile design | Germany | *c.* 1927 **|** Gunta Stölzl
This pen, ink, and watercolor drawing is a design for a jacquard woven wall hanging.
Stölzl's textiles were chiefly woven, rather than printed.

16 | Mexicotton Stripe | USA | 1961 | Alexander Girard
Mexican folk art was a big influence on Girard, who traveled to Mexico to buy artifacts
for interiors he was designing. He created many "Mexidot" and "Mexistripe" patterns.

17 | Hyper Stripe | Japan | 2008 | Tomoko Iida for Nuno
This printed fabric was designed for Nuno. The jaunty striped pattern features a wavering central contrasting strip.

18 | Textile design | Russia | 1975 | Nina Shirokova
Unconventional for Shirokova, whose works usually feature bold, strong colors, this textile is more muted, yet still non-conformist.

19 | Vertical | UK | 2000 | Christopher Farr
This linen furnishing fabric is produced by Christopher Farr Cloth, a company
founded by Farr, Michal Silver, and Matthew Bourne in London in 2000.

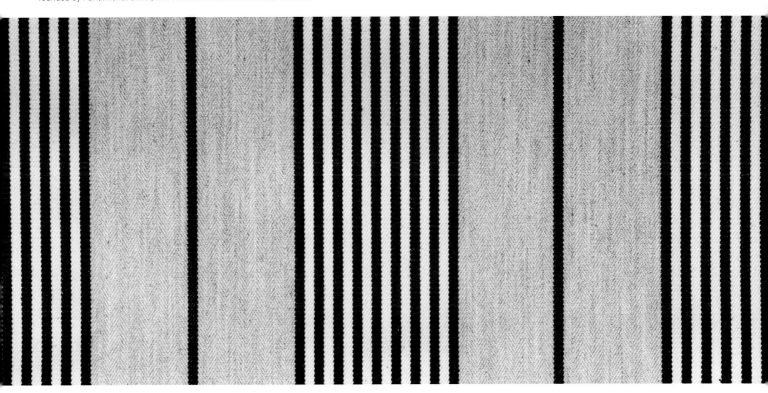

20 | Vintage Stripe 2 Dark Navy | UK | 2015 | Ian Mankin
This tightly woven, cotton furnishing fabric in the time-honored ticking stripe is classic
and unassuming. Ian Mankin's fabrics are woven in their own Lancashire cotton mill.

After the decorative excesses of the Rococo style, with its burgeoning curves and curlicues, stylistic reaction came in the form of a reinterpretation of the classical designs of ancient Greece and Rome. Flat surfaces, restrained ornament, straight edges, and a preponderance of geometric motifs, such as squares, circles, and triangles, expressed the new clean-cut sobriety in architecture, interiors, and furnishings. The Neoclassical style was given a boost by discoveries at Pompeii and Herculaneum in the early 18th century.

Striped patterns were especially prevalent, as wallpapers, furnishing fabrics, and dress materials. At their simplest, they echo the understated ticked fabrics that were used as loose covers to protect fine upholstery. More elegant and delicate versions were also produced that incorporated vegetal or floral motifs in vertical or horizontal banding. Vertically striped wallpaper was particularly associated with the Regency period in England and was a feature of fashionable mid-20th-century interiors where the Regency style was revived.

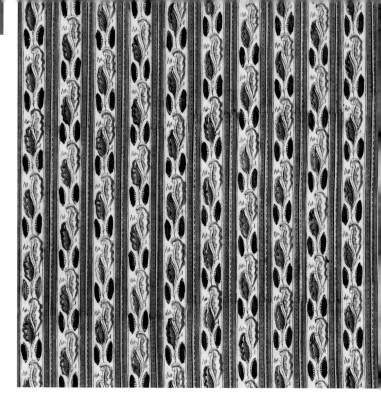

Neoclassicism (1760s–1850s)

Although Neoclassicism took inspiration from the world of classical antiquity, this was not as an end in itself, but as a way of promoting a rational reordering of architecture, design, and the applied arts after the decorative and decadent excesses of Rococo.

Neoclassicism emerged in the middle of the 18th century and had taken hold throughout Europe by the 1770s, from where it spread to the United States. France and Britain, however, were the two countries most in the vanguard, and the pattern books produced by French and British designers served to disseminate the style around the world. Expressing the ideals of the Enlightenment or Age of Reason, Neoclassicism was restrained. Light, uncluttered interiors were in keeping with the prevailing spirit of enquiry. Geometric forms, designs that were flat and linear, and simplicity of ornament brought a sobriety to decorative schemes.

By the mid-18th century, it was fashionable for young gentlemen to take a Grand Tour, which brought exposure to classical sites in Italy and Greece, along with the chance to collect art and artifacts. Neoclassical villas and interiors provided ideal surroundings in which such souvenirs could be displayed. Throughout the period, ongoing archeological discoveries at Herculaneum and Pompeii gave fresh insight into classical schemes of decoration. The Pompeiian palette of black, red, yellow, and white was adopted in fashionable interiors at the end of the 18th century.

Neoclassicism appeared when the Industrial Revolution was underway and with it, an emerging moneyed middle class of consumers. Evoking the three guiding principles outlined by the Roman architect Vitruvius in his treatise *De architectura* (*On Architecture*, c. 27 BCE), designers produced goods that were aesthetically and functionally consistent. Detailing and patterning were derived from classical sources. Swags and festoons of fabric, rosettes, garlands of flowers, and ribbonlike ornamentation were common. So too was the Roman husk motif, which resembled a bud. Beading, used as a trim, was visible in textile designs in the form of dotted outlines. The vase shape, expressed in stylized foliage, was a key motif used by French artists to decorate silk brocades. Stately, symmetrical damasks and polychrome Genoa or *jardinière* velvets were typical accompaniments to the formal, dignified style but simple checks and stripes were not uncommon.

British architect Robert Adam (1728–92) was one of the leading proponents of the new style. His unified schemes for interiors, which extended his individual handling of the Neoclassical style to every element, from wall coverings and floors to architectural detailing, were very influential.

Top The Tapestry Room (1763–71) at Croome Court, Worcestershire after a design by Robert Adam. He was the leading proponent of the Neoclassical style in 18th-century Britain and a fashionable architect. The Tapestry Room was one of three apartments he designed at Croome Court. He designed many notable public buildings, such as the Royal Exchange (1753–54), Edinburgh.

Above "Les Losanges" ("The Diamonds," c. 1800), a copperplate-printed cotton furnishing fabric by French artist Jean-Baptiste Marie Huet (1745–1811).

Opposite A pair of soft-paste porcelain vases with covers (1784–95) by Real Fabrica de Buen Retiro of Madrid. The form of the vases is based on an antique model.

Serapes or sarapes are woven homespun textiles strongly associated with Mexico, although they are produced in other Latin American countries and in areas of the American Southwest. One particular variety is known as the "Saltillo," after the city in northeast Mexico from which it derives. Traditionally, serapes were woven by men and many are still handmade local products, with the patterns and weaving technique passed down through successive generations. Variously used as blankets, ponchos, or shawls, they are typically brightly colored and striped and may also incorporate other indigenous motifs. Originally, serapes were worn by working people of Mexico and Guatemala during colder periods or at higher altitudes.

Serape colors are either naturally occurring shades of sheep's wool, such as black, brown, gray, and tan, or vibrant, brilliant hues achieved by dyeing strands individually before hand-looming. The width of the stripes may vary, with the dominant color generally being the broadest. The ends of traditional serapes are usually fringed.

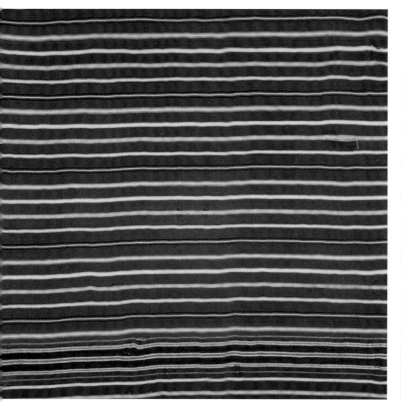

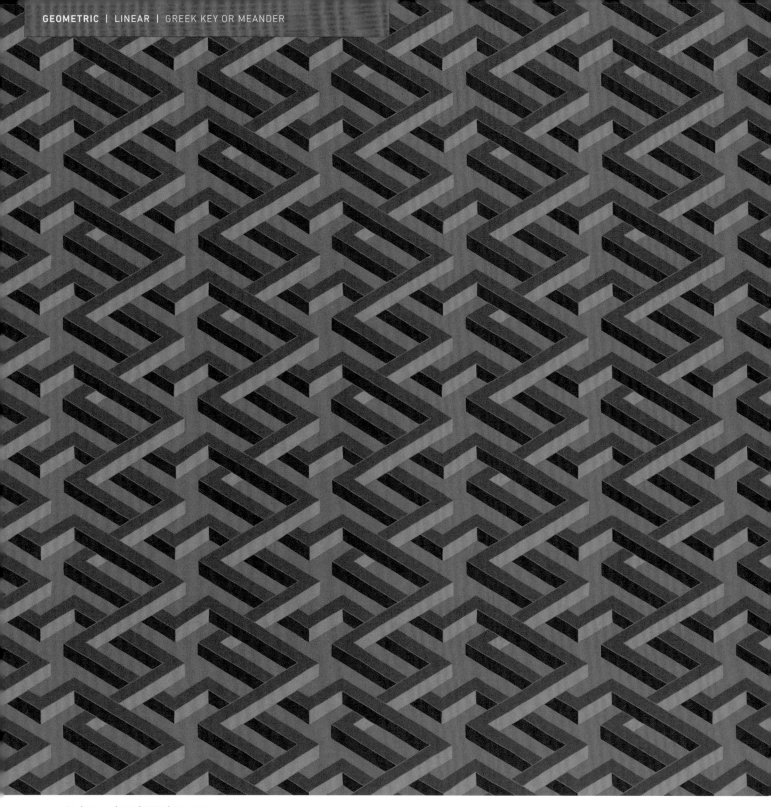

01 | **Luxor** | **UK** | **2015** | Cole & Son

This wallpaper design features an intricate and illusory maze-like pattern, given depth by its use of shading.

04 | Bakst | UK | 2016 | Osborne & Little
The meandering pattern of this furnishing fabric is produced in the jazzy colors that recall Léon Bakst's designs for the Ballets Russes.

02 | Triangulated | USA | Contemporary Revival 2014 | Anni Albers
This linen fabric, with its subtle variation on the Greek key pattern, is produced by Christopher Farr Cloth in association with the Josef and Anni Albers Foundation.

05 | Greek No. 1 | UK | 1856 | Owen Jones
This color lithograph of a Greek key pattern is Plate XV from Jones's global and historical design sourcebook *The Grammar of Ornament* (1856).

03 | Wallpaper | France | 1800–10
Dating from a period when Neoclassical ornament was the height of fashion, this block-printed wallpaper pattern features diamonds bordered by Greek key edging.

06 | Dress fabric | Netherlands | 2017 | Tomi Oladipo
English-Nigerian designer Oladipo created this fabric for Vlisco. The pattern features blocks filled with Greek key motifs alternating with those containing free squiggles.

Anni Albers (1899–1994)

SEE PAGES > 306, 332, 360, 626

Bauhaus-trained weaver, textile designer, and printmaker Anni Albers was a pioneer of modernism. Her experiments with new materials and abstract design redefined fabric as a 20th-century art form.

Born Annelise Fleischmann to a Jewish family in Berlin, Anni demonstrated an early interest in painting and drawing. After studying for a few months at the *Kunstgewerbeschule* (School of Applied Arts) in Hamburg, she enrolled at the Bauhaus in 1922, then based in Weimar. After completing the required foundation courses, Anni joined the weaving workshop in her second year. She had originally wanted a place in the glass workshop, but this was one of the courses barred to women.

Anni was soon absorbed by the technical challenges of weaving, which was taught at that time by Gunta Stölzl (1897–1983; see p. 626). She quickly mastered the hand loom, but understood early on that Bauhaus ideals could only reach a wider public if products and designs could be mass manufactured. Her woven wall hangings featured abstract compositions of lines and solid blocks of color, and she experimented with unusual materials such as horsehair and metallic thread.

Anni met her future husband, Josef Albers (1888–1976), soon after she arrived at the school and in 1925 they were married; eleven years older, Josef was the first Bauhaus student to join the faculty as a master. The next year, the Bauhaus moved into a new building in Dessau designed by Walter Gropius (1833–1969); there, Anni began intensive investigations into the functional side of textiles, such as sound absorption, light reflection, and crease resistance. In 1931, when Stölzl left the Bauhaus, Anni was appointed head of the weaving workshop.

With the rise of Nazism, the Bauhaus came under pressure to conform to the party's repressive policies, which regarded modern art and design as subversive and decadent; rather than submit, the faculty took the decision to close the school in 1933. That same year, Anni and Josef Albers took up an invitation to teach at Black Mountain College in North Carolina. They remained there until 1949. The same year, the Museum of Modern Art in New York put on an exhibition of her work, which then toured major venues in the United States.

In 1950, the Albers moved to Connecticut and Josef took up a post as the chair of the department of design at Yale School of Art. Anni set up a studio at home and devoted the next decade to producing patterns designed for mass production, following a commission from Gropius to create designs for bedspreads and textiles for Harvard. In the early 1960s, she turned her attention to printmaking, and carried on writing and exhibiting her work both in the United States and in Germany.

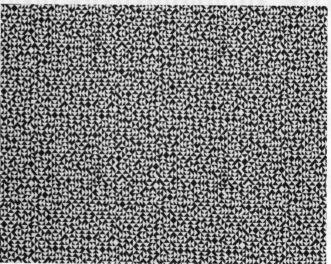

Top Anni Albers in her weaving studio, 1937.

Above "Berry" comes in numerous colorways.

Opposite "Meander" is based on the Greek key motif, with one "meander" superimposed on another lighter one. While the eye is invited to travel along the mazelike paths, the design also has a great sense of stability and repose.

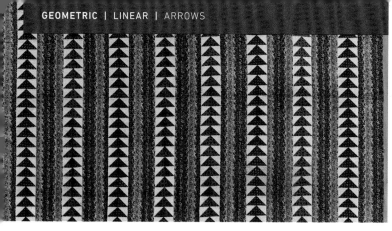

01 | Textile | USA | 1847
Made of a variety of printed cottons, this US comforter features a design that represents geese flying in formation as stylized arrows.

02 | Arrowhead | USA | 1950s | Alexander Girard
Girard's vertically structured furnishing fabric pattern, with its arrowhead motif, has an inherent sense of movement.

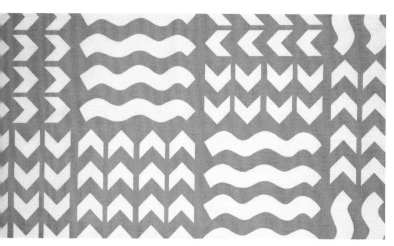

03 | Lucknow | UK | 2014 | Kangan Arora
The pattern of this screen-printed cushion was inspired by early morning sun filtered through a screen, or *jali*, in Uttar Pradesh, India.

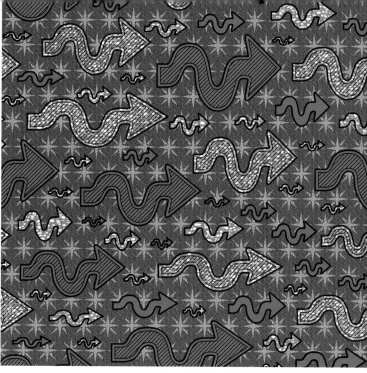

04 | Dress fabric | Netherlands | 2005
A wax-resist fabric manufactured by Vlisco. Arrows of varying sizes and with wiggly tails snake across an asterisked background.

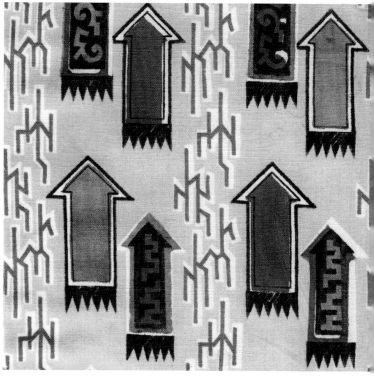

05 | Fabric swatch
This is an unattributed fabric sample from a private archive. Arrow motifs generate patterns with a strong directional emphasis.

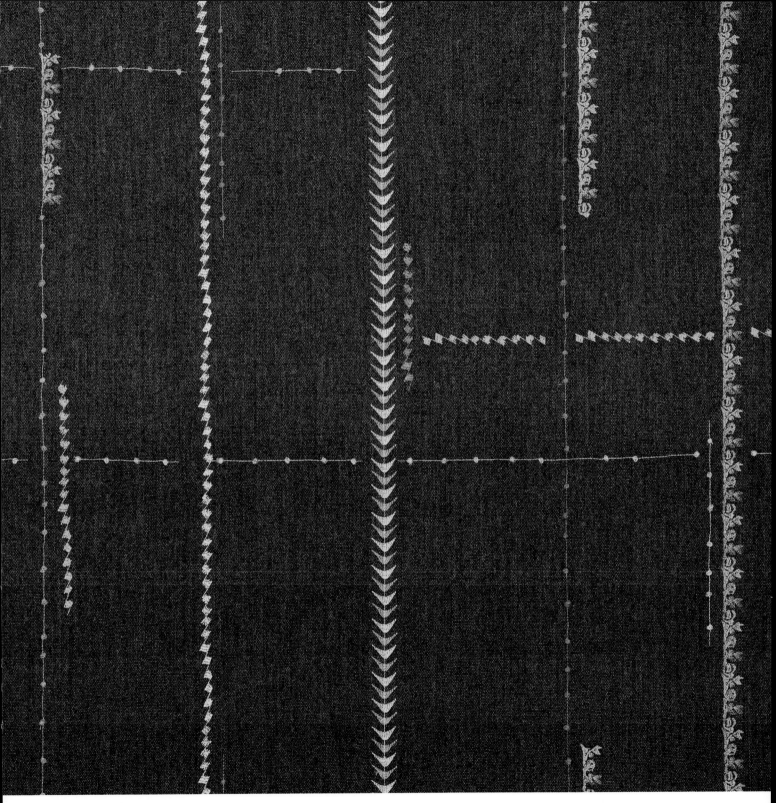

06 | Borders | Netherlands/USA | 2011 | Hella Jongerius for Maharam
Made from wool embroidered with polyester yarn, this furnishing fabric was
designed for Maharam. Jongerius is noted for the textural quality of her designs.

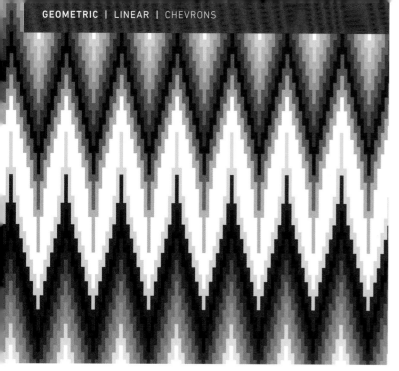

01 | Shaded Chevron | UK | 2010–11 | Eley Kishimoto
Like many of Eley Kishimoto's designs, this pattern has been applied across a wide range of products, both clothing and homeware.

03 | Textile | France | 1920s | Paul Rodier
The House of Rodier was known for its innovative woven fashion and furnishing fabrics, such as this woven silk. Rodier was influenced by Cubism.

02 | Leaded glass | USA | *c.*1911 **|** Frank Lloyd Wright
US architect Wright designed stained-glass windows for many of his Prairie style houses. He called them "light screens" and designed an estimated 4,365 windows.

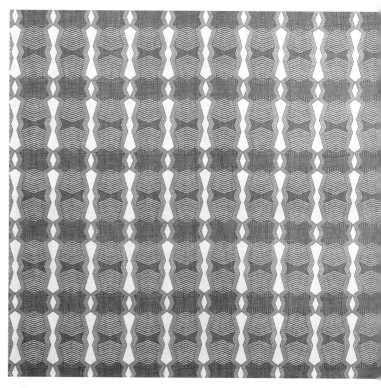

04 | Memphis | UK | 2014 | El Ultimo Grito
A furnishing fabric designed for Christopher Farr Cloth. Founded in 1997 and based in London, El Ultimo Grito produces work across a range of different disciplines.

05 | Jagged Edge | UK | 2006 | Neisha Crosland
The subtle zigzag pattern on this flexo-printed wallpaper has a
three-dimensional *trompe-l'oeil* quality.

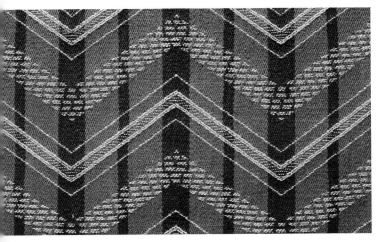

06 | Chevron | UK | 1946 | Enid Marx
This woven cotton furnishing fabric, designed for the Utility Design Panel, was
manufactured by Morton Sundour Fabrics, Carlisle.

07 | Nevis | UK | 2014 | Matthew Williamson at Osborne & Little
The chevron pattern of this imposingly geometric wallpaper is enlivened by tiny
glistening beads .

08 | Embroidered linen | Greece | 18th century
The stylized tree form on this piece of silk embroidery on linen ground features
sawtooth-edge branches that form a chevron pattern.

09 | Zebra | Sweden | 1971 | Sven Fristedt
The design of this furnishing fabric, manufactured by Borås Wäfveri, features bold
chevron stripes interrupted by wavy bands.

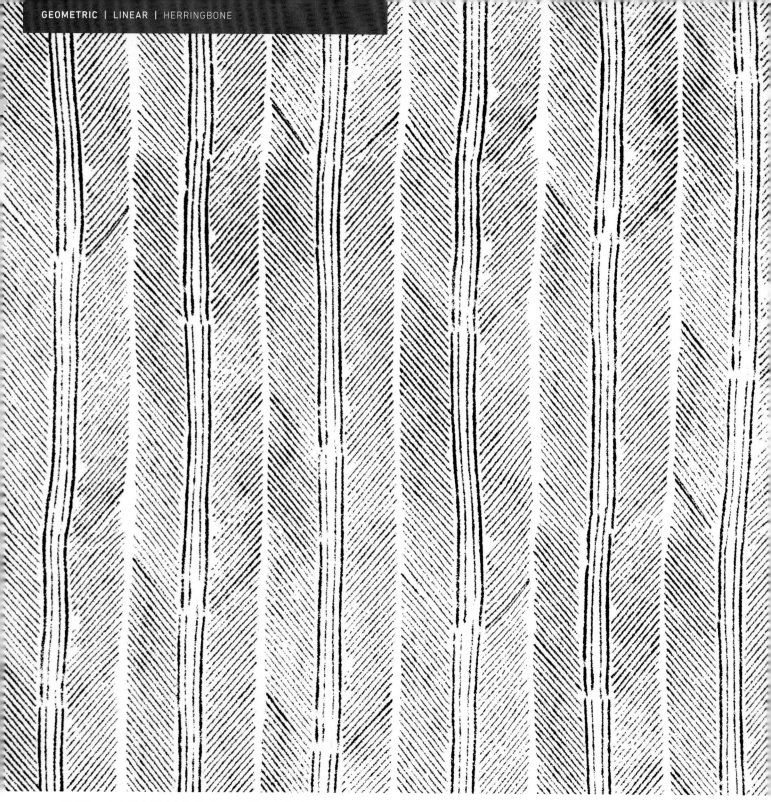

01 | Peacock | UK | 2016 | Phyllis Barron and Dorothy Larcher
This furnishing fabric, produced by Christopher Farr Cloth, is an archived pattern
originally created by Barron and Larcher.

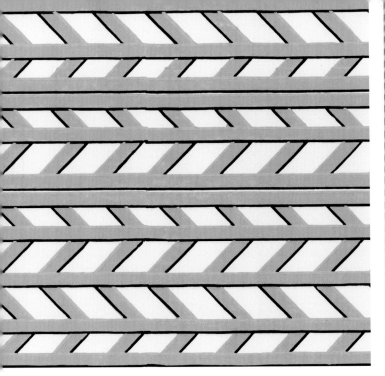

02 | Treillage (Trellis) | France | 1931–32
The herringbone pattern of this simple block-printed French wallpaper has a strong horizontal emphasis.

03 | Small Way | UK | 2016 | Kit Kemp
Kemp, who designed this linen furnishing fabric for Christopher Farr Cloth, is a designer of boutique hotel interiors. Her style is "English eccentric."

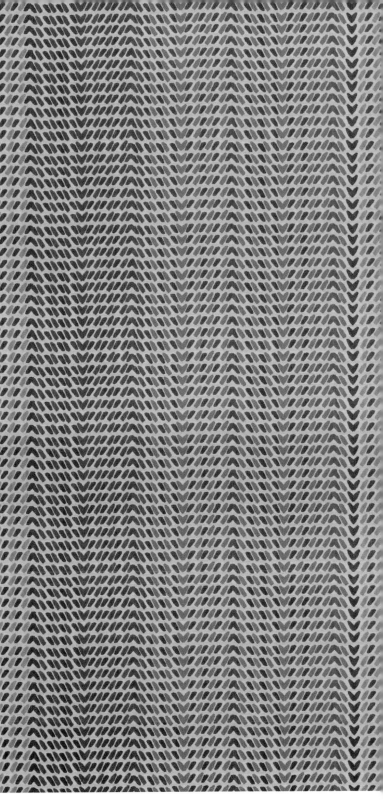

04 | Reef | Netherlands/USA | 2016 | Hella Jongerius for Maharam
Jongerius's furnishing fabric, designed for US textile company Maharam, has a dense herringbone pattern composed of gestural marks, giving it a handmade look.

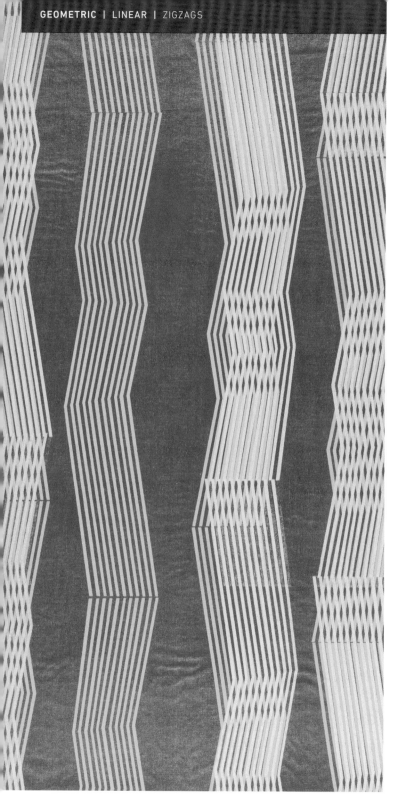

02 | Serpentin (Serpentine) | Austria | 1910–15 | Josef Hoffmann
This gouache design on paper features a geometric zigzag pattern punctuated
by squares. Hoffmann was a friend and admirer of Charles Rennie Mackintosh.

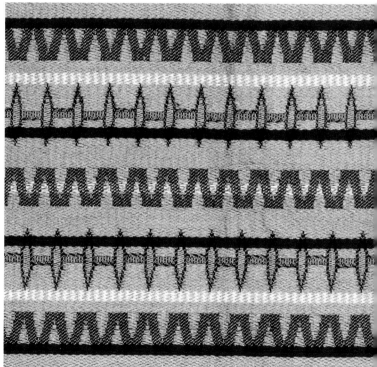

01 | Kinetics | USA | 1965–69 | Ben Rose
Many of Rose's patterns have a strong linear quality, such as this design
for wallpaper screen-printed on vinyl.

03 | Catseye | UK | 1947 | Enid Marx
Marx designed this furnishing fabric for the Utility Design Board, a body set up to
produce clothing and furniture during a time of rationing and material shortages.

04 | Zebra | UK | 2003 | Neisha Crosland
This striking pattern with its strong graphic contrast is available as a wallpaper, furnishing fabric, and carpet.

05 | Ensemble | Italy | *c.*1971 | Missoni
The first Missoni zigzag appeared in 1967. Knitwear patterned with these lightning bolt strikes in bright colors became a brand signature.

06 | Dress fabric | Netherlands | 2017 | Erwin Thomasse
The Dutch company Vlisco, founded in the 19th century, produces dress fabric for the African market using a wax-resist technique.

Eley Kishimoto

SEE PAGES > 19, 31, 101, 116, 120, 130, 137, 178, 208, 213, 214, 253, 256, 294, 296, 314, 318, 323, 358, 380, 399, 422, 425, 434, 438, 498, 549, 566, 568, 637, 647

Founders of the British-based fashion and print design studio Eley Kishimoto, Mark Eley and Wakako Kishimoto met in New York in 1989, where they were working on textile and fashion internships. Three years later, they launched their company on the same day they got married. Their creative partnership, which puts pattern first and foremost, has had an enormous influence on fashion and visual arts.

Kishimoto was born in Sapporo, Japan, and raised in Kobe. In 1986, she went to Britain and studied fashion and print at Central Saint Martins, London, graduating in 1992. Mark was born in Bridgend, Wales, and studied fashion and weave at Brighton Polytechnic, graduating in 1990.

Like many young designers struggling to make ends meet, they first worked out of their home. Soon, however, they attracted attention for the striking prints they created for fashion designers including Joe Casely-Hayford (b.1956), Hussein Chalayan (b.1970), and Alexander McQueen (1969–2010). By 1996, the couple were able to move their studio into a small space in a building in Brixton, south London, which they took over completely when the business grew. With Eley in charge of overall studio direction, Kishimoto focuses on the design side of the business, drawing all the patterns first by hand.

In 1996, the couple launched their collection "Rainwear," which featured printed PVC-coated fabrics made up into umbrellas and waterproof coats. Two years later, the label had grown to include a range of womenswear shown in biannual collections and it has continued to expand. In 2001, they ventured into interiors, with wallpaper and tableware designs. That same year, they launched "Flash," a swirling Op art pattern with contorted houndstooth motifs, which has been applied to various products from clothing and shoes, to motorbikes and motorbike helmets, glasses and cars. This reflects the couple's interdisciplinary approach and abiding interest in extending print across a range of media.

Eley Kishimoto patterns resist categorization. Crisp and graphic, they run the gamut from Op art–inspired geometrics to luxuriant florals; some designs combine contrasting elements like a jigsaw. A three-dimensional quality is evident in the gridded framework of "Venice" (2014) and "Sun-Loving Bollards" (2014), which creates the illusion of raised studs. "Frills" (2014) is a *trompe-l'oeil* pattern composed of tiers of ruffles.

Alongside their own label collections, Eley Kishimoto has continued to collaborate with other fashion designers, such as Marc Jacobs (b.1963) and Jil Sander (b.1943). Between 2008 and 2009, the couple were creative directors for Cacharel, a fashion house based in Paris.

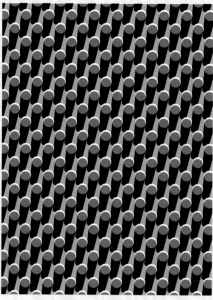

Far Left Wife and husband team Wakako Kishimoto and Mark Eley are known for their quirky styling.

Left "Sun-Loving Bollards," a pattern dating from 2014, has a three-dimensional quality.

Opposite Eley Kishimoto's "Flash" (2001) is typical of their distinctive graphic prints.

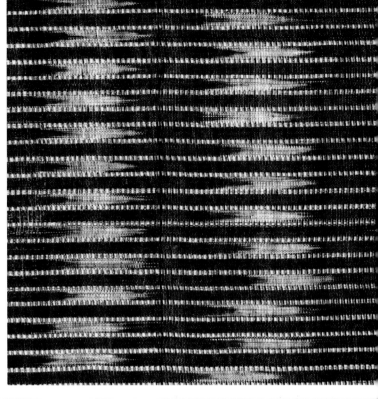

The term *ikat* comes from the Malay word *mengikat*, which means "to tie" or "to bind." *Ikat* is a resist-dyeing technique that gives its name to a family of textiles produced in many areas of Central and Southeast Asia, as well as countries in South and Central America. Thought to be one of the oldest methods of decorating fabric in the world, it involves tying or binding yarns to create a resist. The yarns are then dyed, often multiple times, with the bound areas creating a pattern once the yarns are woven into cloth. In batik or tie-dye, by contrast, the resist is applied to the fabric after it is woven.

There are many different versions of *ikat*, including warp *ikat*, where the warp yarns carry the pattern, weft *ikat*, where the weft yarns carry the pattern, and double *ikat*, where both warp and weft yarns are resist-dyed. Prized for the brilliancy of their colors, *ikat* textiles were traditionally made using dyes derived from natural sources, such as madder, saffron, indigo, and mallow. Another characteristic is a slight blurriness in the design that occurs when the dyes bleed somewhat into the resist areas.

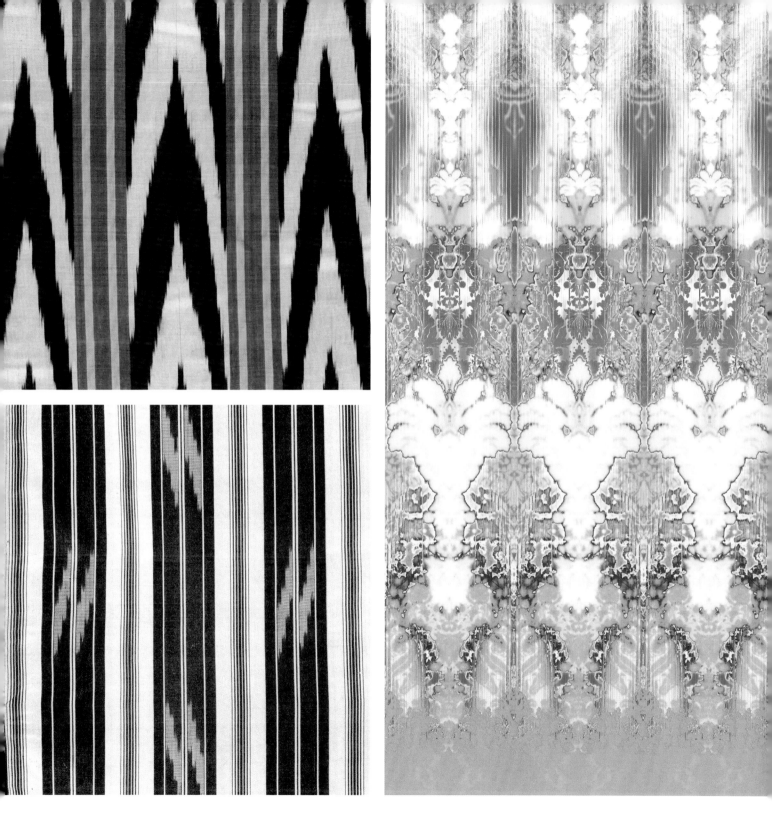

01 | Parure | UK | 2012 | Osborne & Little

This large-scale wallpaper design features a pattern of softly fringed concentric rings in subtle colors. A parure is a set of matching jewelry.

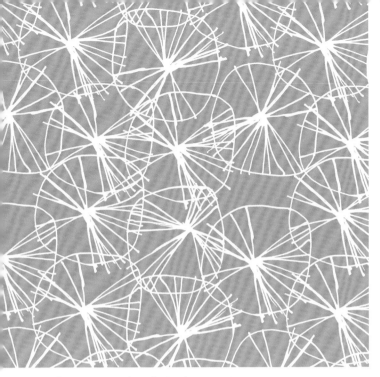

02 | Geo Star Floral | UK | 2014 | Rebecca Hoyes
Hoyes has created a number of print designs for Habitat in her role as senior
designer. She stresses the importance of work that displays "the hand of the maker."

03 | Furnishing fabric | France | c.1931 | Robert Bonfils
Designed for leading French textile manufacturer Bianchini-Férier, this furnishing
fabric displays the fashionable Art Deco style of the 1930s.

04 | Watermark | UK | 1999 | Neisha Crosland
The epitome of subtlety, this flexo-printed wallpaper pattern features pale circles
surrounded by concentric dotted rings.

05 | Textile | Turkey | 16th to 17th centuries
This fabric from the Ottoman Empire is made of silk velvet and features a design of
roundels regularly spaced across the ground.

06 | Textile | USA | 1950
This Amish comforter features a pattern known as the "Double Wedding Ring," one of the
most popular quilting designs. Traditionally, such quilts were given to brides.

Varvara Stepanova (1894–1958)

Painter, photographer, and designer Varvara Stepanova was a leading light in Constructivism, the art movement that emerged after the Russian Revolution in 1917. Her experimental work across all media was devoted to the cause of radical change.

Born in Kovno (now Kaunas), Lithuania, she studied at the Kazan School of Art in Odessa, where she met her future husband Alexander Rodchenko (1891–1956), who was to become one of the most important graphic designers of the period. In 1913, Stepanova moved to Moscow, where she studied at the Stroganov School. Influenced by Cubism and Futurism, by 1917 she was experimenting with abstract art, visual poetry, and collage.

After the revolution, she was swept up in the creative ferment of the time, contributing to exhibitions, illustrating books, and composing "transrational" poetry, in which words were chosen for how they sounded and looked on the page rather than for their meaning. In 1921, along with Rodchenko, she formed the First Working Group of Constructivists. Constructivists rejected fine art and insisted that all art, from architecture to book design to photography to theater, should be agents of social change. Stepanova's graphic sets and costume designs for a production of *The Death of Tarelkin* (1869) in 1922 demonstrated this to great effect.

Throughout the remainder of the 1920s, Stepanova worked as a designer, branching out into photomontage. She also turned her attention to clothing design and, by association, textiles. Although poor economic conditions meant that most of her work never went into mass production, her ideas were years ahead of their time. Her clothing designs were intended to liberate the wearer from gender and class identifiers. Particular attention was paid to functional aspects, such as pockets and belts. Furthermore, the designs, with their bold lines and striking geometric forms, were conceived to highlight the body in action, whether on the stage or engaged in sporting activity.

In 1923, Stepanova worked directly in production as a designer at the Tsindel (First State Textile Printing Factory) near Moscow. Using a limited range of dyes and focusing on geometric motifs, her patterns (more than 150 in total) achieved great depth and vitality. A year later, she was made professor of textile design at the Vkhutemas art and technical school.

With the rise of Joseph Stalin in the late 1920s, and the emergence of Soviet Realism as the sole state-sanctioned form of visual expression, Stepanova's Constructivist approach was sidelined. Although she continued to paint and to design books, magazines, and stage sets until her death, it was from the margins. Her legacy, however, has had a lasting impact on modern graphic design.

Top Varvara Stepanova photographed by her husband, Alexander Rodchenko, in 1924.

Above During the 1920s, Stepanova, who had been an influential artist in the Constructivist movement, turned her attention to textile design.

Opposite While few of Stepanova's textile designs were put into mass production, she revolutionized the way fabric was patterned and clothing was conceived. All of the many patterns she created featured graphic geometric motifs using a limited range of colors.

08 | **Chains** | UK | 2002–03 | Eley Kishimoto
Part of a rug collection designed exclusively for Aram, this bold pattern of linked circles has a graphic punch.

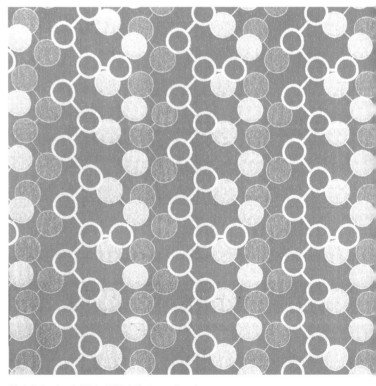

07 | **Recurrence** | UK | 1962 | Barbara Brown
The furnishing fabrics that Barbara Brown designed for Heal's Fabrics epitomized the spirit of the Swinging Sixties.

09 | **Helmsley** | UK | 1951 | Marianne Straub
This furnishing fabric for Warner & Sons displays the abstract patterning typical of Straub's later work. It was inspired by the crystal structure diagram for nylon.

10 | **Bokhen** | UK | 2014 | Emma Jeffs
This printed furnishing fabric, made by Jeffs's studio N & N Wares, features circles
in the form of soft-edged ink blots.

11 | **Circles** | UK | 2016 | Rebecca Hoyes
Shaded multicolored chevrons overlapping adjacent circles add depth of interest
to a simple geometric design.

12 | **Great 8 (Gold)** | UK | 2013 | Jocelyn Warner
Gold circles forming the figure eight have shaded outlines to create
a three-dimensional effect.

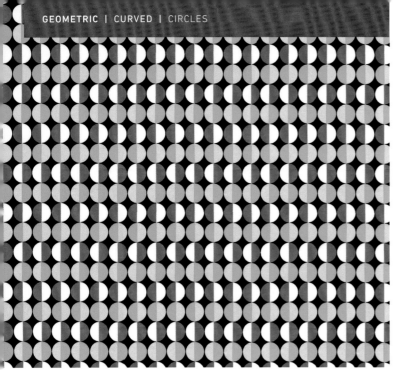

13 | Bola | USA | 2013 | Eleanor Grosch
This cotton fabric was designed for the US textile firm Cloud9 Fabrics, which specializes in organic cotton textiles for quilting and home sewing.

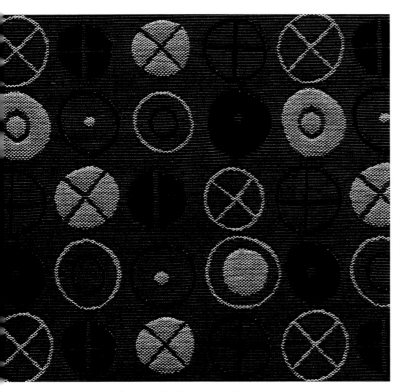

14 | Circles | USA | 1947 | Charles and Ray Eames
Designed by Ray Eames for a textile competition at the Museum of Modern Art, New York, this design is currently produced by Maharam.

15 | Textile design | Russia | 1924 | Alexander Rodchenko
Painter, sculptor, photographer, and graphic designer Rodchenko was a leading practitioner of Constructivism.

16 | Textile | UK | 1930 | Arthur Sanderson & Sons
This roller-printed cotton furnishing fabric features a pattern of overlapping segmented circles in bright colors.

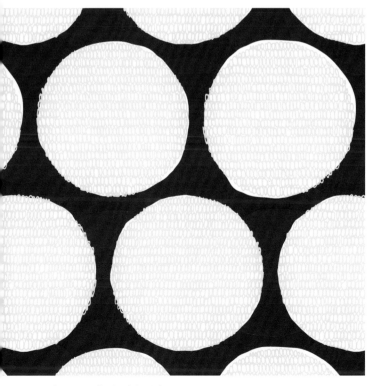

17 | Disguise | USA | 2018 | Sarah Watson
US designer Watson, who is based in São Paulo, Brazil, has created patterns for wallpaper, textiles, and stationery. This fabric is produced by Cloud9 Fabrics.

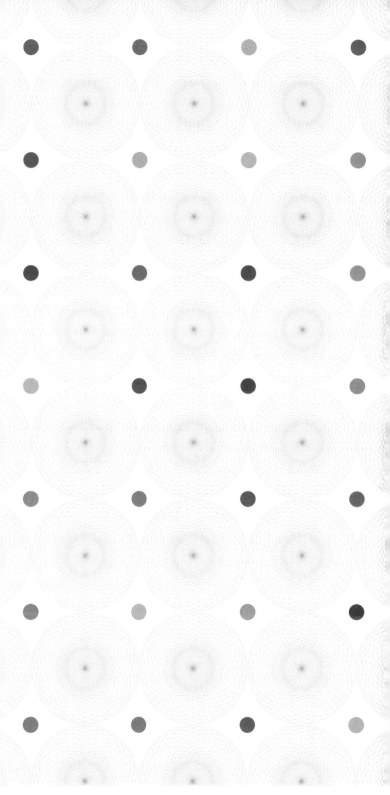

18 | Spiral Spot | UK | 2007 | Sam Pickard
A regularly spaced pattern of small colored spots placed within rows of spirals, this design has a mesmerizing effect.

01 | **Amlapura** | UK | 2014 | Designers Guild

This cotton furnishing fabric, with its pattern of inky paint drops, is part
of a collection inspired by the printed and dyed fabrics of Southeast Asia.

02 | **Textile** | UK | *c.* 1825–35

The circles of this cotton dress fabric are slightly irregular in shape. The dense
pattern of spots has a charming simplicity.

03 | Fabric swatch
Dots and spots in five different sizes are arranged in loose swirling shapes against a crisp white ground.

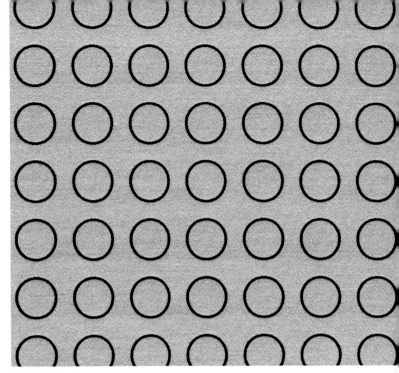

04 | Repeat Dot Ring | Netherlands/USA | 2002 | Hella Jongerius for Maharam
Designed for leading US manufacturer Maharam, this minimal geometric pattern features open circles.

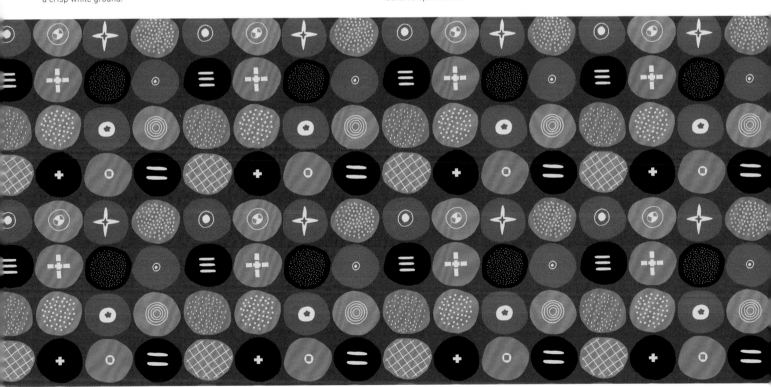

05 | Anpan | Japan | 2014 | Yuki Tsutsumi of Nuno
Designed by Nuno to make use of *kibiso*, the protective outer surface of silk cocoons, typically discarded as too tough to loom. This pattern is named after a type of Japanese sweet roll.

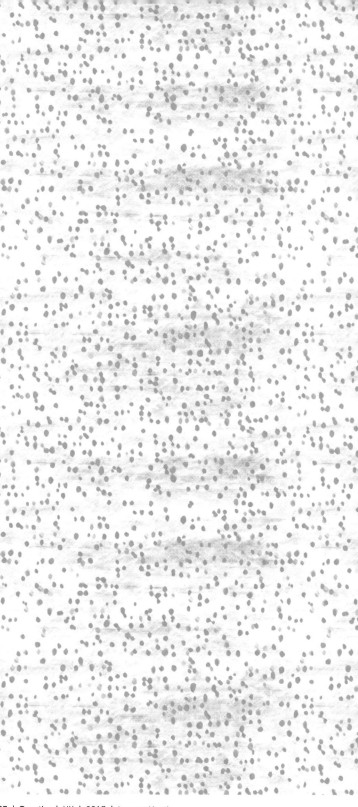

06 | Diagonal Beaded Stripe | UK | 2005 | Neisha Crosland

This pigment printed cotton furnishing fabric has a clean-cut diagonal pattern of spots reminiscent of a screen or bead curtain.

07 | Dorothy | UK | 2017 | Imogen Heath

A contemporary updating of the classic polka dot, this cotton furnishing fabric has a pattern of irregular spots randomly placed across the ground.

08 | Pompoms | USA | 1965–69 | Ben Rose
Rose's designs have the cheerful optimism of mid-century modern. This spotty
pompom wallpaper pattern is screen-printed on vinyl.

09 | Printed design | UK | 2014 | Sally Lloyd-Thomas
This loose painterly design features daubed spots of color arranged across
a roughly drawn grid.

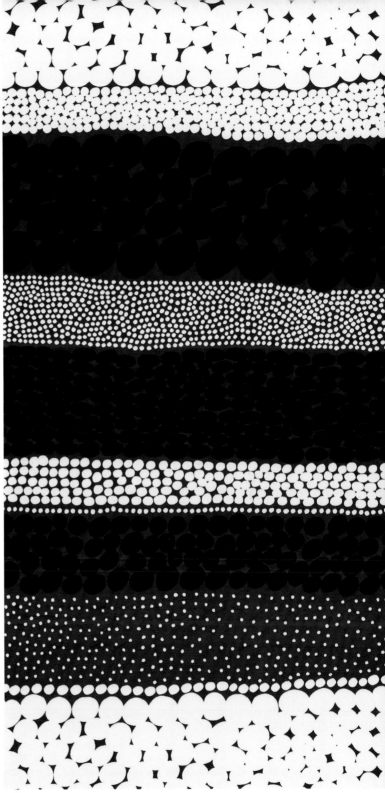

10 | Jurmo | Finland | 2011 | Aino-Maija Metsola
A furnishing fabric designed for Marimekko, this design features vertical bands
of indigo and white spots.

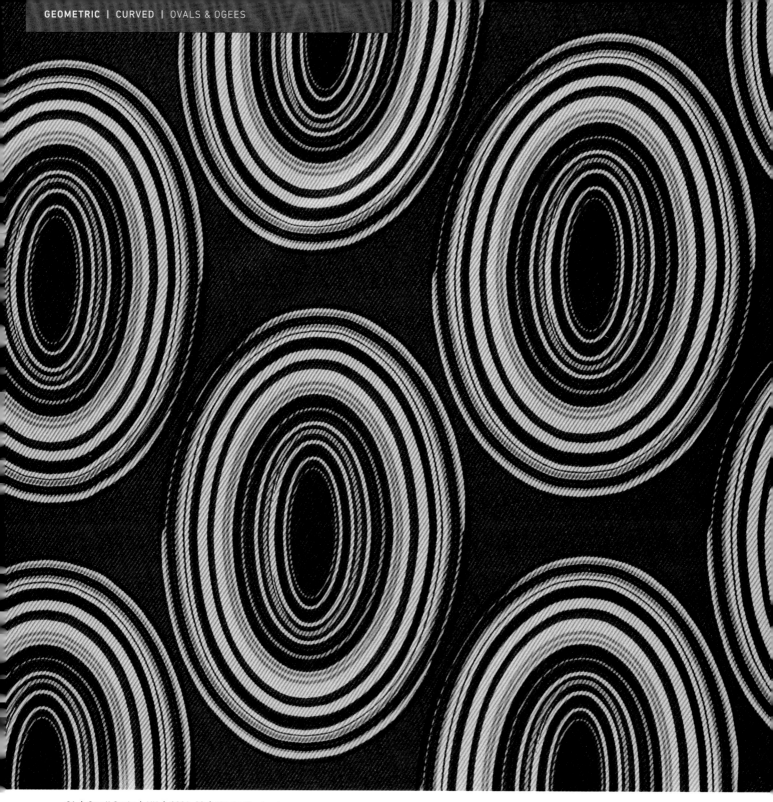

01 | **Small Ovals** | UK | 2001–02 | Neisha Crosland

This woven silk scarf fabric is patterned with concentric oval rings in contrasting
shades of aquamarine, maroon, and burnt orange.

02 | Sgt Pepper | UK | 2016 | Anna Hayman
Hayman cites as influences the work of Aubrey Beardsley and William Morris, as well as the boutique retailer Biba.

03 | Fabric sample
Tiny floral sprigs enliven this vertically structured pattern from a private archive, with its three undulating ribbonlike bands.

04 | Florence | UK | 2010 | Cole & Son
This medium-scale wallpaper design, produced as a one-color surface print, is a reprint of a pattern from the Cole & Son archive dating from 1890.

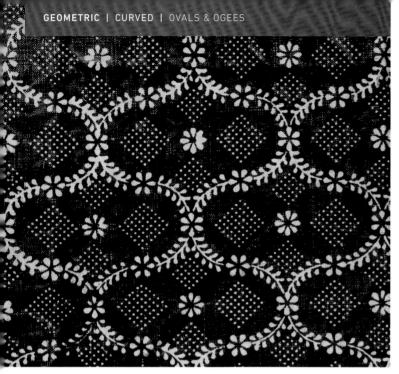

05 | Textile sample | 18th century
This plain woven fabric has been resist-printed with a scrolling pattern of ogee curves enclosing dotted diamonds.

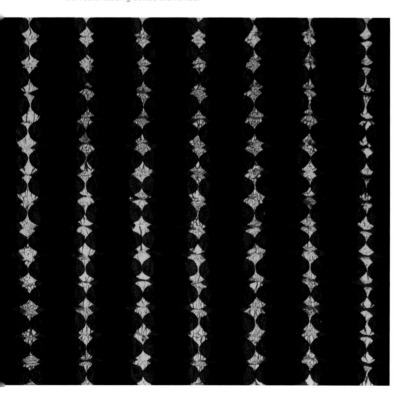

06 | Textile | UK | c. 1960 | Susan Bosence
Bosence's block printed and dyed cotton furnishing fabric features horizontal rows of dark blue ovals intersecting with light ovals.

07 | Wallpaper | USA | 1890–1920
This ogee-patterned wallpaper with foliate motifs was manufactured by M. H. Birge & Sons of Buffalo, New York, one of the most important US wallpaper manufacturers.

08 | Bibana | UK | 2016 | Anna Hayman
Hayman's digitally printed patterns, like this design for wallpaper, have a bohemian
feel. They begin as linocuts.

01 | Border | USA | 1905–15

This machine-printed wallpaper border, with its gold foiled background, was manufactured by the New York Card and Paper Co.

02 | Wallpaper | USA | 1905–15

Wallpaper remained a popular choice for wall decoration well into the 20th century. This reticent demure design is in soft pastel shades.

03 | Carpet design | UK | 20th century
This design for a carpet is symmetrical, contained, and regular, as befits a pattern that is intended to be displayed underfoot.

05 | Color lithograph | UK | 1928 | Edward Bawden
One of the patterns from *A Specimen Book of Pattern Papers Designed for and in Use at the Curwen Press*, this printed design would probably have been used as endpapers.

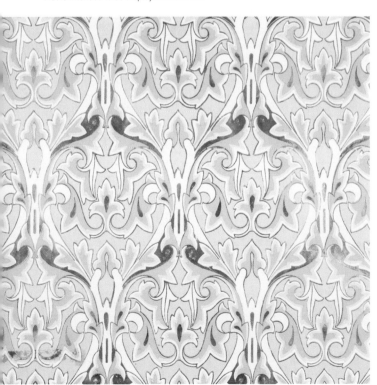

04 | Moresque | UK | 1858 | Owen Jones
This block-printed wallpaper displays vegetal scrolling in a manner that almost prefigures Art Nouveau.

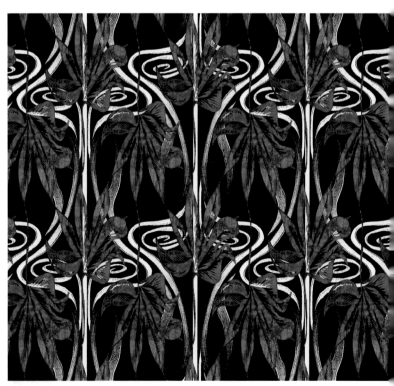

06 | Dianne | UK | 2016 | Anna Hayman
With its Aubrey Beardsley overtones, this rich dark wallpaper design features attenuated scrolling and feathery foliage.

Ancient Egypt (*c.* 3100 – 30 BCE)

The art and architecture of antiquity have captured the imagination of countless designers, who have borrowed motifs, detailing, palettes, and other aspects of ornamentation in stylistic revivals. Ancient Egypt has been a rich source of such inspiration. Egyptian influence is visible in late 18th-century French furniture design, 19th-century architecture, Art Deco, and in the revisited Art Deco style of the late 1960s.

Western interest in ancient Egypt arose at times that coincided with archeological discoveries. During the 18th century, the age of the Grand Tour, travel writers described ancient wonders such as the Pyramids and the Sphinx to their readers. But artifacts that were collected and brought home for exhibition or display in private houses, where they could be studied, attracted particular attention. One such discovery was the Rosetta Stone, which was put on display in the British Museum in 1802. Public interest was similarly sparked in 1821 when the pioneering Italian archeologist Giovanni Belzoni displayed the findings of his excavation at Thebes in London. Nearly a century later, after successive generations of Egyptologists had made their excavations and published their research, Howard Carter's discovery of the tomb of King Tutankhamun in 1922 caused a sensation worldwide.

As more tombs, temples, and mummy cases were uncovered, the variety of ancient Egyptian patterning was revealed. Unsurprisingly, for a civilization that depended on the fertility of the Nile Valley, many of the motifs were based on natural forms and underwritten by symbolic significance. The lotus and the papyrus were symbols of creation and were common in ornamentation. Each temple column at Luxor was decorated to suggest a papyrus plant, with the base the root, the pillar the stem, and the capital the flower. Palm fronds, acanthus leaves, and honeysuckle were also typical, as were feather motifs.

Other patterns, including checks, trellises, zigzags, stripes, and repeats based on triangles were inspired by the warp and weft of woven materials, such as clothing or the floor matting created by braiding together different colored fibers. A version of the volute, the spiral scroll later found on Ionic Greek capitals, is seen in the ancient Egyptian coiled rope motif, while there is a forerunner of the Greek key pattern in mazelike fretwork designs. Stars were widely used to pattern ceilings.

Ancient Egyptian patterning, like the paintings that decorated tombs and temples, was flat and without spatial depth. Colors, derived from mineral sources, were the primary shades of red, blue, and yellow, with the addition of green, set off by the graphic contrast of white and black.

Far Left The ceiling pattern at the Tomb of Qenamun (*c.* 1479–1400 BCE), Thebes, Egypt.

Left A ceiling painting from the Palace of Amenhotep III (*c.* 1390–1353 BCE) at Thebes, Malqata, Egypt.

Opposite A gold, carnelian, turquoise, and lapis lazuli broad collar (332–246 BCE) from the Eastern Delta, Egypt.

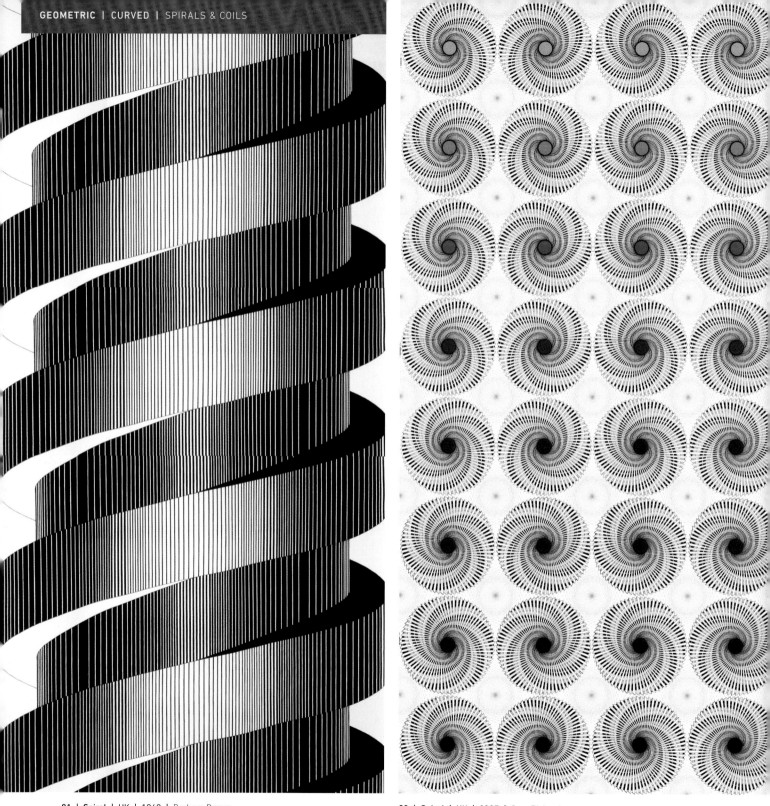

01 | Spiral | UK | 1969 | Barbara Brown

This screen-printed cotton satin furnishing fabric, designed for Heal's, features a black-and-white pattern of an endless screw thread.

02 | Spiral | UK | 2007 | Sam Pickard

Rows of spirals alternate in direction, while the colored central spot appears in shades from yellow through orange to red.

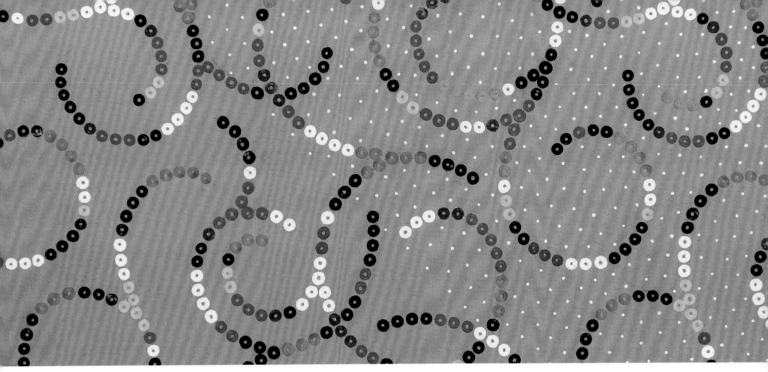

03 | **Textile design** | Russia | 1953 | Nina Shirokova
A gouache on paper sketch for a textile design features an all-over pattern of beaded coils against a dotted background.

04 | **Border** | France | 1835–55
A block-printed and flocked machine-made wallpaper border simulates coiled rope architectural molding.

06 | **Wall decoration** | Egypt | *c.* 1390–1352 BCE
A reconstruction of a wall decoration from the Temple of Amun at Malqata
in Upper Egypt. It is executed in faience, modern plaster, and gold paint.

05 | **Paper** | Japan | **20th century**
This hand-stencil dyed paper reveals the precision and delicacy of this traditional
form of Japanese patterning.

07 | **Textile design** | Russia | 1970 | Nina Shirokova
Shirokova's design for a textile, executed in gouache on paper, shows a clear
influence of Russian folk art and embroidery.

08 | Aztec | UK | 2010–11 | Eley Kishimoto

Eley Kishimoto's hand screen-printed fabric features a characteristically
bold and confident use of color and graphic patterning.

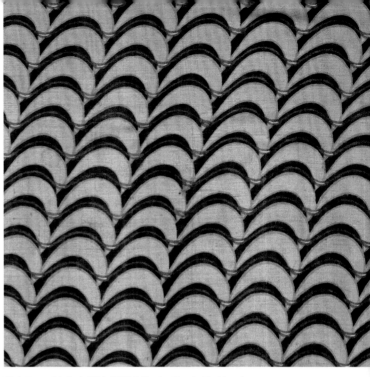

01 | Change Your Life | Netherlands | 1956 | Antoon van Duppen
This fabric was designed for the Dutch company Vlisco, which produces dress materials using a mechanical version of the wax-resist technique.

03 | Dress fabric | UK | 1918 | Charles Rennie Mackintosh
In later years, when his architectural commissions had dried up, Mackintosh made a living designing textile patterns.

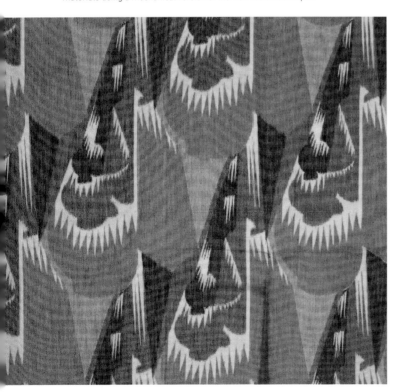

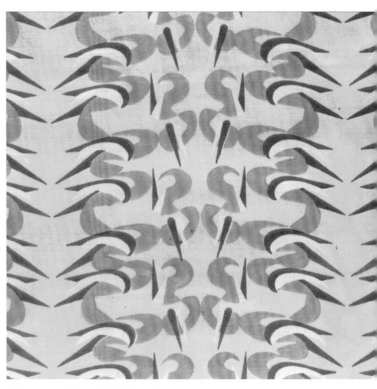

02 | Textile | UK | 1929 | Calico Printers' Association
A warp-printed cotton furnishing fabric made by the Calico Printers' Association. In warp printing, the warp of the fabric is printed prior to weaving.

04 | Maroon | UK | 1938 | Eileen Hunter
Proprietor of Eileen Hunter Fabrics, Hunter was a noted textile designer in the 1930s. Warner & Co. printed her designs.

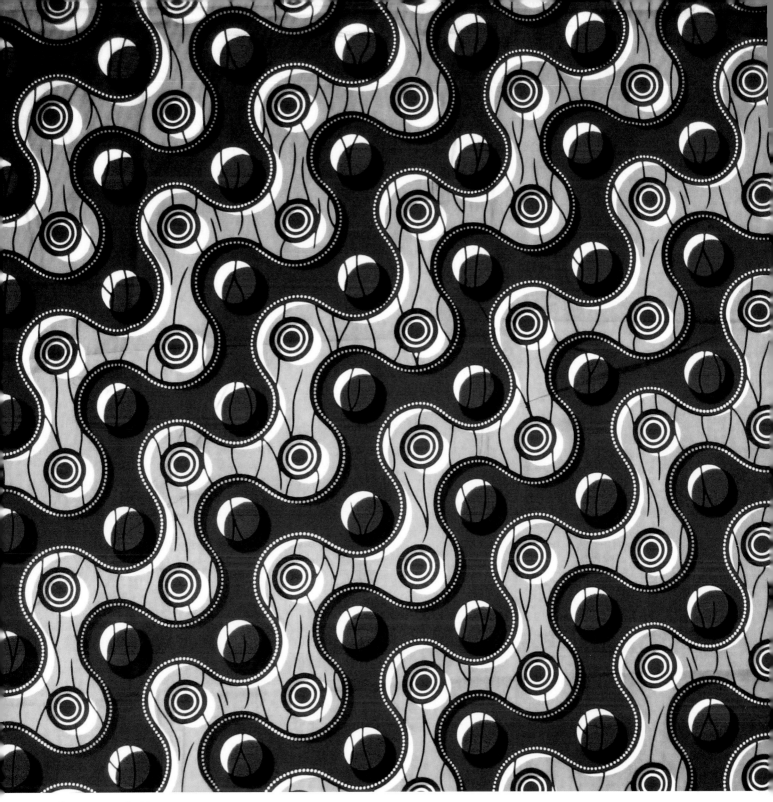

05 | Fabric swatch | Africa
This unusual globular wave pattern has a contoured effect produced by highlighting;
it is overscored by black lines.

Jack Lenor Larsen (b.1927)

SEE PAGES > 315, 616, 619, 648

Weaver and textile designer Jack Lenor Larsen has been a leading force in furnishing fabrics since the 1950s, when his innovative approach to color and texture first appeared on the scene. Responsible for several thousands of designs and with a client list that has included Marilyn Monroe, Frank Lloyd Wright, and Leonard Bernstein, he has gained lifelong inspiration from craft traditions worldwide.

Larsen was born in Seattle to Norwegian-Danish parents who had emigrated from Canada; his father was a building contractor. In 1945, he began studying architecture at the University of Washington; a year later, he took a weaving course that immediately set his future along different lines. "[Weaving] had horizontals and verticals, like architecture, and was dependent on materials and light and shadow, but I had real yarns and real color and real structure," he said.

Following this epiphany, Larsen moved to Los Angeles, where a handcraft revival was underway. After a brief period back in Seattle, where he opened a studio, he went to the Cranbrook Academy of Art in Michigan, where he gained his Master of Fine Arts in 1951. The following year, he arrived in New York, just as the International Style was taking off. Early success came with his winning entry for a drape fabric for Lever House, a translucent material woven with linen cord and gold metal.

By 1954, Larsen had a showroom on New York's Park Avenue. Florence Knoll, who had originally rejected his portfolio for being too original, the colors too earthy, now commissioned him to produce olive-green and burnt-orange weaves for her company's furniture. His use of natural yarns and random repeats struck a chord with contemporary modernist architects and designers. Larsen's first print collection was "Spice Garden" (1955). In 1958, he designed upholstery fabrics for Pan American World Airways's new 707s. A decade later, he designed the interiors and fabrics for Braniff International's Terminal of the Future in Dallas, Texas, and in 1970 created textiles for Braniff's 747.

Larsen has always been inspired both by the very ancient and by the technical cutting edge, a tension that is clearly revealed in his work. Another key influence has been his travels around the world and he has made forty trips to Japan alone. In the 1970s, after traveling to Central Asia, Afghanistan, and Indonesia, he introduced the US market to the then-exotic patterns of *ikat*, *plangi*, and batik. By the mid-1970s, Larsen's company was producing fabrics in thirty different countries. Today, it is part of the US subsidiary of Colefax and Fowler. His design house, Larsen Design Studio, is one of only two to have had an exhibition at the Louvre; examples of Larsen's designs are in many other museum collections.

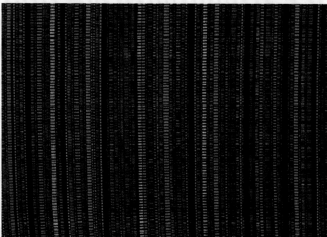

Top US textile designer Jack Lenor Larsen in his studio in New York in 1982.

Above "Leather Cloth" furnishing fabric designed by Larsen in 1955 and woven out of leather, vinyl, and nylon.

Opposite Inspired by a Chinese robe and Ming Dynasty embroideries, this rayon, cotton, and mohair furnishing fabric remained in production for more than twenty years.

06 | Fabric swatch
A highly effective wave pattern features simple broad bands in various shades of indigo, the broken lines suggesting a combed paint finish.

07 | Hedgehog | UK | 2005 | Neisha Crosland
This furnishing fabric has a bristling pattern of spiked waves that generate a peaceful flowing effect.

08 | **Furnishing fabric** | UK | 1922 | F. Gregory Brown
Brown designed this block-printed linen furnishing fabric for William Foxton.
It won a gold medal at the Paris Exposition of 1925.

09 | **Furnishing fabric** | France | 1927–28 | Pierre Chareau
Chareau was a French architect and designer, famous for his Maison de Verre in
Paris, for which he designed furniture and fittings.

10 | **Hanging** | France | c.1930 | Jean Bouzois
This cotton and wool hanging, manufactured by Metz & Co., features a dynamic
pattern of undulating monochromatic waves.

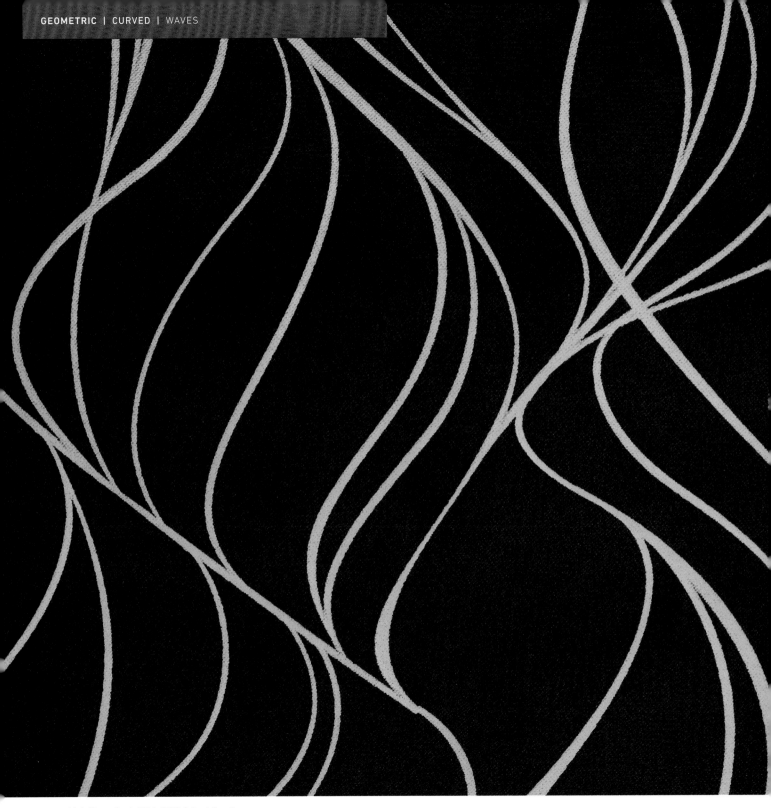

11 | Pirouette | UK | 2009 | Tord Boontje

One of a number of furnishing fabrics that Boontje designed for the Danish textile
manufacturer Kvadrat, this pattern features loose scrolling lines.

12 | Waves | UK | 2017 | Jenny Frean
A printed design produced for Prestigious, this airy pattern displays solid wave shapes that recall birds in flight.

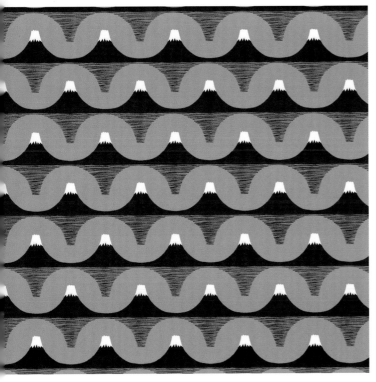

13 | Fujisan | Japan | 2016 | Gaku Masui of Nuno for Steteco.com
This printed fabric was designed by Nuno for Japanese apparel company Steteco.com. The horizontal waves enclose a stylized depiction of Mount Fuji.

14 | Shimmy | UK | 1967 | Natalie Gibson
Gibson designed for a number of leading textile companies, including Heal's Fabrics and Hull Traders. This psychedelic design was produced for Conran Fabrics.

02 | Jali Trellis | UK | 2016 | Matthew Williamson at Osborne & Little
This pattern is available both as a wallpaper and a furnishing fabric. A jali is a
Mughal-style lattice.

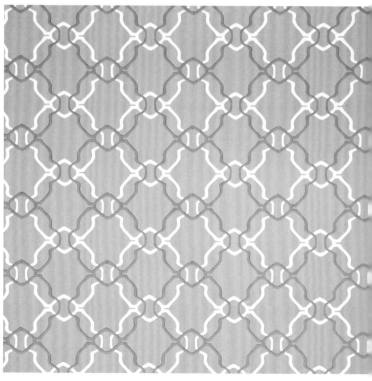

01 | Wallpaper | USA | 1840s
This block-printed wallpaper, with its scrolling cartouches, displays the elegant
Rococo Revival style that was popular in the early 19th century.

03 | Aladdin | UK | 2011 | Neisha Crosland
This subtle wallpaper pattern features two interlinked and superimposed meshes
composed of scrolled frames.

04 | Fabric swatch | Africa
The cartouche or scrolled enclosure derives from ancient Egyptian hieroglyphs, in which it was used to enclose a royal name.

05 | Dress fabric | Netherlands | 2017
This pattern, manufactured by Vlisco using a mechanized wax-resist technique, combines elaborate cartouches with the modern motifs of padlocks and keys.

Art Deco (c. 1920–30s)

Popular worldwide during the interwar years, Art Deco represented the exuberant side of modernism. In its celebration of progress and technology, and its application to the styling of products such as radios, Art Deco was decorative, blending influences as diverse as African tribal art, the architectural forms of Babylonian ziggurats and Egyptian pyramids, and the vibrant set and costume designs of the Ballets Russes.

The term "Art Deco," which refers to the Exposition Internationale des Arts Décoratifs et Industriels Modernes (International Exhibition of Modern Decorative and Industrial Arts) held in Paris in 1925, where Art Deco products and interiors were seen by millions of visitors, was coined retrospectively by British design historian Bevis Hillier in 1966, just at the point where the style was about to be revived by tastemakers such as Barbara Hulanicki (b.1936), founder of clothes store Biba.

Unlike modernism, in which pattern was limited to textile design, and interior and exterior surfaces were left plain and unadorned, Art Deco patterns appeared everywhere and on everything: not only wallpaper and fabrics, but also on the facades of skyscrapers, in the lobbies and interiors of office buildings, theaters and cinemas, and in the design of ocean liners. Geometric, symmetrical, and linear, Art Deco patterning on walls,

ceilings, floors, and doorways commonly featured elements such as triangles and chevrons, radiating sunburst motifs, concentric circles, and semicircles. As the style evolved, it became more curvaceous, borrowing from the aesthetic of streamlining used in the styling of automobiles, locomotives, and airplanes during the interwar period.

One of the leading practitioners of Art Deco was French designer Émile-Jacques Ruhlmann (1879–1933). His furniture, extravagantly patterned carpets, lights, textiles, and wallpaper catered to the luxury market. His furniture in particular—exquisitely made out of exotic woods, such as Macassar ebony and Brazilian mahogany, and inlaid with precious materials such as ivory and shagreen—commanded huge prices.

More affordable were the ceramics produced by British designers Clarice Cliff (1899–1972) and Susie Cooper (1902–95). Cliff's ranges such as "Bizarre" (1927) and "Fantasque" (1928–34), hand-painted in vivid Art Deco colors of orange, green, blue, yellow, and red, featured semiabstract stylized motifs drawn from nature. While Cliff originally worked on standard white blanks, she went on to produce her own shapes which took direct inspiration from the ziggurat-stepped Art Deco profile. Cooper was also a designer of bold, abstract Art Deco patterns before moving on to a more representational style.

Far Left A pochoir print from *Nouvelles Compositions Décoratives* (*New Decorative Compositions*, c. 1930).

Left Another print from *New Decorative Compositions* by Serge Gladky (1880–1930), who worked in France.

Opposite "Latona Red Roses" (c. 1929–30) coffee set by Clarice Cliff is hand-painted in the Art Deco style.

01 | Palmprint | UK | 2016 | Anna Hayman

This vivid furnishing fabric, with its bold palm leaf-shaped motif, has been used
to cover Art Deco-style pendant lights.

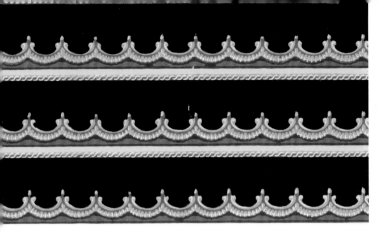

02 | Border | France | c. 1850
Scallops are a traditional edging for window treatments and other forms of soft furnishing. Here, they provide a finishing touch as a wallpaper border.

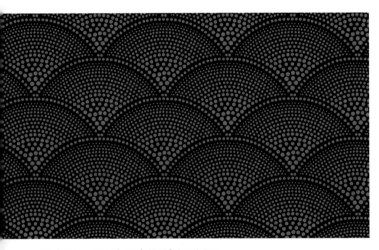

03 | Feather Fan | UK | 2010 | Cole & Son
This elegant wallpaper pattern with repeating fan shapes was inspired by traditional Japanese stencil patterns.

04 | Fabric swatch
Staggered horizontal rows of scalloping are given graphic emphasis by the crisp use of black and white.

05 | Pollen | UK | 2013 | Neisha Crosland
This all-over wallpaper pattern, with its undulating zigzags and clusters of dots, has the effect of old-fashioned marbled paper.

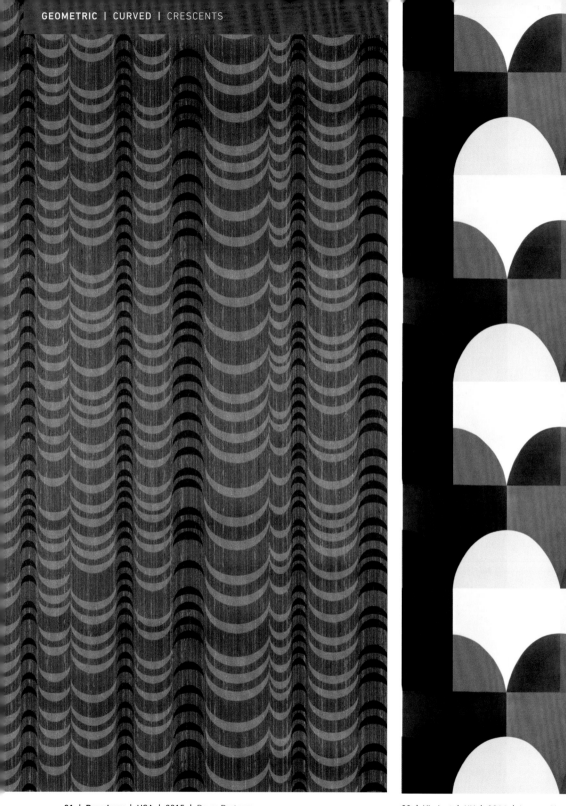

01 | Broadway | USA | 2015 | Boym Partners

Founded by Constantin and Laurene Leon Boym, Boym Partners is an innovative design studio based in New York. This pattern is a rotogravure design on vinyl.

02 | Viaduct | UK | 2014 | Imogen Heath

This furnishing fabric, with its medium-sized repeat, features overlapping viaducts composed of simple crescent shapes.

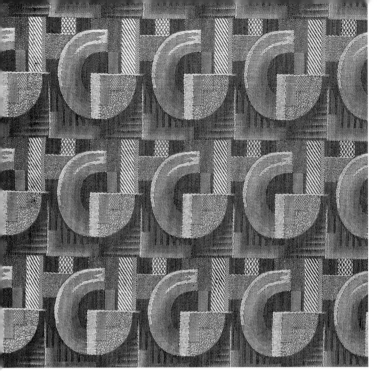

03 | Furnishing fabric | France | 1928
Manufactured in France for British firm Betty Joel, this silk and cotton damask furnishing fabric features Art Deco patterning.

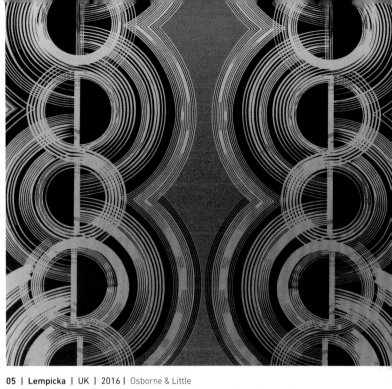

05 | Lempicka | UK | 2016 | Osborne & Little
Concentric crescents create an Art Deco–style wallpaper pattern. Tamara de Lempicka was a Polish painter who worked in Paris during the 1930s.

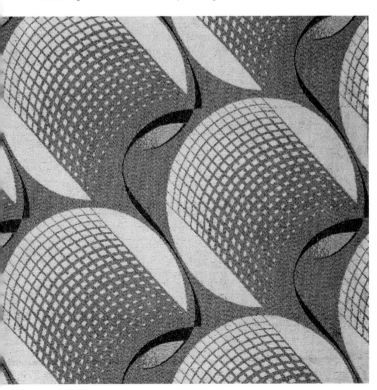

04 | Furnishing fabric | UK | 1931 | O. R. Plaistow
Designed for Courtaulds, this jacquard-woven cotton and rayon furnishing fabric features an Art Deco–style pattern.

06 | Textile | France | 1925–30
The influence of Art Deco is evident in this plush woven cotton furnishing fabric, with its play on geometric shapes.

01 | Wallpaper | France | 1810–20
This block-printed wallpaper features a symmetrical pattern of scrolling arabesques enclosing sunflower heads.

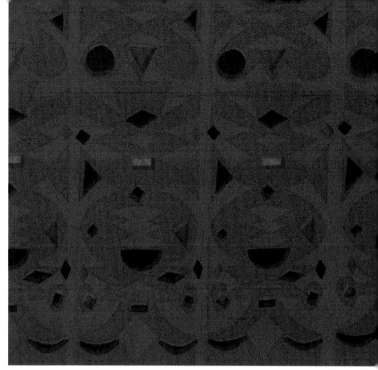

02 | Cutout (Arabesque) | USA | 1954 | Alexander Girard
One of a number of furnishing fabrics designed by Girard for Herman Miller, this design echoes the cutout collages created by Henri Matisse.

03 | Tilework | Iran | 16th to 17th century
The elaborate decorative tilework is a feature of the Imam Mosque in Isfahan, Iran, built by Abbās I, Shah of Persia.

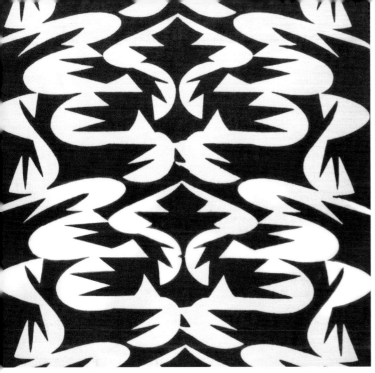

04 | Swans | UK | 1930s | Eileen Hunter
Highly stylized swan shapes comprise a modern interpretation of an arabesque
pattern on a printed cotton furnishing fabric.

06 | Color lithograph | UK | 1856 | Owen Jones
Jones was fascinated by the Alhambra. This plate from *The Grammar of Ornament*
shows a decoration on the Great Arch at the entrance to the Court of the Fishpond.

05 | Furnishing fabric | UK | *c.*1845–51 **|** Augustus Pugin
Pugin, a champion of the Gothic Revival, and a highly prolific designer, created many
patterns for the Houses of Parliament.

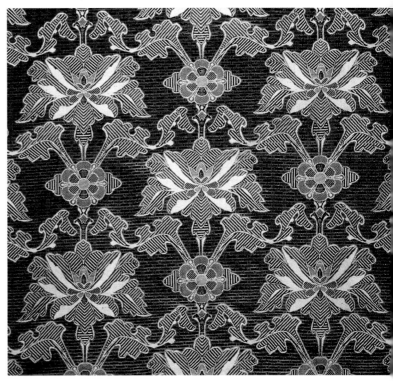

07 | Sultan | UK | *c.*1870 **|** Owen Jones
The flowing interlaced lines, tendrils, or foliage of the arabesque derive originally
from ancient Islamic art.

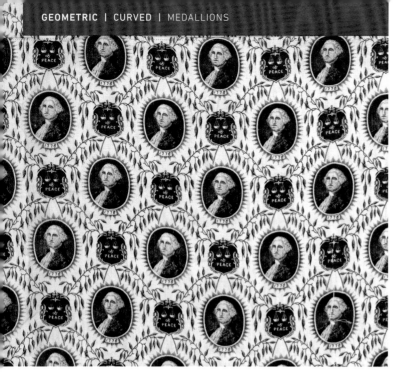

01 | Textile fragment | USA | 1876
Manufactured by American Print Works, this textile fragment displays medallions commemorating George Washington.

03 | Ardmore Cameos | UK | 2017 | Cole & Son with Ardmore Ceramic Art
This cameo wallpaper represents a series of plates featuring animal portraits. It was originally created as a wedding present.

02 | Textile | USA | 1820
Cameos or medallions often served as frames for classically inspired vignettes, as in this printed fabric.

04 | Wallpaper | USA | 1905–15
This machine-printed wallpaper, manufactured by Maxwell & Co., is a delicate design of overlapping medallions.

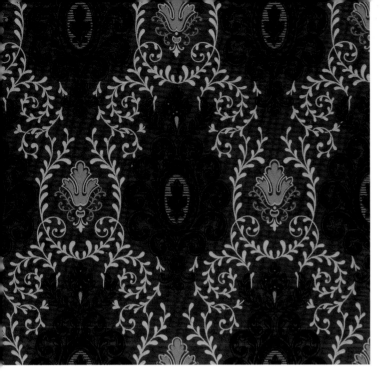

05 | Wallpaper | USA | 1905–15
Manufactured by Wm. Campbell Wall Paper Company, this machine-printed design is a stately classically inspired pattern with scrolling arabesques.

07 | Fabric detail | France | 1921–33
This color print of a fabric detail is taken from the magazine *Art, goût, beauté: feuillets de l'élégance féminine* (*Art, Taste, Beauty: Pages of Feminine Elegance*).

06 | Textile | USA | 19th century
In this fabric sample of unknown origin, scrolling acanthus leaves form the enclosure of the medallion.

08 | Fabric | UK | *c.*1896
A cotton velvet fabric featuring drop-shaped medallions in a dense all-over pattern enlivened with touches of white.

01 | Quatrefoil | USA | 1954 | Alexander Girard

Many of Girard's patterns were abstract or simple geometrics. This early furnishing
fabric anticipates the design trends of the 1960s.

02 | Quatrefoil | UK | 1949–50 | Edward Bawden
This color lithograph is for a wallpaper design produced by Cole & Son.
It was available in a number of different colors.

03 | Fabric swatch
The trefoil or three-leafed shape derives from Gothic architecture and Christian
symbolism, where it represents the Trinity.

04 | Wallpaper | USA | 1800–35
This block-printed wallpaper, thought to be of US origin, is a striking rhythmic
pattern of eye-shaped motifs and quatrefoils.

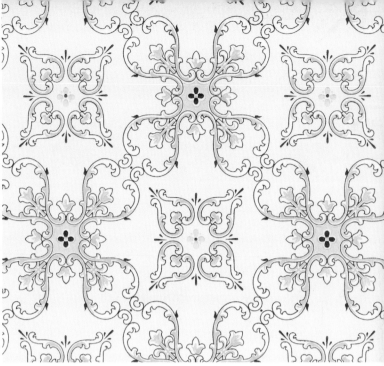

05 | Ceiling paper | USA | 1905–15
Ceiling papers supplied architectural detailing in the absence of ornamental
plasterwork. This example was machine-printed by Janeway & Co.

06 | Wallpaper | UK | 19th century | Owen Jones
Jones was a prolific designer of flat patterns and a prominent design theorist. He
co-founded the South Kensington Museum (later the Victoria and Albert Museum).

02 | Margot | UK | 2016 | Anna Hayman
This wallpaper pattern, with its Art Deco overtones, is a graphic mesh in green and ocher accented with black and white.

01 | Wicker | USA | *c.*1960–69 **|** Tommi Parzinger
Produced by German-born designer Parzinger for Howard & Schaffer, this printed cotton fabric resembles closely woven cane work.

03 | Ropey Heritage | UK | 2012–13 | Eley Kishimoto
Eley Kishimoto's dress fabric has a medium-scale repeat featuring a bold geometric pattern in the form of a rope grid.

04 | Weave | UK | 2011 | Cole & Son
A small-scale wallpaper pattern that recreates the textural effect
of woven basketwork or cane work.

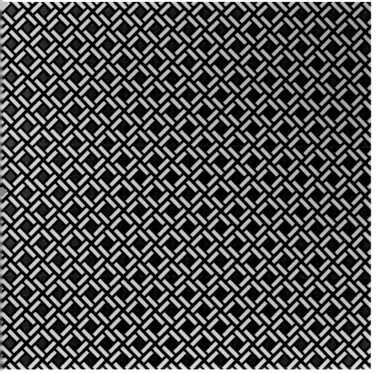

05 | Kelburn | UK | 2013 | Nina Campbell, distributed by Osborne & Little
This elegant wallpaper pattern is a regular woven mesh grid placed diagonally
across the background.

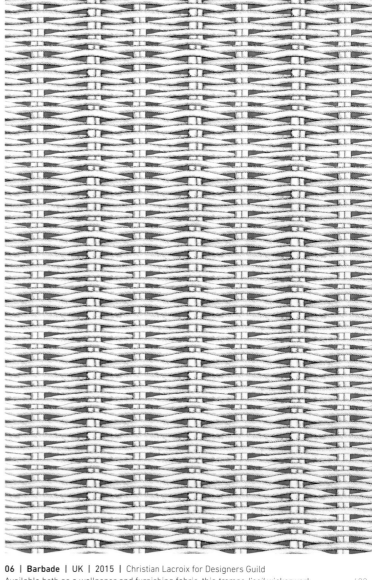

06 | Barbade | UK | 2015 | Christian Lacroix for Designers Guild
Available both as a wallpaper and furnishing fabric, this *trompe-l'oeil* wickerwork
pattern has an exotic tropical aesthetic.

01 | Sloyd | UK | 1947 | Enid Marx
Marx designed this woven cotton furnishing fabric for the Utility Design Panel. It was manufactured by Morton Sundour Fabrics of Carlisle.

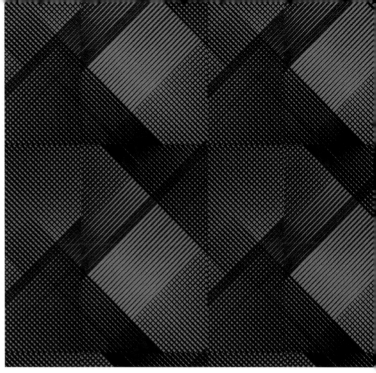

03 | Lattice | UK | 2015 | Emma Jeffs
Jeffs designs under the label N & N Wares, exploring a range of different materials and printing processes.

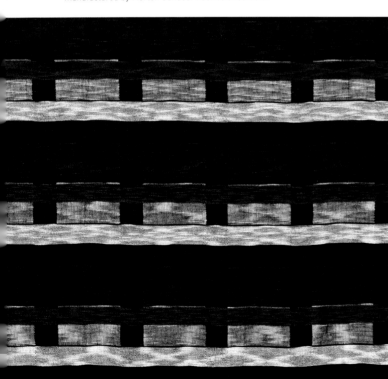

02 | Aleppo | UK | 1954 | Marianne Straub
This woven furnishing fabric was designed for Liberty. Straub's aim was to "design things which people could afford."

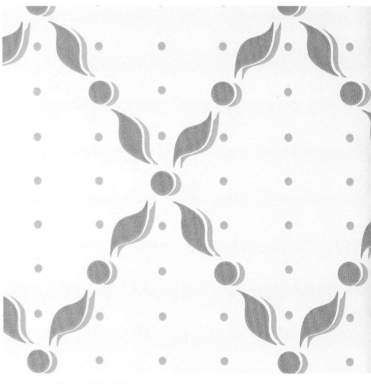

04 | Penton Villas | UK | 2013 | Old Town for St Jude's
Designed for St Jude's by Old Town, a studio based in Norfolk, this open lattice wallpaper has a nostalgic quality.

05 | Light on Lattice | UK | 2014 | Eley Kishimoto
Many of Eley Kishimoto's patterns create bold optical effects, such as this dramatic
and vibrant gridded design.

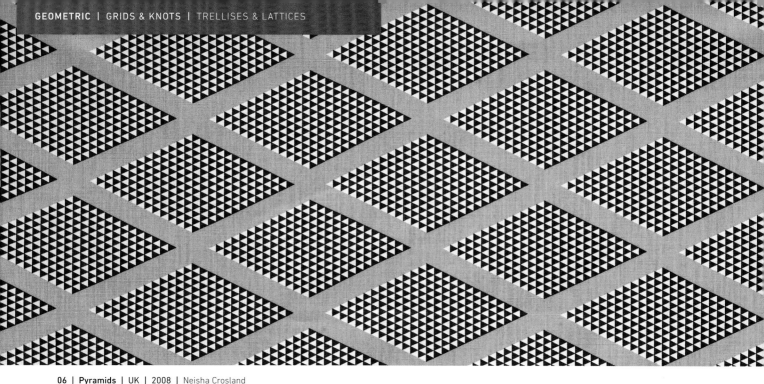

06 | **Pyramids** | UK | 2008 | Neisha Crosland
Crosland's printed linen furnishing fabric has a clean, contemporary lattice pattern
with the grid filled with pyramidal shapes.

07 | **Petipa** | UK | 2016 | Osborne & Little
This modern lattice wallpaper is embedded with tiny metallic beads for a
shimmering, glamorous effect.

08 | **Pompeian** | UK | 2012 | Cole & Son
This classic wallpaper design has been reduced in scale and recolored in shades of
off-white and gray to create a *trompe-l'oeil* effect.

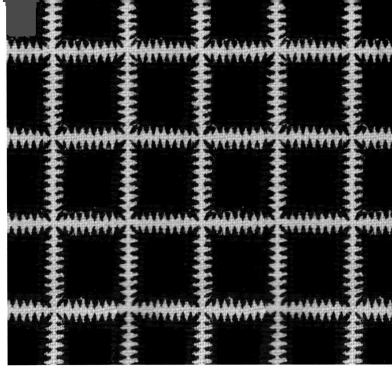

09 | Triangle | USA | 1962 | Alexander Girard
This characteristically crisp Girard furnishing fabric pattern was created for Herman Miller and complemented the clean lines of contemporary furniture.

10 | Fabric swatch
This regular evenly spaced pattern, with the light diamond shapes picking out the grid, has a three-dimensional quality.

11 | Porto | UK | 2014 | Kate Blee for Christopher Farr
Designed for Christopher Farr Cloth, this open, airy lattice wallpaper pattern has an offbeat, wonky charm.

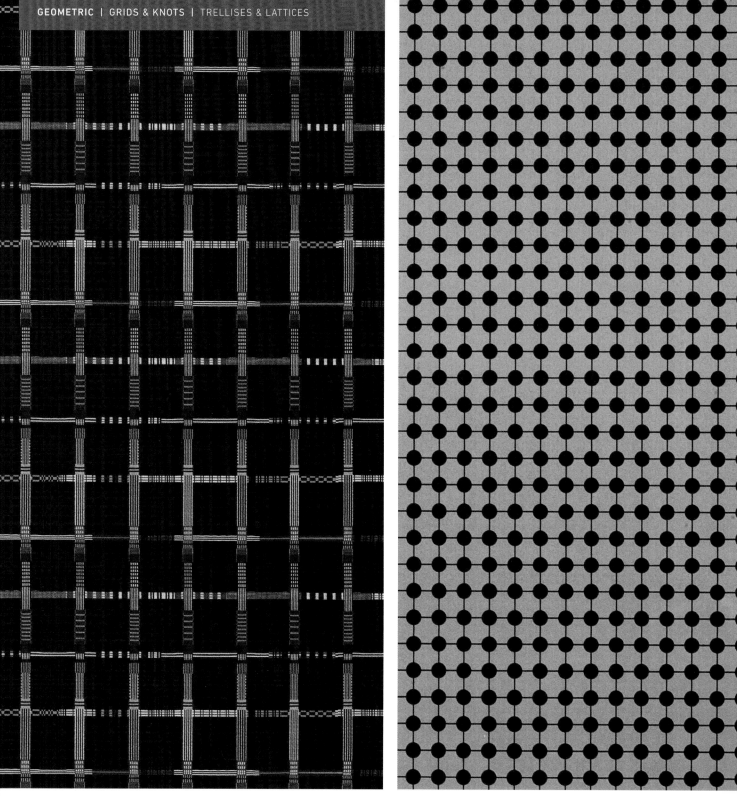

12 | **Inlay** | **USA/Netherlands** | **2016** | Hella Jongerius for Maharam
Designed for Maharam, this furnishing fabric with its dense layers and detailed grids
was inspired by Dutch woven ribbons.

13 | **Gridlock** | **UK** | **2006** | Neisha Crosland
Crosland's flexo-printed wallpaper features a simple, open latticed grid with spots
marking the intersections.

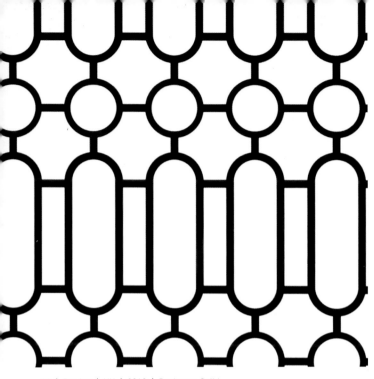

14 | Porden | UK | 2010 | Designers Guild
This wallpaper pattern with its graphic grid of circles and oblongs has a clean, contemporary architectural look.

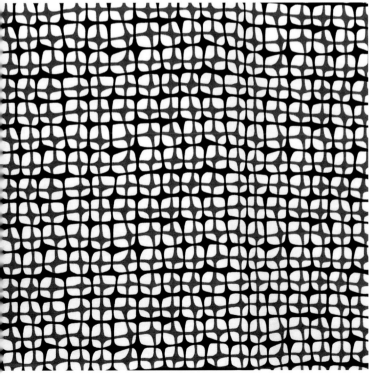

15 | Cello | Sweden | 1953 | Stig Lindberg
Designed for Ljungbergs, this printed cotton furnishing fabric features charming hand-drawn grids overlaying each other.

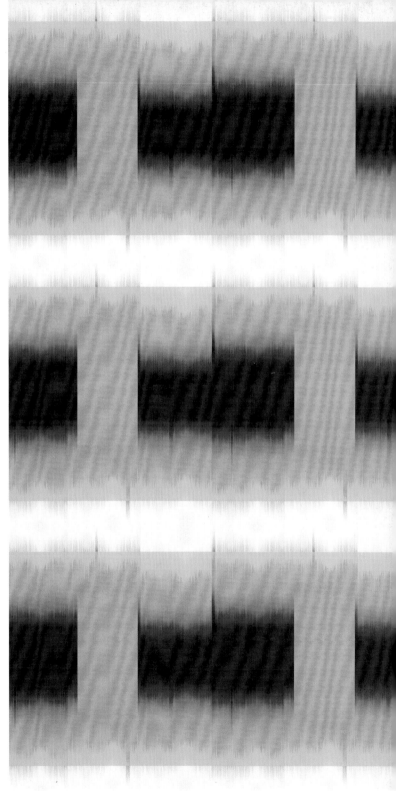

16 | Window Ikat | UK | 2012 | Ptolemy Mann
Textile artist Mann specializes in creating contemporary versions of *ikat* patterns, such as this digital print.

Josef Hoffmann (1870–1956)

SEE PAGES > 349, 370, 625

Best known as an architect, Josef Hoffmann was a prolific designer across a wide range of disciplines, including metalwork, silver, furniture, glass, porcelain, and textiles. While his architectural training gave him an acute sense of form and proportion, he was also a superb designer of pattern and surface decoration.

Born in Pirnitz, Moravia (now Czech Republic), Hoffmann trained as an architect at the Academy of Fine Arts in Vienna. After completing his studies, he worked for the architect-designer Otto Wagner (1841–1918) before setting up his own practice. In 1899, he was appointed a professor at Vienna's School of Applied Arts, a post he held until 1936. Hoffmann was also a founder member of the Vienna Secession in 1897, a group of artists, including Gustav Klimt and Koloman Moser (1868–1918), who rejected the reliance on historicism in art and design.

A visit Hoffmann made to Britain in 1900, during which he met Charles Rennie Mackintosh (1868–1928; see p. 102), along with figures in the Arts and Crafts movement, had a huge influence on him. His unifying notion of the *Gesamtkunstwerk* (total work of art), a building whose contents, furnishings, and decoration share the same aesthetic, became the cornerstone of his design approach.

In 1903, together with Moser, and with the financial backing of textile manufacturer Fritz Wärndorfer, Hoffmann founded the Wiener Werkstätte (Vienna Workshops), an experimental artist-led collective whose mission was to reform the applied arts and foster interdisciplinary collaborations. As artistic director, he was responsible for many designs, along with two major buildings, the Purkersdorf Sanatorium (1904–05) on the outskirts of Vienna and the Stoclet Palace (1905–11) in Brussels.

Hoffmann's early textiles were jacquard weaves, produced as furnishing fabrics. A very early design for chenille, "Curving Roses" (1900), bears a striking similarity to Mackintosh's favorite rose motif, both in theme and execution. In 1910, following the opening of a fashion and textile department at the Workshops, Hoffmann turned his hand to block-printing, with the results used as dress fabrics. His textiles display a strong geometric bias; grids often feature in his patterns, as do cubes and squares. Stylized flowers, leaves, and other natural forms are also common. While some designs are dense, others are much lighter and airier, with black lines graphically contrasting with areas of white ground.

Hoffmann remained a key figure at the Workshops until it closed in 1932. During his time there, and throughout the remainder of his life, he continued to design buildings, notably urban housing projects in Vienna.

Far Left Josef Hoffmann was a co-founder of the Wiener Werkstätte in Vienna.

Left "Florida," a carpet and fabric design Hoffmann created for Backhausen & Söhne of Vienna in 1908.

Opposite Hoffmann produced his "Notschrei" ("Cry for Help") textile design in 1904.

01 | Crosses | USA | 1957 | Alexander Girard

Warm colors, such as pink, red, orange, and magenta, were among Girard's favorites,
combined here in this furnishing fabric to create a plaid effect.

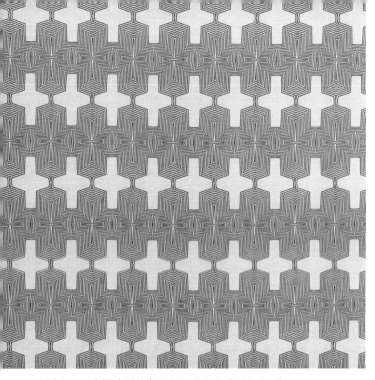

02 | Laguna | UK | 2014 | El Ultimo Grito for Christopher Farr
Designed for Christopher Farr Cloth, this furnishing fabric features an intricate
pattern of cruciform shapes.

03 | Stenciled paper | Japan | 20th century
This hand-stenciled dyed paper is patterned with a small-scale grid of circles and
diamonds filled with crosses.

04 | Richard Nixon | USA | 2013 | Jonathan Adler
Designed by New York lifestyle retailer Adler, this Peruvian llama flat weave rug
features a simple cross motif.

02 | **Ropey** | **UK** | **2002** | Eley Kishimoto
This asymmetric coiled rope pattern was designed for Aram and appears
on a hand-tufted pure new wool rug.

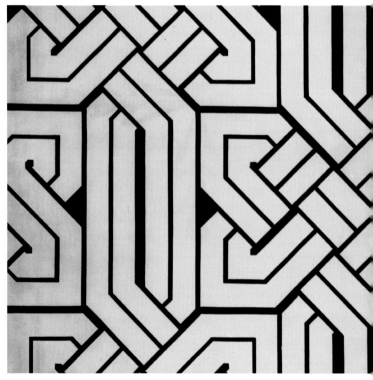

01 | **Fabric swatch**
This loose knotted pattern features thin white ribbons and beaded lines sparsely
arranged on a dark ground.

03 | **Book illustration** | **UK** | **1876** | Christopher Dresser
This lithograph taken from *Studies in Design* and published by Cassell & Co. shows
a traditional knotted pattern.

04 | Interlace pattern | Germany | pre 15th century | Albrecht Dürer
This intricate laced pattern with its white central medallion is a woodcut
block-printed on paper.

Celtic (7th century – 9th century)

Dating back to the European Iron Age, Celtic art, displayed in pottery, metalwork, and stonework, was made by tribes who spoke Celtic languages and originated in eastern France, the Low Countries, western Germany and Austria. Today, the Celtic style of ornament and decoration is more commonly associated with the culture of the Celtic peoples of early Britain. After the introduction of Christianity, elements of Celtic design were incorporated into religious artifacts.

Celtic art reached its peak in the 7th, 8th, and 9th centuries, before Viking raids disrupted monastic life. This was the era that produced the richly decorative jewelry found at Sutton Hoo, Suffolk, in 1939, which has been dated to the 7th century, along with other early medieval masterpieces such as the Book of Kells (c. 800) and the Lindisfarne Gospels (c. 650–750). Aside from monastic manuscripts, most of what survives of Celtic design is in the form of exquisitely wrought metalwork: highly embellished helmets, shields, swords, cups, chalices, mirrors, and jewelry.

While Celtic art shows influences from other civilizations, including those of the Mediterranean region, such as the Scythians, Greeks, and Etruscans, it is remarkably consistent in its design motifs and patterning. Unlike classical design, in which naturalistic forms, such as those based on acanthus leaves, are common, Celtic design was strongly geometric and only occasionally symmetric. Patterns of circles, dots, and spirals were common, with the intertwined triple spiral or triskele a characteristic feature. Ornament was intricate and elaborately worked, even on the smallest scale, covering the surface of objects evenly so that positive and negative elements were balanced in a harmonious whole.

Knotwork, or strapwork, was another distinguishing feature of Celtic design: interlaced ribbons and spirals forming complex patterns. Where animal forms occurred, these were stylized, fantastical creatures whose elongated crests, tongues, and tails curved round to create intertwined knots. Later, as motifs based on foliage, buds, and stems crept in, these too were interwoven into knot-like patterns. Other linear designs include those formed by evenly spaced diagonals creating a Z-pattern, and angled lines creating stepped patterns.

The discovery of the celebrated Tara Brooch, dating from the 8th century, which was found in Ireland in 1850, was significant in fostering a Celtic revival in the late 19th century. Interlaced or knotwork patterns were taken up by artists and designers of the Glasgow School and featured in Art Nouveau. Celtic design was also championed by Irish nationalists seeking Home Rule.

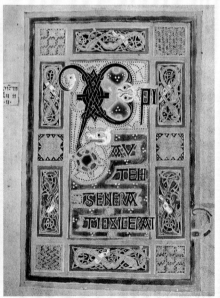

Far Left A medieval masterpiece, the Book of Kells (c. 800) is a decorated copy of the Gospels in Latin.

Left Frontispiece of the Gospel of St Matthew from the Mac Durnan Gospels (9th century), an Irish manuscript.

Opposite The Tara Brooch (8th century) was found in County Meath. It sports scrolls and triple-spiral motifs.

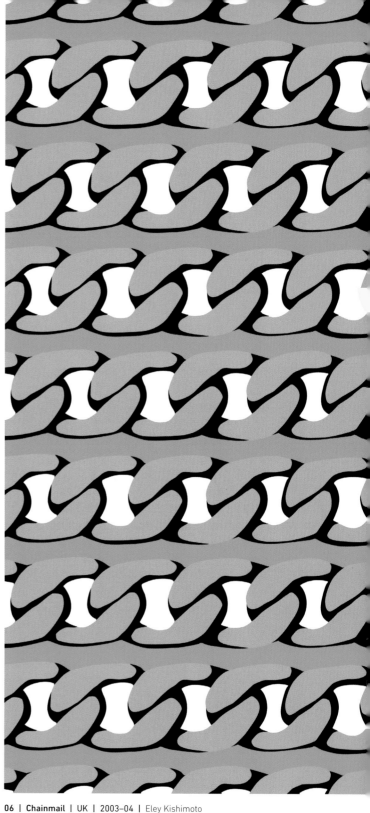

05 | Wallpaper | USA | 1950

Manufactured by the Artcraft Wallpaper Company, this wallpaper combines
crosshatched squares with open knotted meshwork.

06 | Chainmail | UK | 2003–04 | Eley Kishimoto
The judicious use of shading around the links in the chain mail gives this printed
fabric design a three-dimensional quality.

07 | **Equinox** | UK | 2015 | Mini Moderns
This wallpaper design was inspired by the Kent countryside, specifically by braided corn dollies and other traditional braided straw ornaments.

08 | **Carpet page** | Ireland | *c.* 650–700
Geometrically ornamented carpet pages were placed at the beginning of each Gospel in illuminated manuscripts. This example comes from the Book of Durrow.

09 | **Lithograph** | UK | 1856
Celtic ornament was distinguished to a great extent by interlaced knotwork. This form of decoration appeared across a wide range of artifacts.

02 | Wallpaper | UK | 19th century | Owen Jones
A formal floral design arranges four petal motifs to form a diaper pattern.
Diaper patterns tend to have small-scale repeats.

01 | Textile | Iran | 17th century
This lustrous silk brocade woven with metallic threads features a traditional
diamond-shaped diaper pattern.

03 | Wallpaper | USA | 1890–1920
Manufactured by M. H. Birge & Sons, this wallpaper is a classic diaper pattern,
featuring scrolled foliate forms.

04 | Crace Diaper | UK | *c.*1848 | Augustus Pugin
With its blue on white diaper pattern, this block-printed wallpaper is one of the many that Pugin designed for the Houses of Parliament.

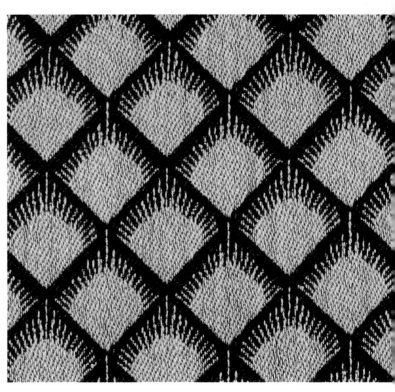

06 | Lee Priory | UK | 2010 | Cole & Son
This small-scale early Victorian wallpaper design from the Cole & Son archive has Gothic overtones.

05 | Fabric | France | 19th century
Diaper designs can be composed of any tightly arranged or interlocking elements, such as these floral forms.

07 | Maize | UK | 2007 | Neisha Crosland
This linen furnishing fabric features a diaper pattern, with stylized natural motifs inspired by maize heads.

Enid Marx (1902–98)

SEE PAGES > 311, 367, 370, 424, 567

Best remembered for the textiles she designed for London bus and tube seats, Enid Marx had a career spanning more than seventy years. As well as a textile designer, she was a painter, printmaker, author, illustrator, and a designer of trademarks, book jackets, and postage stamps.

Pattern absorbed her from an early age. A collection of ribbon samples, given to her when she was four years old, was a childhood treasure. While a boarder at Roedean during World War I, she was encouraged to draw. Subsequently, she attended the Central School of Art and Design and then the Royal College of Art (RCA). There, she met the British painter Eric Ravilious (1903–42), who shared many of her interests, particularly in folk art. By then, she had encountered the work of Pablo Picasso (1881–1973) and Georges Braque (1882–1963), and her fascination with abstraction set her at odds with the RCA's insistence on naturalism. She failed to get her diploma for this reason and decided to become a textile designer.

In 1925, Marx went to work for renowned designers Phyllis Barron (1890–1964) and Dorothy Larcher (1884–1952; see p. 132) at their textile studio in Hampstead. After a year's apprenticeship, she set up her own workshop making block-printed fabric. Her crisp, vivid modernist designs, first sold through a Sloane Street gallery and then through a gallery in Albemarle Street, captured the spirit of the age and became fashionable. She gained her first commissions for book jackets and produced a range of patterned papers.

In 1937, the London Passenger Transport Board invited Marx to design textiles for the upholstered seating on buses and underground trains. The chosen fabric was a hard-wearing cotton/velvet blend known as "moquette." The patterns had to be striking enough to hide superficial dirt, but not so eye-catching that they caused passengers to feel ill at ease. She used strong tonal and textural contrasts in small geometric repeats.

During World War II, as a member of the design panel of the Utility Furniture Advisory Committee, Marx was given the task of designing textiles for the serviceable "Utility" pieces produced to address the furniture shortage caused by the Blitz. She was appointed a Royal Designer for Industry in 1944.

After the war, more commissions came from publishers, notably Penguin Books. Marx was asked to design commemorative postage stamps for Queen Elizabeth II's coronation in 1953. Other work in the postwar period ranged from packaging to calendars, posters, and prints. From 1965 to 1970, she was head of the dress, textiles, and ceramics department at Croydon School of Art.

Far Left Enid Marx at her drawing table.

Left The cover and inside pages of *Quiz*, a chapbook lithographed by Marx for Faber & Faber in 1942.

Opposite Marx designed the "Spot and Stripe" (1945) furnishing fabric for the wartime Utility Scheme.

02 | Alcazar | UK | 2013 | Christian Lacroix
Replicating the effect of Moorish tiles, this multicolored printed linen furnishing fabric was created for Designers Guild.

01 | Ceramic tiles | Spain | 14th century
This intricate geometric tilework is a feature of the Alcázar of Seville, Spain, a royal palace built by Moorish kings.

03 | Color lithograph | France | 1877
An illustration from *L'Art Arabe (Arab Art)* by French Orientalist Émile Prisse d'Avennes, which depicts the wall tiles of a mosque in the Qasr Rodouan quarter of Cairo.

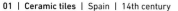

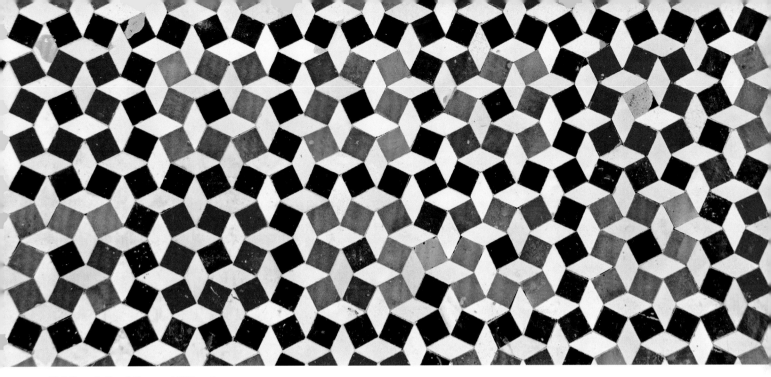

04 | Ceramic tiles | Morocco | 19th century
This vivid tilework from Bahia Palace, Marrakech, Morocco, combines white diamond shapes with colored squares.

05 | Ceramic tiles | Spain | 19th century
These Moorish tiles from Toledo, Spain, feature hexagons patterned with floral scrolls with blue square inserts.

06 | Oriel | UK | 2016 | Imogen Heath
Heath's printed furnishing fabric is a monochromatic abstracted design that recalls traditional tiled pavements.

Islamic (7th century – 13th century)

Islam, founded in the 7th century, spread rapidly, and by 800 held sway over a vast area stretching from Iberia to the Indus River in Asia. During its Golden Age, which lasted until the 13th century, new forms of architecture were created for worship.

While Islamic patterning shows Greek, Byzantine, and Roman influences, it evolved into a distinct style in terms of motifs and their application. Seen in carpets, rugs, and other textiles, it was also a feature of tilework, ceramics, metalwork, woodwork, mosaics, and, most significantly, in the decoration of mosques, whose walls, floors, vaults, and arches were covered in intricate polychromatic ornament.

While figurative or representational patterning is not absent from Islamic patterns, symmetrical geometric designs predominate. At its finest, Islamic patterning exhibits a perfectly judged relationship between ornament and ground; all-over decoration of objects and buildings is common. The Mosque of Süleyman the Magnificent (1550–57) in Istanbul and the 14th-century Alhambra Palace in Granada are two supreme examples of structures transformed by shimmering tessellated patterning. The tessellated patterns of the Alhambra inspired Dutch artist M. C. Escher (1898–1972; see p. 260) to create his puzzles of perception.

Islamic designs are usually based on geometric shapes: circles, squares, pentagons, and octagons. Repeated, overlapped, and interlaced to form pointed stars and lozenges, they may be combined with arabesques and calligraphy. Simpler were diaper patterns, repeats composed of geometric shapes, often diamonds. Floral or vegetal designs, such as stylized flowers and flowering trees, occur in ceramics and textiles. Flat-weave tribal rugs, such as kilims, often feature an angular wolf's-mouth or wolf's-foot motif, a symbol to ward off wolf attacks on flocks of sheep. Bird motifs are common.

In the 19th century, Persian textiles and carpets were sought after, while Orientalists such as Frederic, Lord Leighton (1830–96) amassed collections of Islamic tiles from sites in the Middle East. British architect Owen Jones (1809–74) made extensive studies of the decoration at the Alhambra in his quest to develop a non-historic contemporary style distinct from Neoclassicism or the Gothic Revival. The twelve-part publication of his book *Plans, Elevations, Sections and Details of the Alhambra* (1836–45) made use of the new process of chromolithography. For the Great Exhibition of 1851, where he was a Superintendent of Works, he chose a controversial red, yellow, and blue color scheme for the interior ironwork, based partly on what he had observed at the Alhambra.

Far Left Mosaic ornament from the Court of the Lions, Alhambra, from *The Arabian Antiquities of Spain* (1815).

Left This 15th-century polychrome marble mosaic wall panel with geometric interlace is from Cairo.

Opposite An early 16th-century Turkish mirror with a split-leaf palmette design inlaid with gold.

07 | Tiles | Iran | 14th century
This decorative tilework appears on the Jameh Mosque of Yazd, which boasts the highest minarets in Iran.

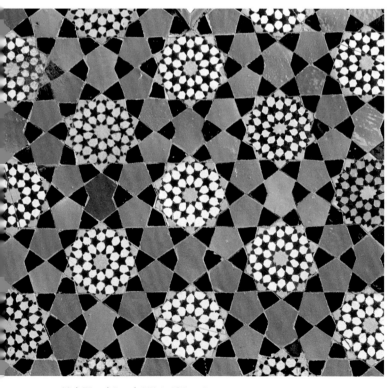

08 | Tiles | Iran | 11th to 12th century
The Jameh Mosque of Isfahan dates from the 8th century but has been rebuilt over the centuries. Decorative glazed tiles cover many of the building's surfaces.

09 | Tiles | Spain
These Moorish-style tiles are from Santander, Cantabria. The Moors conquered the Iberian Peninsula in the 8th century.

10 | Tiles | Spain | 14th century
Ceramic tilework such as this is a feature of the Alcázar of Seville, a royal palace built by Moorish kings.

11 | Mosaic | Spain | 14th century
This mosaic detail can be found at the Alhambra in Granada, Spain. Such complicated mathematical patterning covers the lower portion of the palace walls.

12 | Tiles | Morocco
Tilework is a common feature of buildings in hot climates as it serves to keep exteriors and interiors cool.

Iznik, once known as Nicaea, a town southeast of Istanbul, has been a center of ceramic production since the 14th century. Iznik ware itself dates from about a century later.

The first Iznik vessels were made to imitate Chinese porcelain, which was highly prized by the Ottoman sultans. Originally characterized by blue patterning over a white ground and under a glossy colorless glaze, more colors were gradually added to the palette, including purple, sage green, and turquoise. Later still, a bright green replaced the sage green and a bold red was added.

While Iznik wares included many ceramic products, from bowls and platters to ewers and lamps, the principal output of the factory was tiles, employed in great quantities in the decoration of Istanbul's mosques. Many were also used extensively to clad the walls, entrances, and other surfaces of the Topkapi Palace in Istanbul. In addition to geometric patterns, Iznik tiles and other Iznik wares were decorated with arabesques of leaves and flowers. Stylized tulips, carnations, and roses were popular motifs.

Azulejo tiles, which originated in 13th-century Moorish Spain, spread to Portugal during the 14th century. Today, they are strongly associated with the exteriors and interiors of many Spanish and Portuguese buildings. When Lisbon was rebuilt after the devastating earthquake of 1755, panels of azulejos were installed on royal palaces, public buildings, and domestic housing.

The Alhambra Palace in Granada, Spain, features early examples of such tilework. There, tiles glazed in single colors were pieced together to form the type of bold geometric patterns or tessellations that would later captivate the Dutch artist M. C. Escher (see p. 260). In the 15th century, when Italian potters introduced the majolica technique, pictorial azulejos were produced, featuring religious, mythological, or historical scenes, along with those patterned with floral or geometric designs. A particular feature of grand Portuguese houses were azulejo panels portraying life-sized figures, placed at entrances to welcome visitors. Similar tilework can be found in Mexico and some South American countries.

Suzani is a form of embroidered textile that has its origins in Central Asia. The word "suzani" comes from the Persian *suzan*, which means "needle." With a history that dates back to the days of the medieval Silk Road, the old merchants' trading link between Asia and the West, suzani is particularly associated with Uzbekistan, notably the city of Bukhara, which is also well known for its rugs. These large tribal embroideries, commonly used as bedcovers or wall hangings, are traditionally worked by female family members for a bride's dowry and are so elaborate that they may take many years to complete.

Suzani embroidery is generally executed in cotton or silk thread on a cotton or silk base. Stitches include chain, satin, and buttonhole, as well as couching, or areas of raised embroidery. Patterns typically include flowers and foliage, particularly brightly colored tulips, irises, and carnations, while leaves tend to appear on borders. Suns and moons are other common motifs, and fruit, such as pomegranates, and birds and animals occasionally feature.

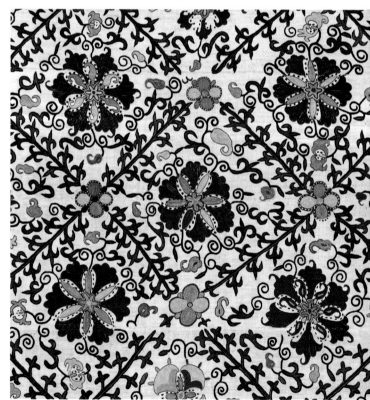

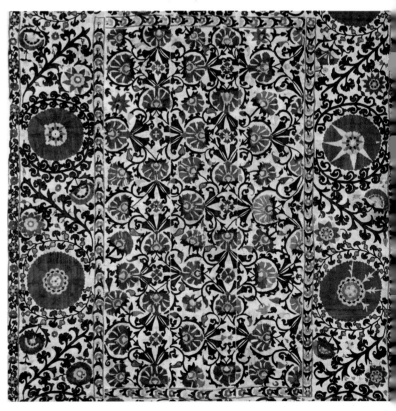

Tapa cloth, made in Tonga, Samoa, Tahiti, Fiji, and other islands in the Pacific Ocean, is a barkcloth that is decorated with a number of traditional, usually geometric, patterns. Depending on the island from which it originates, it goes by a variety of different names. For centuries it was employed to make clothing, but its primary use today is decorative and for ceremonies such as weddings and funerals.

Bark, which typically comes from the paper mulberry tree, is stripped, dried, soaked, and then beaten thin. Several strips are beaten and glued together to form a large sheet. The barkcloth is decorated, either by painting, dyeing, stenciling, or smoking. Paints and vegetable dyes are usually light brown, red, or black in color. A common method of decorating is to place successive sections of the sheet over a ribbed stencil and then rub with paint to transfer the pattern. Gridded squares containing individual geometric patterns occur frequently in the tapa cloth produced in Tonga, Samoa, and Fiji. Stylized fish, animals, and birds also feature in some designs. Symbols and designs are often specific to a particular island.

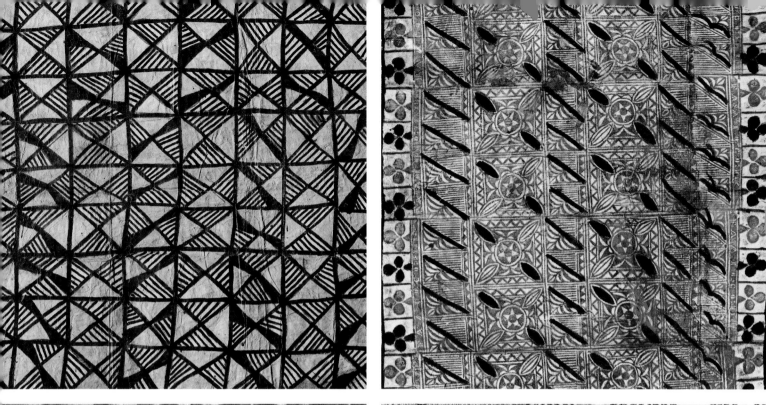

Fair Isle, a tiny island in the Shetlands, the most northern Scottish archipelago, gives its name to a traditional knitting technique that results in multicolored geometric patterns. Locals have been knitting commercially since the 1600s, when they are reported to have bartered knitwear with passing ships. Fair Isle knitwear became fashionable in the 1920s after the then-Prince of Wales (later King Edward VIII) was pictured wearing a Fair Isle jumper. Soon, Fair Isle sweaters, cardigans, and sleeveless tops became a British wardrobe staple for both men and women.

Patterns range from simple symmetrical two-color designs to those involving as many as five different shades. Despite the pattern's apparent complexity, it is not particularly difficult to execute. In traditional designs, no more than two colors are worked in any given row, with one yarn being "carried" or "stranded" across the back and the other knitted with. This results in a knitted item of double thickness for extra warmth. Crosses and lozenge-shaped hexagons are often incorporated within designs to form a basic OXO pattern.

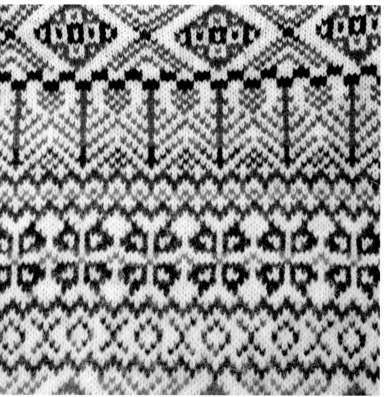

Kente cloth is a traditional Ghanaian weave, whose origins date back nearly 400 years. The word "kente" comes from the Akan dialect and means "basket." One of the most important centers of production is a village called Bonwire in the south of the country in the Ashanti Region. Originally, Kente cloth was a high-status product, worn exclusively by kings and tribal chiefs.

Specific patterns or motifs have individual meanings that correspond to Ashanti beliefs. The "king's eye" and the "golden stool" are two motifs associated with power. Master weavers of Kente cloth must become fluent in such symbolic language.

All Kente cloth patterns are bold geometrics, typically stripes, banding, and zigzags. Traditional colors, derived from vegetable dyes, are black (for Africa), red (for ancestral blood), yellow (for gold), and green (for the forest). Although the fabric was originally woven from silk thread, a wider range of cheaper materials is used in the 21st century, such as cotton and rayon, and commercial applications include bags, sandals, and shirts.

Quilting, a technique that involves sewing layers of fabric together, often around inner padding, has been employed to make warm clothing and bedcovers for millennia. At its most basic, the individual fabric layers consist of bolts of whole cloth sewn together across their width and length. More elaborately, patchwork quilting entails piecing together geometric shapes, which may be made of different types of fabric, into striking compositions of color and form, often with the addition of appliqué.

Quilting became especially popular in the United States during the late 18th and 19th centuries. Quilts were used to frugally extend the serviceable life of scraps of fabric and as a means of creating heirloom treasures for special occasions. Quilt-making was often done communally, and quilting bees were social events that allowed participants to finish several quilts in a day rather than weeks or months. Different types of pattern were associated with specific locations and groups. Amish quilts, for example, typically only feature solid colors arranged in simple geometric patterns.

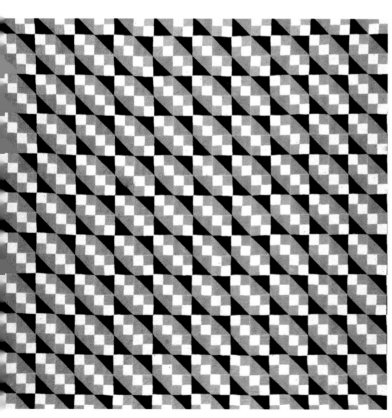

Although quilt-making and patchwork have traditionally been seen as the creative pastimes of women, either individually or collectively as in "quilting bees," from the middle of the 19th century onward, such activities were increasingly adopted by male military personnel during their leisure hours or recuperative time. Posted overseas far from home, soldiers were encouraged to adopt such pursuits rather than alleviate their boredom or loneliness in less productive and potentially more troublesome ways. There is also the possibility that sewing intricate and precise patterns of pieced fabric served as a form of post-combat therapy or helped to while away hours spent recovering from injuries sustained in battle. The Great Exhibition held in London in 1851 included "more than thirty examples submitted by military personnel."

Most of the military quilts were made from the thick wool or worsted fabric used to manufacture uniforms, materials that are bulky and unwieldy to sew. Quilts produced by men stationed in India during the latter half of the 19th century displayed brighter colors than so-called "Crimea quilts."

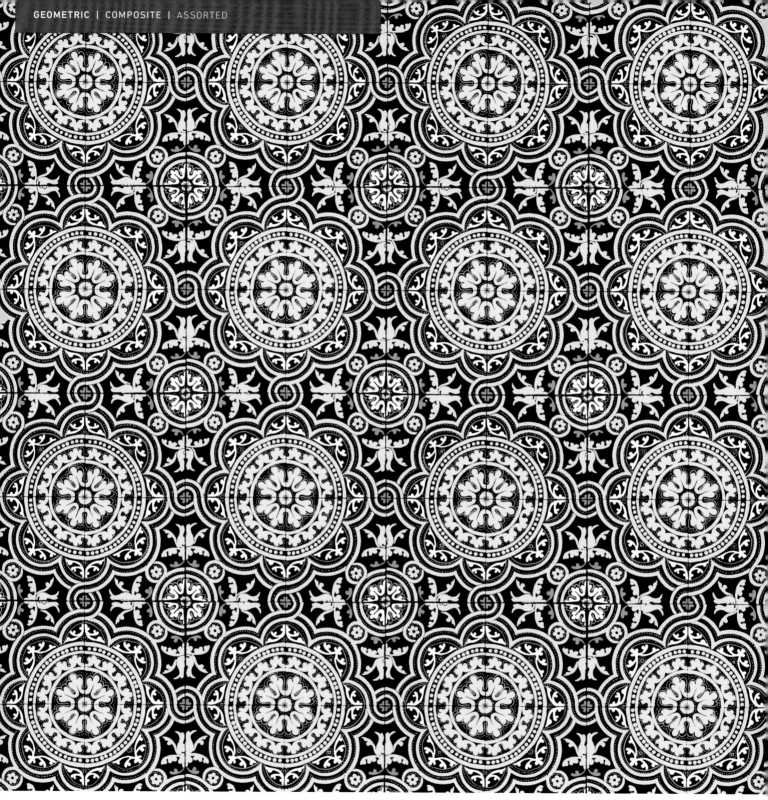

01 | Piccadilly | UK | 2012 | Cole & Son
This wallpaper pattern, available in five colorways, is reminiscent of traditional
blue-and-white tiling.

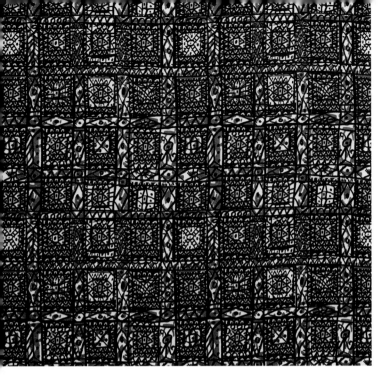

02 | Mosaic | UK/Spain | 2012 | Javier Mariscal for Christopher Farr
Created by Spanish designer Mariscal for Christopher Farr Cloth, this furnishing
fabric features a dense and detailed design suggestive of mosaic or tilework.

04 | Moorish Circles | UK | 2006 | Neisha Crosland
Also available as a rug, this design for a Surflex-printed wallpaper combines organic
and geometric elements.

03 | Darjeeling | UK | 2014 | Mini Moderns
A striking wallpaper design featuring a tessellation of pattern elements taken from
Mini Moderns' Paisley Crescent wallpaper.

05 | Tiles | Spain | 20th century | Antoni Gaudí
An example of a style known as Catalan Modernism, this decorated tilework was
designed by Gaudí for the Güell Palace in Barcelona.

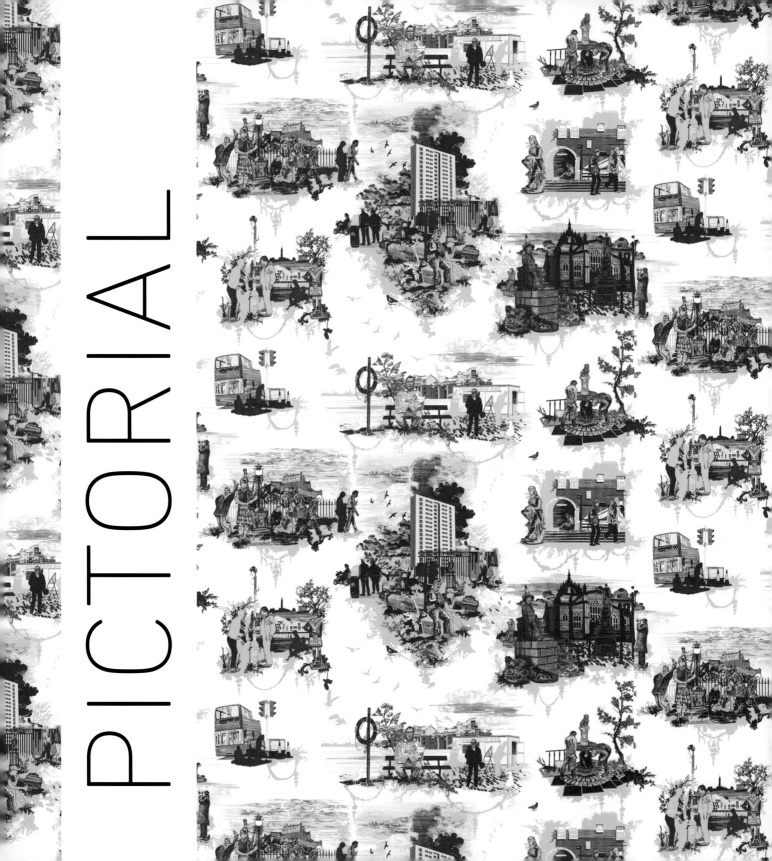

PICTORIAL

01 | Piscatore | UK | 1953 | John Drummond

The design of this satin furnishing fabric, designed for Anne Loosely, in which the
fisherman merges with his nets, is clearly influenced by modern sculpture.

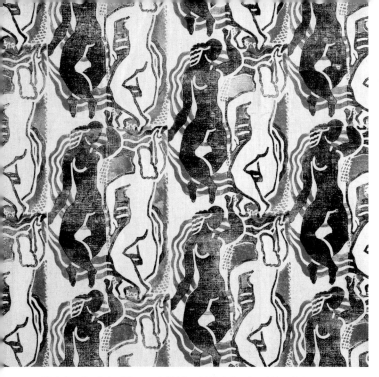

02 | **Dancing Naked Figures** | UK | *c.* 1938 | Frank and Mary Dobson
Frank Dobson was a sculptor who produced designs for furnishing fabrics, which
were subsequently block-printed by his wife, Mary.

03 | **Statues** | UK | *c.* 1934 | Frank Dobson
This screen-printed furnishing fabric was designed for Allan Walton Textiles.
Allan Walton commissioned many artists to produce textile designs.

04 | **Color lithograph** | Austria | 1901 | Koloman Moser
Moser's illustration, titled *Wanddecor December* (*December Wall Decoration*), is Plate
27 from *Die Quelle: Flächen Schmuck* (*The Source: Ornament for Flat Surfaces*).

02 | Transport | UK | 1945 | Feliks Topolski
Produced by the Ascher Studio, this lively pictorial design for printed rayon dress fabric expresses the vitality of the original artwork.

01 | Dress fabric | UK | 1945 | Feliks Topolski
A printed rayon crêpe dress fabric designed for the Ascher Studio. In the postwar period, Zika Ascher commissioned leading artists to provide original textile patterns.

03 | Family Groups | UK | *c.* 1945 | Henry Moore
This screen-printed silk scarf was one of Ascher's well-known "Artists' Squares." They were affordable fashion items during the rationed postwar era.

04 | **Dress fabric** | UK | *c.* 1945 | Henry Moore
One of Zika Ascher's particular strengths was his ability to render an artist's vision
accurately through the medium of screen-printing.

05 | **Furnishing fabric** | UK | *c.* 1945 | Henry Moore
Moore, world famous for his abstract sculptures based on the human figure, had
a long association with the Ascher Studio.

01 | Festival | UK | 1938
This printed cotton furnishing fabric, produced by Tootal, Broadhurst, Lee & Co., depicts dancing women in traditional dress.

02 | Lustgärden (The Garden of Eden) | Sweden | c. 1947 | Stig Lindberg
One of Lindberg's best-loved patterns, this furnishing fabric, originally manufactured by Nordiska Kompaniet, has a folk art quality.

03 | Textile | USA | 1949 | Ruth Reeves
Reeves was inspired by the folk art of Central and Southern America. This bold large-scale design incorporates Peruvian motifs including llamas.

04 | **Textile design** | Russia | 1962 | Nina Shirokova
Unlike many artists working under the Soviet regime, Shirokova's design shows the influence of traditional folk art.

05 | **Town of Zagorsk** | Russia | 1961 | Nina Shirokova
Richly colored, tightly framed vignettes depicting elements of village life are arranged in horizontal bands.

06 | **Kalamkari** | India | 1879
A *kalamkari* is a type of traditional hand-painted or block-printed cotton textile. This example comes from Machilipatnam in Andhra Pradesh.

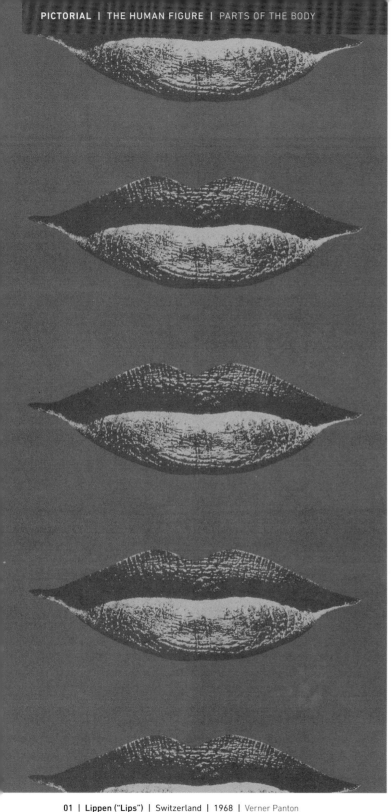

02 | Masks | UK | 1954 | Robert Stewart
One of many textile designs created by Stewart for the London retailer Liberty, this pattern features bands of totemic masks.

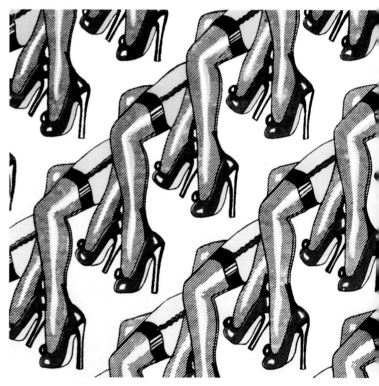

01 | Lippen ("Lips") | Switzerland | 1968 | Verner Panton
Panton created a screen-printed cotton textile for "Visiona 0," a futuristic exhibition at the Cologne Furniture Fair. The lips were modeled by Panton's wife, Marianne.

03 | Legs | UK | 1973 | Jane Wealleans
This screen-printed satin fabric was produced by OK Textiles, a firm founded by Wealleans and Susan Saunders, which specialized in short runs.

04 | Bachelor's Wallpaper | USA | 1902 | Charles Dana Gibson
Manufactured by M. H. Birge & Sons, this wallpaper features images of four "Gibson
Girls," fictional popular Edwardian New Women and early commercial pin-ups.

02 | Wallpaper | Germany | 20th century
This idiosyncratic wallpaper design encloses scenes portraying firemen at work within a grid formed by braided stems.

01 | Wallpaper | France | 1788 | Jean-Baptiste Réveillon
This block-printed, hand-painted, and hand-gilded wallpaper was produced by Réveillon, a highly successful wallpaper manufacturer.

03 | Pallas and Venus | France | *c.* 1805 | Jean-Baptiste Huet
Designed by Huet, this Neoclassical printed cotton was manufactured in Jouy-en-Josas in northern France by German-born industrialist Christophe-Philippe Oberkampf.

04 | **Textile** | France | early 19th century
This printed cotton fabric features a pair of lovers set within a frame against a floral background. Cupid flies overhead.

05 | **Greek Procession** | France | early 20th century | Raoul Dufy
The French artist Dufy created many patterns for textiles. This design has horizontal bands of figures in red, black, and white, the colors of ancient Greek pottery.

06 | **Frieze** | France | 1795–1801
Manufactured by Pierre Jacquemart, this Neoclassical frieze depicts figures resembling Greek caryatids.

The Classical World (8th century BCE–5th century CE)

The classical civilizations of ancient Greece and Rome have influenced and inspired generations of Western designers and architects from the Renaissance onward. Coinciding with periods of archeological discoveries, revivals of classical styles have often reflected a desire to return to fundamental architectural principles, where beauty derives from an ideal of proportion known as "the golden mean."

In ancient Greece, with the development of the city-state in *c.* 700 BCE, temples and other public buildings appeared. Of post and lintel construction, where columns support roof beams, these were conceived in three distinct styles or "orders": Doric, Ionic, and Corinthian. Although the orders are distinguishable by the differences in the capitals of their columns—Doric is plain, Ionic fluted, and Corinthian foliate—they also functioned as schemes of design, dictating form, proportion, and detailing.

First described by the Roman architect Vitruvius, the formal vocabulary of the Greek orders served as a blueprint for later interpretations. The familiar vertical division of the wall plane in 18th- and 19th-century interiors by means of skirting board, dado, picture rail, frieze, and cornice echoes the principal elements of classical entablature and their proportional relationships.

Most of what is known about ancient Greek pattern derives from the decoration of temples and pottery. Stylized summaries of plant structure were common motifs. The anthemion or honeysuckle ornament was a decorative flourish expressed in simple, curved lines to suggest a flower-like cluster. The acanthus leaf, which occurs in Corinthian capitals, was another prevalent motif. Other natural forms found in decoration include lotus buds, palmettes, laurel leaves, ivy, and aloe.

The most significant type of Greek patterning was the Greek key or fret, used to border friezes and vases. This continuous meander, which traces out a labyrinth in linear form, bending at right angles on itself, is thought to have been a symbol of unity or infinity. The fret pattern occurs as a single fret, as a double fret where two lines are interlaced, and in a rounded version termed a running scroll. The scroll or volute that forms the top of Ionic columns was a common feature of Greek decoration. Rope ornament was used as a border.

The architecture of ancient Rome adhered to the Greek vernacular, but decoration on villas, public buildings, and monuments was more elaborate and expressive of imperial might. Acanthus leaves proliferated, applied in exaggerated surfaces where leaves nestled within leaves. From the 1st century BCE, mosaic was the vehicle for pictorial wall and floor decoration.

Far Left A Roman mosaic floor panel, comprised of stone, tile, and glass, from the 2nd century.

Left An illustration from a *Handbook of Coloured Ornament in the Historic Styles* (*c.* 1880).

Opposite A perfume bottle (*c.* 510–500 BCE) attributed to the Group of the Paidikos Alabastra of ancient Greece.

01 | Love Comic | USA | 1970 | Nicky Zann

Manufactured by Concord Fabrics, this printed cotton fabric features original comic strip art, conceived, drawn, and rendered for the design by Zann.

02 | True Romance | UK | 2017 | Mini Moderns

Part of the Saturday Night/Sunday Morning collection, this wallpaper design was inspired by the designers' sisters' romantic comics.

03 | Faces | USA | 1971
This printed fabric, produced by Avondale Mills, depicts a graphic black and white sea of faces, reminiscent of a pop festival scene.

04 | Raspberry Lips | UK | 1973 | Jane Wealleans
Produced by Wealleans's company, OK Textiles of London, this furnishing fabric depicts a bold graphic pattern.

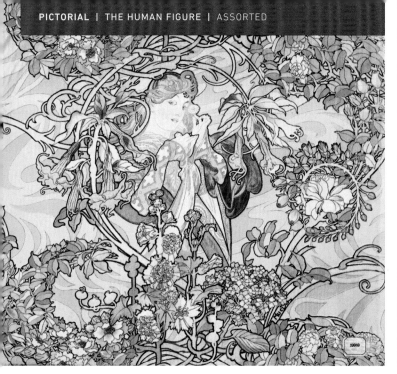

01 | Femme à Marguerite (Woman with Daisy) | France | 1898–1900 | Alphonse Mucha
Mucha's design on printed velvet fabric portrays a woman holding a daisy amid scrolling Art Nouveau–style vines and branches.

03 | Hands | UK | 1986 | Helen David
Helen and Colin David founded the British fashion label English Eccentrics in 1983. This design was for a dress fabric.

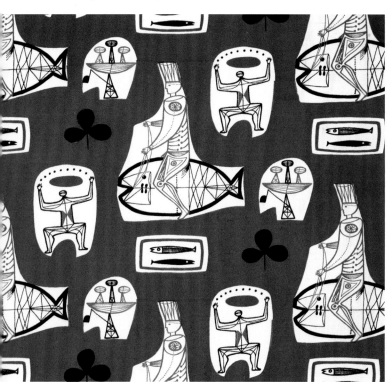

02 | Macrahanish | UK | 1955 | Robert Stewart
This screen-printed linen and cotton furnishing fabric was designed for Liberty. Stewart was one of Liberty's chief postwar designers.

04 | Textile | UK | mid-19th century
A cotton fabric featuring a chinoiserie-style pattern of roses, female figures, and children playing, arranged in vivid vertical bands.

05 | Wallpaper | Austria | 1914–15 | Anny Schröder
This illustration of a wallpaper design is from *Wiener Werkstätte Mode 1914–15*
(*Vienna Workshops Fashion 1914–15*), published in Vienna by Eduard Kosmack.

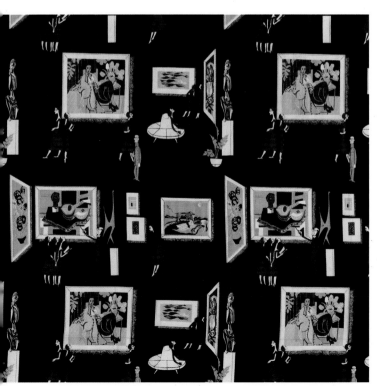

06 | Fabric | 1950s
This unusual fabric design of unknown provenance portrays groups of people
viewing paintings and sculpture at an art gallery.

07 | Wallpaper | USA | 19th to 20th century
A turn-of-the-century wallpaper pattern features a rather risqué motif of a half-nude
young woman among bouquets of flowers.

02 | Red House | UK | 1914 | Claud Lovat Fraser
Fraser, an artist and designer, created this pattern for a silk furnishing fabric for Liberty. It was reissued, recolored by Susan Collier, in 1973.

01 | London | UK | 2007 | Cath Kidston
This charming design for fabric and wallpaper features recognizable London landmarks, from Tower Bridge and Buckingham Palace to the London Eye.

03 | Gaudí | UK | 1984 | Helen David
This dress fabric, designed by David of English Eccentrics, is based on the broken mosaic ornamentation seen in the buildings of Catalan architect Antoni Gaudí.

04 | Dress fabric | Netherlands | 2017 | Francesca Franceschi
This vibrant pyramidal pattern was designed by Italian-born Franceschi for Vlisco.
It is a Dutch wax block print.

05 | NYC | UK | 2008 | Chloe Geary-Smith
Chloe Geary is an illustrator with a particular interest in street scenes. This all-over
pattern appears on a silk and chiffon scarf.

06 | Do You Live in a Town? | UK | 2006 | Mini Moderns
This highly graphic wallpaper design resembles an architectural blueprint. Stylized
trees punctuate the cityscape.

07 | Les Monuments de Paris (The Monuments of Paris) | France | 1816–20
This printed cotton fabric, depicting famous Parisian monuments and landmarks, was manufactured by Hartmann et Fils.

09 | Watercolor | UK | 20th century
A stylized version of a willow pattern, this design for a carpet includes multicolored overlays of oriental fretwork and medallions.

08 | Prefab Stripe | UK | 1998 | Sharon Elphick
Artist and designer Elphick has advocated the use of wallpaper in modern settings. This pattern depicts the facade of a prefab 1960s apartment block.

10 | Village Church | UK | 1954 | Hilda Durkin
Durkin was one of the designers who created textile patterns for Heal's under the inspired direction of Tom Worthington.

01 | Aftermath | USA | 2013 | Studio Job for Maharam
This furnishing fabric designed for US textile firm Maharam features
a postapocalyptic cityscape. Studio Job is based in the Netherlands.

02 | Billie Goes to Town | UK | 2014 | Cath Kidston
In this light-hearted print, Billie, the brand founder's Sealyham Terrier, is a tourist visiting London landmarks, parks, and shops.

03 | Urban Chaos | UK | 2013 | Timorous Beasties
A pastiche of Victorian silhouette paper-cuts, this wallpaper pattern features crash barriers, aerials, skateboarders, cyclists, and traffic lights in a frantic cityscape.

05 | **NYC** | **UK** | **2008** | Chloe Geary-Smith
This printed border depicts Geary-Smith's illustrations of New York skyscrapers, executed in a loose painterly style.

06 | **Welwyn Garden City** | **UK** | **1926** | Doris Gregg
This block-printed furnishing fabric portrays a section of Welwyn Garden City, with terraced housing surrounding a factory.

04 | **Metropolis** | **USA** | **1955** | Elenhank
Elenhank, founded by Henry and Eleanor Kluck, created many textile patterns in the postwar period. Henry's architectural background is evident in this design.

07 | **Metroland** | **UK** | **2017** | Mini Moderns
This linear repeat of suburban houses is available as printed window film. The motif originally occurred on Paisley Crescent wallpaper.

08 | Miami | UK | 2015 | Cole & Son
This vibrant wallpaper pattern, inspired by Miami's retro style, features terraced
colonnades and lush tropical vegetation.

01 | New York City Toile | UK | 2012 | Timorous Beasties
Familiar New York landmarks, including the Flatiron Building, the New York Stock
Exchange, and the Empire State Building, feature in this contemporary urban toile.

02 | London Toile | UK | 2016 | Cath Kidston
London is a constant source of inspiration for the Cath Kidston design team, and flecks of green add a touch of freshness to a classic blue and white toile print.

03 | La Fête de la Fédération | France | 1790–91 | Jean-Baptiste Huet
This block-printed fabric, "The Festival of the Federation," commemorates a festival held throughout France in 1790 in celebration of the French Revolution.

04 | New York Toile 2 | UK | 2012 | Timorous Beasties
Another example of Timorous Beasties' provocative urban toiles, this combines recognizable Manhattan landmarks with gritty street scenes.

01 | **Textile** | UK | 1935
This printed cotton fabric was manufactured by Tootal, Broadhurst, Lee & Co. Bands of anchors against a shaded blue ground are linked by the scrolling lines of ropes.

02 | **Dungeness** | UK | 2015 | Mini Moderns
This wallpaper design, with its lighthouses, cabins, huts, and fishing boats, evokes the shingle coastline at Dungeness, Kent.

03 | **Deep Sea** | UK | 2011 | Emily Sutton for St. Jude's

This screen-printed linen furnishing fabric was designed for St. Jude's. Sutton's "Curiosity Shop" won Best British Pattern at the British Design Awards in 2011.

04 | Great Wave | UK | 2010 | Cole & Son
This dramatic wallpaper pattern is an homage to the woodblock print by Katsushika Hokusai, *Under the Wave off Kanagawa* (*c*. 1830–32).

05 | Marmara | UK | 2015 | Osborne & Little
This beautifully evocative wallpaper is a depiction of a seascape surrounded by the Turkish mainland.

06 | Brighten Up Your Day | UK | 2013 | Cath Kidston
The title is a wordplay on "Brighton," but it is also one of the brand's guiding principles.
It features an array of picture postcards from the popular British seaside resort.

07 | Ocean View | UK | 2002 | Eley Kishimoto
Triangular ocher and orange sails are adrift on sparkling waves. Stylized gulls bring depth to the pattern.

08 | High Seas | USA | 2012 | Michéle Brummer Everett
Designed for US textile firm Cloud9 Fabrics, this printed organic cotton is a simple and highly effective stylized wave pattern in three colors.

09 | Dress fabric | UK | 1940 | Calico Printers' Association
This jaunty printed cotton dress fabric, manufactured by the Calico Printers'
Association, depicts fish, boats, anchors, and buoys enclosed in fan shapes.

11 | Lifeboats | UK | 1938 | Calico Printers' Association
Life preservers frame a view of gulls swooping over the water in this printed cotton
furnishing fabric produced by the Calico Printers' Association.

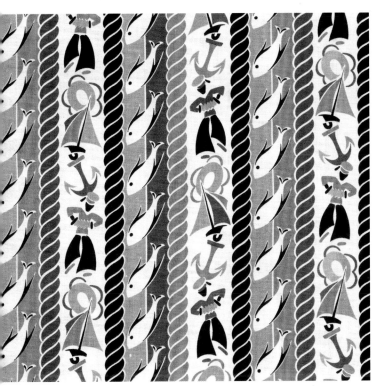

10 | Nautical | UK | 1940 | Calico Printers' Association
This dress fabric features anchors, ships, life preservers, and sailors wearing
bell-bottomed pants, arranged between vertical rows of fish and coiled rope.

12 | Porto Fino | UK | 1952 | Mary Oliver
Oliver was a British designer who designed prints for a range of leading textile
manufacturers. She founded her own firm, Mary Oliver Textiles, in 1967.

Collier Campbell

SEE PAGES > 122, 291

Founders of British design company Collier Campbell, Manchester-born sisters Susan Collier (1938–2011) and Sarah Campbell worked in artistic partnership all their lives. Susan was a self-taught painter whose love of nature and unerring eye for color was in evidence from an early age. Sarah had no formal textile training, studying fine art and then graphic design at Chelsea College of Art. Both showed an intuitive rapport with pattern and color.

In 1961, after a brief stint working for designer Pat Albeck (1930–2017), during which time she sold sketches to scarf companies such as Jacqmar, Collier took her portfolio to Liberty, which bought six of her designs and commissioned more. In the late 1960s, Campbell, who had already been assisting her sister, had similar success when Liberty bought a design she produced for her graduation. Collier was retained by the company in 1968 and appointed design and color consultant in 1971; Campbell was retained as a freelance designer in the early 1970s.

A breakthrough came when Yves Saint Laurent (1936–2008) commissioned the sisters to create original patterns for his ready-to-wear collection of 1971. Six years later, they left Liberty to work under their own names, and in 1979/80 formed their company Collier Campbell. What made Collier Campbell patterns distinctive was their painterly quality. Full of vitality and freshness, the vibrancy of the designs reflected Collier Campbell's careful control of the printing process, which ensured that even brushmarks were retained in the final result (all the original designs were hand-painted). In this context, their insistence on "cheating the repeat" helped create depth and fluidity.

Collier Campbell designs reflected the trend for fashion and interior styles to grow ever closer, and many of the patterns, which were created for a variety of different fabrics, from silk to linen union, were used in a range of applications: as cushion covers, drapes, wallpaper, and duvet covers, as well as dresses, scarves, and accessories. An early Liberty pattern, "Cottage Garden" (1974), anticipated this shift, its moody colors and floral motifs echoing the vogue for period styles that was sweeping through fashion at the time. Almost a decade later, "Cote d'Azur" (1983), one of Collier Campbell's best-known patterns, captured the more optimistic and outward-looking spirit of the 1980s. The company had a long and fruitful association with British designer and retailer Terence Conran (b.1931), who commissioned them to create the carpet designs for Gatwick Airport's North Terminal in 1988, as well as producing many designs for his Habitat stores. After Collier's death, Campbell has continued to design, paint, teach, and write under her own name.

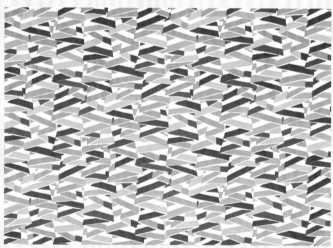

Top Sarah Campbell and Susan Collier in 1984; the sisters co-founded one of the most successful textile design businesses in Europe.

Above "Havana" is a furnishing fabric from the "Six Views" (1983) collection.

Opposite Infused with Mediterranean light and displaying a painterly delight in mark-making reminiscent of French painter Henri Matisse, "Cote d'Azur" (1983) won the designers the Prince Philip Designers Prize in 1984. Produced by luxury Swiss textile firm Christian Fischbacher, it was one of the patterns in the "Six Views" (1983) collection.

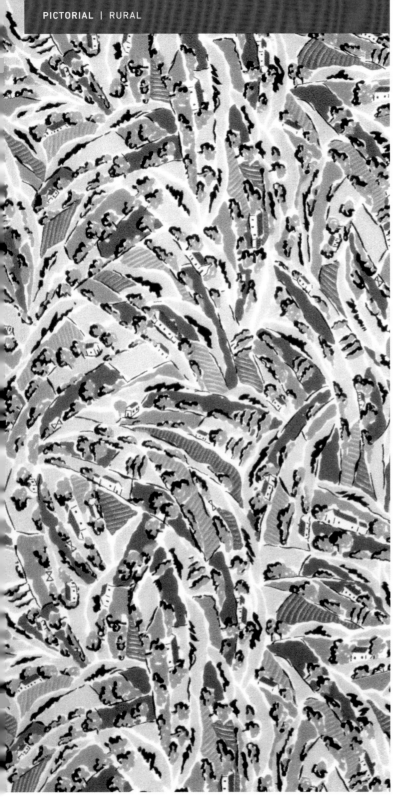

01 | Aerial View | UK | 1936 | Calico Printers' Association
This printed cotton dress fabric, manufactured by the Calico Printers' Association, is an abstract impression of a landscape viewed from the air.

02 | Fabric | USA | 1930s | L. Kahn
This printed cotton fabric, produced in conjunction with the Educational Alliance, Art School, New York, shows a country scene with houses and ploughed fields.

03 | Carnac | UK | 2016 | Phyllis Barron and Dorothy Larcher
One of the Barron and Larcher patterns revived by Christopher Farr Cloth, this
delicate design features stalks set against a dotted ground.

04 | Cowboy | UK | 1999 | Cath Kidston
One of Cath Kidston's most recognizable prints, "Cowboy" is inspired by vintage
American style from the 1950s and 1960s.

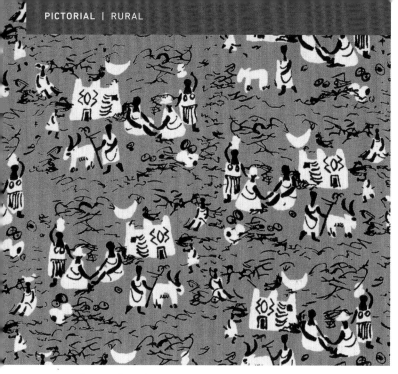

05 | Textile | UK | 1948 | Julian Trevelyan
Trevelyan was one of the artists who designed patterns for Ascher Studio. This screen-printed spun rayon dress fabric was used by Horrockses Fashions.

06 | Sussex Downs | UK | 2012 | Jenny Frean, First Eleven Studio
A spontaneous line drawing of the countryside was the starting point for this beautiful voile furnishing fabric produced by Sanderson.

07 | Cornish Farm | UK | *c.* 1930 | Alec Walker
Walker founded Cryséde, a textile firm based in St. Ives. The design of this block-printed silk dress fabric was taken from one of his paintings.

08 | La Chasse (The Hunt) | France | 1913 | Raoul Dufy
Dufy's furnishing fabric, designed for the leading French silk manufacturer
Bianchini-Férier, depicts a hunting scene.

09 | Moordale | UK | 2017 | Mini Moderns
This sweeping landscape wallpaper pattern features Roseberry Topping, a distinctive
hill in North Yorkshire, UK, and The Cow and Calf pub at Ilkley, West Yorkshire.

Edward Bawden (1903–89)

SEE PAGES > 393, 421

Illustrator, painter, and designer Edward Bawden had a long creative career that embraced both fine art and applied art disciplines. Working in media as diverse as book and poster illustration, wallpaper, and pattern design, ceramics, metalwork, mural painting, and watercolor, he portrayed a distinctly English way of life.

Born in Braintree, Essex, Bawden was educated at the Friends' School in Saffron Walden. Excused from sports owing to a heart problem, he devoted much of his spare time to drawing, displaying a facility that encouraged his teachers to arrange for him to spend a day a week at Cambridge School of Art, which he subsequently attended full time between 1919 and 1921. In 1922, he was awarded a scholarship to the Royal College of Art in London, where he studied illustration and calligraphy, taking his diploma in 1925. There, he was taught by Paul Nash and met Eric Ravilious (1903–42), the latter of whom became a close friend until his premature death in World War II.

An early prestigious commission came about in 1928 when Bawden and Ravilious were asked to create a mural for the refectory at Morley College. Around the same time, Bawden also produced tiles for London Underground. His introduction to commercial work came via Curwen Press, where he, Ravilious, and Nash contributed illustrations for clients including London Transport, Penguin Books, and Shell-Mex.

Bawden began designing wallpaper in the mid-1920s, producing printed rolls from his own linocuts and selling them through Elspeth Anne Little's shop Modern Textiles in South Kensington. From 1926 onward, Curwen Press published these designs as color lithographs. Whimsical, pictorial, and quintessentially English patterns such as "Woodpigeon" (1927) and "Knole Park" (1929) show a light graphic touch. A subsequent collection, "Plaistow Wallpapers" (1932), was more textural in character.

In 1932, Bawden married Charlotte Epton and soon after the couple left London to settle in Great Bardfield, Essex. Together with Ravilious and his wife, they established what was to become an artist's colony. By the end of the 1930s, he had joined forces with John Aldridge (1905–83), another village artist, to produce a series of lino-printed wallpapers, Bardfield Papers, featuring architectural motifs. War intervened and it was not until 1946 that Cole & Son, which had acquired the blocks, was able to put them into production on a commercial basis.

During the war, Bawden served as an official war artist in France and the Middle East. During the post-war years, in addition to teaching at the Royal College of Art and elsewhere, producing illustrations, murals, and paintings, he remained a leading light of the Great Bardfield Artists.

Top Designer and painter Edward Bawden photographed with some of the designs he created for Queen Elizabeth II's coronation in 1953.

Above Bawden's "Orcades" furnishing fabric was designed in 1954, when he was living at Great Bardfield, Essex.

Opposite Bawden began creating wallpaper designs in the 1920s, initially hand-printing them from linocuts onto rolls of paper. From 1926, the Curwen Press produced his designs, printing them in the form of sheets of color lithographs. "Desert and Camels" (c. 1930) is a whimsical design featuring an all-over pattern of undulating sand dunes in yellow dotted about by camel trains in red and black.

10 | Textile | France | c. 1840
This printed cotton textile depicts rural scenes within a floral grid, including a woman with a watering can, a boy with a butterfly net, and children with a bird's nest.

11 | The Drinking Trough | France | c. 1792 | Jean-Baptiste Huet
Manufactured in Jouy-en-Josas by Christophe-Philippe Oberkampf, this classic *toile de Jouy* depicts rustic figures in bucolic scenes.

12 | Japanese Garden | UK | 2017 | Osborne & Little
This wallpaper design is a contemporary version of the Japonaiserie style and
portrays kimono-clad Japanese women by an ornamental brook.

13 | Exotisme | UK | 2017 | Christian Lacroix
Lacroix produced this eccentric scenic wallpaper for Designers Guild. It features
vignettes overlaid with branches of exotic foliage.

Originating in the Netherlands in the 16th century, Delftware—largely, but not exclusively, tiles—is a type of tin-glazed earthenware similar to majolica, in which the clay is covered with a white tin glaze, then hand-painted, usually in blue, and fired. Occasionally other colors, such as green, crimson, and sepia, were also used. The white ground, which was sometimes covered with a clear glaze after painting, was a simulation of porcelain.

As the name suggests, the main center of production was the Dutch town Delft, where an estimated 800 million tiles were produced before the end of the 18th century. The technique was introduced to Britain by Dutch potters, where an English version became established.

A key characteristic of Delft tiles are the charming rural scenes the tiles depict. Windmills, canals, sailing ships, drawbridges, milkmaids, and other representations of country life are typical; occasionally, individual tiles make up a panel that forms a complete picture.

01 | Hunting Toile | UK | 2012 | Timorous Beasties

Hunters and fishermen go after their prey in this contemporary subversion of the traditional *toile de Jouy*.

02 | La Route de Poissy | France | 1815
This copperplate-printed cotton fabric features a number of roadside scenes, including a horse and carriage, and a man playing the bagpipes.

03 | La Promenade en Bois | France | 1920s | Raoul Dufy
Fashionably dressed women stroll through a wooded park in this design for a woven silk furnishing fabric, manufactured by Bianchini-Férier.

04 | Versailles Grand | UK | 2014 | Cole & Son
Inspired by Jean de La Fontaine's fables, this wallpaper is a contemporary version of 18th-century French scenic engravings. It features birds and animals in a wooded setting.

Baroque and Rococo (mid-16th century–mid-18th century)

Baroque and Rococo were ornamented styles that dominated European architecture and design from the mid-16th to the mid-18th century. Originating in Italy, the Baroque style of painting was soon echoed in architecture and design, and by 1620 had reached northern Europe.

Luxurious textiles were prevalent in Baroque interiors as upholstery materials, wall coverings, and bed hangings. Fabrics in rich, dark colors and with symmetrical relief patterning, such as damasks, figured velvets, and brocades, were typical of the style, as were embroideries in silk and crewel work. Other textiles featured motifs that drew on nature, with floral sprays and garlands, and curling foliage densely covering the ground.

One of the leading exponents of the style was French architect and designer Daniel Marot (1661–1752), who spent most of his career in the Netherlands and England. His engravings helped to disseminate the Baroque style in Britain, where he oversaw the redecoration of state rooms and the design of garden parterres at Hampton Court Palace.

Rococo, the style that immediately succeeded Baroque, was prevalent during the first half of the 18th century in France, from where it spread throughout Europe. Lighter and more delicate than its predecessor, the style takes its name from *rocaille*, the French term for decorative

rockwork of the type seen in shell grottoes. Exotic marine shells were collected at this time, and the shell shape was a key feature of Rococo ornament and patterning. So, too, were free C- and S-shaped curves, curlicues, and flourishes, often suggestive of running water. The style was associated with schemes of interior decoration and with furniture design.

Unlike Baroque, which was austere and solemn, Rococo designs had a light, sensuous quality. Bright colors were set off by airy expanses of white or pale pastel colors. Repeats were often asymmetric, with motifs placed seemingly randomly on the ground, deliberately unbalanced compositions that created a sense of playfulness.

Floral sprays and sprigs, leaves and vines, naturalistically rendered, were typical motifs, but figures were also depicted—groups of musicians or idealized shepherds and shepherdesses. Chinoiserie elements—Chinese figures, dragons, and pagodas—were common features.

In Britain, chinoiserie Rococo was the most popular version of the style and is seen in the flowered silks created by Huguenot weavers in London's Spitalfields. Anna Maria Garthwaite (1688–1763) was one of the leading fabric designers of her day, and one of the first whose name is known. Employing a technique devised in the 1730s, she introduced tonal shading, giving her floral motifs greater naturalism.

Far Left Hand-blocked English chinoiserie Rococo wallpaper from the 18th century.

Left This English wallpaper design, with its scattered flowers, dates from the 18th century.

Opposite This painted silk English *robe à la Française* from the 1740s shows the taste for chinoiserie.

01 | **Tractor** | Russia | 1930 | Sergei Burylin

Burylin was one of a number of Soviet designers producing industrial-themed patterns.
This printed cotton was manufactured at the Ivanovo-Voznesensk Mills in west Russia.

02 | **Motor Bike** | 2015 | Sholto Drumlanrig

London-based print designer Drumlanrig has worked with a range of clients,
including Diane von Furstenberg and Liberty.

03 | Bicycles | 2015 | Sholto Drumlanrig
Many of Drumlanrig's patterns, which have found a wide range of applications on clothing and other products, have a strong graphic character.

04 | Textile | Russia | 1920–30
Printed textiles produced in the late 1920s in the Soviet Union celebrated industrial progress in graphic stylized patterns.

01 | Sailing Boats | UK | *c.* 1920 | Doris Carter
Carter's block-printed cotton furnishing fabric, with its overlapping billowing sails, was manufactured by Footprints.

02 | Baraka | UK | 1992
Designed for Liberty, this printed cotton furnishing fabric features a flotilla of old sailing vessels amid shoals of fish.

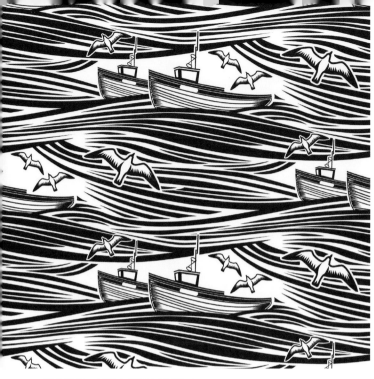

03 | Whitby | UK | 2010 | Mini Moderns
This lively seaside pattern, with its fishing trawlers and gulls, has appeared on a wide range of products, including fabric, wallpaper, enamelware, and packaging.

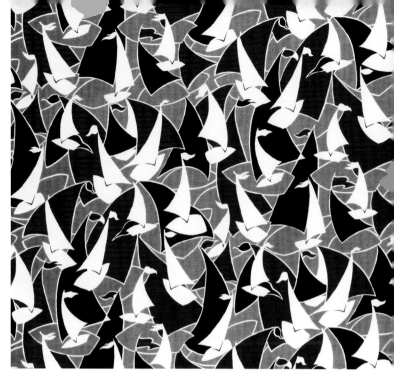

05 | Yacht | UK | 1941
Manufactured by Tootal, Broadhurst, Lee & Co., this cotton pique dress fabric features a pattern whose directional changes evoke a tacking yacht.

04 | Textile | UK | 1930
Boats, waves, and billowing clouds animate this printed linen furnishing fabric produced by Edinburgh Weavers.

06 | Fabric | USA | 1930s | Rose Taibbi
This street and water scene was hand screen-printed by Taibbi, a student at the Educational Alliance Art School in New York, when she was eleven years old.

01 | Swoop | UK | 2015 | Sholto Drumlanrig
The original image for this graphic pattern was executed in felt tip pen. Drumlanrig
has created many fabric designs for menswear and womenswear.

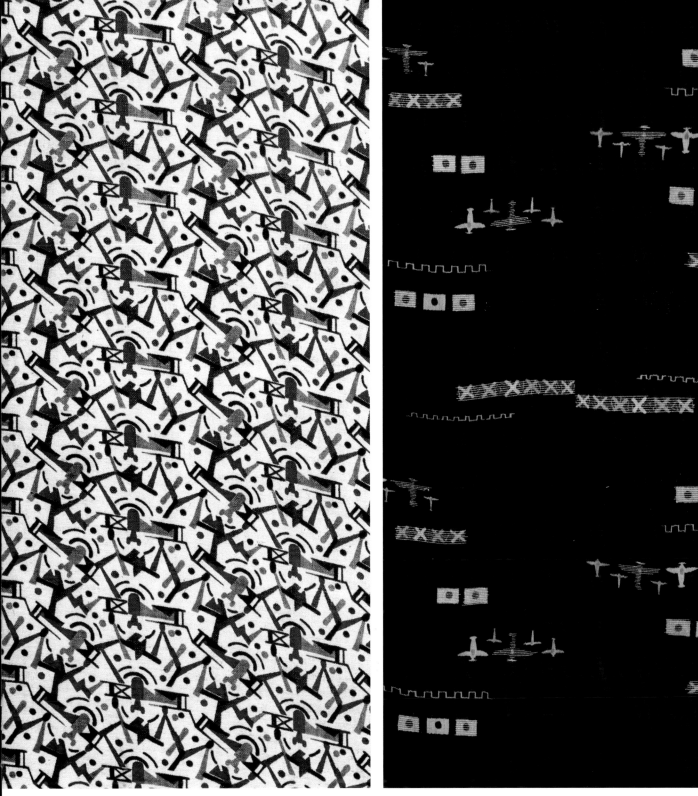

02 | Fabric | Russia | 1927
Typical of the themed patterns that celebrated Soviet industry, this printed cotton
fabric is a lively stylized design of aeroplanes.

03 | Kimono | Japan | *c.* 1940s
This silk kimono features a striking pattern of planes, the crenellations of the Great
Wall of China, barbed wire, and the *Hinomaru* (circle of the Sun) flag of Japan.

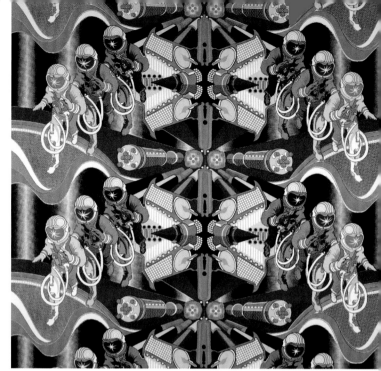

02 | Space Walk | UK | 1969 | Sue Thatcher Palmer
Palmer, who designed this dramatic printed cotton furnishing fabric for Warner Fabrics, was very influenced by Pop art.

01 | Wallpaper | USA | c. 1950
Space travel was still largely within the realms of science fiction when this machine-printed wallpaper was designed.

03 | Astronauts and Spaceships | USA | 1954
This pictorial wallpaper pattern, manufactured by The Prager Company, features comic book–style illustrations.

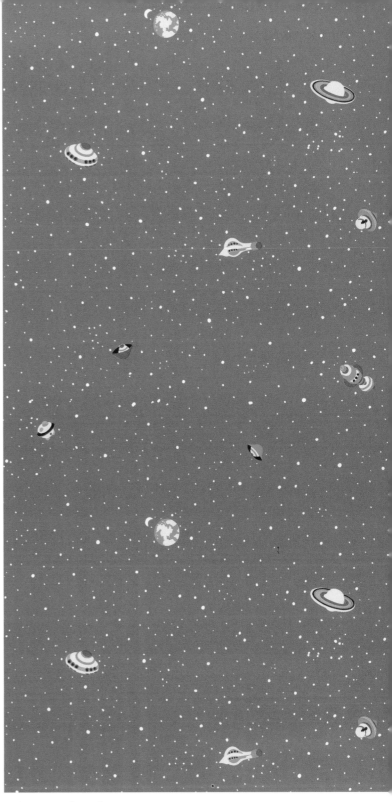

04 | Lunar Rocket | UK | 1969 | Eddie Squires
Designed for Warner and Sons to commemorate the first moon landing, this printed cotton features a detailed pattern. Squires later become the director of the company.

05 | Wallpaper | USA | 1992
Manufactured by leading interiors company F. Schumacher & Co., this machine-printed wallpaper depicts objects in space.

01 | Flying Colours | USA | 2012 | Michéle Brummer Everett
Everett is a South African-born designer based in the United States. This flag pattern
was created for Cloud9 Fabrics.

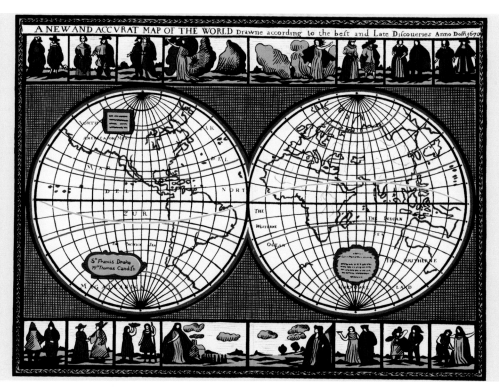

02 | Bon Voyage | USA | 1958
This screen-printed wallpaper, manufactured by F. Schumacher & Co., features
steamship and airline labels surrounding a map of the two hemispheres from 1670.

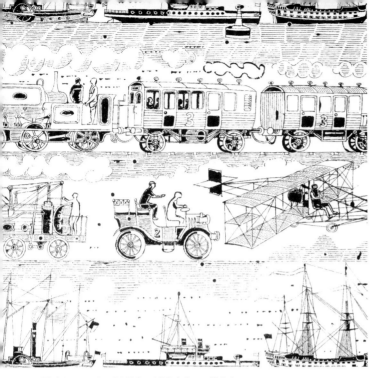

03 | Locomotion | UK | *c.*1955 | Roger Nicholson
Nicholson's screen-printed wallpaper features a variety of early forms
of transportation, from motor cars to biplanes, graphically rendered in outline.

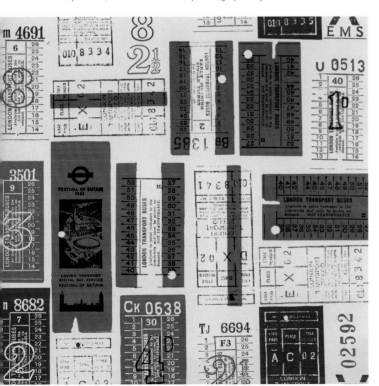

04 | Hold Tight | UK | 2014 | Mini Moderns
This vintage-style wallpaper design, with its medium-scale repeat, is patterned with
images of old bus tickets.

05 | Flags | UK | 1956 | Jane Edgar
This printed linen furnishing fabric was designed for Gerald Holtom, one of the
British textile companies producing contemporary designs in the 1950s.

02 | **Matrinah** | UK | 2017 | Cole & Son with Ardmore Ceramic Art
Named after Ardmore designer Matrinah Xaba, this wallpaper design reproduces
ceramic decoration by Ardmore Ceramic Art of South Africa.

01 | **Ceramica** | UK | 2017 | Matthew Williamson at Osborne & Little
One of the many Williamson designs produced by Osborne & Little, this wallpaper
creates a pattern from porcelain plates.

03 | **Pots** | France | 1925 | André Duranceau
French-American artist and textile designer Duranceau is best known for *Inspirations*
(1928), a collection of pochoir (stencil-based) prints.

04 | Malaga | UK | 1955
Progressive British firm Wallpaper Manufacturers produced this wallpaper. It is part of the company's Palladio range of hand screen-printed wallpapers.

05 | Wallpaper | USA | 1950
This machine-printed embossed and flocked wallpaper, manufactured by M. H. Birge & Sons, puts domestic objects in the frame.

06 | Batterie de Cuisine (Cookware) | USA | 1965–68 | Piazza Prints
Piazza Prints was founded in New York in 1946. Cartoonist Saul Steinberg created designs for a number of pictorial wallpapers produced by the company.

02 | **Heirlooms** | USA | 1952 | Albert John Pucci
Produced by Associated American Artists, this printed cotton furnishing fabric
depicts a collection of antiques and curios loosely arranged on a blue-green ground.

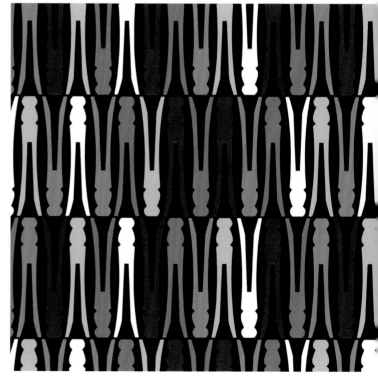

01 | **Wallpaper** | UK | 1950s to 1960s
This mid-century modern wallpaper from Arthur Sanderson & Sons features
contemporary vases and dishes within a rounded grid of hand-drawn lines.

03 | **Peggy** | USA | 2013 | Michelle Engel Bencsko
The humble wooden clothespin forms the basis of this horizontally structured
pattern produced for Cloud9 Fabrics.

04 | Safety Pins | France | 1918–25 | Paul Poiret
Poiret was a leading French couturier who revolutionized women's dress. This
pattern features randomly scattered dressmaking and safety pins on a black ground.

Stig Lindberg (1916–82)

SEE PAGES > 179, 182, 429, 474, 643

Stig Lindberg's work in ceramics, textiles, and glassware typifies the Scandinavian modern esthetic, particularly the version of the style that arose in postwar Sweden, which brought an organic sensibility back to modernism. Pattern—even representational pattern—was permissible again, and Lindberg, who was a supreme pattern-maker, was one of its most influential designers.

Born in Umeå, Sweden, Lindberg studied at the University College of Arts, Crafts and Design in Stockholm between 1935 and 1937, with the intention of becoming a painter. After graduation, he began what was to be a long association with the Gustavsberg ceramics factory, when he went to work there as a faience painter, training under the direction of Wilhelm Kåge (1899–1960). Kåge, who was a great influence on Lindberg, had dedicated his career to producing affordable functional cookware and dinner services for ordinary households, democratic ideals that lay at the heart of the emerging Scandinavian design ethos.

Sweden's neutrality during World War II meant that domestic production was not disrupted or placed on a war footing, as was the case elsewhere in Europe. Local industry also benefited from the fact that the country served as a refuge for talented designers fleeing Nazism, such as Arne Jacobsen (1902–71) and Josef Frank (1885–1967; see p. 238). A spirit of resistance—or perhaps a hope for eventual peace and recovery—is evident in the textile designs produced in Sweden during the war, a time when floral and naturalistic patterns were at the forefront.

Lindberg's first textile designs of note were produced in 1947 for an exhibition curated by Astrid Sampe (1909–2002), head of the textile studio at Nordiska Kompaniet, or "NK," a leading department store with branches in Stockholm and Gothenburg. A textile designer herself, Sampe pioneered the notion of "signed textiles"—designs commissioned from named designers and produced for the contract market. The two textiles Lindberg designed for Sampe were "Pottery" (1947) and "Lustgården" (Garden of Eden, c. 1951). "Pottery," with its repeating bottle and vase shapes, wittily combines the media in which Lindberg specialized: ceramics and textiles. There are elements, too, of folk art, equally evident in "Garden of Eden." Both the subject matter and representational style of Lindberg's textile patterns echo his work in ceramics.

Lindberg succeeded Kåge as creative director of Gustavsberg in 1949, holding the post until 1957. He returned to the same job in the company in 1972, before finally leaving in 1980. Between 1957 and 1970, he was a senior lecturer at the University College of Arts, Crafts and Design.

Far Left Noted Swedish postwar designer Stig Lindberg in his Gustavsberg studio in 1956.

Left The table top is covered by a reissued Lindberg design, "Lustgården" (1954).

Opposite "Pottery" (1947) is one of Lindberg's best-known textile patterns.

05 | Dress fabric | Netherlands | 2017 | Simone Post

532
533

Designed for Vlisco, this Dutch wax-print fabric is patterned with electric lights suspended in front of hanging fabrics.

06 | Wound Up | USA | 2016

This printed cotton fabric for Cloud9 Fabrics features an economically executed design of balls of wool in soft colors.

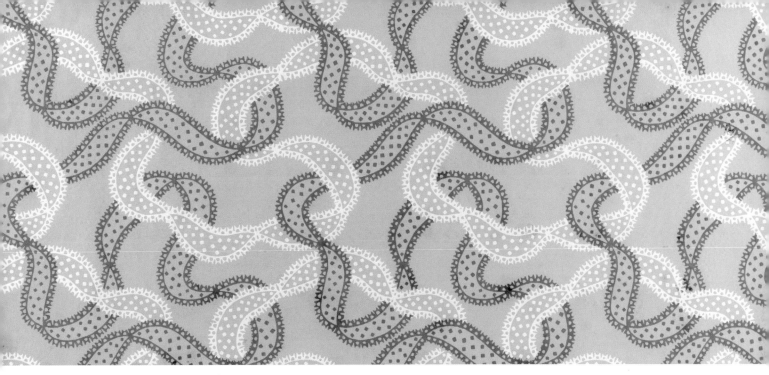

07 | **Ribbon and Lace** | **UK** | **20th century** | John Aldridge
British artist and designer Aldridge collaborated with Edward Bawden in the
production of the Bardfield collection of wallpaper designs.

08 | **Khulu Vases** | **UK** | **2017** | Cole & Son with Ardmore Ceramic Art
Part of the Ardmore collection from Cole & Son, this dramatic wallpaper design depicts
classical vases decorated with African animals.

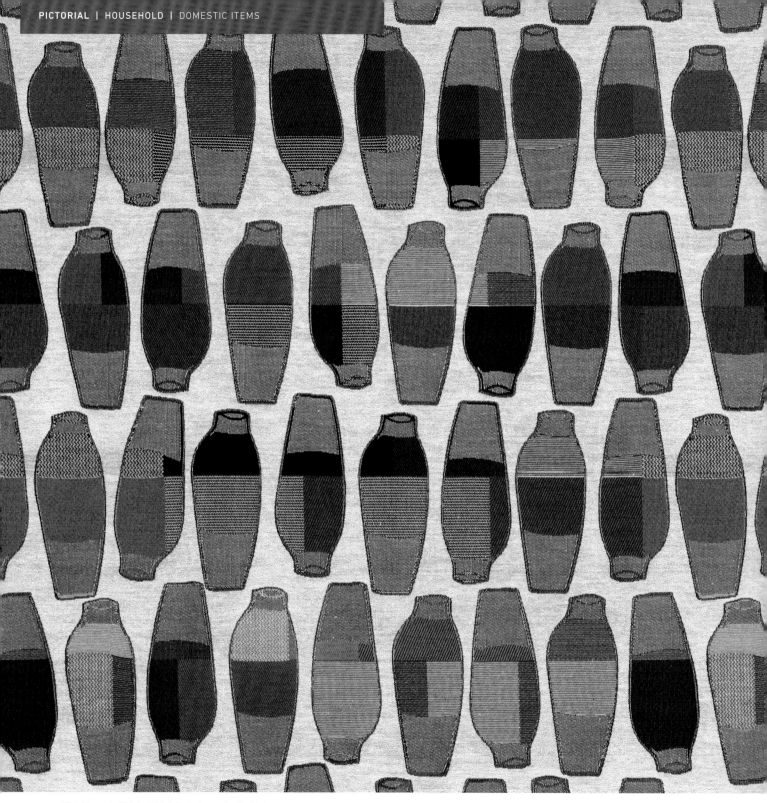

09 | Vases | USA | 2013 | Hella Jongerius for Maharam

Designed for US textile company Maharam, this furnishing fabric has a horizontally
structured pattern of earthenware vases.

10 | Bottle and Jar Bouquets | USA | 2017 | Emily Isabella
Isabella is an illustrator, packaging designer, and textile designer. She produced this pattern of silhouette bouquets for Cloud9 Fabrics.

11 | Dress fabric | UK | *c.* 1945 | Henry Moore
This screen-printed rayon dress fabric, produced by Ascher Studio, is one of a number of textile patterns that Moore designed in the immediate postwar years.

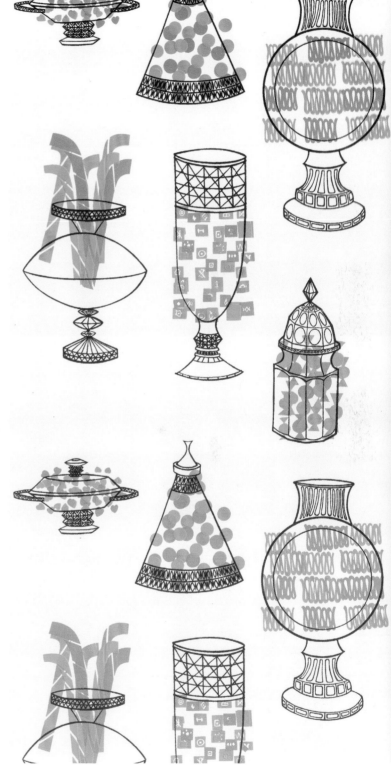

12 | Penny Candy | USA | 1960–67 | Ben Rose
This wallpaper, screen-printed on vinyl, features stylized outlines of storage jars overprinted by multicolored candy in bright colors.

01 | Buttons | USA | 1952
A small company based in New York, Piazza Prints, produced this hand
screen-printed wallpaper.

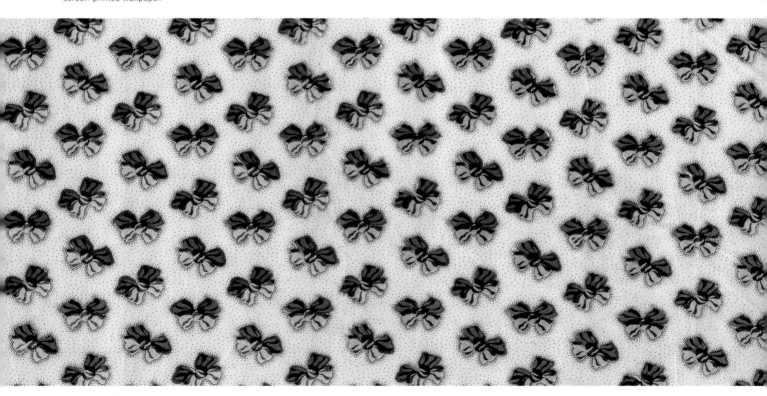

02 | Textile | 19th century
The all-over pattern of pink and blue bows, with a scattering of black dots
on roller-printed cotton fabric, creates a demure feel.

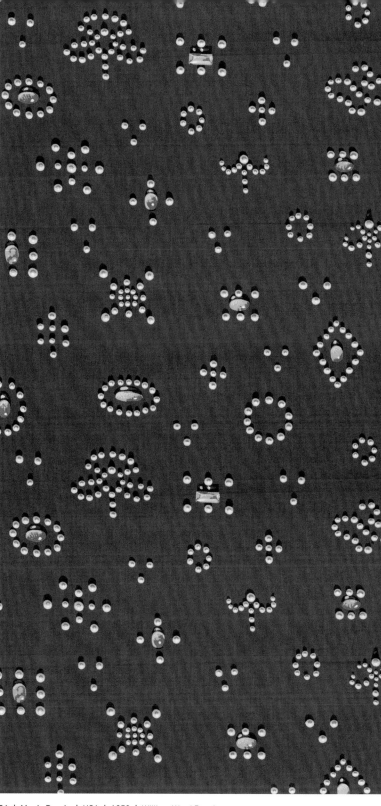

03 | Dress fabric | Netherlands | 2017 | Francesca Franceschi
Franceschi's lively pattern of hats and gloves, printed using the Dutch wax-resist technique, was designed for Vlisco.

04 | Magic Pearls | USA | 1953 | William Ward Beecher
Beecher designed this printed cotton fabric for Associated American Artists. The pearls and gems look three-dimensional, as if they had been sewn onto the cloth.

06 | Textile | India | 18th century
This printed cotton fabric features a lattice of twisting ribbons enclosing small sprays of flowers.

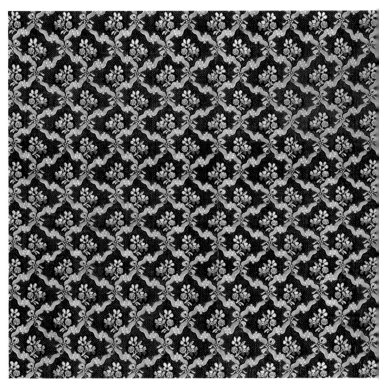

05 | Cocarde | UK | 2016 | Christian Lacroix

538
539

Lacroix produced this pattern depicting emblems, rosettes, and badges for Designers Guild. It is available as a wallpaper and furnishing fabric.

07 | Textile | France | 18th century
In this woven silk fabric, the diamond grid formed by the ribbons features bows at the intersections.

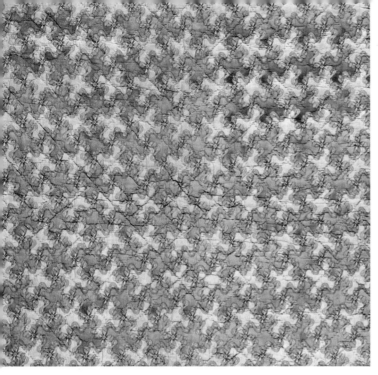

08 | Quilt | 19th century
The top fabric of this three-layer comforter has an all-over pattern of violet bows and ribbons. Its provenance is unknown.

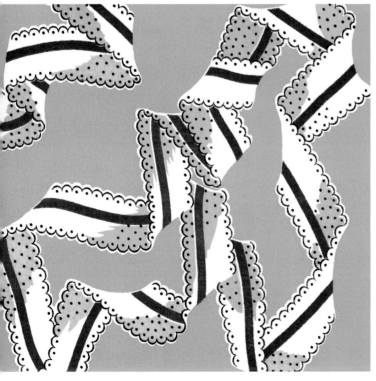

09 | Textile | UK | 1947 | Alastair Morton
Morton, the influential director of Edinburgh Weavers textile company, designed this pattern to cover a booklet accompanying Horrockses Fashions' second collection.

10 | Shoes | UK | 2015 | Sholto Drumlanrig
Drumlanrig's eye-catching design of scattered women's shoes packs graphic punch with its use of bright clashing colors.

02 | Textile | Japan | 19th century
Patterned using a silk dye-resist technique, this fabric features an all-over design
of fans and peonies.

01 | Fan Fantasy | USA | 1947 | Schier and Doggett

This wallpaper, made by Robinson & Barber, features randomly arranged fans from
the Cooper Union collection.

03 | Panel | Japan | late 19th century
Fans are a common Japanese motif. This delicate silk panel combines fans, flowers,
and ferns in an all-over pattern.

04 | Textile design | USA | 1950–70 | Tommi Parzinger
Parzinger's gouache and graphite drawing is based around a repeating fan motif.
He is best known for his furniture design.

01 | Pocket Change | USA | *c.* 1970 | Jack Denst
Denst is an award-winning wallpaper designer who began his career in 1947. His
screen-printed mylar foil wallpaper border features all the denominations of US coins.

02 | Dress fabric | Netherlands | 2012 | Tomi Oladipo
English-Nigerian Oladipo studied at the Royal College of Art in London before
working in Vlisco's design department.

03 | Curio | UK | 2017 | Osborne & Little
Squirrels and owls overrun the shelves of a dresser, crowded with ornaments and
collectibles, in this whimsical wallpaper pattern.

04 | Sitting Comfortably | UK | 2008 | Mini Moderns
This spare wallpaper pattern includes iconic mid-century modern chair designs,
from Arne Jacobsen's Ant Chair (1952) to Harry Bertoia's Diamond Chair (1952).

542
543

06 | Penguin Library | UK | 2013 | Osborne & Little
The covers of Penguin Books paperbacks are instantly recognizable the world over.
This wallpaper reproduces a range of vintage covers.

05 | Textile | UK | 1954 | Jacqueline Groag
Groag's printed linen furnishing fabric features a lively graphic design of book
spines. The white space between rows suggests shelving.

07 | Library | USA | 2012 | Rob Bancroft
A subtle variant on a basket-weave pattern, this printed cotton fabric, designed for
Cloud9 Fabrics, evokes stacked books.

08 | **Beauty Parlour** | UK | 2015 | Sholto Drumlanrig
Clashing hot pink and orange-red gives this crisp graphic pattern of hairdryers, lipsticks, and manicured hands added punch.

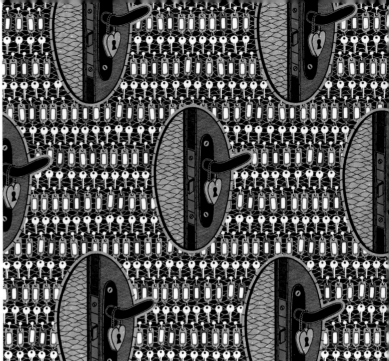

10 | **Dress fabric** | Netherlands | 2017 | Cor van den Boogaard
Van den Boogaard has designed for Dutch textile firm Vlisco for more than forty years, and is responsible for many of its iconic patterns.

09 | **Keys** | UK | 2010 | A. Richard Allen
Allen is an award-winning British artist and illustrator. He executed this vibrant design in mixed media.

11 | **Open Sesame** | USA | 1952 | Anton Refregier
Produced for Associated American Artists, this screen-printed cotton furnishing fabric features a small-scale pattern of stylized keys and locks.

01 | **International Women's Day** | Russia | 1930 | Darya Preobrazhenskaya
Preobrazhenskaya, a graduate of Moscow State Stroganov Academy of Industrial and Applied
Arts, was one of the Soviet textile designers producing thematic patterns during the late 1920s.

02 | Textile | Russia | *c.* 1928–30 | Sergei Burylin
Burylin was a Soviet designer of propaganda patterns. This fabric was manufactured at the Ivanovo-Voznesensk textile mills.

04 | Industrial | Russia | 1930 | Darya Preobrazhenskaya
This printed dress fabric, designed to promote the first Five-Year Plan for Soviet economic development, includes motifs of hammers, sickles, cogs, and factories.

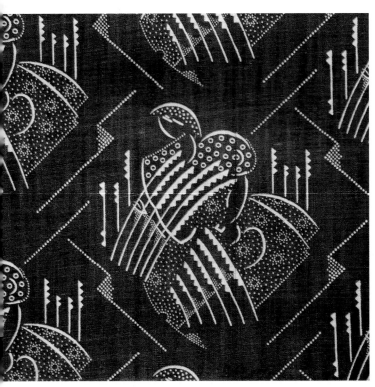

03 | Reaping Women | Russia | *c.* 1920–*c.* 1930 | L. Sillich
Many Soviet thematic patterns were printed only in a single color. Fabrics were chiefly intended for use as dress materials.

05 | Transport | Russia | 1927 | Darya Preobrazhenskaya
Soviet propaganda patterns have a dynamic quality. Preobrazhenskaya's lithograph is a design for a printed dress fabric.

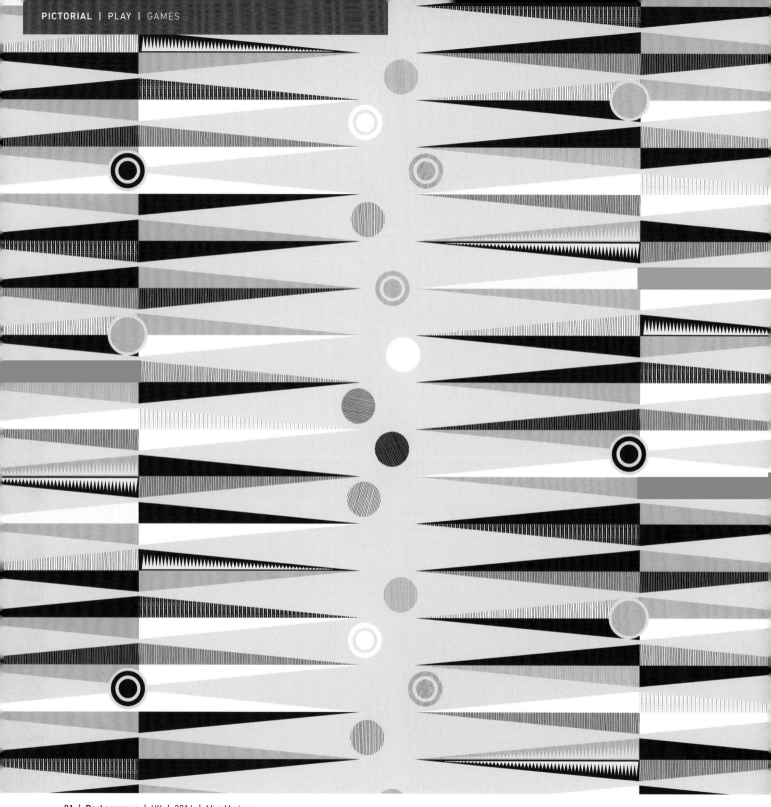

01 | **Backgammon** | **UK** | **2014** | Mini Moderns
Available as a wallpaper and furnishing fabric, this striking design features
an interplay between chevrons and discs.

02 | Marbles | UK | 2002–03 | Eley Kishimoto
Eley Kishimoto's beguiling printed textile referencing the popular small spherical
glass toy has been applied to a wide range of products.

03 | Wallpaper | Belgium | 1910–20
This lively haphazard pattern features playing cards, poker chips, and dice, along
with hearts, spades, clubs, and diamond motifs.

04 | Fun and Games | UK | 1936 | Calico Printers' Association
Colorful party streamers, flags, cards, and paper lanterns are arranged against
a black ground on this printed rayon crêpe dress fabric.

05 | Maison de Jeu (Gambling House) | UK | 2016 | Christian Lacroix
Produced for Designers Guild, this wallpaper and furnishing fabric pattern depicts
vintage French playing cards.

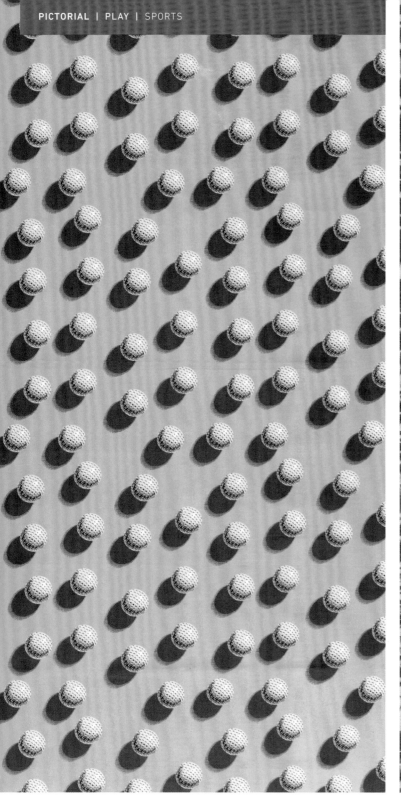

01 | Golf Magic | USA | c. 1953 | Brian Connelly
Produced by Associated American Artists, this printed cotton has a *trompe-l'oeil* pattern featuring dimpled golf balls on an acid yellow ground.

02 | Stadium | USA | 1927 | René Clarke
Produced by Stehli Silks, an innovative textile company, this printed silk crêpe de Chine is part of the groundbreaking Americana Print collection.

03 | Play Ball Two | USA | 1972 | Joe Martin
This screen-printed vinyl wallpaper, manufactured by Piazza Prints, features
a collection of baseballs autographed by major league players.

04 | Textile | Russia | 1920–30
This printed fabric has a lively pattern of figure skaters, with much of the dynamism
of the design coming from its diagonal emphasis.

01 | C60 | UK | 2009 | Mini Moderns
Designed as an homage to the cassette tape, this graphic pattern is available as a wallpaper and a window film.

02 | The Angel with the Trumpet | UK | c. 1884 | Herbert Horne
Horne was an architect, typographer, designer, and poet. This pattern shows clear Arts and Crafts influences.

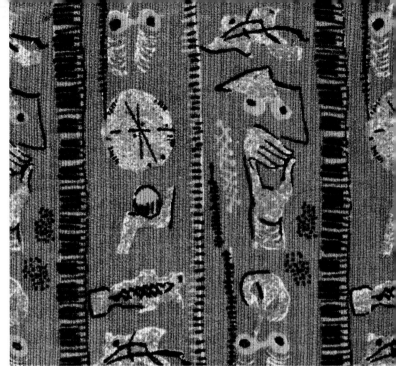

04 | Keyboard | UK | 1945–46 | Henry Moore
Moore's design for a furnishing fabric produced by Ascher Studios was one of many created by leading contemporary artists for the company.

03 | Treasure Trove | USA | 1952 | William Ward Beecher
This printed cotton fabric, produced by Associated American Artists, includes candlesticks, violins, and metronomes among various other treasures.

05 | Pet Sounds | UK | 2008 | Mini Moderns
A guitar neck sprouts a tree where a bird perches, a badger gazes into a trumpet, and a squirrel scampers along a trombone in this whimsical wallpaper pattern.

01 | Opera | UK | 20th century | Joyce Clissold

Clissold was a leading designer for Footprints at Durham Wharf on the River Thames. The company specialized in block-printed textiles.

02 | Last Waltz | UK | 1942

This dress fabric, manufactured by Tootal, Broadhurst, Lee & Co., features a couple waltzing amid streamers and balloons.

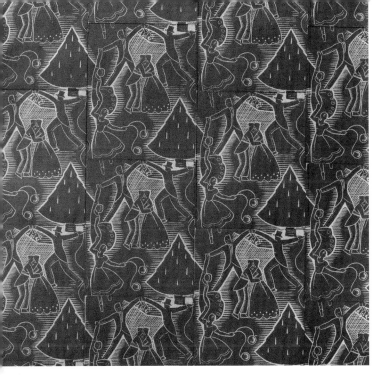

03 | Block print | UK | c. 1920–30 | K. McDonald
This block-printed endpaper features motifs of couples dancing around a tree. A judicious use of white gives a sense of depth.

05 | Fayres Fair | UK | 2008 | Mini Moderns
Stylized carousel horses prance across this appealing wallpaper design. The pattern has a rhythmic musical quality.

04 | Reciprocal Dancers | Austria | 1901 | Koloman Moser
Plate 5 from *Die Quelle: Flächen Schmuck* (*The Source: Ornament for Flat Surfaces*) depicts a swirling Art Nouveau–style pattern of highly abstracted dancers.

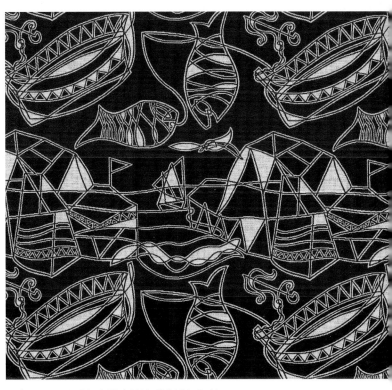

06 | Fisherman's Tale | UK | 1930–40 | Hilda Durkin
Along with Edinburgh Weavers, for which this pattern was produced, Durkin also designed for Heal's and Turnbull & Stockdale.

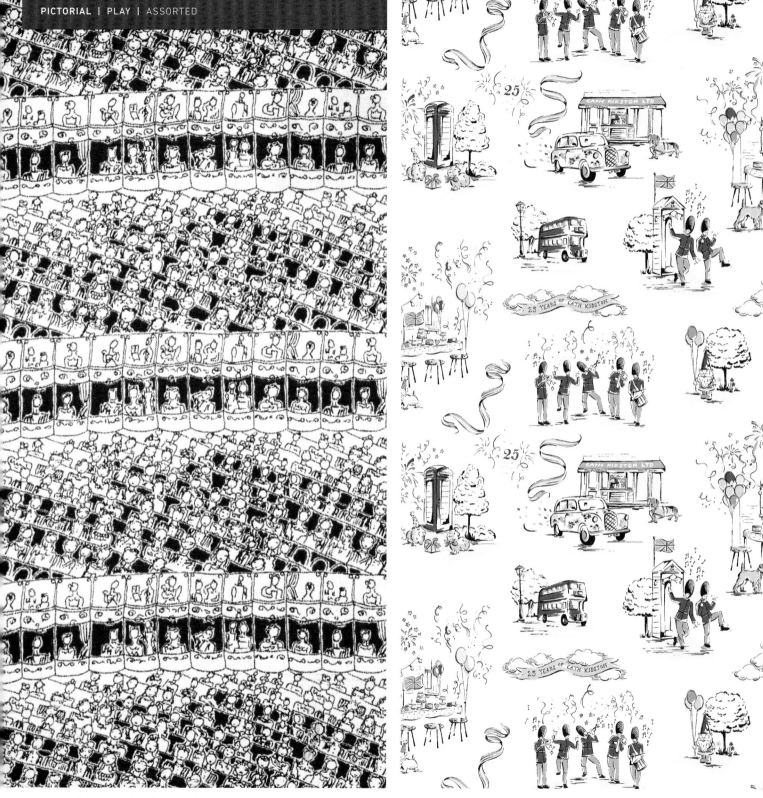

07 | Gala Night | UK | *c.* 1947 | Jacqueline Groag
Groag's dress fabric, with its amusing repeat of a gala night audience seated in the stalls and in boxes, was manufactured by F. W. Grafton & Co. of Manchester.

08 | Big Birthday Party | UK | 2017 | Cath Kidston
Created to mark the brand's 25th birthday, "Big Birthday Party" sees Cath Kidston's iconic Guards celebrating in style at a British street party.

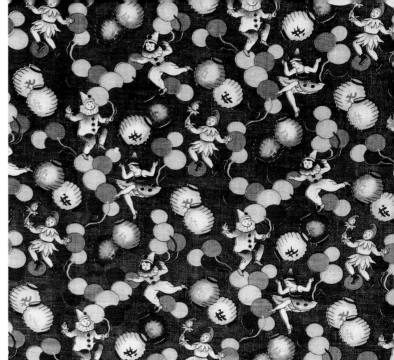

10 | Dress fabric | UK | 1924
This printed cotton fabric features children in fancy dress, lanterns, and balloons. It was made by F. Steiner & Co, which was founded in Lancashire in the 1840s.

09 | Kites and Mites | USA | 1954 | Paul McCobb
McCobb's printed cotton furnishing fabric, made by L. Anton Maix, features an all-over pattern of kite shapes and stick figures.

11 | Paints and Palettes | UK | 1974 | Rae Spencer-Cullen
Manufactured by Squeekers, this vivid printed satin dress fabric has an all-over pattern of paints, palettes, pencils, and squiggles.

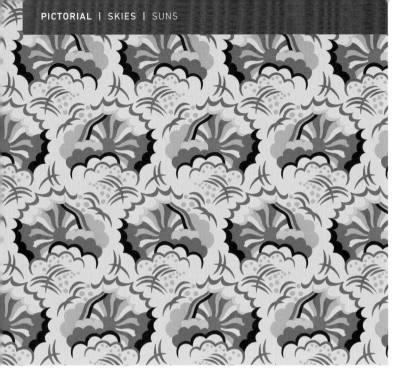

01 | Sunset | UK | 2015 | Sholto Drumlanrig
Drumlanrig designs patterns for a wide range of clients, including Liberty, COS, Lulu Guinness, Royal Doulton, and the Royal Collection.

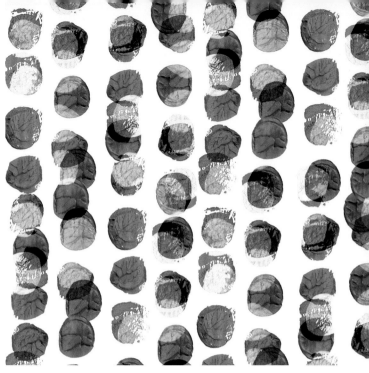

03 | Solar Flare | UK | 2017 | Catherine Worsley
Worsley's mixed-media print features irregular brightly colored blobs that occasionally overlap one another.

02 | Sunburst | UK | 1997 | Neisha Crosland
This pattern, which featured on a silk scarf, echoes one of Crosland's early designs, a star pattern she created for Osborne & Little.

04 | Morn's Rays | USA | 2015 | Michelle Engel Bencsko
Bencsko produced this tightly spaced regular design depicting sunbursts for US textile company Cloud9 Fabrics.

05 | Sunrise | UK | 1969 | Lucienne Day
Day designed the pattern on this roller-printed cotton furnishing fabric for Heal's, the
British firm that produced most of her designs.

06 | Pyramid Sunrise | UK | 2015 | Sholto Drumlanrig
This dense all-over pattern depicts a sunrise over a pyramid through the use
of semicircles and triangles filled in with stripes and diamond shapes.

07 | Birds, Cloud, Sun, Rain | UK | 1938 | Frank Dobson
A pattern with a lively sense of movement, this design for a printed furnishing fabric
portrays birds flying through changeable weather.

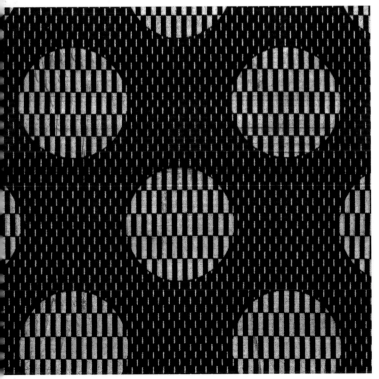

08 | Midnight Sun | France | *c.* 1915 | Herman A. Elsberg
Elsberg was a US collector and textile designer. This silk velvet textile was woven
at his factory in Lyon, France.

09 | Solar | USA | 1974 | Elenhank
Elenhank's screen-printed linen furnishing fabric features a radiating design
of elongated oval shapes.

01 | Clouds | UK | 2014 | Cath Kidston
This pattern features a soft, painterly take on fluffy white clouds. As with most
Cath Kidston prints, it has been applied to everything from bags to homeware.

02 | The Fool | USA | 1970-71 | Marijke Koger

This synthetic dress fabric, with its pattern of white cloud shapes, hints at Koger's
love of psychedelic colors.

04 | **April** | USA | *c.*1927 | Clayton Knight
Produced by Stehli Silks, this silk crêpe de Chine dress fabric is a stylized scene of April showers, complete with rainbows.

03 | **Big Sky** | USA | 1975 | Elenhank
Clouds mass on the horizon in this screen-printed polyester furnishing fabric. Elenhank's later work was inspired by nature.

05 | **Cloud Toile** | UK | 2012 | Timorous Beasties
Available as a wallpaper and as a furnishing fabric, this atmospheric cloud pattern is a modern take on 18th-century French toiles.

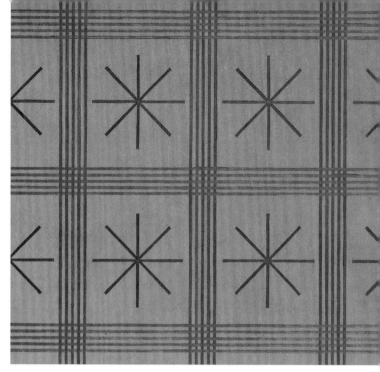

02 | Textile design | USA | 1950–70 | Tommi Parzinger
Bands of five gold lines divide the surface into a grid. At the center of each square is a stylized gold snowflake.

01 | Textile | USA | 1930–39 | Educational Alliance
The Educational Alliance, originally set up in New York in 1920 as a center for Jewish immigrants, ran courses for children in screen-printing and applied arts.

03 | Snowflakes Falling in a Winter Landscape | Japan | 1882
Color woodblock prints such as this were common in Japanese pattern books for kimono design. Unusually, the snowflakes are red.

04 | Wallpaper | USA | 1950
This machine-printed embossed and flocked wallpaper was manufactured
by M. H. Birge & Sons.

05 | Snowflakes | USA | 1952–57 | Charlotte Sternberg
Sternberg's screen-printed cotton fabric, featuring white snowflakes on a gray
ground, was designed for Associated American Artists.

06 | Crystals | USA | 1953 | Janice Hart White
Manufactured by Bassett & Vollum, this screen-printed wallpaper depicts snowflakes
and crystals of varying sizes widely spaced on a white ground.

01 | Air Rave | UK | 2006 | Eley Kishimoto
Eley Kishimoto's patterns, which have been applied across a wide range of products, are naturally eclectic in their sources of inspiration.

02 | Ceiling pattern | UK | 1874 | Christopher Dresser
Dresser's color lithograph depicts a design for a ceiling pattern and appears in his influential book *Studies in Design* (1874), published by Cassell & Co.

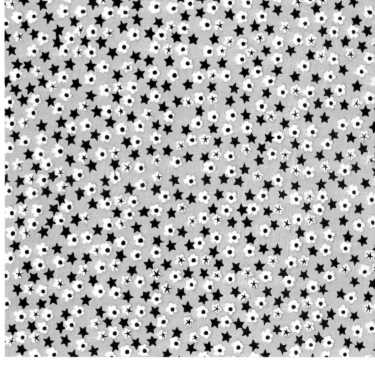

03 | Block print | Japan
This illustration of red stars on a peach background is taken from the Olga Hirsch Collection of Decorated Papers, dating from the 16th century onward.

04 | Star Ikat | UK | 2012 | Ptolemy Mann
British textile artist and designer Mann uses digital printing to produce
contemporary versions of traditional *ikat* patterns.

06 | Star and Stripe | UK | 1945 | Enid Marx
This utility furnishing fabric was produced at a time of materials shortages. The
Utility Design Panel was disbanded in 1952 with the end of rationing.

05 | Dress fabric | USA | 1927 | Helen Wills Moody
Moody was a tennis champion turned designer. This printed crêpe de Chine was
manufactured by Stehli Silks.

07 | Evenstar | USA | 1972 | Wendy Klein
Klein worked at the Larsen Design Studio, which produced this printed cotton design,
with its offset rows of stars.

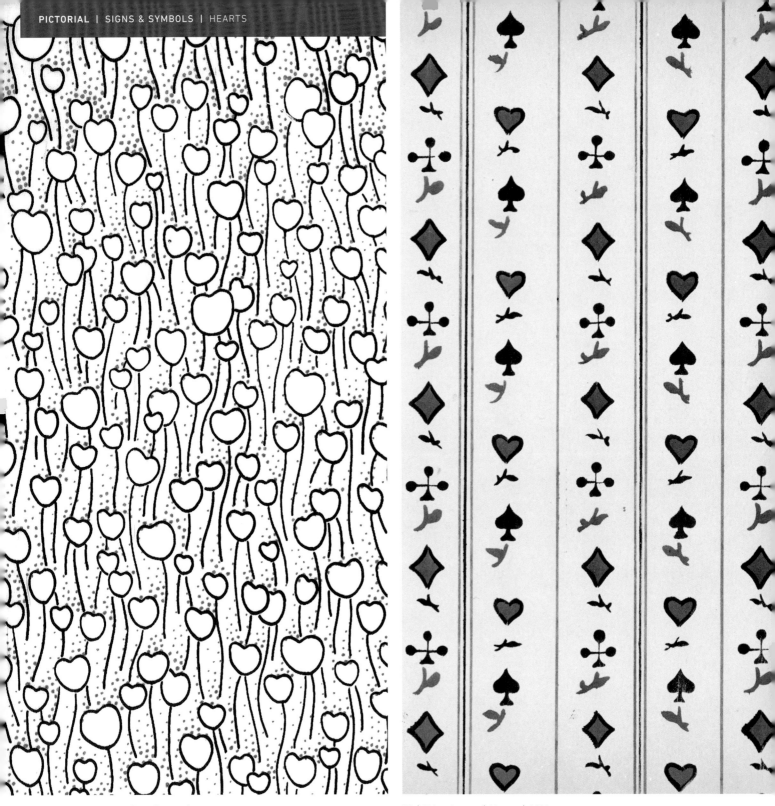

01 | Love Field | UK | 2003 | Eley Kishimoto

This charming pattern portrays love as heart-shaped flowers blooming in a field. Eley Kishimoto use a mixture of analog and digital techniques.

02 | Printed paper | France | 1920

Manufactured by Maison Maunoury et Cie, this machine-printed paper is a sample from *Patria Papiers de Fantaisie* (*Patria Fancy Papers*).

03 | Happy Dreams | UK | 1967 | Natalie Gibson
This printed cotton furnishing fabric, with its psychedelic overtones, was designed for Conran Fabrics.

04 | Love Boat | Netherlands | 2016 | Gabriela Sánchez y Sánchez de la Barquera
De la Barquera is a Mexican-Dutch textile print and jewelry designer based in Eindhoven, the Netherlands. She is a member of the Vlisco design team.

01 | **Alphabet Stripe** | USA | 1953 | Alexander Girard
Girard designed a number of patterns based around the alphabet. In this design,
random characters arranged in horizontal rows read as a texture.

03 | **Pause** | USA | 2004 | 2x4
This wallpaper pattern based around punctuation was designed for Knoll Textiles
by 2x4, a graphic design firm based in New York.

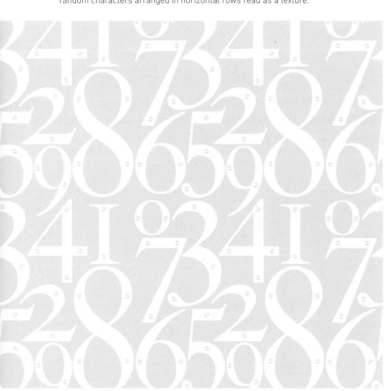

02 | **Knock Knock** | UK | 2006 | Mini Moderns
Mini Moderns' contemporary wallpaper design features an assortment of door
numbers, complete with screw heads.

04 | **Names** | USA | 1957 | Alexander Girard
Girard designed this linen furnishing fabric featuring a pattern based on cursive
script while he was director of design at Herman Miller.

05 | Letters | Denmark | 1955 | Gunnar Aagaard Andersen
This furnishing fabric was produced by Kvadrat and manufactured by Maharam in 2002. Andersen was a Danish artist, designer, and architect.

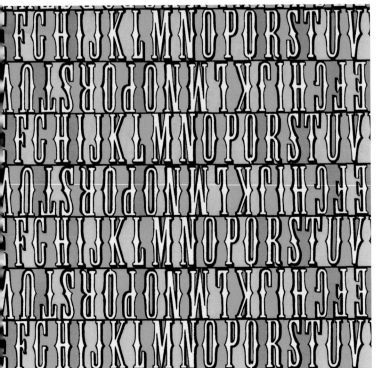

06 | Alpha Omega | USA | 1965–68 | Joe Martin
Produced by Piazza Prints, this screen-printed vinyl wallpaper depicts a random collection of letters in alternating right-side up and upside-down rows.

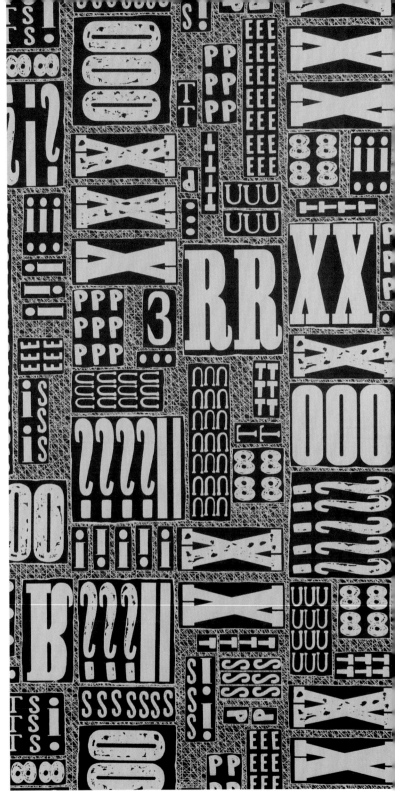

07 | Letter (Boutique) | UK | 2013 | Jocelyn Warner
Reminiscent of the arrangement of letter press blocks in a printer's tray, this large-scale wallpaper has a lively textural effect.

Alexander Girard (1907–93)

SEE PAGES > 120, 145, 147, 248, 330, 349, 351, 364, 416, 420, 427, 433, 570

Initially trained as an architect, Alexander Girard is best known for the textile designs he created for Herman Miller during the 1950s and 1960s, when his work helped to establish the American modern esthetic that emerged in the postwar years. A passionate, life-long collector of folk art, he drew particular inspiration from dolls, toys, textiles, and other artifacts across a range of cultures, especially Mexico. These interests informed his color and pattern sensibilities.

Born in New York to a US mother and French-Italian father, Girard grew up in Florence. In 1917, he was sent to school in England, then studied architecture at the Architectural Association in London between 1924 and 1929. After further architectural studies in Stockholm and Rome, he returned to the United States in the early 1930s, moving to Detroit in 1937 to work for an interior design studio. A commission to redesign the canteen for radio manufacturer Detrola in 1943 led to him becoming chief designer for the company in 1945. He also established friendships with Charles (1907–78) and Ray Eames (1912–88; see p. 308) and Eero Saarinen (1910–61), leading figures at the nearby Cranbrook Academy of Art.

In 1951, George Nelson (1908–86) appointed Girard head of the textiles department at Herman Miller, the furniture company that produced many designs by Eames, Saarinen, Nelson, and other US modernists. Girard's textiles, which were eventually to number some 300 different patterns, were used as upholstery, drapes, and wall panels.

Early designs for fabric reflected Girard's architectural training and featured geometric motifs, such as the pattern "Rain" (1953), composed of overlapping triangles in brown, black, and yellow. Many of his designs also depicted buildings executed in colored line, as well as graphic elements, symbols, and letters, of which "Alphabet" (1960) is an early example. As his work progressed, the folk art influence became more apparent, and doll-like figures became recurring motifs. Girard's vibrantly colored "Mexidot" and "Mexistripe" patterns evolved during a collaboration with a traditional Mexican cotton mill. Many of his fabrics were made by Maharam, a leading North American textile company.

Independent of his work for Herman Miller, Girard also designed corporate identities and environments. In 1960, he designed the interior and overall theme of La Fonda del Sol restaurant in Manhattan's Time-Life Building, a visual concept based around sun motifs that extended to menus, matchbooks, and wall tiles. Similarly, in 1965, his rebranding work for Braniff International Airways gave him immense scope. The project, based around the central idea of "the end of the plain plane," saw him design every detail, from plane liveries to sugar packets.

Top Alexander Girard selecting works for the "Own Your Own" exhibition in 1963.

Above The Detroit home of Girard and his wife, photographed for *Vogue* in 1950, is a classic mid-century modern open-plan interior, complete with picture window.

Opposite Girard designed furnishing fabrics for Herman Miller between 1952, when the company first launched its textile division, and 1973. This graphic design, "Alphabet" (1960), is a dense repeat of random letters, numbers, and symbols.

CKUY67DX9CKUY
R3MOT2V5LR3M
&FSPBJ8NC&FS
ZQ1WAH4EIZQ1W
CKUY67DX9CKUY
R3MOT2V5LR3M
&FSPBJ8NC&FS
ZQ1WAH4EIZQ1W
CKUY67DX9CKUY
R3MOT2V5LR3M
&FSPBJ8NC&FS
ZQ1WAH4EIZQ1W
CKUY67DX9CKUY
R3MOT2V5LR3M

Although representations of living creatures are rare in Islamic art, writing is not. This reflects the central importance of the written text in Islam. Arabic calligraphy is a common decorative feature of Islamic tiles, other ceramics, and metalwork, where it typically spells out prayers, sacred names, passages from the Koran, or lines of poetry. Over the centuries, Arabic scripts have evolved from the angular Kufic, to the more familiar curved *thuluth* form in common use today.

Kufic script originated in the 8th century and is the oldest form of Arabic script. It is named for Kufa, Iran, where it is believed to have been developed. Kufic went out of general use in the 12th century, although it continued to be employed as a decorative element. A distinctive variant known as "squared Kufic" can be seen on many panels of decorative tilework, particularly in mosques, and resembles Greek key motifs or maze-like patterns. By contrast, *thuluth*, which was developed from the 15th to the 19th centuries, is a cursive, flowing script that was first used to write sura headings, religious inscriptions, and princely titles and epigraphs.

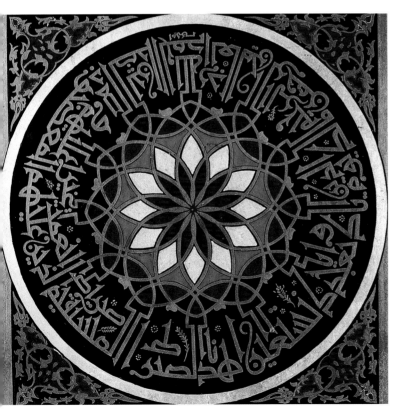

02 | The Fleur-de-lis | 1875
This block-printed wallpaper features the fleur-de-lis motif in a diaper pattern. The symbol represents a stylized lily.

01 | Tudor Rose and Fleur-de-lis | UK | 1848–60 | Augustus Pugin
Pugin's pattern features alternating crowned fleur-de-lis and Tudor roses. Both motifs are heraldic devices of various English monarchs.

03 | Textile | France | c. 1925 | Herman A. Elsberg
Elsberg's woven silk furnishing fabric has an all-over fleur-de-lis pattern connected with serpentine lines.

04 | Ceiling paper | USA | 1907–08
Manufactured by S. A. Maxwell & Co., this machine-printed wallpaper was designed to stand in for plasterwork decoration on the ceiling.

06 | Wallpaper | France | c. 1850
Although the fleur-de-lis has appeared on coats-of-arms in many European countries, it is especially associated with France.

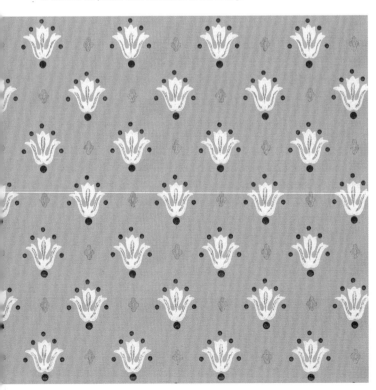

05 | Wallpaper | USA | 1950
Made by M. H. Birge & Sons, this embossed flocked wallpaper has a diaper pattern. The origin of the fleur-de-lis symbol is unknown.

07 | Apparel for an Alb | UK | c. 1845–50 | Augustus Pugin
Pugin was a convert to Catholicism. This fabric, made of colored silk on gold, was designed for St. Augustine's Abbey in Ramsgate, Kent. An alb is a liturgical vestment.

ABSTRACT

01 | Breakwater | UK | 2011 | Christopher Farr

Available as a wallpaper and as a printed linen furnishing fabric, this loose painterly
design features a pattern of overlapping brushstrokes.

02 | Impasto | UK | 2017 | Designers Guild

This small-scale wallpaper pattern, with its subtle marks and dabs of color, has the
textural effect of old distressed walls.

03 | Painter | UK | 2015 | Kangan Arora

This screen-printed linen union furnishing fabric features a bold design of free, broad
brushstrokes. Arora grew up in India; her work celebrates color and abstract pattern.

04 | Salvage | UK | 2011 | Cole & Son

This mottled textural wallpaper design features soft colors reminiscent of stripped
wall surfaces and tarnished metal.

Modernism (late 19th – mid-20th centuries)

Modernism had its roots in several different progressive European art and design movements. Associations of artists, designers, and architects, such as the Deutscher Werkbund (German Association of Craftsmen), De Stijl (The Style) in the Netherlands, and the Constructivists in Russia were precursors of the modern movement that emerged in the 1920s.

A key notion of modernism was "form follows function." Taking inspiration from products of the machine age, such as the airplane, modernist architects and designers adopted a rationalist approach. "A house is a machine for living in," said Swiss-French architect and designer Le Corbusier (1887–1965), meaning that it should be designed to facilitate activities such as cooking, bathing, and eating. Architectural detailing, like cornicing and skirting boards with little practical purpose, was removed.

There had been a growing rejection of ornamentation in design from the start of the 20th century due to the influence of the Arts and Crafts movement, with its focus on the honest expression of construction. Austrian architect Adolf Loos's (1870–1933) controversial manifesto *Ornament and Crime* (1913), German architect and designer Peter Behrens's (1868–1940) statement "less is more," which was adopted and made famous by German-American architect Ludwig Mies van der Rohe (1886–1969), and the emphasis on simplicity and geometric form promoted by De Stijl, inspired a move away from surface decoration and embellishment toward smooth planes and clean lines.

By the time of the Bauhaus, the radical school founded in Weimar in 1919, there was a shift toward rationalism among the design avant-garde. Yet neither pattern nor color went away. Anni Albers (1899–1994; see p. 362) and Gunta Stölzl (1897–1983; see p. 626) were active in the textile department, creating woven and printed fabrics that were vibrant rhythmic exercises in geometric composition. Influenced by the teachings of Paul Klee, who believed that weaving was similar to music, Albers introduced a dynamic quality to her designs. Few Bauhaus textiles, however, were put into mass production.

A cross-fertilization occurred between modern art movements like Cubism and pattern design. Artists Sonia Delaunay (1885–1979; see p. 338) and Vanessa Bell (1879–1961; see p. 588) produced dazzling abstract patterns between the two world wars. The adoption of screen printing by the British textile industry made short runs of adventurous designs cost-effective and so brought a modernist esthetic within reach of a wider public. Enid Marx (1902–98; see p. 442) and Marion Dorn (1896–1964; see p. 228) created textile patterns for seating on London buses and tube trains that brought abstract, geometric design to the masses.

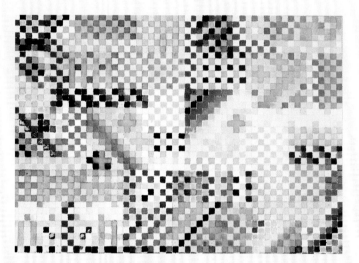

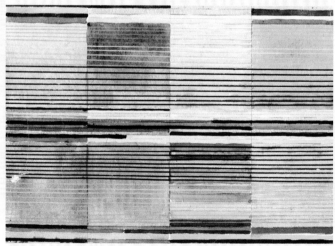

Top A working design for a woven carpet (*c.* 1927) by Gunta Stölzl.

Above A design for a wall hanging (*c.* 1928) by Stölzl. Under Stölzl's direction, the weaving workshop at the Bauhaus in Dessau became one of its most successful departments. While modernists eschewed representational patterns, their vivid geometric designs were vibrant and dynamic.

Opposite *Composition* (1917–18) by Theo van Doesburg (1883–1931). A Dutch artist, designer, architect, and poet, van Doesburg was most famous as a co-founder of the avant-garde movement De Stijl. Although Walter Gropius (1833–1969) refused to allow him to become a Bauhaus master, he taught the school's students for a time.

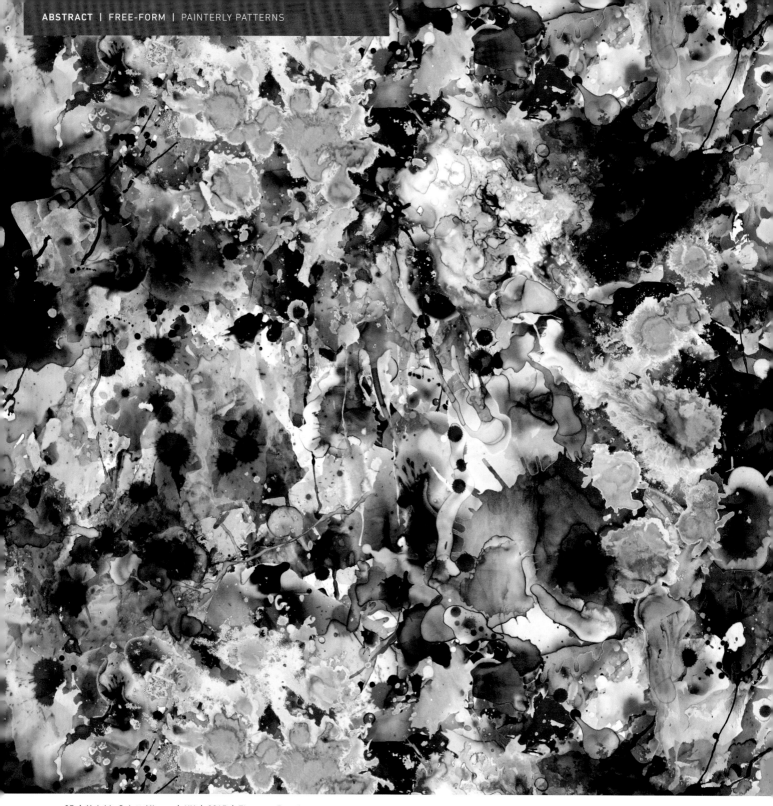

05 | Kaleido Splatt Allover | UK | 2015 | Timorous Beasties

This exuberant design, available both as a wallpaper and furnishing fabric, is
patterned with abstract blotches and splodges of water-based inks and body color.

06 | **Furnishing fabric** | UK | *c.* 1933 | Calico Printers' Association
The Manchester-based Calico Printers' Association comprised a number of different printworks and was founded to produce cheap fabric for export.

08 | **Speckled** | USA | 2016 | Holly DeGroot
Designed for Cloud9 Fabrics, a company set up to supply fabric for the home sewing market, this speckled pattern has a light airy quality.

07 | **Printed design** | UK | 2014 | Rebecca Hoyes, First Eleven Studio
Produced for First Eleven Studio, this printed design in indigo is reminiscent of the abstract patterning of traditional *ikat* fabrics.

09 | **Raindrop Flowers** | UK | 2017 | Jenny Frean
Hovering on the border between representational and abstract, this floral printed design has a feeling of freshness.

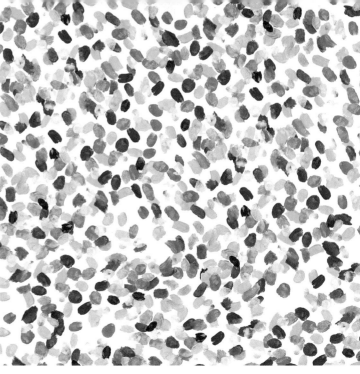

10 | Watermarks | UK | 2016 | Catherine Worsley
Yorkshire-born Worsley trained in graphic design and illustration before specializing in bold colorful pattern design.

12 | Orange Orchard | Australia | 2017 | Marni Stuart
Stuart is a textile designer and design lecturer. All her patterns originate as handmade artworks using a diverse range of media.

11 | Ormeggio (Mooring) | Italy | 1954
This printed cotton furnishing fabric has all the hallmarks of mid-century modern pattern design, with its abstract umbrella-like motifs.

13 | Paint Blobs | UK | 2017 | Marni Stuart
Stuart's balanced abstract pattern features overlapping dabs of color offset by generous amounts of white space.

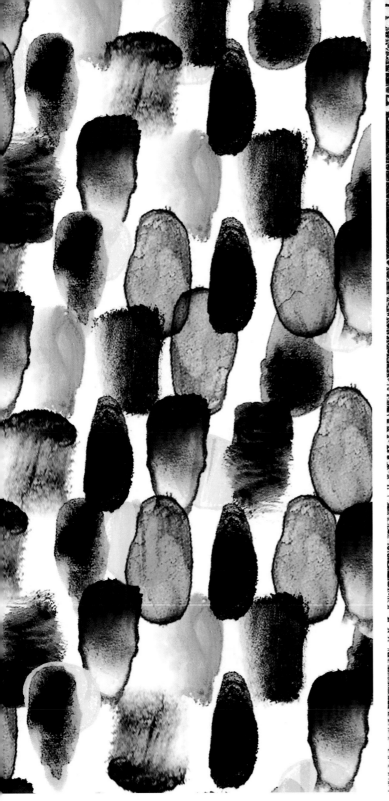

14 | Sea Glass | UK | 2016 | Catherine Worsley
Reminiscent of fragments of colored glass worn smooth by the sea, or of fingerprints, this pattern features luminous shades of blue, green, and yellow.

15 | Paper | UK | 19th century
Marbling is a technique of creating decorative patterns on paper. Each design is unique. Marbled papers are often used in bookbinding and as endpapers.

Vanessa Bell (1879–1961) | Duncan Grant (1885–1978)

SEE PAGES > 96, 623, 625

Vanessa Bell and Duncan Grant, key members of the Bloomsbury Group, a freethinking circle of artists, intellectuals, and writers that flourished in London between the world wars, are best known for their paintings and for the transformation of their rural retreat, Charleston, into a masterpiece of applied decorative art. But both were also significant designers, producing many textile patterns for the artist-led collective Omega Workshops, founded in 1913.

Vanessa, the elder sister of the novelist Virginia Woolf, was born Vanessa Stephen into a wealthy London family and educated at home. From an early age, she was interested in drawing and attended Arthur Cope's art school in South Kensington in 1896 before going on to study painting at the Royal Academy in 1901. After the death of her parents, she sold the family home in Hyde Park Gate and moved with her siblings to Gordon Square in Bloomsbury. What would later be termed the Bloomsbury Group began there in Thursday evening meetings. In 1906, Vanessa set up the Friday Club, a painting salon, and she married art critic Clive Bell in 1907.

Duncan, who came from an impoverished military background, had a varied upbringing, which was partly spent in India and Burma and partly at boarding schools in Rugby and London. He attended Westminster School of Art between 1902 and 1905, spent the following year studying art in Paris, and attended the Slade for a term in 1908.

Vanessa and Duncan met in 1905 and were both influenced by the art critic Roger Fry's "Manet and the Post-Impressionists" exhibition, which he put on at the Grafton Galleries in 1910. When Fry founded the Omega Workshops in Fitzroy Square, London, both Vanessa and Duncan produced work for it. The collective was intended to dissolve the conventional boundaries between decorative and fine art. In addition to painted furniture, stained glass, and mosaics, Omega produced furnishing fabrics. Bell and Grant's bold, painterly textile designs were sought after by an avant-garde clientele. Many were also later produced as dress fabrics. Omega, however, closed in 1919 because of financial difficulties.

Clive and Vanessa Bell had an open marriage, and both had other lovers. Grant was homosexual, which did not prevent Vanessa from falling in love with him and eventually having a daughter by him. In 1916, Clive, Vanessa, Duncan, and his lover David Garnett went to live at Charleston in Sussex, chiefly so that the young men could escape conscription by working on the land. Over the years, this unusual menage, aided by many visiting Bloomsbury Group members, transformed the farmhouse into a living work of art, every surface patterned and painted in a vivid exuberant expression of art for art's sake.

Top Members of the Bloomsbury Group at Charleston in c. 1920. Vanessa Bell cuts writer Lytton Strachey's hair while (left to right) Roger Fry, Clive Bell, Duncan Grant, and an unidentified guest look on.

Above This watercolor dating from the early 1940s is a fabric design by Bell.

Opposite Created for the Omega Workshops design collective in 1913, this printed linen furnishing fabric, "White," was designed by Bell. Like many of Bell and Grant's designs, it displays Fauvist and Cubist colors and shapes. The irregular painterly splodges of red and ocher are arranged randomly across a white ground crisscrossed by hatching. "White" was possibly named after the suffragette Amber Blanco-White,

The Japanese decorative technique of marbling is known as *suminagashi* and originated in the 12th century. It is a method of creating dappled, mottled, or spattered patterns that bear a close resemblance to the grain of marble, granite, and other types of stone. It is thought to have spread to Turkey, from where it reached the West in the 17th century. The art became popular in the 19th century after Charles W. Woolnough published *The Art of Marbling* (1853), in which he describes how he adapted a method of marbling onto book cloth. Marbling is typically applied to sheets of paper for use as book covers and endpapers. Each marbled pattern is unique.

Methods of marbling vary. Commonly, a shallow tray is filled with a sized liquid containing powdered seaweed and other chemicals. Pigments are then dropped onto the surface of the liquid, which naturally prevents the colors from running into one another. Subsequently, the colors are raked, feathered, combed, or brushed to create intricate swirling patterns. A prepared sheet of paper is laid across the surface to transfer the pattern, then lifted off and dried.

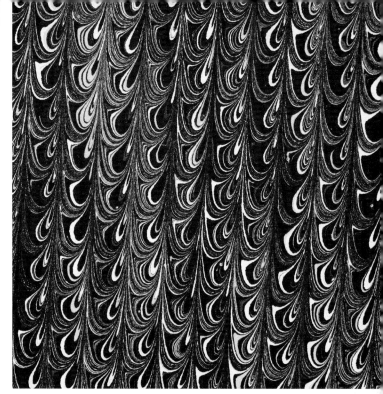

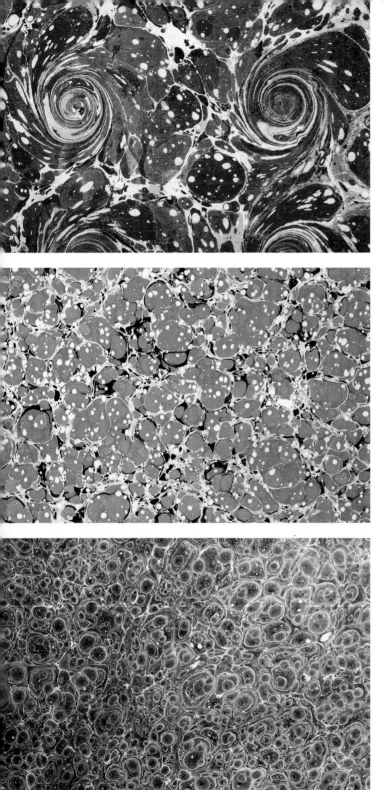
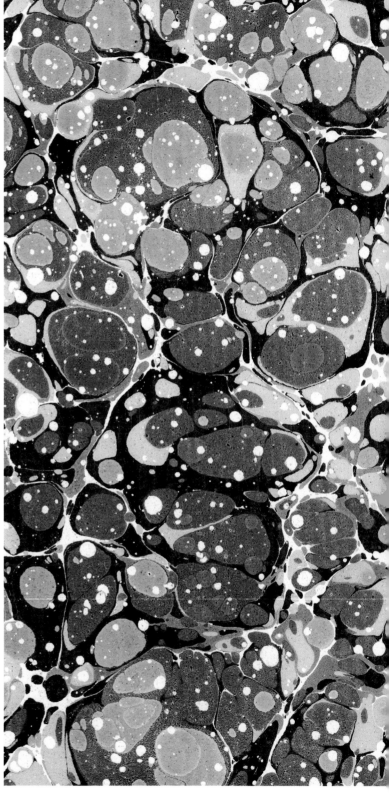

Shibori is a method of Japanese resist-dyeing used to create patterns on fabric. Dating to the 8th century, it comprises a range of techniques that can be used singly or in combination to create more intricate designs. Traditionally, *shibori* patterns were executed using indigo and, to a lesser extent, madder; fabrics were silk, hemp, and cotton.

At its most basic, *shibori* involves tying or binding sections of fabric to create a resist before dyeing: this method is familiar in the West as tie-dye (see p. 594). In Japan, thread is traditionally used for binding.

Other variants involve braiding and binding the fabric before dyeing; using a hook to pluck up small sections of fabric, then binding them with unknotted thread, which gives a watery effect; stitching sections of cloth and pulling the stitching tight; winding the cloth diagonally around a pole, then wrapping it in thread; and binding the cloth between solid shapes. Each method is chosen to work with the type of cloth used and to achieve a particular type of pattern. Sometimes techniques are used together to obtain an elaborate effect.

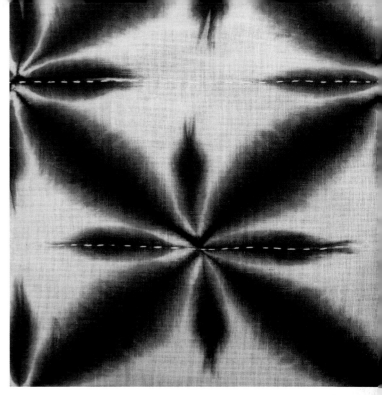

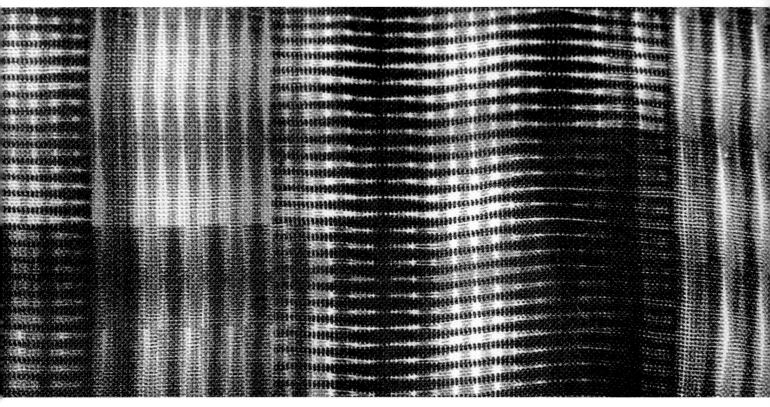

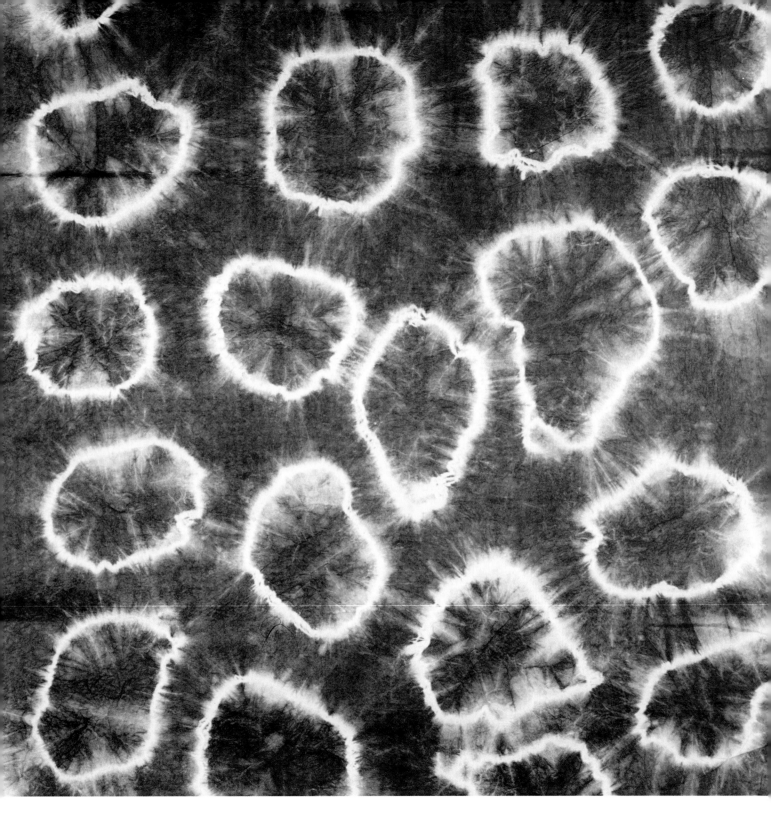

Resist-dyeing has been practiced for centuries and in countries all around the world; the earliest examples of resist-dyed fabric, dating from as early as 500 CE, are thought to be Peruvian. In the West, however, tie-dye was a term that came into widespread use in the United States during the 1960s and 1970s, when it was adopted by the flower children of California and rock singers such as Janis Joplin and the founder of The Lovin' Spoonful, John Sebastian. Tie-dye became strongly associated with the hippy movement, psychedelia, and counterculture in general.

Western tie-dye produced during this period was characterized by simple shapes such as concentric circles or spirals and brilliant primary colors, often used together in the same design. Cheap fast dyes suitable for use by amateurs helped to popularize the technique: many tie-dye designs were homemade, with elastic bands or string employed to create the resist. While the typical tie-dye mass-market product was the cotton T-shirt, upmarket designers also created tie-dye silk, velvet, and chiffon.

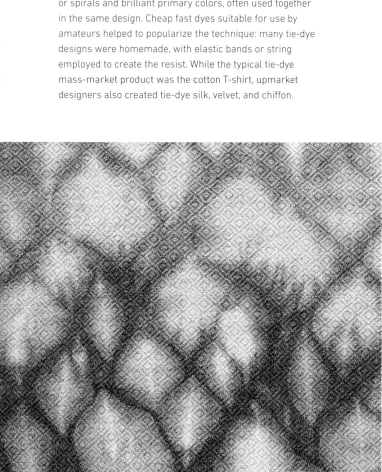

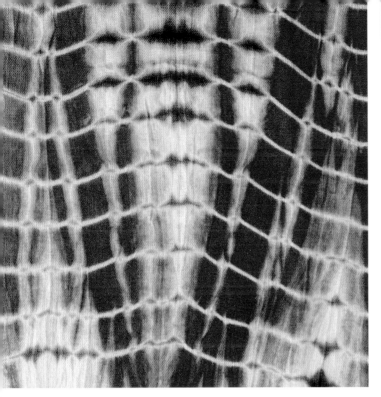

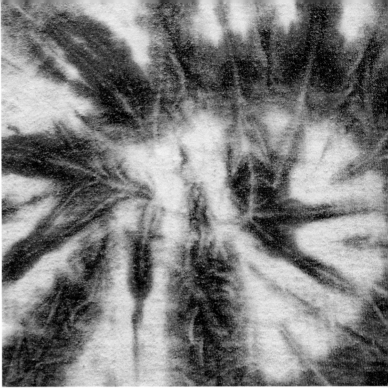

Plangi or *pelangi* is a form of tie-dyeing that has been practised for centuries in Indonesia. The term means "rainbow": vibrant multicolored patterns are typical of *plangi*-dyed cloths. So, too, are complex geometric designs, which are produced in Sumatra, Java, and Bali, among other Indonesian islands, where representational patterning is prohibited under the laws of Islam. A traditional product that features this type of patterning is the Sumatran s*lendang*, or silk shoulder wrap, decorated with resist-dyeing and resist-stitching. Most dramatic are the lozenges and squares of Balinese *plangi* cloths, which are bold and simple in design.

A variant method is known as *tritik*, a Javanese term meaning "water drops." Here, the areas of resist are stitched using strong thread or even plastic, which is then pulled tight. This creates a mirror-image effect resembling small water drops forming lines across the cloth. *Tritik* is often combined with other tie-dyeing methods, with the white dotted lines separating areas of strong color.

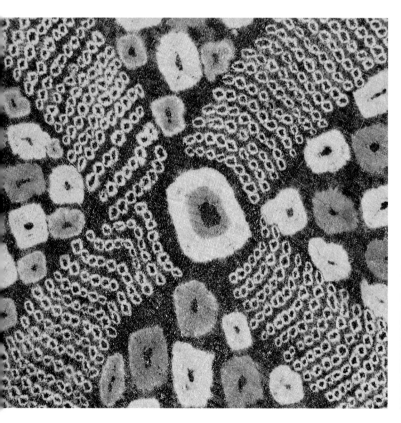

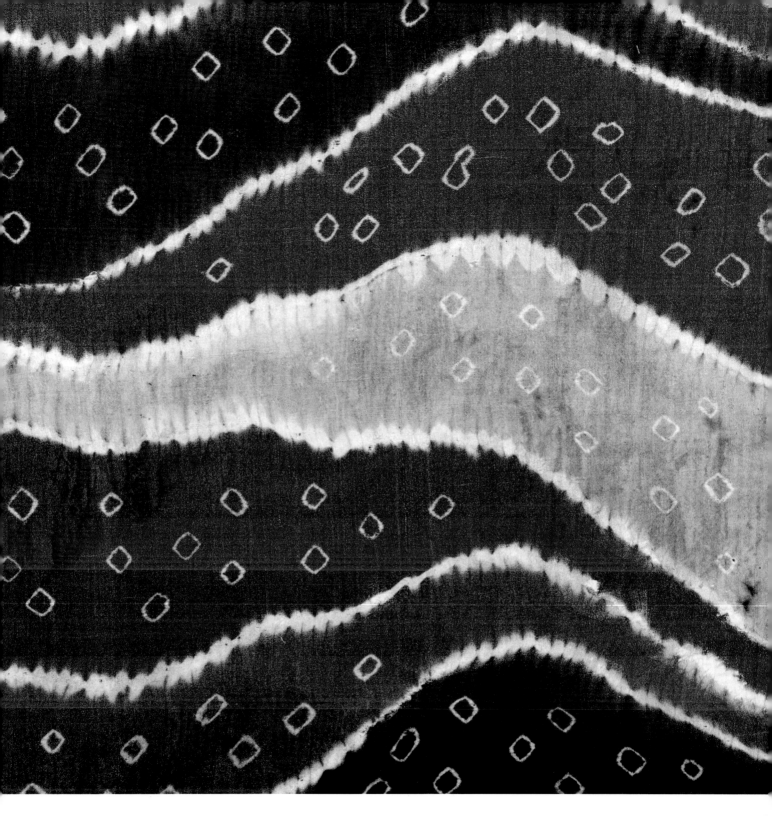

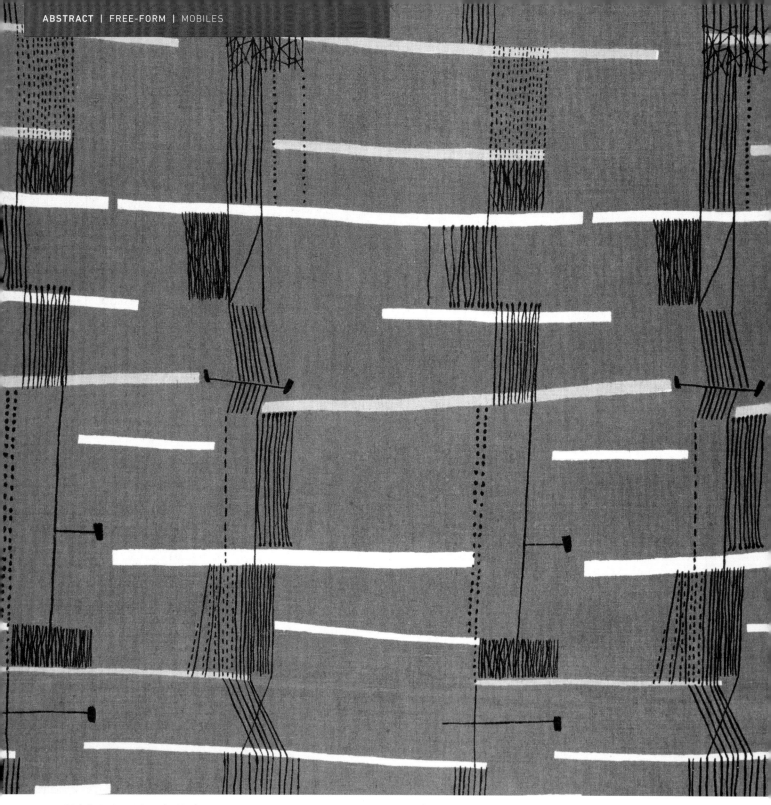

01 | Springboard | UK | 1954 | Lucienne Day

Postwar textile designers explored a new visual vocabulary, drawn from
contemporary art, for example the mobiles created by US artist Alexander Calder.

02 | Raimoult | UK | 1954 | Robert Stewart
Stewart designed this screen-printed linen and cotton furnishing fabric for Liberty.
During the 1950s, he was Liberty's most prolific designer.

03 | Flotilla | UK | 1952 | Lucienne Day
This screen-printed rayon furnishing fabric was produced for Heal's. Day created
many inventive designs for Heal's during the 1950s.

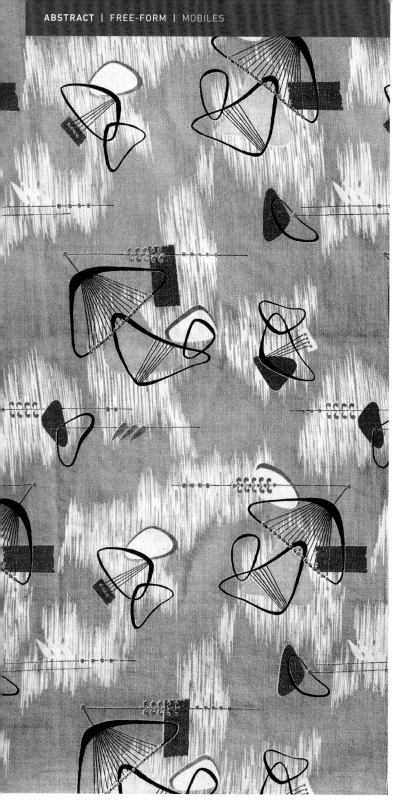

05 | Treehouse | UK | 2008 | Alice Stevenson
Stevenson's screen-printed linen union furnishing fabric was designed for St. Jude's.
Her work includes book jackets, illustration, stationery and packaging.

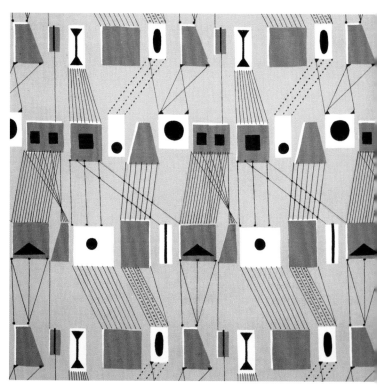

04 | Furnishing fabric | unknown | 1950s
The curved boomerang-type shapes are typical of patterns inspired by the mobiles
of US artist Alexander Calder, with their suspension of organic forms in space.

06 | Rig | UK | 1953 | Lucienne Day
Day was inspired by contemporary artists such as Paul Klee and Joan Miró. This
printed linen furnishing fabric was designed for Heal's.

07 | **Espace** | Germany | 1954 | Elsbeth Kupferoth
This screen-printed furnishing fabric was designed for the German firm Pausa,
founded in Mössingen, West Germany in 1911.

Lucienne Day (1917–2010)

SEE PAGES > 69, 108, 124, 172, 351, 499, 503, 518, 559, 598, 599, 600, 609, 613, 624, 644

One of the leading British pattern designers of the 20th century, Lucienne Day enjoyed a critically and commercially successful career that spanned more than sixty years. Her patterns, applied to textiles first and foremost, but also to carpets, wallpaper, ceramics, table linen, and dish towels, transformed traditional English natural plant-based motifs into fresh contemporary designs that echoed themes in modern art and expressed the optimistic progressive mood of the immediate postwar period.

Born Désirée Lucienne Conradi to an English mother and a Belgian father, Day grew up in south London, where she was educated at a convent school. From there she went on to study at Croydon School of Art, before attending the Royal College of Art from 1937 to 1940, where she specialized in textile design. During her final year at the Royal College, she met her future husband, Robin Day (1915–2010); their long creative life together was not so much a joint endeavor to a shared end as a parallel exploration along similar independent lines.

After World War II, a new generation of young designers was eager to make its mark, and Lucienne was among them. She found inspiration in the imagery, rhythms, and colors of the abstract paintings of Paul Klee and Joan Miró. After designing a number of dress fabrics, she shifted her attention to furnishing textiles, which offered the potential for reaching a wider public. That opportunity arrived with the Festival of Britain in 1951. The festival was a celebration of progressive national spirit at a time when rationing was still in place, widespread bomb damage was evident, and industrial materials were in short supply. "Calyx" (1951), the first of Lucienne's patterns to bring her widespread acclaim, was created for a contemporary dining room in the Homes and Gardens Pavilion, a setting designed by Robin and that featured his molded plywood furniture. The screen-printed fabric was manufactured by Heal's, although the firm was initially skeptical of its radical departure from traditional floral prints. "Calyx" went on to win a gold medal at the Milan Triennale and the prestigious International Design Award of the American Institute of Decorators; equally telling, it was a popular success. Lucienne continued to collaborate with Heal's for twenty years.

In subsequent decades, she designed for many other manufacturers, both in Britain and abroad, including Edinburgh Weavers, Royal Wilton, Crown, and Rosenthal. Aside from highly stylized natural forms, she also experimented with typographical prints and pure abstracts. Lucienne and Robin were design consultants to John Lewis from 1962 to 1987. In 1987, she became the first female Master of the Royal Designers for Industry.

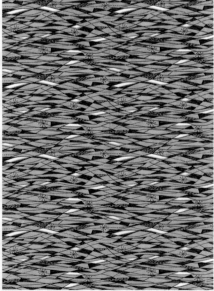

Far Left Lucienne Day with her husband Robin, a noted furniture designer.

Left This furnishing fabric, "Acres," was designed by Lucienne in 1952.

Opposite Lucienne designed the Calderesque "Perpetua" furnishing fabric in 1953 for British Celanese.

Memphis, the leading design group associated with Postmodernism (see p. 606), was launched in Italy in the early 1980s. It was influenced by Studio Alchimia, headed by the designer Alessandro Mendini, who rejected the minimalist approach of early 20th-century modernism and sought to reawaken an interest in decoration and pattern. In this he took inspiration from a range of sources, including 19th-century dress fabrics; a compendium of such designs was published in the "Decorattivo" (1976) series.

Based in Milan, Memphis comprised an influential group of designers, which included Italian architect and designer Ettore Sottsass, French painter Nathalie du Pasquier, and British designer George J. Sowden. Sottsass's most famous pattern, "Bacterio" (1978), was designed to be used on a plastic laminate, and later appeared on his furniture. Like Sottsass, Sowden was interested in the way the application of pattern could enrich products, whereas Du Pasquier's hectic textile patterns drew inspiration from sources as diverse as rock music, African textiles, and cartoons.

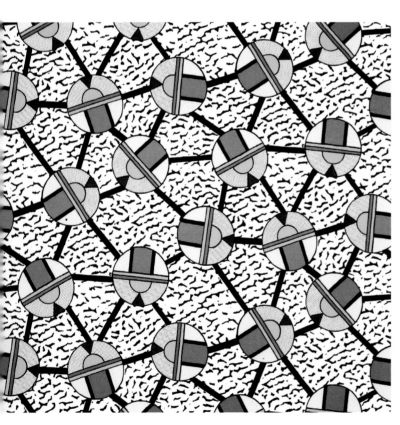

Postmodernism (mid- to late 20th century)

Originating in the field of architecture in the late 1970s, Postmodernism began as a backlash against modernism, which had become a sterile cul-de-sac, resulting in bland, uniformly conceived buildings that did not respond to their sites or express the diversity of the cultures in which they existed. From architecture, the Postmodern movement spread rapidly to art, design, literature, film, music, graphics, and fashion.

By the 1980s, consumerism was aided and abetted by sophisticated branding and marketing campaigns. Postmodernists working in various disciplines both critiqued this aspect of contemporary culture and participated in it. Sampling and bricolage were used to create new work out of a diverse range of elements. Parody, wit, humor, and subversion were evident in the work of artists such as Keith Haring (1958–90), whose cartoonlike figures and barking dogs brought the street to the art world. Haring produced a number of patterns for fabric, including "USA" (1988).

The design group most strongly identified with Postmodernism, and which was responsible for many of its most famous products and patterns, was the Memphis Group. A Milan-based association of designers loosely grouped around the Italian Ettore Sottsass (1917–2007), Memphis founders included the French painter Nathalie Du Pasquier (b.1957) and British product designer George J. Sowden (b.1942). Studio Alchimia, led by Alessandro Mendini (b.1931), was another Milan group that devised influential Postmodern projects. Just as Postmodernist architects challenged the supremacy of modernism by quoting from historical styles, Postmodernist designers questioned notions of value, practicality, and good taste. Sottsass's Carlton room divider (1981) has sloping shelves which seem to disregard its function and is made from cheap processed wood covered with bright plastic laminate.

The style unleashed a taste for decoration. Patterned surfaces became fashionable. Sottsass designed many patterns for Memphis; the "Bacterio" pattern that covers the base of the Carlton divider was first produced for Studio Alchimia in 1978. Du Pasquier, another prolific Memphis pattern designer, produced Postmodern patterns for American Apparel and Wrong for Hay, a branch of Hay, a Danish interiors company.

Postmodern patterns were typically bright and featured clashing primary colors, eye-popping fluorescents, and neon shades. Geometric shapes, squiggles, flashes and zigzags, and mottled designs that replicated the effect of plastic laminate brought a new focus of attention to the surface.

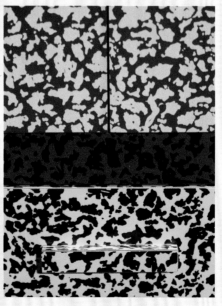

Far Left Digital illustration (2015) by Japanese artist Yoko Honda (b.1984) inspired by a Memphis pattern.

Left A detail of the Casablanca sideboard, designed by Ettore Sottsass for the Memphis Group in 1981.

Opposite The Poltrono di Proust (1981) hand-painted chair by Alessandro Mendini.

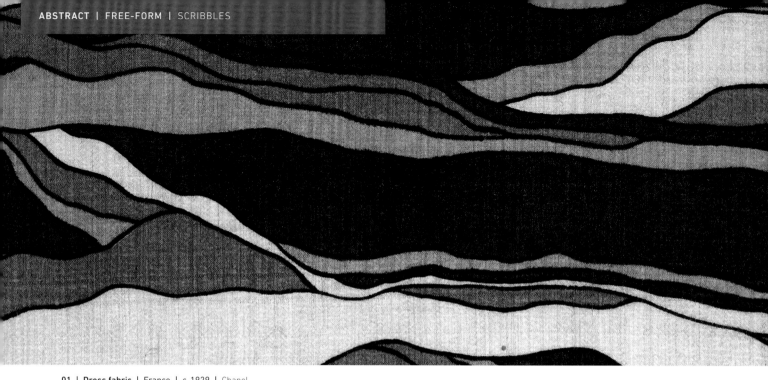

01 | Dress fabric | France | c. 1929 | Chanel
This wool and silk dress fabric with an undulating pattern was produced for the well-known French couturier Coco Chanel.

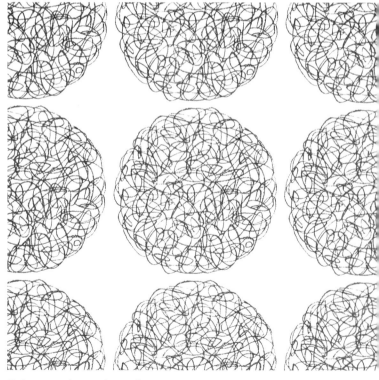

02 | Scribble | UK | 2012 | Orla Kiely
Kiely's finely crosshatched wallpaper pattern has an appealing hand-drawn quality. The effect is textural, akin to hessian or other open weaves.

03 | Basketry | Japan | 2002 | Reiko Sudo
Sudo's flock-printed cotton dress fabric was designed for leading Japanese firm Nuno and comes in three subtle colors.

04 | Graphica | UK | 1953 | Lucienne Day
This screen-printed furnishing fabric for Heal's, reminiscent of buzzing electricity pylons, was one of Day's own personal favorites.

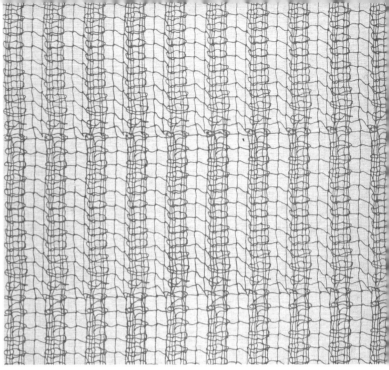

06 | Fishnet | USA | 1954 | Ben Rose
Fine lines produce a fishnet-like pattern, with vertical columns alternating in density. Rose was a leading designer and textile producer in the 1950s and 1960s.

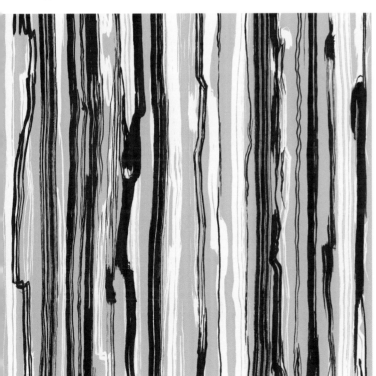

05 | Strand | UK | 2016 | Cole & Son
This dramatic wallpaper pattern features alternating metallic and matt vertical ribbons or irregular brushmarks.

07 | Mirage | UK | 1954 | Robert Stewart
Stewart created this spiky vertically structured pattern for a screen-printed linen and cotton furnishing fabric produced by Liberty.

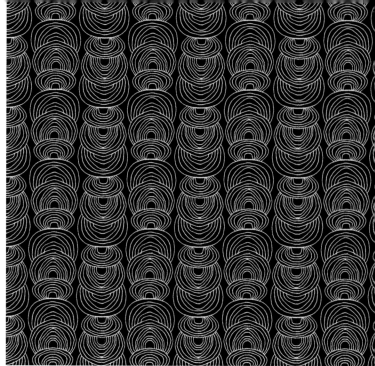

09 | Ripple | USA | 2015 | Anna Graham
Designed for Cloud9 Fabrics, this organic cotton printed fabric features a vertically structured pattern of concentric overlapping circles.

08 | Scribble (Gray) | UK | 1999 | Jocelyn Warner
Warner's abstract wallpaper pattern, with its loose interlaced lines, has a 1950s architectural feel. It is part of the "Larger Than Life" collection.

10 | Basuto | UK | 1955
This graphic wallpaper pattern was designed by the British firm Palladio Wallpapers and produced by the Wallpaper Manufacturers.

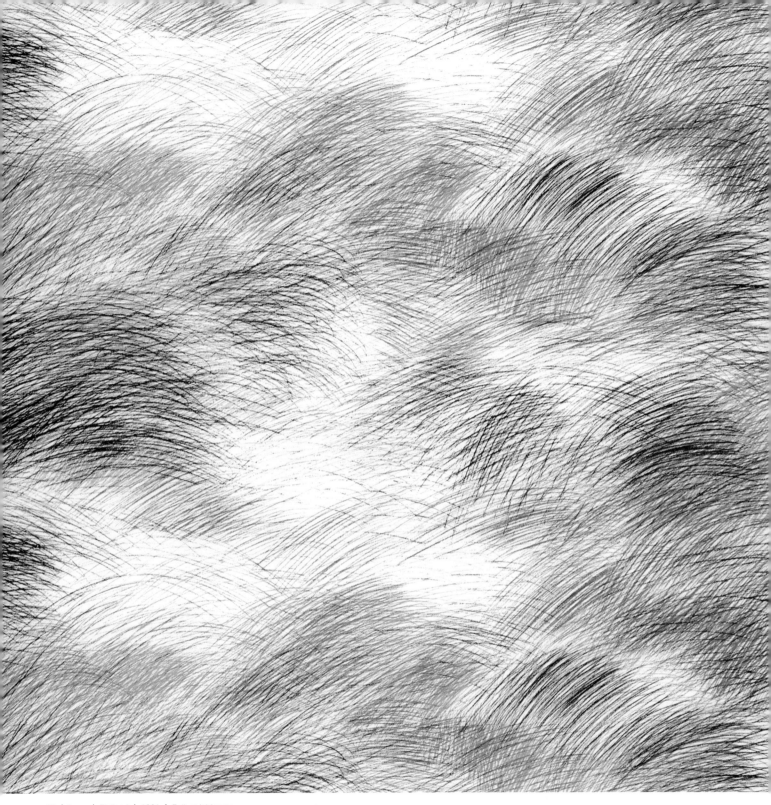

11 | Lepo | Finland | 1991 | Fujiwo Ishimoto
Designed for Marimekko, this monochromatic scribbled pattern was inspired by the
soft grasses Ishimoto knew as a child growing up on a farm.

01 | Furnishing fabric | UK | 1947 | Henry Moore
During the 1950s, just as designers were inspired by art, artists also turned their hands to design. This screen-printed, spun-rayon fabric was produced by Ascher Studios.

03 | Bird IN-A Box | USA | 1953 | Hans Moller
This cotton furnishing fabric, produced by Associated American Artists, was designed by German-born Moller, an abstract artist.

02 | The Dance | USA | 1950s | Angelo Testa
Testa was a leading US textile designer who studied under László Moholy-Nagy. This design recalls musical notation, or Paul Klee's phrase "taking a line for a walk."

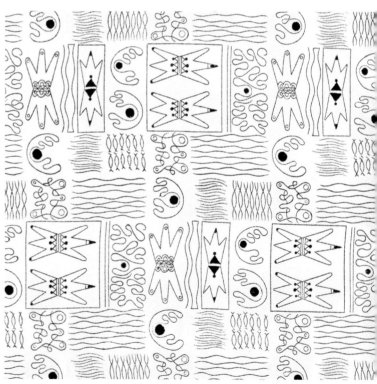

04 | Dress fabric | UK | 1947 | Paule Vézelay
Vézelay was one of the artists commissioned by Ascher to create patterns for dress fabrics. "Doodles" was a recognized category of postwar pattern design.

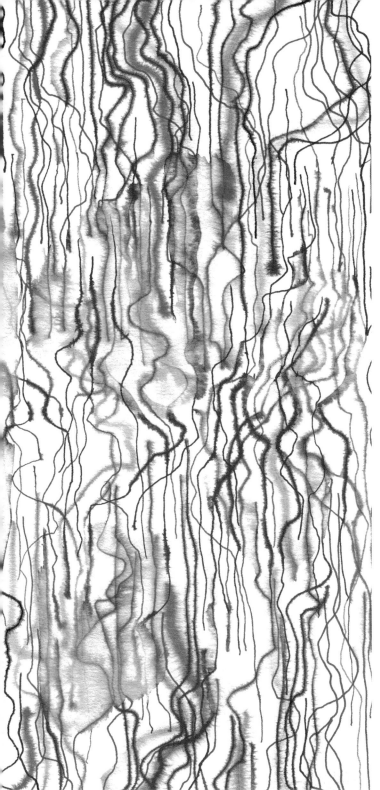

05 | Tarentel | UK | 2009 | Tord Boontje
Designed for Kvadrat, this furnishing fabric with its loose, streaked pattern is one of a number of designs inspired by the natural world.

04 | Palisade | UK | 1953 | Lucienne Day
This printed rayon taffeta was designed for British Celanese. Day was influenced by artists Joan Miró and Paul Klee.

06 | Joonas | Finland | 1961 | Maija Isola
This bold design for a furnishing fabric, produced by Marimekko, features eye-like motifs that form almost concentric rings.

In the natural world, camouflage is the means by which both prey and predators hide their presence: the tiger's stripes, the fawn's dappled coat, the leopard's spots all simulate patterns of light and shade to help conceal them in their habitats. Other animals, notably the octopus and the chameleon, are able to change their patterning or coloration to blend in with their surroundings and disappear from view. Some, like the snowshoe hare, change seasonally, with white fur in winter and brown fur in summer.

Camouflage in the military sense arose in the 19th century as weapons became more accurate over longer distances. During both world wars, artists were employed to disguise guns, tanks, fighter planes, and other assets from aerial observation. The term "camouflage" is thought to derive from *camoufler*, the Parisian slang for "to disguise," and may have been influenced by the French term *camouflet*, meaning "smoke blown in someone's face." Camouflaged textile patterns, used in battledress, are designed to blend in with specific types of terrain, from jungle and woodland to desert.

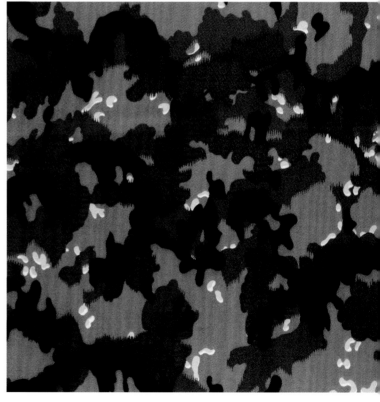

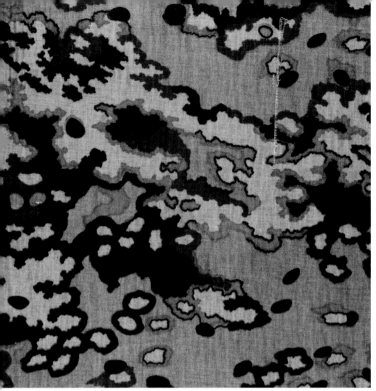

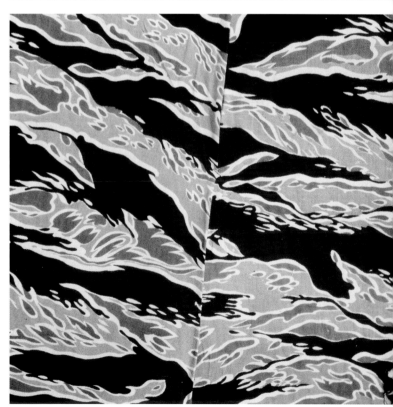

01 | Round Tower | USA | 1970s | Larsen Design Studio
Larsen Design Studio, the studio founded by Jack Lenor Larsen, produced this wool
furnishing fabric with a psychedelic pattern.

02 | Wallpaper | UK | 1968
Bright bands of color swirl along a central axis in this screen-printed wallpaper
manufactured by the Wallpaper Manufacturers.

03 | **Grand Blotch Damask** | UK | 2011 | Timorous Beasties
Available either as wallpaper or furnishing fabric, this subversion of a damask
pattern is reminiscent of a Rorschach or inkblot test.

04 | **Cotton fabric** | USA | 1970s
This printed cotton fabric recalls the psychedelic patterning popularized by Biba,
a highly fashionable and influential British retailer in the 1960s and 1970s.

06 | Dolores | UK | 1964 | Eddie Squires
Squires's screen-printed cotton furnishing fabric was designed for Warner & Sons.
He was contributing to the "Theme on the Thirties" collection.

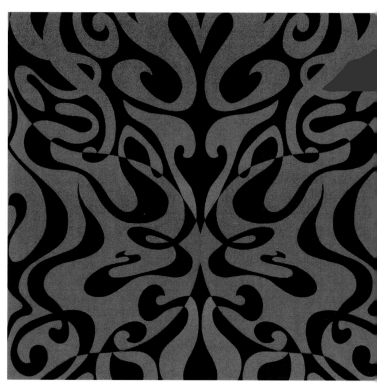

05 | Galleria | UK | 1969 | Barbara Brown
Like many of Brown's patterns, this design for a furnishing fabric, produced
by Heal's, has a three-dimensional quality.

07 | Woodstock | UK | 2005 | Cole & Son
This contemporary wallpaper pattern was inspired by the psychedelic designs of the
Swinging Sixties.

08 | Bojangles | USA | 1967 | Larsen Design Studio
Designed to upholster organically shaped furniture, this pattern is screen-printed
onto Caprolan stretch nylon bonded to a foam backing.

Shirley Craven (b.1934)

SEE PAGE > 622

Drawing inspiration from sources as varied as Abstract Expressionism and free jazz, Shirley Craven's bold painterly patterns sum up the explosive creative energies of the 1960s. As color and design consultant for Hull Traders, her designs, along with those she commissioned from some forty other leading designers and artists of the day, transformed textiles into a vibrant new art form.

Born in Hull, Craven studied at Hull College of Art before training in printed textiles at the Royal College of Art from 1955 to 1958. Time spent as a freelance designer left her frustrated by the demands of commercial clients, who wanted her to alter her designs to suit market taste.

In 1959, Craven found a sympathetic outlet for her talents at Hull Traders, a progressive firm dedicated to promoting good design, which had been set up two years previously and was owned by Peter Neubert. Hull Traders took its name from its entrepreneurial founder, Tristram Hull, and not the Yorkshire city; its premises were in Willesden, London, with a showroom off Oxford Street, although it later relocated to Trawden, Lancashire. Craven's first design for Hull Traders was the overscale abstract "Le Bosquet" (1959), for which she won a Design Centre Award in 1960. Two further Design Centre Awards followed: for "Shape" (1964),

"Division" (1964), and "Sixty-Three" (1963) in 1964, and for "Five" (1966) and "Simple Solar" (1967) in 1968. As well as winning critical acclaim, her patterns were commercial successes.

By 1963, she had been made chief designer of Hull Traders and been given full control over the company's creative output. Over the next two decades, she exploited the flexible process of hand screen-printing in her own fabrics, designs that amounted to a third of the firm's production. "Kaplan" (1961), with its gestural mark-making, and "Pascoe" (c. 1960–69), resembling a Matisse-like collage of brightly colored torn tissue, exemplified the eclecticism of her approach. "Curtain Up" (1970) was a psychedelic essay in vivid green and orange.

One of Craven's strengths is her dedication to getting each colorway exactly right. Another related quality is the way in which her designs resemble variations on musical themes or emotional moods. Craven is also responsible for using up-and-coming artists and designers, including Althea McNish (b.1933).

Hull Traders also produced original furniture. One best-selling range, designed by Craven's husband Bernard Holdaway (1934–2009), was "Tomotom": brightly colored cardboard furniture, which was launched at the Ideal Home Exhibition in 1966 and became an icon of Pop design.

Far Left Shirley Craven and Prince Philip, Duke of Edinburgh at London's Design Centre in 1960.

Left "Shape" (1964) was a printed cotton satin furnishing fabric that Craven designed for the progressive London firm Hull Traders.

Opposite Craven's "Kaplan" cotton furnishing fabric (1961) was produced by Hull Traders.

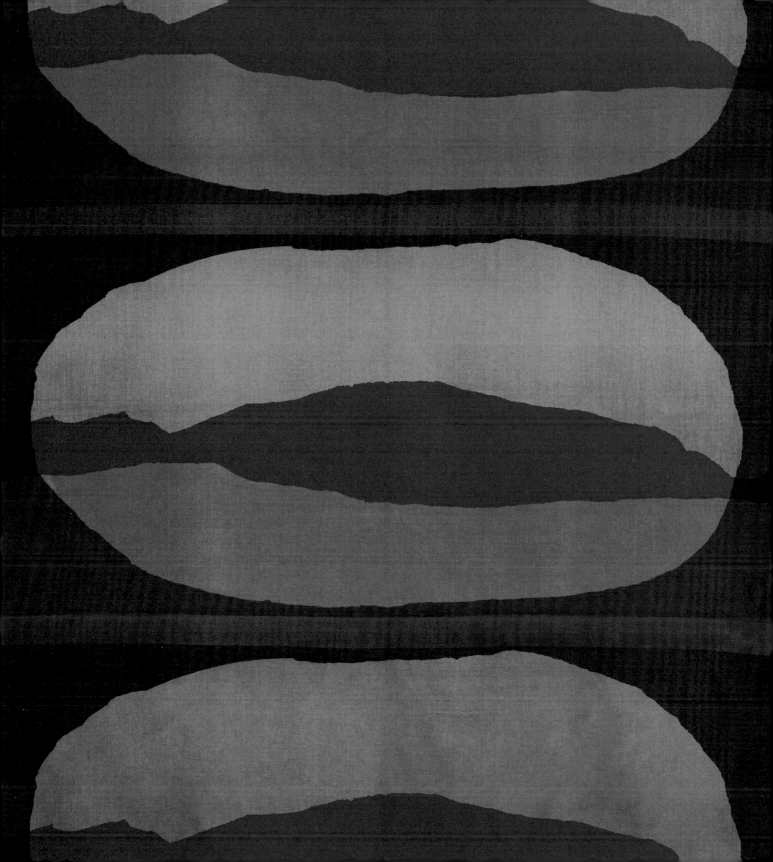

01 | Kaléidoscope (Kaleidoscope) | France | 1926 | Maurice Pillard-Verneuil
French designer Verneuil was known for his Art Deco patterns. This is Plate 10 from his *Kaléidoscope: Ornements Abstraits* (*Kaleidoscope: Abstract Ornaments*).

03 | Simple Solar | UK | 1968 | Shirley Craven
Craven's design for a screen-printed cotton satin produced by Hull Traders won her a Design Centre Award in 1968.

02 | Get Lost | USA | 2017 | Jessica Jones
Jones's printed organic cotton, designed for Cloud9 Fabrics, features a simple interlocking maze-like motif.

04 | Textile | Russia | 1973 | Nina Shirokova
Shirokova is a Russian artist and textile designer, who draws on abstract and folk motifs. This is a textile design of gouache on paper.

05 | Furnishing fabric | UK | 1913 | Vanessa Bell
One of the patterns created by the artist Vanessa Bell for Omega Workshops, this
painterly printed linen furnishing fabric was manufactured in France.

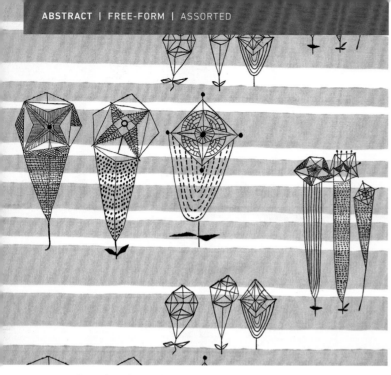

06 | Trio | UK | 1954 | Lucienne Day
Day's Roller-printed furnishing fabric has a lyrical, musical quality, as if flowers were the notes on a stave.

08 | Spago | Italy | 1957 | Gigi Tessari
This furnishing fabric, designed for Manifattura JSA, has a loose painterly quality. Italian artists, sculptors, and architects all designed textiles in the postwar period.

07 | Petrus | UK | 1967 | Peter Hall
This large-scale pattern, screen-printed on cotton crêpe, fills the width of the fabric. Hall was a regular designer for Heal's.

09 | Brazil | UK | *c.* 1935 **|** Eileen Hunter
This printed cotton sateen furnishing fabric was designed by Eileen Hunter for her own textile firm, Eileen Hunter Fabrics.

10 | Fabric design | UK | 1913 | Vanessa Bell
Bell's fabric design for the Omega Workshops shows the clear influence
of Postimpressionism.

11 | Foreshore | UK | 1952 | Lucienne Day
Designed for Edinburgh Weavers, this printed cotton furnishing fabric features Day's
characteristic calligraphic mark-making.

12 | Triangel (Triangle) | Austria | 1910–13 | Josef Hoffmann
In this printed silk design, black-and-white triangles overlap squares. Twisting vines
occupy a vertical row.

13 | Textile | UK | 1875 | Christopher Dresser
Dresser's printed silk damask features a pattern in the Japanese style. He was an
avid collector of Japanese artifacts.

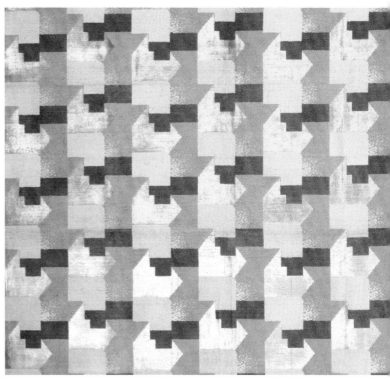

14 | Furnishing fabric | France | *c.* 1925
The pattern of this woven cotton plush furnishing fabric makes the most of the
sensuous texture and the way it catches the light.

Gunta Stölzl (1897–1983)

SEE PAGES > 306, 351, 582

A leading figure at the Bauhaus, the German design school founded in 1919, Gunta Stölzl played a key role in establishing weaving as a modern design discipline. She was the first woman to become a full master at the school and fostered the talents of other female textile artists. Her works typify the abstract geometric emphasis of modernist design.

Stölzl was born in Munich, Germany. In 1914, she enrolled at Munich's *Kunstgewerbeschule* (School of Applied Arts), taking courses in glass painting, decorative arts, and ceramics. After spending nearly two years serving as a Red Cross nurse during World War I, Stölzl returned to the school. It was at this time that she came across the *Bauhaus Manifesto* (1919) and decided to pursue her studies there.

The Bauhaus was set up in Weimar as a radical modernist experiment in art and design education. Its "preliminary course" encouraged students to work across different disciplines. When Stölzl won a place on the preliminary course in 1920, it was headed by Johannes Itten (1888–1967), who taught art theory in the weaving workshop, laying the emphasis on the use of geometric form and primary colors. Itten left the school in 1922 and was replaced by László Moholy-Nagy (1895–1946).

In its early days, the Bauhaus was informally structured and students were expected to teach themselves and each other. It was also divided along gender lines. Stölzl had gravitated to the weaving workshop, then a neglected department headed by Georg Muche (1895–1987) because women were welcome there. At first, Bauhaus textiles were hand-crafted and pictorial. Soon, however, students began to move in a more abstract geometric direction. Within the weaving workshop, Stölzl was a mentor and in 1921 she reopened the Bauhaus dye studio. Before long, she was effectively running the department alongside Muche. Two years after the Bauhaus moved to Dessau, Stölzl was made a junior master; she became a full master the following year.

Under her direction, the weaving workshop became one of the Bauhaus's most successful departments. She experimented with synthetic materials, included mathematics as part of the technical weaving course, and moved further in the direction of industrial production. By the early 1930s, with the rise of Nazism, the radical teachings of the school were coming under political pressure and in 1931 Stölzl was dismissed.

She moved to Switzerland, where she had mixed success, opening a couple of hand-weaving businesses, exhibiting at the Paris Exposition in 1937, and receiving a commission to make drapes for a Zurich cinema, but she never regained the position of influence she had held at the Bauhaus.

Top A group photograph of the Bauhaus masters taken by Walter Gropius with a self-timer on the roof of the Bauhaus building in Dessau in 1926. Left to right: Josef Albers, Marcel Breuer, Gunta Stölzl, Oskar Schlemmer, Wassily Kandinsky, Gropius, Herbert Bayer, László Moholy-Nagy, and Hinnerk Scheper.

Above A jacquard-woven silk and cotton wall hanging (1926–27) designed by Stölzl.

Opposite A tapestry design created by Stölzl in 1928. Although the output at the Bauhaus weaving workshop was all hand-crafted, she was moving in the direction of mass manufacture.

16 | Textile | UK | *c.* 1920–30 | E. Geggs
This block-printed paper, with its combination of curved and squared-off forms and banding, is a design for a textile.

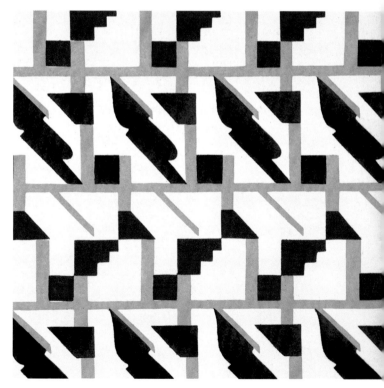

15 | Focus | UK | 1965 | Doreen Dyall
Designed for the progressive firm Heal's, this screen-printed cotton satin furnishing fabric features a bold abstract design with a strong vertical emphasis.

17 | Pochoir print | France | late 1920s | Serge Gladky
Gladky's pochoir print was published in his collection of abstract designs *Nouvelles Compositions Décoratives* (*New Decorative Compositions*).

18 | Applecross | UK | 1954 | Robert Stewart
Instantly recognizable as a mid-century modern pattern, this design by Stewart
for Liberty is reminiscent of the work of Lucienne Day, among others.

Jacqueline Groag (1903–86)

SEE PAGES > 202, 544, 556

With her background in modernist European art and design movements, Jacqueline Groag was one of the progressive designers whose work put an entirely different stamp on the British textile industry in the postwar period. Although she is noted for her designs for furnishing and dress fabrics, she also created patterns for wallpaper, carpets, greetings cards, ceramics, and plastic laminate for table tops and cabinets.

Born in Prague, Czechoslovakia, to Jewish parents, Groag's given name was Hilde Pilke—she changed her first name to Jacqueline when she married Jacques Groag (1892–1962), a modernist architect, in 1939. In the 1920s, she studied textile design in Vienna, and became one of the students of Josef Hoffmann (1870–1956; see p. 430), head of the Wiener Werkstätte (Vienna Workshops).

By the late 1920s, Groag was hand-printing dress fabric for many of the leading Parisian couturiers. Critical acclaim followed soon after: she won a gold medal at the Milan Triennale in 1933 for textile design and another for printed textiles at the Paris Exposition in 1937.

Following the Anschluss in 1938, when the German Army entered Austria and war was imminent, the newly married Groags were forced to flee Vienna, first to Prague and then to London. There, they established strong links with many of the leading lights of British design, including Gordon Russell (1892–1980), who became a close friend, and Jack Pritchard (1899–1992), founder of Isokon.

Groag's avant-garde designs featured in the influential "Britain Can Make It" exhibition in 1946 and reached an even wider public when they were displayed at the Festival of Britain in 1951. Her patterns drew heavily on stylized natural forms, as well as motifs from abstract and contemporary art. Much of her work displays finely drawn gridded patterns. The human form is another recurring theme. "Gala Night" (1947) shows a crowded auditorium before curtain up. Another design, "Garden Party" (1968), features a doll-like figure densely overlaid by natural motifs. Confident handling of line and bold color combinations made the designs immediately appealing to a new generation of consumers.

By the mid-1950s, Groag was a major figure in British textiles, designing for retailers such as Liberty. Many of her textile patterns were also applied to wallpaper. Her association with Misha Black (1910–77) at the Design Research Unit led to her designing interiors for boats and aeroplanes. Through her US clients, notably Associated American Artists and Hallmark Cards, her work gained international recognition. Groag was made a Royal Designer for Industry in 1984, two years before her death.

Far Left Jacqueline Groag's progressive designs came to prominence in the 1950s.

Left "Kiddies Town," a wallpaper Groag designed in 1951 for John Line & Son.

Opposite "Melody," a cotton furnishing fabric designed in 1960 for Edinburgh Weavers.

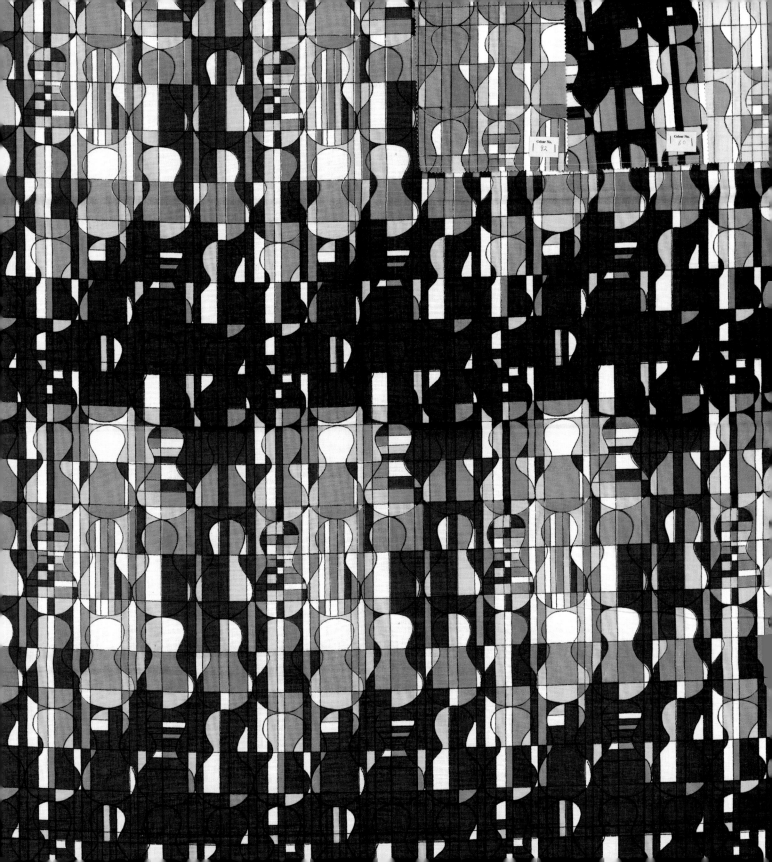

Colour No. 92

Colour No. 60

01 | Compendium | UK | 1968 | Rosemary Newsom
The optical effect of this screen-printed wallpaper, designed for Wallpaper
Manufacturers, owes much to the clashing shades of red and pink.

02 | Dress fabric | Netherlands | 2016 | Vlisco
The shaded rectangles increase and flatten toward the middle of this pattern for
Vlisco, which has an Escher-like quality.

04 | Kernoo | UK | 1962 | Victor Vasarely
Vasarely was an influential Op artist who produced a number of textile designs, such as this screen-printed cotton furnishing fabric for Edinburgh Weavers.

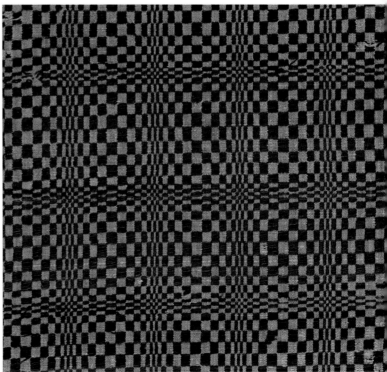

03 | Extension | UK | 1967 | Haydon Williams
This printed cotton furnishing fabric, designed for Heal's, has a three-dimensional quality similar to that seen in the work of Barbara Brown.

05 | Coverlet | *c.* 1850
This wool and cotton coverlet of unknown provenance, dating from the mid-19th century, features a pattern that might have been designed in the 1960s.

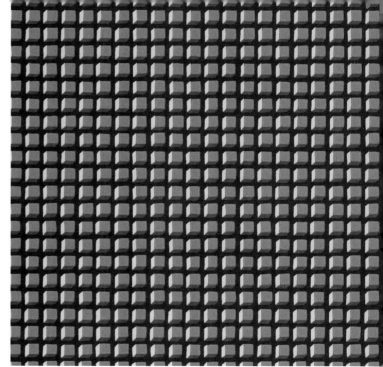

07 | Mosaic | UK | 2015 | Cole & Son
This small-scale highly regular wallpaper pattern features an all-over design of tiny cubes, shaded to give a three-dimensional quality.

06 | P.L.U.T.O. (Pipeline Laid Under The Ocean) | UK | 2015 | Mini Moderns
In this wallpaper pattern, the copper line represents a fuel pipe laid under the Channel for the D-Day invasion. The background is dazzle camouflage used on ships.

08 | Indigo Blur | UK | 2015 | Ptolemy Mann
Mann produces contemporary versions of traditional *ikat* patterns. This is a design for a cushion produced by MADE.

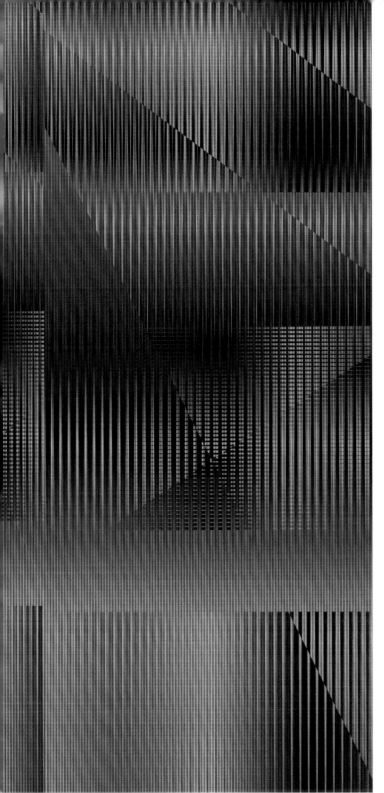

10 | Textile | UK | *c.* 1920 | Claud Lovat Fraser
Fraser was a multitalented artist and designer who produced vivid abstract patterns.
This design was revived in 1973 by Liberty.

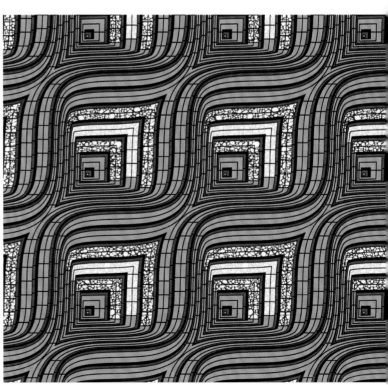

09 | Haze | UK | 2014 | Emma Jeffs, N&N Wares
Jeffs's sophisticated design for a furnishing fabric has an illusory feel and
an intense shimmering quality.

11 | Dress fabric | Netherlands | 2015 | Michiel Schuurman
Dutch designer Schuurman's paisleylike pattern is one of the Real Dutch Super-Wax
fabrics Vlisco produced for the African market.

12 | Decor | UK | 1966 | Barbara Brown

Like many of Brown's designs, this optical pattern has a three-dimensional effect.
It was produced as a cotton satin furnishing fabric by Heal's Fabrics.

13 | **Moonlight Daisy** | UK | 2009–10 | Eley Kishimoto
Eley Kishimoto's deceptively simple pattern makes use of a small all-over circle motif to generate a three-dimensional quality.

15 | **Ruhlmann** | UK | 2016 | Osborne & Little
This diamond trellis wallpaper pattern is named after French Art Deco furniture designer Émile-Jacques Ruhlmann.

14 | **Riley** | UK | 2000–01 | Neisha Crosland
In this design for printed silk, the optical effect is reliant on the spacing of the narrow diagonal lines and the way they appear to step across the fabric width.

16 | **Braided** | UK | 2002–03 | Neisha Crosland
Crosland began her career designing patterns for scarves. This billowing design was produced in woven silk lurex.

Barbara Brown (b.1932)

SEE PAGES > 380, 396, 618, 636

One of Britain's most prolific textile designers, Barbara Brown created patterns that epitomized the optimistic spirit of the 1960s. During a period that saw British youth culture explode onto the international scene, her large-scale, Op art–inspired prints said "Swinging Sixties" every bit as much as pop music by The Beatles or clothes by Mary Quant.

Brown studied at Canterbury College of Art, then enrolled at the Royal College of Art in 1953. Talent-spotted by Tom Worthington, director of Heal Fabrics, she sold her first fabric to Heal's before she had completed her course. She went on to work for the company for the following two decades, although she also acted as a consultant for other companies in Europe and the United States.

Heal's, originally a family-owned company based in London's Tottenham Court Road, was established in the early 19th century. Under the chairmanship of Ambrose Heal (1872–1959), an exponent of Arts and Crafts ideals, the business was transformed in the early 20th century into a leading manufacturer and retailer of good quality, well-designed furniture and furnishings. There could have been no better showcase for the work of a young designer and, by 1967, Brown was being hailed in the company's catalog as the "golden girl of Heal Fabrics."

Like Lucienne Day (1917–2010; see p. 602), Brown did not conceive her designs with specific fashion or commercial markets in mind. Instead, she worked more like a painter, with her patterns evolving over time. The designs were specifically produced for machine manufacture, not hand-printing, which made them affordable.

Although her early work featured characteristically mid-century modern motifs, such as organic plant-like forms, Brown quickly left representational art behind, making her name with large-scale geometric patterns. A particular characteristic is their three-dimensional quality: they swirl and ripple, echoing on a flat plane the quality of hanging material. With time, her patterns also moved away from hot contrasting colors in favor of tonal shades and monochrome. The obvious inspiration was Op art, whose leading exponents—for example, Bridget Riley and Victor Vasarely—were creating work that explored illusory optical techniques.

Brown did not design patterns exclusively for textiles. In 1964, she created the pattern "Focus" for use on a range of ceramic tableware designed by David Queensbury (b.1929) and manufactured by Midwinter Pottery. In the latter part of her career, she taught at Medway College of Art, Guildford School of Art, and Hornsey College of Art.

Far Left Barbara Brown created iconic designs of the Swinging Sixties.

Left "Complex," a 1967 furnishing fabric designed by Brown for Heal Fabrics.

Opposite Brown designed the "Frequency" furnishing fabric with its swirling bands for Heal Fabrics in 1969.

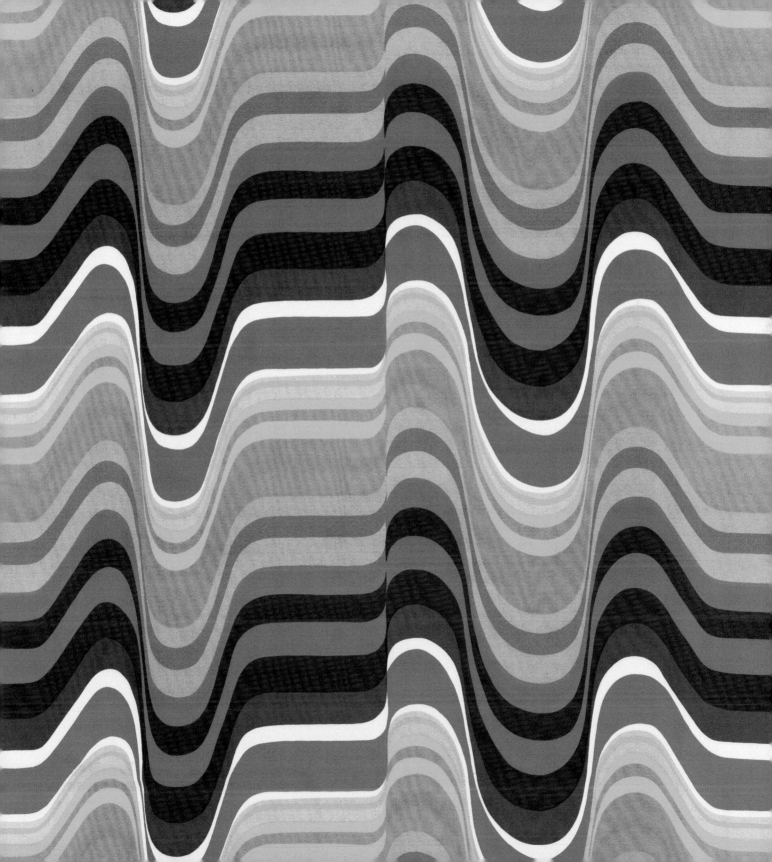

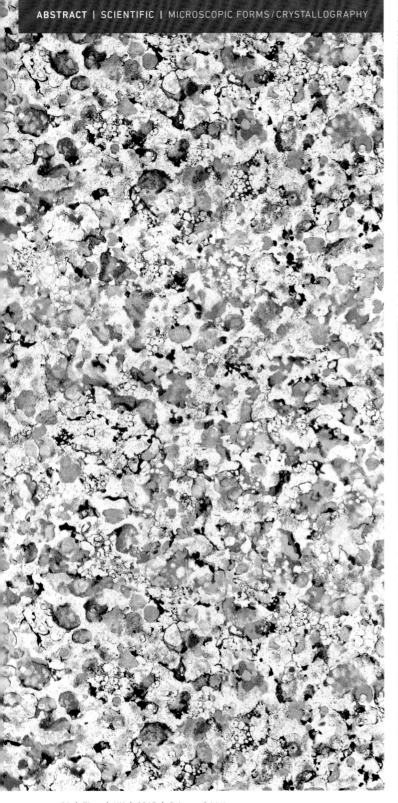

01 | Ebru | UK | 2015 | Osborne & Little

Part of Osborne & Little's Pasha collection, this colored marble-effect wallpaper has metallic highlights for a lively surface texture.

02 | Earthforms | USA | 1954 | Ben Rose

Rose's screen-printed plain weave furnishing fabric features horizontal bands of white and three shades of green with undulating black lines.

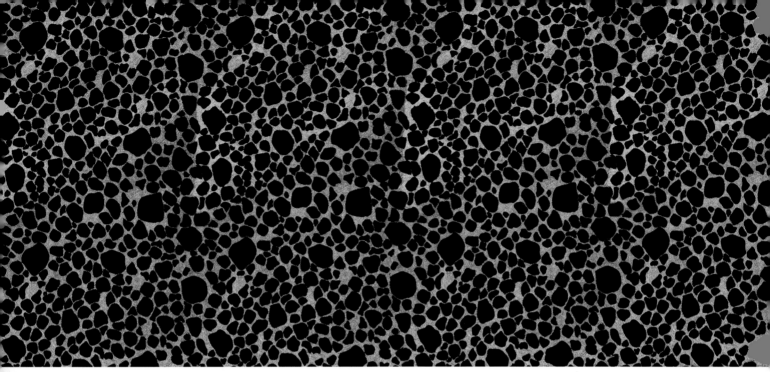

03 | Lampas | France | 1925 | Émile-Jacques Ruhlmann
Ruhlmann's color lithograph is taken from *Etoffes d'Ameublement Tissues et Broches*
(*Woven and Brocaded Upholstery Fabrics*). Lampas is figured silk with a special warp.

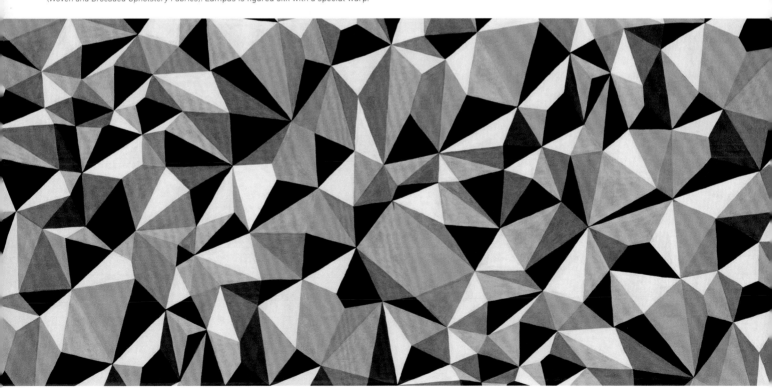

04 | Quartz | UK | 2016 | Cole & Son
This dramatic wallpaper depicting the crystalline facets and shards of quartz is
available in a range of colors.

Mid-century Modern (1946–1970s)

After World War II, modernism was reinvented for a forward-looking age. Architects and designers who had fled Nazism to settle and work in the United States had a significant impact, producing buildings in the International Style. Graduates of the modernist Cranbrook Academy, such as Charles Eames (1907–78), Ray Eames (1912–88), and Eero Saarinen (1910–61), created furniture that expressed the same progressive spirit.

Thrown into the mix was the work of Scandinavian designers such as Hans Wegner (1914–2007), Finn Juhl (1912–89), and Børge Mogensen (1914–72), which first came to international audiences through exhibitions in the late 1940s. Danish Modern, with its simple lines, emphasis on craft, and organic, natural sensibility was a hit with the US public.

This second wave of modernism was characterized by an explosion of creativity in pattern design. Just as Scandinavian modern furniture designers brought nature back into the picture, postwar pattern designers, including British designer Lucienne Day (1917–2010; see p. 602), Swedish designer Stig Lindberg (1916–82; see p. 530), and Finnish designer Maija Isola (1927–2001; see p. 66), created updated versions of natural motifs, often in distilled, graphic, or abstracted forms, focusing on patterns of growth expressed in calligraphic line.

The postwar period was a time of optimism, when scientific breakthroughs in fields from molecular biology to space exploration promised a brighter future. In Britain, the Festival Pattern Group, part of the Festival of Britain in 1951, was formed to encourage manufacturers to decorate their products with scientific patterns, particularly those derived from X-ray crystallography diagrams. Patterns featuring ball-and-spoke atomic structures, along with more globular designs, were used on textiles, wallpaper, ceramics, and other products.

Contemporary art was equally influential. Day's work recalls the sculptural mobiles of Alexander Calder and the work of abstract artists Paul Klee and Joan Miró. Czech-born designers Zika (1910–92) and Lida Ascher (1910–83; see p. 288) commissioned artists including Henry Moore (1898–1986) to create original patterns for textiles that expressed their artistic vision. Textiles with free-form patterns drawn from the work of Abstract Expressionists such as Jackson Pollock were another way of bringing a modern sensibility to a wider public.

Another significant strand that affected pattern design during this time was folk art. US textile designer Alexander Girard (1907–93; see p. 572), who created many fabrics for Knoll, was an avid collector of Mexican folk art. Doll-like motifs occur in his designs, along with vibrant Mexican-style colors and graphic elements.

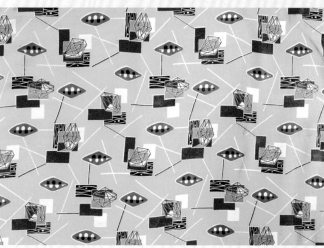

Top This 1956 screen-printed cotton furnishing fabric entitled 'Herb Antony' is from designer Lucienne Day.

Above This early 1950s printed cotton furnishing fabric resembles those produced by the Festival of Britain Pattern Group.

Opposite These leaf-shaped ceramic plates were designed by Stig Lindberg for the Swedish ceramic manufacturer Gustavsberg. Lindberg first went to work as a faience painter at the factory in the late 1930s, eventually becoming its creative director for two long periods in the 1950s and 1970s.

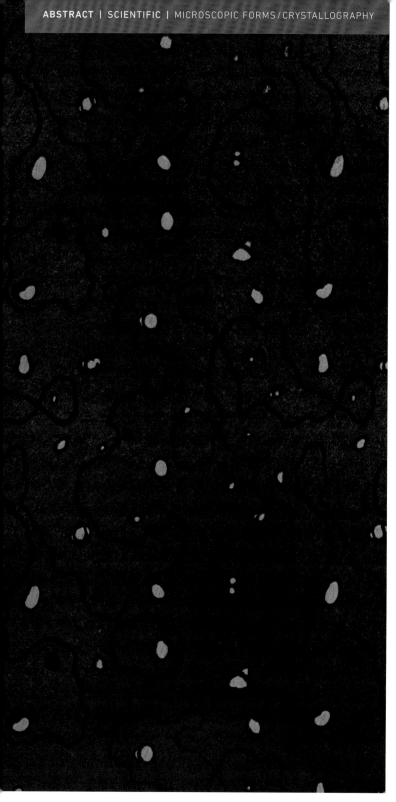

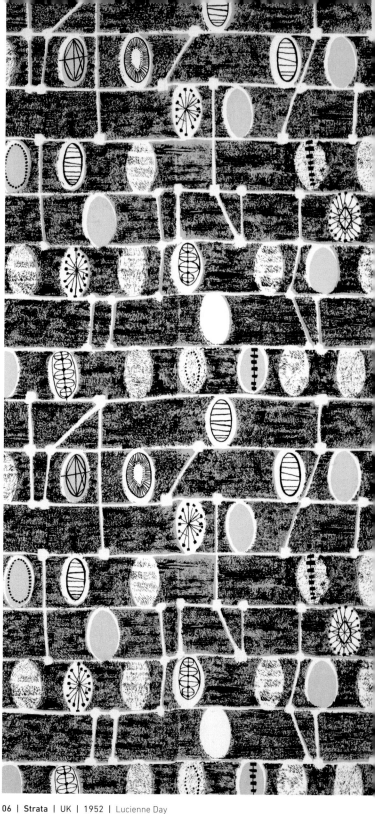

05 | **Textile** | France | 1925 | Émile-Jacques Ruhlmann
Published in *Woven and Brocaded Upholstery Fabrics* (1925) by Leon Moussinac, this is a design for a lampas, or luxury silk fabric.

06 | **Strata** | UK | 1952 | Lucienne Day
Day's screen-printed cotton furnishing fabric, designed for Heal's, features horizontal layers with egg-shaped forms inset with geometric patterns.

07 | Abstract Malachite | UK | 2013 | Christian Lacroix
This digitally printed cotton furnishing fabric created by Lacroix for Designers Guild
features a bold geometric pattern inspired by malachite crystals.

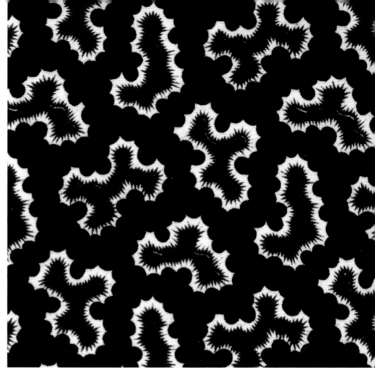

01 | Haemoglobin | UK | 1951
One of many postwar patterns inspired by scientific diagrams, this roller-printed cotton organdie dress fabric was manufactured in Manchester by Barlow & Jones.

03 | Fabric swatch
This unattributed fabric swatch from a private archive features rotating ameba- or cellular-like motifs.

02 | Textile | UK | 1951 | Bernard Rowland
Rowland's fabric design for silk, produced for the Festival Pattern Group, was based on the crystal structure diagram of chalk.

04 | Haemoglobin 8.26 | UK | 1951 | Bernard Rowland
Manufactured by Vanners and Fennell Bros of Suffolk, this silk tie pattern was based on the crystal structures of haemoglobin 8.26, chalk, and insulin.

05 | Time Capsule | USA | 1954 | Ben Rose
Scientific motifs were a feature of many mid-century modern patterns. This furnishing fabric depicts polyhedrons of varying sizes.

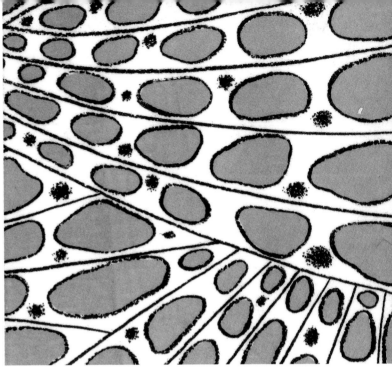

07 | Cells | UK | 2004 | Eley Kishimoto
Eley Kishimoto's patterns always display a bold hand-drawn quality. The irregular shapes and opposing diagonals create a great sense of liveliness.

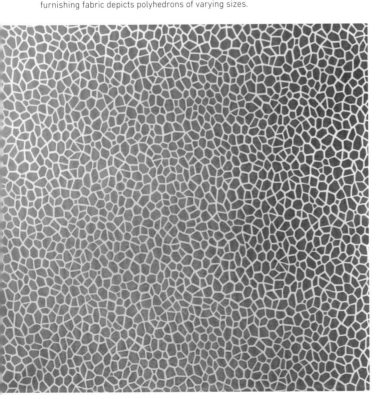

06 | Kairi | UK | 2014 | Matthew Williamson at Osborne & Little
Inspired by the patterning of a dragonfly's wing, this cellular design creates an understated all-over organic effect.

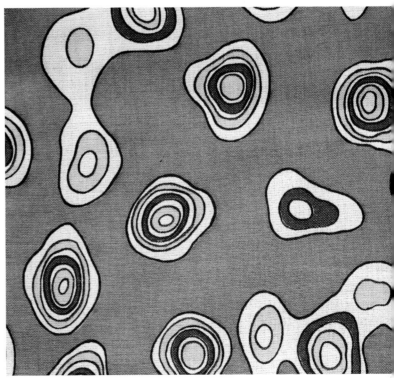

08 | Afwillite 8.45 | UK | 1951 | S. M. Slade
Slade's abstract cellular design for a dress fabric, with motifs widely spaced on the ground, was manufactured for British Celanese.

02 | Aurora | USA | 1970 | Larsen Design Studio
Jack Lenor Larsen was a leading US textile designer during the 1960s and 1970s. Many of his patterns were inspired by textiles of other cultures.

01 | Tiger Moon | UK | 2008 | Neisha Crosland
This flexo-printed wallpaper, with its shimmering foiled surface and large-scale motif, simulates the effect of the moon appearing through clouds.

03 | Pluto | UK | 1998 | Neisha Crosland
Crosland's textile and wallpaper designs display an elegant simplicity. This pattern appeared on a silk scarf.

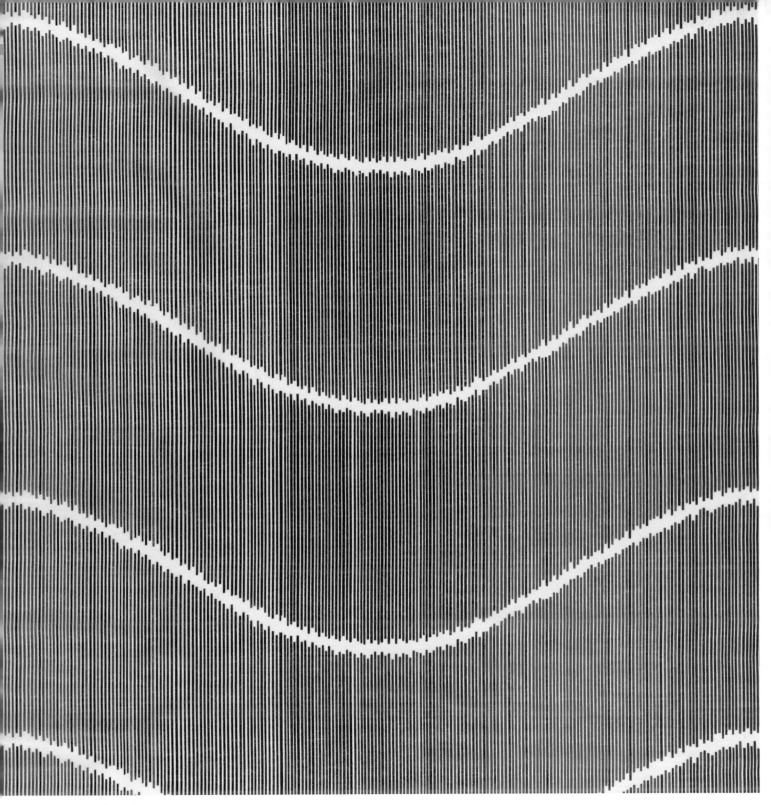

04 | Borealis | USA | 1979 | Elenhank
Elenhank's polyester furnishing fabric evokes in a very economical way the
phenomenon of the Northern Lights.

Index by Date

Unknown dates

Textile, 169
Saluki design, 209
Fabric swatch, 311
No title, 317
Fabric swatch, 364
Fabric swatch, 385
Fabric sample, 389
Fabric swatch, 401
Fabric swatch, 404
Fabric swatch, 409
Fabric swatch, 413
Fabric swatch, 421
Fabric swatch, 427
Fabric swatch, 434
Tiles, 448
Mosaic, 449
Tiles, 449
Siapo, or Tapa cloth, 457
Ashanti Kente cloth, 461
Block print, 566
Fabric swatch, 646

BCE

c. 1479–1400 BCE
Ceiling Pattern, Tomb of
　Qenamun, 394
c. 1390–1353 BCE
Ceiling from the palace of
　Amenhotep III, 394
c. 1390–1352 BCE
Wall decoration, 398
c. 510–500 BCE
Terracotta alabastron
　(perfume vase), 481
332–246 BCE
Miniature broad collar, 395

2nd century

Mosaic floor panel, 480

7th century

Book of Kells, 436
Carpet page, 439

8th century

Tara Brooch, 437

9th century

Frontispiece of the Gospel of
　St. Matthew, Armagh, 436

11th century

Tiles, 448

12th century

Embroidered silk
　textile, 290

14th century

Interlace pattern with
　white medallion, 435
Ceramic tiles, 444
Tiles, 448
Tiles, 449

15th century

Folding game board, 325
Wall panel with geometric
　interlace, 446

16th century

Furnishing fabric, 39
Pillow cover, 54
Textile, 377
Tilework, 416
Mirror with split-leaf
　palmette design inlaid
　with gold, 447

17th century

Damask sample, 113
Textile, 440
Wall tile, 510

18th century

Printed cotton, 32
Textile fragment, 38
Palampore, 38
Textile, 39
Sarasa, 120
Textile design, 130
Textile design, 135
Fabric panel, 142
Pichhwai, 219

Table top, 325
Table top, 325
Fragment, 355
Embroidered linen, 367
Textile sample, 390
Tile (figure), 510
Tile (house), 510
Chinoiserie rococo paper
　and border, 514
Wallpaper design with
　scattered flowers, 514
Textile, 538
Textile, 538

1720s

Six tin-glazed earthenware
　tiles, with Chinoiserie
　scenes, 300

1730s

Dress fabric, 27
Porcelain book
　cover, 299

1740s

Robe à la Française, 515

1760s

Domino paper, 90
Chinoiserie decorated
　teapot, 301
Tapestry Room from
　Croome Court, 356

1770s

Printed cotton, 47
Wallpaper, 93

1780s

Wallpaper, 193
Textile, 234
Vase with cover, 357
Wallpaper, 478

1790s

Royal Oak and Ivy, 176
Textile, 354

Frieze, 479
La Fête de la
　Fédération, 495
The Drinking Trough, 508

19th century

Chrysanthemums
　papercut, 20
Kimono detail, 21
Futon fabric, 21
Textile, 37
Temple altar cloth, 49
Blue and Gold Cherry
　Blossom on a Pond, 52
Wallpaper, 72
Winter Berry, 76
Textile design, 84
Wallpaper, 109
Textile, 119
Textile, 119
Stencil cloth, 119
Textile design, 139
Foliage, 154
Athenian, 161
Fabric design, 167
Textile pattern, 169
Paisley design, 170
The Fairyland Design, 175
Papercut, 176
Endpaper, 223
Silk fabric, 225
Damask, 272
Textile design, 299
Silk hanging, 303
Panel, 324
Wallpaper, 333
Textile, 341
Textile, 341
Textile, 375
Textile, 419
Wallpaper, 421
Wallpaper, 440
Fabric, 441
Ceramic tiles, 445
Ceramic tiles, 445
Bedcover suzani, 455
Hiapo, 456

Bark cloth, 456
Bark cloth, 457
Textile, 479
Wallpaper, 485
Delft tile showing a draw-
　bridge over a canal, 511
Textile, 536
Quilt, 539
Textile, 540
Paper, 587
Decorative end paper, 590
Decorative end paper, 591

1800s

Wallpaper border, 38
Textile, 92
Cotton textile, 121
Les Losanges furnishing
　fabric, 356
Wallpaper, 361
Wallpaper, 421
Shakhrisyabz suzani, 454
Pallas and Venus, 478

1810s

Wallpaper, 166
Wallpaper, 247
Wallpaper, 416
Mosaic ornament in the
　south side of the Court of
　the Lions, Alhambra, 446
Les Monuments de Paris
　(The Monuments of
　Paris), 489
La Route de Poissy, 513

1820s

Textile, 244
Textile, 322
Textile, 384
Textile, 418

1830s

Wallpaper, 50
Pattern design, 97
Cotton textile, 121
Textile, 138

Textile, 138
Birds of America, 250
Border, 397

1840s

Quilt, 139
Lithograph, 329
Textile, 364
Wallpaper, 408
Furnishing fabric, 417
Crace diaper, 441
Textile, 508
Tudor Rose and Fleur-de-lis, 576
Apparel for an alb, 577

1850s

Quilt, 31
Lotus, 37
Wall stencil, 38
Scarf, 42
Textile, 92
No title, 111
Whig Rose quilt, 121
Shawl, 169
Detail of a skirt, 170
Fighting Stags, 217
Rapids at Naruto, 232
Wallpaper, 302
Wallpaper, 343
Sarape, 359
Moresque, 393
Border, 413
Color lithograph, 417
Lithograph, 439
Textile, 484
Wallpaper, 577
Marbled end paper, 591
Coverlet, 633

1860s

Trellis, 16
Daisy, 24
Wallpaper, 151
Quilt, 163
Indian, 169
Pomegranate, 185
Quilt, 343
Sarape, wearing blanket, 359
Gulbadan, 374
Clarice Cliff, 411
Hiapo, or Tapa cloth, 457
Quilt, 465

1870s

Wallpaper, 23
Daisy, 24
Lily, 28
Tulip, 30
Sunflower, 35
Iris and Kingfisher, 44
Marigold, 46
African Marigold, 47
Peony tile, 50
Peony, 51
Stafford, 53
Honeysuckle, 54
Snakeshead, 58
Larkspur, 63
Bluebell, 80
Pimpernel, 81
Marigold, 82
Wallpaper, 88
Wreath, 134
No title, 141
Bramble, 145
Unknown, 153
Tile panel, 164
Acanthus, 165
Apple, 178
Wallpaper, 184
Willow, 194
Vine, 199
Kimono detail, 204
Dove and Rose, 226
Pair of round bottles, 232
Tile, 233
Textile, 249
Billow, 264
Wallpaper, 271
Lithograph, 298
Sarape, 358
Sultan, 417
Textile fragment, 418
Book illustration, 434
Color lithograph, 444
Kalamkari, 475
Marbled end paper, 590
Ceiling pattern, 566
The Fleur-de-lis, 576
Textile, 625

1880s

Chrysanthemum Blossoms, 22
Chrysanthemum, 23
The Lily, 29

Sunflower Stalks, 34
Kennet, 35
Ceramic tile, 37
Bird and Anemone, 41
Iris, 42
Tiles, 47
Wallpaper, 49
Bamboo and Cherry Blossoms, 53
Honeysuckle, 54
Fabric sample, 55
Strawberry Thief, 59
Poppy, 64
Fabric sample, 71
Fabric sample, 71
Corncockle, 80
Cray, 84
Arcadia, 84
Lodden, 97
Autumn Flowers, 116
Furnishing fabric, 117
Christchurch, 136
Flowerpot, 140
Leaf Pattern, 150
Detail of a skirt, 170
Textile, 170
Wallpaper, 173
No title [pear], 182
Brer Rabbit, 212
Yellow and Green Trees with Cranes, 231
Cranes Flying in an Abstract Pattern, 231
The Peacock Garden, 245
Peacock Feathers, 246
Woodblock print, 248
Textile design, 258
Silk textile, 264
Bees with Honeycomb, 272
Hydrangeas and Butterflies, 275
Tile panel, 298
Peacock and Dragon, 299
Illustration for a *Handbook of Colored Ornament in the Historic Styles*, 480
Angel with the Trumpet, 552
Snowflakes Falling in a Winter Landscape, 564

1890s

Water lily wallpaper and tiles, 26

Day Lily, 27
Golden Lily, 28
Sunflower, 34
Cestrefeld, 35
Irises, 43
Irises, 45
Wallpaper, 45
The Oswin, 49
Wallflower, 56
Fabric sample, 57
Batchelor's Button, 62
The Iolanthe, 63
Dandelions, 69
Daffodil, 71
Teazle, 74
Thistle, 74
Meadow Flowers, 79
The Well at the World's End, 82
Plate, 83
Galahad, 87
Pink and Rose, 92
The Lerena, 113
Wallpaper, 164
Granville, 164
Oak Tree, 176
Viper Grass, 204
Fabric sample, 209
The Duleek, 217
Cockatoo, 234
Strawberries and Birds, 250
The Owl, 257
Wallpaper, 390
Femme à Marguerite (Woman with Daisy), 484

Late 19th century

Wallpaper, 22
Anemone, 41
Peony, 48
Furnishing fabric, 56
Hyacinth, 60
Clover, 72
Obi, 74
Thistle, 75
Tile design, 75
Blackberry, 76
Textile design, 128
Blossom, 193
Pichhwai, 219
Almond Blossom and Swallow, 224
Purple Bird, 226

Wallpaper, 230
The Peacock, 244
Silk fragment, 242
Peacock, Grapevine and Vases, 242
Panpipes, 303
Stripes on kimono, 375
Fabric, 419
Wallpaper, 440
Panel, 540

20th century

Chrysanthemums & Snow Circles, 22
A "Cherry Blossom" table lamp, 99
Stenciled paper, 157
Wallpaper, 174
Furnishing fabric, 179
Wild Olive, 189
Shirt panel (mola), 293
Textile, 312
Reflections: 1, 315
Circle Motif, 379
Carpet design, 393
Paper, 398
Stenciled paper, 433
Detail of a length of Kente cloth, 460
Tiles, 467
Greek Procession, 479
Watercolor, 489
Ribbon and Lace, 533
Opera, 554
German oak leaf pattern—*Eichenlaubmuster*, 615
Three Gustavsberg leaf-shaped dishes, 643

1900s

Color lithograph, 35
Wallpaper, 39
Wallpaper, 42
Color lithograph, 44
Textile, 47
Silk fragment, 53
Crocus, 57
Frieze, 64
Wallpaper, 64
Poppies, 64
Wallpaper, 69
Arlette, 72
Clover, 72

1900s cont.

Fool's Parsley, 76
Woodland Weeds, 81
The Furrow, 86
Seaweed, 88
Wallpaper, 90
Columbine, 96
The Precious Stones: Topaz, 98
The Precious Stones: Amethyst, 98
Plate 33 from "Documents Decoratifs," 98
Wallpaper design, 105
Minto, 123
Furnishing fabric, 136
The Formal Garden, 141
Small pattern, 148
Wallpaper design with repeating leaves, 158
Wallpaper with heart shaped leaves, 159
Silvanus, 166
Tulip Tree, 177
The Orange Tree, 180
Wallpaper, 219
Printed endpaper, 219
Macaw, 235
Brown Birds Perched on Holly, 250
Die Tausend Raben (A Thousand Ravens), 257
Notschrei ("Cry for Help"), 349
Border, 391
Wallpaper, 392
Wallpaper, 418
Wallpaper, 419
Ceiling paper, 421
Kente cloth, 460
Color lithograph, 471
Bachelor's Wallpaper, 477
Reciprocal Dancers, 555
Ceiling paper, 577

1910s

Rose and Teardrop, 18
Tulip and Lattice, 31
Textile, 61
Textile design, 63
Osterlocken (Narcissus), 70
Textile, 104
Cockpen, 108
Arbutus, 144

Textile, 175
Wallpaper, 235
Chinese Magpie, 236
Cedar Tree, 243
La Jungle (The Jungle), 287
Leaded glass, 366
Serpentin (Serpentine), 370
Dress fabric, 400
Wallpaper, 485
La Chasse (The Hunt), 505
Safety Pins, 529
Wallpaper, 549
Midnight Sun, 561
Composition, 583
White, 588
Furnishing fabric, 623
Fabric design, 625
Triangel (Triangle), 625

1920s

Briar, 18
Rose, 19
Buttercup and Daisy, 25
Les Arums (The Arum Lilies), 29
Furnishing fabric, 31
Furnishing fabric, 32
Nure, 81
Textile, 84
Primavera, 93
Austria, 96
Les Cornets, 101
Untitled, 103
Furnishing fabric, 104
Furnishing fabric, 124
Furnishing fabric, 130
Wallpaper, 130
Wallpaper, 139
Unknown, 140
Grand Feuillages, 150
Wallpaper (Hedera), 154
Dress fabric, 180
Bird and Pomegranate, 181
Falcon Hunt, 216
Wallpaper, 225
Pots, 526
Textile design, 234
Furnishing fabric, 242
Printed design, 244
Block print, 263
Crabs, 266
Les Conques, 268
Paper sample, 269

Wallpaper, 271
L'Eau (Water), 271
Furnishing fabric, 275
Pochoir print, 275
Dress fabric, 276
Design on paper, 284
Sheep, 284
Furnishing fabric, 291
Dress fabric, 297
Dress fabric, 306
Woven hanging, 306
No title, 317
Ziprian, 326
Cabinet detail, 327
Textile, 330
Pochoir print, 334
Pochoir on paper, 341
Quilt, 344
Textile design, 351
Textile, 366
Unknown, 378
Textile design, 382
Color lithograph, 393
Textile, 400
Textile, 415
Furnishing fabric, 415
Fabric detail, 419
Furnishing fabric, 405
Kente cloth, 461
Welwyn Garden City, 492
Sahara, 507
La Promenade en Bois, 513
Textile, 517
Sailing Boats, 518
Fabric, 521
Reaping Women, 547
Transport, 547
Textile, 547
Stadium, 550
Textile, 551
Block print, 555
Dress fabric, 557
April, 563
Dress fabric, 567
Printed paper, 568
Textile, 576
Design for a Wall Hanging, 582
Working Design for a Carpet, 582
Dress fabric, 608
Furnishing fabric, 625
Wall hanging, 626

Design for a hanging, 627
Textile, 628
Pochoir print, 628
Textile, 635
Kaléidoscope (Kaleidoscope), 622
Textile, 629
Lampas, 641
Textile, 644

1930s

Furnishing fabric, 25
Dress fabric, 25
Dress fabric, 26
Printed cotton/rayon, 31
Dress fabric, 31
Wallpaper, 32
Wrapping paper design, 56
Fabric sample, 65
Furnishing fabric, 85
Dress fabric, 85
Dress fabric, 92
Dress fabric, 93
Multifloral, 96
Dress fabric, 78
Dress fabric, 96
Dress fabric, 105
Dress fabric, 129
Feather pattern, 132
Rustic, 146
Stylized leaf and flower design, 146
Sans Souci, 150
George and Rufus, 209
Spencerian Horses, 214
Horses Head, 214
Jumping Horse, 215
Elefant (Elephant), 220
Doves, 227
Three Poppies, Four Wheat Sheaves, 228
Avis, 229
Wallpaper, 230
Scarf, 247
Feathers, 249
Mandalay, 264
Sea Horses, 271
No title, 320
Mosaic, 329
Pochoir on paper, 337
Pointed Pip, 350
Treillage, 369
Furnishing fabric, 377

Textile, 383
Maroon, 400
Hanging, 405
Furnishing fabric, 415
Swans, 417
Statues, 471
Dancing Naked Figures, 471
Festival, 474
Textile, 496
Lifeboats, 499
Fabric, 502
Aerial View, 502
Cornish Farm, 504
Tractor, 516
Textile, 519
Fabric, 519
International Women's Day, 546
Industrial, 547
Fun and Games, 549
Fisherman's Tale, 555
Birds, Cloud, Sun, Rain, 561
Textile, 564
Furnishing fabric, 585
Design for fabric, 588
Maroon, 624

1940s

Krysantemer (Chrysanthemums), 21
Pansy, 32
Stjärnmattan (Star Canvas), 40
Klöverblad (Cloverleaf), 73
Söndagsmorgon, 81
Eldblomman, 93
Millom, 94
Adelaide, 95
Paradiset (Paradise), 125
Attica, 140
Fruktlåda (Fruitbox), 179
Vegetable Tree, 185
Sagoträdet, 188
Jockeys, 215
Varklockor (black), 238
Lizard, 259
Shells and Starfish, 270
Butterfly, 276
Girafters, 282
Bird Zoo, 283
Jungle, 289
Crosspatch, 309
Thisbe, 311

Totley, 337
Walpole, 344
Lindfield, 348
Chevron, 367
Catseye utility furnishing
    fabric, 370
Circles, 382
Quatrefoil, 421
Sloyd, 424
Spot and Stripe, 443
Dress fabric, 472
Transport, 472
Family Groups, 472
Dress fabric, 473
Furnishing fabric, 473
Lustgärden (The Garden of
    Eden), 474
Textile, 474
Nautical, 499
Sea Shanties, 499
Textile, 504
Yacht, 519
Kimono, 521
A textile pottery, 531
Dress fabric, 535
Textile, 539
Fan Fantasy, 540
Keyboard, 553
Last Waltz, 554
Gala Night, 556
Star and Stripe, 567
Dress fabric, 612

1950s
Pallida, 44
Dandelion Clock, 69
Provence, 108
Hand-stencil-dyed paper,
    118
Mikado, 120
Flower Show, 124
Tuscany, 142
Seedpods, 167
Forest, 172
Kier, 180
Summer Stock, 187
Isabella, 202
Heinä, 205
Altamira, 215
Enara, 217
Buffalo, 219
Stenciled paper, 230
Furnishing fabric, 241

Happy Family, 241
Furnishing fabric, 241
Feathers, 248
Swan, 253
Aircraft, 256
Lizard, 259
Turtle, 259
LizardFishBat, 261
A Fish Is a Fish, 262
Fish, 262
Aquaria, 263
Fish, 265
Poisson (Fish), 265
Shrimp, 267
Sea Shells, 268
Sea Things, 270
Beetle, 280
Animal Kingdom, 283
Dress fabric, 288
Wallpaper, 290
Parade, 291
Shirt Panel (mola), 292
Unicorn, 303
Tenayuca, 306
Toccata, 312
Tartan textile sample, 320
Trapeze, 330
Prisma, 330
Multi Triangles, 330
Oomph, 332
Textile, 334
Design 706, 335
Arrowhead, 364
Textile, 377
Helmsley, 380
Textile design, 397
Change Your Life, 400
Leather cloth, 402
Cutout (Arabesque), 416
Quatrefoil, 420
Aleppo, 424
Cello, 429
Crosses, 433
Wallpaper, 438
Piscatore, 470
Masks, 476
Macrahanish, 484
Fabric, 485
Village Church, 489
Metropolis, 492
Porto Fino, 499
Orcades, 506
Astronauts and

Spaceships, 522
Wallpaper, 522
Bon Voyage, 524
Locomotion, 525
Flags, 525
Malaga, 527
Wallpaper, 527
Wallpaper, 528
Heirlooms, 528
Buttons, 536
Magic Pearls, 537
Textile design, 541
Textile, 544
Open Sesame, 545
Golf Magic, 550
Treasure Trove, 553
Kites and Mites, 557
Textile design, 564
Crystals, 565
Snowflakes, 565
Wallpaper, 565
Names, 570
Alphabet Stripe, 570
Letters, 571
Wallpaper, 577
Ormeggio (Mooring), 586
Marbled end paper, 591
Hand tie-dyed paper, 593
Springboard, 598
Raimoult, 599
Flotilla, 599
Furnishing fabric, 600
Rig, 600
Espace, 601
Acres, 602
Perpetua, 603
Fishnet, 609
Mirage, 609
Basuto, 610
The Dance, 612
Bird IN-A Box, 612
Palisade, 613
Camo, 614
Trios, 624
Spago, 624
Foreshore, 625
Applecross, 629
Kiddies Town, 630
Earthforms, 640
Festival of Britain style
    furnishing fabric, 642
Strata, 644
Haemoglobin, 646

Textile, 646
Afwillite 8.45, 647
Time Capsule, 647

1960s
Wallpaper, 33
Hydrangea, 56
Clematis, 61
Hyasintti (Hyacinth), 61
Unikko, 67
Verdure, 104
Leaves, 145
Eden, 147
Tallyho (orange), 182
Fabric design, 217
BirdFish, 260
Shells & Sand, 269
Chinese Dragon, 298
Zambezie, 307
Textile, 313
Box Plaid, 320
Nairobi, 345
Meteoric, 346
Treads, 349
Mexicotton Stripe, 351
Causeway, 351
Kinetics, 370
Recurrence, 380
Pompoms, 387
Textile, 390
Spiral, 396
Happiness, 403
Shimmy, 407
Wicker, 422
Triangle, 427
Town of Zagorsk, 475
Textile design, 475
Lippen ("Lips"), 476
Space Walk, 522
Lunar Rocket, 523
Batterie de Cuisine 527
Penny Candy, 535
Sunrise, 559
The Fool, 562
Happy Dreams, 569
Alpha Omega, 571
Unknown (Tie-dyed), 595
Joonas, 613
Camo, 614
DPM Camo, 614
Tiger Stripe Camo, 615
Wallpaper, 616
Galeria, 618

Dolores, 618
Bojangles, 619
Shape, 620
Kaplan furnishing fabric, 621
Simple Solar, 622
Petrus, 624
Melody, 631
Compendium, 632
Kernoo, 633
Extension, 633
Decor, 636
Unnamed, 638
Frequency, 639

1970s
Red House, 48
Cottage Garden, 122
Tuuli, 173
Wood's Edge, 173
Small Elephants, 220
Dress fabric, 266
Gouache on paper, 290
Wallpaper design, 311
Matrix, 315
Zebra, 367
Ensemble, 371
Textile design, 398
Legs, 476
Love Comic, 482
Raspberry Lips, 483
Faces, 483
Côte d'Azur, 501
Pocket Change, 542
Play Ball Two, 551
Paints and Palettes, 557
Solar, 561
Big Sky, 563
Evenstar, 567
Round Tower, 616
Cotton fabric, 617
Textile, 622
Aurora, 648
Borealis, 649

1980s
Dress fabric, 268
Hands, 484
Gaudi, 486
Havana, 500
Casablanca sideboard,
    detail, 606
Poltrona di Proust, 607
Unknown 615

1990s

Happy, 17
Rosetta Glory, 17
Secret Garden, 18
Lily (Blue), 29
Queuing Tulips, 31
Anemone, 41
Clematis, 61
Dandelion Two, 68
Dandelion One, 68
Grand Thistle, 75
Cow Parsley, 77
Wilderness, 89
Seaflower, 89
Botanica, 97
Checkered flower, 100
Angolese Starflower, 101
Tulip, 106
Shadow, 108
Birdcage, 116
Galaxy Bouquet, 130
Heaven Scent, 135
Itsy Bitsy, 137
Charleston Flowers, 142
Banana Leaf, 157
Leaf (Black/Gold), 157
Caterpillar Leaf, 162
Belladonna, 162
Rajapur, 168
Mandara, 173
Tree of Life, 177
Still Life, 178
Hollywood Grape, 178
Fiki (Fig), 179
Apple Tree, 184
Birdtree, 191
Until Dawn, 194
Nectar, 196
Prince, 197
Twine, 198
Lumimarja, 202
Floral Pattern, 202
Bamboo, 205
Gräs (Grass), 205
Antique Rose Blossom, 210
Horses, 214
Bunny Dance, 213
Doveflight, 226
Iguana, 258
Papillon, 275
Zebra, 371
Watermark, 377
Prefab Stripe, 489

Cowboy, 503
Baraka, 518
Wallpaper, 523
Sunburst, 558
Lepo, 611
Scribble (Grey), 610
"Daguet" Camo, 615
Pluto, 648

2000s

Wallflower Stripe, 57
Hedgerow, 76
Briar, 120
Hawthorn Rusts, 161
Puutarhurin Parhaat, 186
Cascade (Ivory Black), 189
Boomerang, 190
Blossom (Renaissance
    Gold), 202
No title, 236
Bird Garden, 250
Gulls, 256
Moths, 279
Caterpillars, 280
Monster Skin, 296
Moo, 284
Graphic Croc, 294
Optical, 313
Checkerboard, 314
Dogtooth, 318
Printed design, 332
Geotaxis, 335
Fez, 340
Repeat Classic Stripe, 347
Hyper Stripe, 353
Vertical, 353
Empire 1 Navy, 354
Arrows, 364
Jagged Edge, 367
Flash, 373
Chains, 380
Spiral Spot, 383
Repeat Dot Ring, 385
Diagonal Beaded Stripe, 386
Small Ovals, 388
Spiral, 396
Hedgehog, 404
Pirouette, 406
Pyramids, 426
Gridlock, 428
Ropey, 434
Chainmail, 438
Maize, 441

Moorish Circles, 467
London, 486
NYC, 488
Do You Live in a Town?, 488
NYC, 492
Ocean View, 498
Sitting Comfortably, 543
Marbles, 549
C60, 552
Pet Sounds, 553
Fayres Fair, 555
Air Rave, 566
Love Field, 568
Knock Knock, 570
Pause, 570
Treehouse, 600
Basketry, 608
Tarentel, 613
Woodstock, 618
Braided, 637
Moonlight Daisy, 637
Riley, 637
Cells, 647
Tiger Moon, 648

2010

Ramblas, 18
Water Lily, 26
Baudard, 37
Bloomsbury, 101
Sudbury, 140
Ludlow, 192
Dogs, 209
Tropical Birds, 252
Exaggerated Plaid, 321
Florence, 389
Feather Fan, 413
Porden, 429
Lee Priory, 441
Great Wave, 497
Whitby, 519
Keys, 545
Shaded Chevron, 366
Aztec, 399
Shuttle and Shaft, 358

2011

Dandy (Lemony), 19
No title, 126
Pepper Trail, 188
Wisteria (Lilac Rose), 199
Bamboo, 204
Ascension, 253

Wild Honey Bee Allover, 272
Butterflies, 277
Zig Zag Moth, 278
White Moth Circle, 279
Parterre, 326
Blotch Stripe, 346
Borders, 365
Jurmo, 387
Aladdin, 408
Weave, 423
Deep Sea, 496
Breakwater, 580
Salvage, 581
Grand Blotch Damask, 617

2012

Mini Mean Roses, 19
Summer Lily, 28
Pansy Stripe, 32
Kentish Rose, 85
Meadow Day, 90
Requena, 105
Happy Flowers, 105
Striped Petal, 107
Aldwych, 117
Rhododendron, 137
Amapola, 137
Palm Jungle, 147
Multi Acorn Spot, 157
Komorebi, 162
Kompotti, 166
Wild Strawberry, 180
Woods & Pears, 185
Multi Stem, 203
Pedigree Entourage, 208
Byron, 243
Little Birds, 254
Coral and Shells, 269
Tsunotombo (Owlfly), 281
Zoo, 283
Harvest Hare, 285
Misty Ikat, 315
Allegro, 322
On Point, 334
Kites, 336
Samoa, 340
Hicks' Grand, 342
Scaffold, 346
Ottoman Stripe, 350
Vortex, 374
Ikat Damask, 375
Parure, 376
Ropey Heritage, 422

Pompeian, 426
Window Ikat, 429
Piccadilly, 466
Mosaic, 467
New York City Toile, 494
New York Toile 2, 495
High Seas, 498
Sussex Downs (Landscape),
    504
Hunting Toile, 512
Flying Colors, 524
Dress fabric, 542
Library, 544
Cloud Toile, 563
Star Ikat, 567
Scribble, 608

2013

Rosa, 18
La La Lyon, 116
Cellini, 113
Royal Garden, 123
Ivy Block, 155
Lochwood, 174
Bavaria Stripe, 186
Great Vine, 199
Cellini, 200
Printed design, 212
Rambo Blacks, 218
Tyger Tyger, 222
Les Jardins Majorelle, 258
Butterflies, 276
Bavaria, 284
Merian Palm, 287
Celestial Dragon, 298
Cube Star (Coral), 329
V Stripe, 350
Great 8 (Gold), 381
Bola, 382
Pollen, 413
Kelburn, 423
Penton Villas, 424
Richard Nixon, 433
Alcazar, 444
Aftermath, 490
Urban Chaos, 491
Brighten Up Your Day, 498
Peggy, 528
Vases, 534
Penguin Library, 544
Letter (Boutique), 571
Tracks, 581
Abstract Malachite, 645

2014

Rose, 16
Sakura Flower, 53
Bluebell, 80
Trailing rose, 129
Eden, 145
Odhni, 147
Jardin Exo'chic, 151
Tribe, 160
Jindai, 160
Bird Branch Stripe, 189
Tiara, 193
Japoneries, 201
Sausage Dogs, 209
Starling, 249
Imperial Apiary, 273
Camberwell Beauty, 276
Dragonfly Dance, 280
Printed design, 315
Staggered Gingham, 316
32:64, 318
Cuteboy, 323
Geometric design, 328
Intaglio, 332
Triangulated, 361
Lucknow, 364
Memphis, 366
Nevis, 367
Sun Loving Bollards, 372
Geo Star Floral, 377
Bokhen, 381
Amlapura, 384
Anpan, 385
Printed design, 387
Viaduct, 414
Light on Lattice, 425
Porto, 427
Laguna, 432
Darjeeling, 467
Billie Goes to Town, 491
Versailles Grand, 513
Hold Tight, 525
Backgammon, 548
Clouds, 562
Printed design, 585
Haze, 635
Kairi, 647

2015

Shanghai Garden, 50
French Meadow, 79
Marble Damask, 112
Damsel Damask, 115

Culpeper, 127
Kayin, 154
Tropicana, 163
Parati, 182
Habanera [pineapple], 183
Billie, 211
Parrot with Pineapple, 236
Arini, 237
Leopardo, 247
Feathers, 249
The Fruit Looters, 251
Flock, 254
Gulls, 256
Amazon, 258
Nicaragua, 259
Nautilus, 265
Inky Insects, 279
Pardus (Leopard), 295
Pantigre, 297
Essex Check
    Dark Navy, 316
Houndstooth, 319
Puzzle, 322
Lorenzo, 322
Zirconia, 331
Jali, 340
Vintage Stripe 2
    Dark Navy, 352
Luxor, 360
Broadway, 414
Barbade, 423
Lattice, 424
Equinox, 439
Miami, 493
Dungeness, 496
Marmara, 497
Motor Bike, 516
Bicycles, 517
Swoop, 520
Shoes, 539
Beauty Parlour, 545
Sunset, 558
Morn's Rays, 558
Pyramid Sunrise, 560
Kaleido Splatt Allover, 584
Tracey, 592
Memphis pattern, 606
Reflect, 609
Ripple, 610
P.L.U.T.O. (Pipeline Laid
    Under The Ocean), 634
Mosaic, 634
Indigo Blur, 634

Dress fabric, 635
Ebru, 640

2016

Fleur de Lotus, 36
Antoinette, 43
Field, 79
Masson, 90
Elizabeth, 91
A New Language, 100
Majella, 104
Balabina, 113
Bloomsbury Garden, 124
Mughal Garden, 127
Garden, 127
Corsage, 129
Windflower bunch, 131
Bouquet, 133
Versailles Garden, 145
Armature Feuille, 146
Chrysler, 163
Birch Wood, 172
Korpi, 174
No title (pear), 183
A Discreet Revival, 188
Ruskin Floral, 195
Rabbit, 212
Leopards, 222
Birds, 225
Chickens, 240
Birds on Branch, 253
Tropical Fish Stripe, 262
Sea Bed, 266
Charonda, 274
Fantasque, 286
Giraffe, 295
Dress fabric, 296
Assembled Check, 310
Bar Line, 311
Checkerboard, 314
Ripon Dark Navy, 318
No title, 330
Mera, 333
Normandie, 337
Color Dance, 344
Crochet, 349
Skate, 349
Bakst, 361
Peacock, 368
Small Way, 369
Reef, 369
Circles, 381
Sgt. Pepper, 389

Bibana, 390
Dianne, 393
Fujisan, 407
Jali Trellis, 408
Palmprint, 412
Lempicka, 415
Margot, 422
Petipa, 426
Inlay, 428
Oriel, 445
London Toile, 495
Carnac, 503
Wound Up, 532
Cocarde, 538
Maison de Jeu (Gambling
    House), 549
Love Boat, 569
Speckled, 585
Watermarks, 586
Sea Glass, 587
Strand, 609
Dress fabric, 632
Ruhlman, 637
Quartz, 641

2017

Mizukusa, 37
Fritillaria, 80
Snowdrops, 81
Delft Flower, 97
Noailles Nuit, 117
Annabelle, 122
The Rainbow, 122
Arabesque, 123
Art Room, 143
Evergreen, 144
Woodland, 160
Zaffera, 161
Montracy, 171
Dress fabric, 184
A Forest, 194
Safari Dance, 221
Leopard Walk, 222
Quill, 248
Narina, 248
Star-ling, 254
Aviary, 255
Savuti, 286
Veljekset
    (Brothers), 286
Zambezi, 287
Zulu Border, 295
Reveries, 302

Vista, 307
Homework, 307
Frith, 314
Detail of black marquetry
    surface, 324
Folded Geometric, 334
Veren, 336
Marker Hexagon, 343
Jodphur Blue, 348
Greek No. 1, 361
Dress fabric, 371
Dorothy, 386
Waves, 407
Dress fabric, 409
Ardmore Cameos, 418
True Romance, 482
Dress fabric, 487
Metroland, 492
Moordale, 505
Japanese Garden, 509
Exotisme, 509
Ceramica, 526
Matrinah, 526
Dress fabric, 532
Khulu Vases, 533
Bottle and Jar Bouquets,
    535
Dress fabric, 537
Curio, 542
Dress fabric, 545
Birthday Party, 556
Solar Flare, 558
Impasto, 580
Raindrop Flowers, 585
Orange Orchard, 586
Paint Blobs, 586
Get Lost, 622

2018

Kolkata Fern, 150
Disguise, 383

Index by Designer

A

Adam, Robert, 356
Adler, Jonathan, 322, 433
Albeck, Pat, 179
Albers, Anni, 306, 332, 360, 362, 363, 362
Albers, Josef, 626
Aldridge, John, 533
Allen, A. Richard, 545
American Print Works, 418
American Wall Paper Manufacturers' Association, 88
Andersen, Gunnar Aagaard, 571
Apponaug Company, 268
Ardmore Ceramic Art, 221, 222, 248, 286, 287, 295, 418, 526, 533
Armfield, Diana, 219
Arora, Kangan, 336, 340, 364
Artcraft Wallpaper Company, 438
Ascher, Lida, 288
Ascher, Zika, 288
Ascher Studio, 288, 289, 313, 320, 472, 473, 504, 535, 553, 612
Associated American Artists, 528, 545, 550, 565, 537, 553, 617
Associated Artists, 71
Associes, Paris, 90
Astrom, Maria, 97, 179
Atelier Martine, 104, 108
Audubon, John James, 250
Avondale Mills Inc., 483

B

Bacon, John Henry Frederick, 86
Bancroft, Rob, 544, 629
Barlow & Jones, 646
Barron, Phyllis, 132, 133, 349, 350, 368, 502
Bassett & Vollum, 283
Battersby, Martin, 266
Battle, Sarah, 183, 240
Bawden, Edward, 393, 421, 506, 506, 507
Bayer, Herbert, 626
Beecher, William Ward, 537, 553
Bell, Vanessa, 96, 588, 589, 623, 625
Bencsko, Michelle Engel, 334, 528, 558
Bianchini-Férier, 149
Bicât, André, 146

Birge & Sons Co., M. H., 390, 440, 527, 577, 565
Blee, Kate, 160, 346, 427, 581
Blinds 2 Go, 585
Boontje, Tord, 17, 79, 89, 108, 127, 135, 194, 196, 197, 406, 613
Bonfils, Robert, 377
van den Boogaard, Cor, 545
Bosence, Susan, 390, 595
Bouzois, Jean, 405
Boym Partners, 414
Bradburn, Neil, 220
Brayley, Francis, 465
Breuer, Marcel, 626
British Celanese Ltd., 647
British Disruptive Pattern, 614
Brown, Barbara, 380, 396, 618, 636, 638, 639
Brown, Gregory, 405
Burylin, Sergei, 516, 547
Butterfield, Lindsay P., 56, 64

C

Calico Printers' Association, 25, 31, 31, 65, 78, 85, 96, 129, 215, 227, 271, 400, 499, 499, 499, 502, 549, 585
Campbell, Nina, 174, 423
Campbell, Sarah 291
Campbell Wall Paper Co., Wm., 419
Carpenter, Carrie, 34
Carter, Doris, 263, 518
Castellani, Aki Ueda, 212, 225, 253
Cath Kidston, (See Kidston, Cath)
Chanel, 306, 608
Chareau, Pierre, 405, 628
Clarinval, Yvonne, 271
Clarke, René, 550
Clegg, Christine, 215
Clissold, Joyce, 554
Cloud9, 334, 344, 383, 524, 532, 544, 558, 585, 609, 610, 622, 629
Cole & Son, 26, 28, 77, 113, 117, 123, 140, 147, 168, 185, 192, 199, 221, 222, 243, 248, 286, 287, 295, 322, 336, 342, 360, 389, 413, 418, 421, 423, 426, 441, 466, 493, 497, 513, 526, 533, 537, 581, 609, 618, 634, 641

Colley, Jacqueline, 258, 259, 266
Collier Campbell, 122, 500, 501
Connelly, Brian, 550
Conran Fabrics, 407, 569
Conran, Terence, 486
Cooper, Margaret, 241
Courtaulds, 415
Crane, Walter, 27, 44, 74, 79, 141, 164, 180, 224, 234, 235, 245, 264, 271
Craven, Shirley, 620, 621, 622
Crosland, Neisha, 16, 41, 61, 100, 127, 157, 162, 178, 188, 190, 191, 326, 340, 367, 371, 377, 386, 388, 404, 408, 413, 426, 428, 441, 467, 558, 637, 637, 648, 648
Cullen, Rae Spencer, 557

D

David, Helen, 484, 486
Day, Lewis Foreman, 150, 161, 177
Day, Lucienne, 69, 108, 124, 172, 351, 503, 518, 559, 598, 600, 602, 603, 613, 624, 625, 644
Day, Robin, 602
Dearle, John Henry, 28, 42, 60, 71, 76, 81, 88, 117, 164, 176, 181
DeGroot, Holly, 585
Delaunay, Sonia, 313, 337, 338, 339, 341
De Morgan, William, 34, 75, 83, 152, 153, 164, 242, 298
Denst, Jack, 542
Desfossé, Jules, 320
Designers Guild, 18, 32, 36, 37, 43, 50, 80, 90, 97, 104, 105, 113, 117, 129, 145, 147, 151, 160, 161, 171, 182, 200, 201, 248, 274, 297, 302, 314, 336, 384, 423, 429, 444, 509, 538, 549, 580, 645
Dilkusha, 214
Dilnot, John, 276, 279, 280
Dobson, Frank, 471, 561
Dobson, Mary, 471
Doccia, 301
van Doesberg, Theo, 583
Donald Brothers Ltd., 146
Dorn, Marion, 228, 229, 256
Dresser, Christopher, 232, 258, 434, 566, 625

Drumlanrig, Sholto, 516, 517, 520, 539, 545, 558, 560
Drummond, John, 56, 470
Ducharne, François, 25, 26, 105
Dufy, Raoul, 29, 101, 123, 146, 148, 149, 150, 268, 287, 349, 479, 505, 513
Dunn, Tirzah, 249
Du Pasquier, Natalie, 604, 605
Duranceau, André, 266, 526
Dürer, Albrecht, 435
Durkin, Hilda, 489, 555
van Duppen, Antoon, 400

E

Eames, Charles, 270, 308, 309, 382
Eames, Ray, 270, 308, 309, 382
Edgar, Jane, 525
Edinburgh Weavers, 140, 150, 229, 241, 519, 631
Educational Alliance, 564
Elenhank, 173, 492, 561, 563, 649
Eley, Mark, 372
Eley Kishimoto, 19, 31, 101, 116, 120, 130, 137, 178, 208, 213, 214, 253, 256, 294, 296, 314, 318, 323, 358, 366, 372, 373, 380, 399, 422, 425, 434, 438, 498, 549, 566, 568, 637, 647
Elphick, Sharon, 489
Elsberg, Herman A., 175, 216, 561, 576
El Ultimo Grito, 366, 433
English Eccentrics, 18
Ericson, Estrid, 220
Erismann & Co., 158
Escher, M. C., 253, 259, 259, 260, 261, 262, 270, 280, 303
Everett, Michéle Brummer, 498, 524

F

Farr, Christopher, 105, 123, 137, 146, 160, 346, 349, 353, 366, 369, 427, 433, 467, 580
Faulkner, Kate, 50, 51, 156, 193
First Eleven Studio, 126, 183, 209, 236, 249, 283, 314, 328, 330, 377, 381, 585
Footprints, 518
Franceschi, Francesca, 296, 487

Frank, Jean-Michel, 327
Frank, Josef, 21, 40, 73, 81, 93, 93,
    125, 185, 188, 238, 239, 276
Fraser, Claud Lovat, 635
Frean, Jenny, 53, 81, 254, 407, 504,
    585
Fristedt, Sven, 367

G

Garcelon, André, 334
Gaudí, Antoni, 47, 467
Geary-Smith, Chloe, 488, 492
Geggs, E., 628
Gerald Holton Ltd., 525
Gibson, Charles Dana, 477
Gibson, Natalie, 407, 569
Girard, Alexander, 120, 145, 147,
    248, 330, 349, 351, 364, 416, 420,
    427, 433, 570, 572, 573
Gladky, Serge, 628
Gledhill Wall Paper Co., 42
Goncharova, Natalia, 235
Goodman, Francis, 288
Gotto, Felix C., 264
Grafton & Co., F. W., 130
Graham, Anna, 610
Grantil Company, J., 317
Gråsten, Viola, 332
Grasset, Eugène, 26, 43, 45, 69, 74
Gregg, Doris, 492
Groag, Jacqueline, 202, 311, 544,
    556, 630, 631
Gropius, Walter, 626
Grosch, Eleanor, 382
Groult, André, 32
Guild, Tricia, 18, 32, 36, 37, 43, 50,
    80, 90, 97, 104, 105, 113, 129,
    145, 147, 160, 161, 171, 200, 201,
    248, 274, 314, 336
Gustavsberg, 643

H

Haité, George, 57, 169, 170
Hall, Peter, 104, 624
Harben Papers, Inc., 291
Harper, Mary A., 44, 61
Hartmann et Fils, 489
Haward, Sidney, 32, 96
Hayman, Anna, 295, 389, 391, 393,
    412, 422
Heal's, 396, 618, 624, 633, 636, 638,
    639
Hearld, Mark, 226, 250, 285
Heath, Imogen, 18, 79, 80, 90, 144,
    249, 307, 322, 333, 386, 414

Helios Ltd., 95, 348
Hicks, David, 342
Hiroshige, Utagawa, 232
Hirvi, Erja, 193, 202
Hoffmann, Josef, 349, 370, 430, 431,
    625
Hollyer, Frederick, 58
Honda, Yoko, 236, 606
Horne, Herbert, 552
Hough, Sarah, 275
Howard & Schaffer, 422
Howell and Brothers, 49
Hoyes, Rebecca, 314, 328, 330, 377,
    381, 585
Huet, Jean-Baptiste, 478, 495, 508
Hull Traders, 620, 621, 622
Hunter, Eileen, 400, 417, 624
Hutton, Dorothy, 291

I

Ian Mankin (see Mankin, Ian)
Iida, Tomoko, 353
Imperial Wallcoverings, 23
Irving, Constance, 19
Isabella, Emily, 535
Ishimoto, Fujiwo, 611
Isola, Maija, 66, 67, 173, 205, 613
Ito, Fumi, 281

J

Jacquemart, Pierre, 479
Janeway & Co., 421
Jeffrey & Co., 141
Jeffs, Emma, 311, 381, 424, 592, 635
Joel Ltd., Betty, 415
Jones, Jessica, 622
Jones, Owen, 37, 72, 109, 141, 151,
    329, 333, 343, 361, 393, 417, 417,
    421, 440
Jongerius, Hella, 145, 347, 365, 369,
    385, 428, 534
Justema, William, 33, 269

K

Kahn, L., 502
Kandinsky, Wassily, 626
Katzenbach and Warren, 187
Kemp, Kit, 369
Kersey, Kathleen, 144
Kidston, Cath, 85, 129, 131, 180, 209,
    210, 210, 211, 254, 486, 491, 495,
    498, 503, 556, 562
Kiely, Orla, 106, 107, 137, 157, 203,
    608
Kilburn, William, 128, 130, 135, 193

Kishimoto, Wakako, 372
Klein, Wendy, 567
Knight, Clayton, 563
Knoll Textiles, 570
Kronholm, Varpu, 222, 279
Kupferoth, Elsbeth, 601
Kvadrat, 196, 197, 406, 613

L

Lacroix, Christian, 117, 151, 182,
    297, 302, 423, 509, 538, 549, 645
Larcher, Dorothy, 132, 133, 349,
    368, 502
Larsen, Jack Lenor, 315, 402, 403
Larsen Design Studio, 402, 403, 616,
    619, 648
Laverne Inc., 330
Lewin, Angie, 68, 76, 177
Liberty & Co., 72, 84, 92, 424, 476,
    484, 518, 599, 609, 629
Liedgren, Birgitta, 205
Lindberg, Stig, 179, 182, 429, 474,
    530, 530, 531, 643
Line & Son Ltd., John, 630
Little, Anthony, 298
Ljungberg, 97, 179, 429, 182, 330,
    332
Lloyd-Thomas, Sally, 315, 332, 387
Lorca, 340
Louekari, Maija, 186, 286

M

Mackintosh, Charles Rennie, 18, 31,
    102, 103, 400
MADE, 634
Maggiolini, Giuseppe, 325
Maharam, 145, 186, 284, 319, 321,
    347, 350, 365, 369, 385, 428, 534,
    571
Mahler, Marian, 140
Mairs & Co., William H., 64
Maison Maunoury et Cie, 269, 568
Maix, L. Anton, 557
Malta, Vincent, 263
Manifattura J. S. A., 624
Mankin, Ian, 316, 318, 352, 354
Mann, Ptolemy, 315, 348, 374, 429,
    567, 634
Marimekko, 66, 193, 205, 387, 611
Mariscal, Javier, 105, 137, 467
Markelius, Sven, 330
Martin, Joe, 283, 551, 571
Marx, Enid, 32, 311, 367, 370, 424,
    442, 443, 567
Masui, Gaku, 316, 343, 407

Maxwell & Co., S. A., 418, 577
McAuley, Alistair, 114
McClelland, Nancy, 139
McCobb, Paul, 557
McDonald, K., 555
McLeish, Minnie, 31, 104, 275
McSparran, Kimberly, 269
Meissinger, Lilli, 217
Memphis, 604, 605, 606
Mendini, Alessandro, 607
Mergentime, Marguerita, 214
Metsola, Aino-Maija, 166, 174, 387
Miller, Edgar, 283
Mini Moderns, 143, 194, 249, 254,
    256, 276, 284, 307, 439, 467,
    482, 488, 492, 496, 505, 519,
    525, 543, 548, 552, 553, 555,
    570, 634
Minton, John, 142
Missoni, 371
Moholy-Nagy, László, 626
Mollemans, Jan, 268
Moller, Hans, 612
Moody, Helen Wills, 567
Moore, Henry, 472, 473, 535, 553,
    612
Morris, May, 64, 84
Morris, William, 16, 23, 24, 28, 30, 35,
    35, 41, 41, 46, 47, 54, 56, 58, 59,
    62, 63, 64, 75, 80, 81, 82, 82, 84,
    92, 97, 116, 117, 134, 136, 140,
    154, 164, 165, 178, 185, 194, 199,
    212, 226, 299
Morris & Co., 35, 51, 54, 154, 169,
    180
Morton, Alastair, 539
Morton & Co., Alexander, 86, 87
Morton Sundour Fabrics, 140, 443
Moser, Koloman, 72, 166, 257, 471,
    555
Mucha, Alphonse, 35, 44, 98, 98, 98,
    484
Muncaster, Jenny, 142
Munsell, Richard, 263
Murphy, James Cavanagh, 446

N

N & N Wares, 311, 381, 424, 635
Napper, Harry, 303
Newson, Rosemary, 632
New York Card and Paper Co., 392
Nicholson, Ben, 209
Nordiska Kompaniet, 474
Nuno, 37, 162, 343, 385, 608

O

Oberkampf, Christophe-Philippe, 478, 508

Oberkampf & Cie, 495

OK Textiles Ltd., 476, 483

Oladipo, Tomi, 361, 542

Old Town, 424

Oliver, Mary, 499

Osborne & Little, 127, 154, 160, 163, 163, 173, 174, 183, 222, 237, 247, 255, 280, 286, 295, 298, 298, 331, 337, 340, 361, 367, 376, 408, 415, 423, 426, 497, 509, 526, 542, 544, 637, 640, 647

P

Palmer, Sue Thatcher, 522

Panton, Verner, 476

Parker, Robyn, 262

Parzinger, Tommi, 259, 422, 541, 564

Pausa, 601

Piazza Prints, 527, 551, 536

Picasso, Pablo, 265

Pickard, Sam, 17, 57, 89, 150, 155, 161, 198, 205, 313, 335, 350, 383, 396

Plaistow, O. R., 415

Poiret, Paul, 104, 529

Post, Simone, 532

Prager Company, Inc., 522

Preobrazhenskaya, Darya, 546, 547

Prestigious, 407

Pucci, Albert John, 528

Pugin, Augustus, 110, 111, 417, 441, 576, 577

Q

Quaintance & Co., W. B., 262

de Quénetai, Claire, 91, 100, 122, 188

Qveflander, Anneli, 61

R

Rabier, Benjamin, 219

Racinet, Albert Charles August, 298

Real Fabrica de Buen Retiro, 357

Record, Anne, 343

Reeves, Ruth, 474

Refregier, Anton, 545

Réveillon, Jean-Baptiste, 478

Riemerschmid, Richard, 61, 158, 159, 174

Robinson & Barber, 540

Rodchenko, Alexander, 382, 378

Rodier, Paul, 366

Rombola, John, 291

Rose, Ben, 282, 306, 307, 345, 346, 370, 387, 535, 609, 640, 647

Rowland, Bernard, 646

Ruhlmann, Émile-Jacques, 641, 644

S

St. Jude's, 68, 76, 177, 226, 250, 285, 424, 496, 599

Sanchez y Sanchez de la Barquera, Gabriela, 569

Sanderson & Sons, Arthur, 53, 85, 154, 234, 254, 290, 330, 383, 504, 528

Saunders, Liza, 212, 218

Schepe, Hinnerk, 626

Schier and Doggett, 540

Schlemmer, Oskar, 626

Schröder, Anny, 485

Schumacher & Co., F., 283, 523, 524, 525

Schuurman, Michiel, 635

Scott, George Gilbert, 169

Scott, Ken, 262

Scull, Doris, 284

Séguy, E. A., 275

Sewell, Matt, 249

Shinohara, Teruyo, 22

Shirokova, Nina, 290, 352, 397, 398, 475, 622

Shuttleworth, Peter, 312

Sillich, L., 547

Silver, Arthur, 246

Silver, R., 244

Silver Studio, 230

Simmons, Paul, 114

Simon, Mary Hergenroder, 139

Slade, S. M., 647

Smith, Joshua, 124

Smith, Paul, 310, 319, 321, 350

Snischek, Max, 326

Sottsass, Ettore, 606

Spiers, Charlotte Horne, 22, 48

Squeekers, 557

Squires, Eddie, 523, 618

Stahl, Louis, 243

Standard Papers, 392

Stead McAlpin & Co., 522

Stehli Silks Co., 180, 550, 563, 567

Steiner & Co., F., 47, 124, 242, 557

Stepanova, Varvara, 378, 379

Sternberg, Charlotte, 565

Steteco.com, 37, 162, 385, 407

Stevenson, Alice, 599

Stewart. Robert, 180, 476, 484, 599, 609, 629

Stölzl, Gunta, 306, 351, 582, 626, 627

Strachey, Lytton, 588

Straub, Marianne, 94, 95, 315, 337, 348, 380, 424

Strengell, Marianne, 334

Stuart, Marni, 334, 586

Studio Houndstooth, 318

Studio Job, 186, 284, 490,

Sudo, Reiko, 162, 608

Sugiura, Ryoko, 101, 184

Sutton, Emily, 496

T

Taibbi, Rose, 519

Talbert, Bruce James, 53, 145, 182

Taniguchi, Yuka, 202

Tessari, Gigi, 624

Testa, Angelo, 612

Thomas Strahan Co., 344

Thomasse, Erwin, 371

Thomson, Alexander "Greek," 38

Tiffany Studios, 99

Tillett, D. D., 320

Tillett, Leslie, 320

Timorous Beasties, 75, 112, 114, 114, 115, 116, 124, 172, 177, 189, 195, 204, 251, 258, 272, 273, 277, 278, 279, 287, 346, 375, 491, 494, 495, 512, 563, 584, 617

Tisdall, Hans, 241

Tootal, Broadhurst, Lee & Co., 25, 93, 474, 496, 519, 554

Toploski, Feliks, 289, 472

Trevelyan, Julian, 504

Trickey, Tony, 126, 209, 236, 283

Tsutsumi, Yuki, 37, 385

Turnbull & Stockdale Ltd., 150

Turner, William, 236

2x4, 570

V

Vanners & Fennel Bros. Ltd., 646

Vasareley, Victor, 633

Vashkov, Sergei, 312

Vera, Paul, 225

Verneuil, Maurice-Pillard, 622

Vézelay, Paule, 612

Vigers, Allan, 96

Vlisco, 167, 215, 265, 267, 364, 400, 409, 487, 532, 537, 542, 569, 632, 635

Voysey, C. F. A., 18, 25, 35, 49, 63, 63, 76, 81, 86, 86, 87, 105, 108, 113, 123, 136, 175, 189, 217, 226, 250, 250, 257

W

Walker, Alec, 504

Wallpaper Manufacturers, 527, 610, 632

Warner, Jocelyn, 19, 29, 157, 189, 199, 202, 329, 381, 571, 610

Warner & Sons, 94, 141, 522, 523, 618

Watson, Sarah, 383

Wealleans, Jane, 476, 483

Weir, Harrison William, 24

Wheeler, Candace, 71, 272

White, Janice Hart, 565

Wiener Werkstätte, 276, 326

Wilcock, Arthur, 29, 55, 57, 204

Wilkinson, Charles K., 394

William, Haydon, 633

Williamson, Matthew, 127, 163, 173, 183, 222, 237, 247, 280, 298, 367, 408, 526, 647

Willinger, Karen, 217

van Winden, Sanne, 184

Winter and Kurth, 324

Worsley, Catherine, 558, 586, 587

Wright, Frank Lloyd, 335, 366

Y

Yasui, Yumi, 162

Z

Zann, Nicky, 482

Zuber & Cie, 50

von Zülow, Franz, 70

Index by Country of Pattern Origin

Unknown location

not known, Textile fragment, **38**
not known, Wallpaper, **39**
not known, Silk fragment, **53**
not known, Wrapping paper design, **56**
not known, Damask sample, **113**
not known, Cotton textile, **121**
not known, Fabric panel, **142**
not known, Textile, **169**
not known, Wallpaper, **173**
not known, Design on paper, **284**
not known, Embroidered silk textile, **290**
not known, Fabric swatch, **311**
not known, Fabric swatch, **364**
not known, Fabric swatch, **385**
not known, Fabric sample, **389**
not known, Textile sample, **390**
not known, Fabric swatch, **404**
not known, Fabric swatch, **413**
not known, Fabric swatch, **421**
not known, Fabric swatch, **427**
not known, Fabric swatch, **434**
not known, Fabric, **485**
not known, Textile, **536**
not known, Quilt, **539**
not known, Coverlet, **633**
not known, Fabric swatch, private archive, **646**

Africa

Africa, Unknown country, Fabric swatch, **401**
Africa, Unknown country, Fabric swatch, **409**
Egypt, Ceiling pattern, Tomb of Qenamun, Charles K. Wilkinson, **394**
Egypt, Ceiling painting from the palace of Amenhotep III, **394**
Egypt, Miniature broad collar, **395**
Egypt, Wall decoration, not known, **398**
Egypt, Cairo, Wall Panel with Geometric Interlace, **446**
Ghana, Detail of a length of Kente cloth, Ashanti People, **460**
Ghana, Kente cloth, Akan People, **460**

Ghana, Kente cloth, Akan People, **461**
Ghana, Kente cloth, Ewe People, **461**
Ghana, Ashanti Kente cloth, Ghana, **461**
Ivory Coast, Tie-dye Plangi textile on raffia Dida pane, **596**
Morocco, Ceramic tiles, **445**
Morocco, Tiles, **449**

Asia

China, Textile, not known, **37**
China, Porcelain book cover, not known, **299**
China, Textile design, not known, **299**
China, Silk hanging, not known, **303**
India, Printed cotton, India, **32**
India, Palampore, not known, **38**
India, Textile, not known, **39**
India, Printed cotton, not known, **47**
India, Sarasa, not known, **120**
India, Detail of a skirt, not known, **170**
India, Textile, not known, **170**
India, Pichhwai, not known, **219**
India, Pichhwai, not known, **219**
India, Shirt panel (mola), Kuna Indian Culture, **292**
India, Shirt panel (mola), Kuna Indian Culture, **293**
India, Gulbadan, Bengal, India, **374**
India, Quilt, **465**
India, Kalamkari, not known, **475**
India, Textile, not known, **538**
Japan, Chrysanthemums papercut, not known, **20**
Japan, Kimono detail, not known, **21**
Japan, Futon fabric, not known, **21**
Japan, Chrysanthemums & Snow Circles, Teruyo Shinohara, **22**
Japan, Chrysanthemum Blossoms, not known, **22**
Japan, Mizukusa, Yuki Tsutsumi of Nuno for Steteco.com, **37**
Japan, Temple altar cloth, **49**
Japan, Blue and Gold Cherry Blossom on a Pond, **52**
Japan, Bamboo and Cherry Blossoms, not known, **53**

Japan, Obi, not known, **74**
Japan, Angolese Starflower, Ryoko Sugiura, **101**
Japan, Hand-stencil-dyed paper, **118**
Japan, Textile, **119**
Japan, Stencil cloth, **119**
Japan, Stenciled paper, not known, **157**
Japan, Belladonna, Reiko Sudo, **162**
Japan, Komorebi, Yumi Yasui of Nuno for Steteco.com, **162**
Japan, Papercut, not known, **176**
Japan, Floral Pattern, Yuka Taniguchi, **202**
Japan, Kimono detail, not known, **204**
Japan, Silk fabric, not known, **225**
Japan, Stencilied paper, not known, **230**
Japan, Yellow and Green Trees with Cranes, not known, **231**
Japan, Cranes Flying in an Abstract Pattern, not known, **231**
Japan, Rapids at Naruto, Utagawa Hiroshige, **232**
Japan, Woodblock print, not known, **248**
Japan, Silk textile, not known, **264**
Japan, Hydrangeas and Butterflies, **275**
Japan, Tsunotombo (Owlfly), Fumi Ito, **281**
Japan, Staggered Gingham, Gaku Masui for Nuno, **316**
Japan, Textile, not known, **341**
Japan, Marker Hexagon, Gaku Masui, **343**
Japan, Hyper Stripe, Tomoko Iida for Nuno, **353**
Japan, Stripes on kimono, **375**
Japan, Anpan, Yuki Tsutsumi of Nuno for Kibiso, **385**
Japan, Paper, not known, **398**
Japan, Fujisan, Gaku Masui of Nuno for Steteco.com, **407**
Japan, Stencilled paper, El Ultimo Grito for Christopher Farr, **433**
Japan, Kimono, not known, **521**
Japan, Textile, not known, **540**
Japan, Panel, not known, **540**

Japan, Snowflakes Falling in a Winter Landscape, not known, **564**
Japan, Block print, not known, **566**
Japan, Japanese tie-dyeing fabric, **592**
Japan, Hand tie-dyed paper, **593**
Japan/Italy, Memphis pattern, Yoko Honda, **606**
Japan, Basketry, Reiko Sudo, **608**
Thailand, Fabric with indigo dye background, **594**
Vietnam, Tiger Stripe Camo, Vietnamese camouflage, **615**

Central Asia/Middle East

Iran, Textile, not known, **92**
Iran, Tilework, not known (built by Shah Abbas I), **416**
Iran, Textile, not known, **440**
Iran, Tiles, not known, **448**
Iran, Tiles, not known, **448**
Iran, Friday mosque, **575**
Syria, Arabic writing, **574**
Tajikistan, Uzbekistan or Kazakhstan, Bedcover suzani, **455**
Turkey, Furnishing fabric, not known, **39**
Turkey, Textile, not known, **377**
Turkey, Mirror with split-leaf palmette design inlaid with gold, **447**
Turkey, Iznik tiles, **450**
Turkey, Stylized flower motifs, **451**
Turkey, Iznik tiles, **451**
Turkey, Selimne Mosque, **574**
Uzbekistan, Shakhrisyabz suzani, **454**
Uzbekistan, Ceremonial hanging, Uzbek, **454**
Uzbekistan, suzani, **454**
Uzbekistan, suzani, **455**
Uzbekistan, Madrasa of Ulugh Beg, **574**

Europe

Austria, Osterlocken (Narcissus), Franz von Zülow, **70**
Austria, Arlette, Koloman Moser, **72**
Austria, Silvanus, Koloman Moser, **166**

Europe cont.

Austria, Die Tausend Raben (A Thousand Ravens), Koloman Moser, 257

Austria, Dress fabric, 276

Austria, Notschrei ("Cry for Help"), Josef Hoffman, 349

Austria, Serpentin (Serpentine), Josef Hoffmann, 370

Austria, Small pattern, Josef Hoffmann, 430

Austria, Color lithograph, Koloman Moser, 471

Austria, Wallpaper, Anny Schröder, 485

Austria, Reciprocal Dancers, Koloman Moser, 555

Austria, Triangel (Triangle), Josef Hoffmann, 625

Austria/Sweden, Varklockor (black), Josef Frank, 238

Austria/Sweden, Gröna Fåglar, Josef Frank, 239

Belgium, Wallpaper, 549

Czech Republic, Plate 33 from "Documents Decoratifs," Alphonse Mucha, 98

Czech Republic, The Precious Stones: Topaz, Alphonse Mucha, 98

Czech Republic, The Precious Stones: Amethyst, Alphonse Mucha, 98

Denmark, Letters, Gunnar Aagaard Andersen, 571

Finland, Hyasintti (Hyacinth), Anneli Qveflander, 61

Finland, Unikko, Maija Isola, 67

Finland, Kompotti, Aino-Maija Metsola, 166

Finland, Tuuli, Maija Isola, 173

Finland, Korpi, Aino-Maija Metsola, 174

Finland, Puutarhurin Parhaat, Maija Louekari, 186

Finland, Tiara, Erja Hirvi, Marimekko, 193

Finland, Lumimarja, Erja Hirvi, 202

Finland, Heinä, Maija Isola, Marimekko, 205

Finland, Veljekset (Brothers), Maija Louekari, 286

Finland, Jurmo, Aino-Maija Metsola, 387

Finland, Lepo, Fujiwo Ishimoto, 611

Finland, Joonas, Maija Isola, 613

Finland, Camo, Finnish camouflage, 614

France, Furnishing fabric, François Ducharne, 25

France, Dress fabric, François Ducharne, 26

France, Water lily wallpaper and tiles, Eugène Grasset, 26

France, Les Arums (The Arum Lilies), Raoul Dufy, 29

France, Wallpaper, André Groult, 32

France, Color lithograph, Alphonse Mucha, 35

France, Wallpaper border, 38

France, Scarf, 42

France, Color lithograph, Alphonse Mucha, 44

France, Irises, Eugène Grasset, 45

France, Wallpaper, 50

France, Dandelions, Eugène Grasset, 69

France, Winter Berry, 76

France, Textile design, 84

France, Domino paper, 90

France, Les Cornets, Raoul Dufy, 101

France, Textile, 104

France, Dress fabric, François Ducharne, 105

France, Atelier Martine, 108

France, Noailles Nuit, Christian Lacroix for Designers Guild, 117

France, Cotton textile, 121

France, Arabesque, Raoul Dufy/ Christopher Farr, 123

France, Textile design, 139

France, Small pattern, Raoul Dufy, 148

France, Raoul Dufy, 149

France, Grand Feuillages, Raoul Dufy, 150

France, Wallpaper, 166

France, Fabric design, 167

France, Printed endpaper, Benjamin Rabier, 219

France, Endpaper, 223

France, Wallpaper, Paul Vera, 225

France, Wallpaper, 247

France, Textile, 249

France, Les Conques, Raoul Dufy, 268

France, Paper sample, 269

France, Wallpaper, 271

France, L'Eau (Water), Yvonne Clarinval, 271

France, Damask, 272

France, Pochoir print, E. A. Séguy, 275

France, La Jungle (The Jungle), Raoul Dufy, 287

France, Lithograph, Albert Charles August Racinet, 298

France, Wallpaper, 302

France, Dress fabric, Chanel, 306

France, no title, Jules Desfossé, 320

France, Cabinet detail, Jean-Michel Frank, 327

France, Mosaic, 329

France, Pochoir print, André Garcelon, 334

France, Pochoir on paper, Sonia Delaunay, 337

France, Dress by Sonia Delaunay, 338

France, Cloth, Sonia Delaunay, 339

France, Pochoir on paper, Sonia Delaunay, 341

France, Fragment, France, 355

France, Les Losanges furnishing fabric, French, 356

France, Wallpaper, 361

France, Textile, Paul Rodier, 366

France, Treillage, 369

France, Furnishing fabric, Robert Bonfils, 377

France, Border, 397

France, Furnishing fabric, Pierre Chareau, 405

France, Hanging, Jean Bouzois, 405

France, Border, 413

France, Furnishing fabric, 415

France, Textile, 415

France, Wallpaper, 416

France, Fabric detail, 419

France, Fabric, 441

France, Color lithograph, 444

France, Wallpaper, Jean-Baptiste Réveillon, 478

France, Pallas and Venus, Jean-Baptiste Huet, 478

France, Textile, 479

France, Greek Procession, Raoul Dufy, 479

France, Frieze, 479

France, Femme à Marguerite, Alphonse Mucha, 484

France, Les Monuments de Paris, 489

France, La Fête de la Fédération, Jean-Baptiste Huet, 495

France, La Chasse, Raoul Dufy, 505

France, Textile, 508

France, The Drinking Trough, Jean-Baptiste Huet, 508

France, La Route de Poissy, 513

France, La Promenade en Bois, Raoul Dufy, 513

France, Pots, André Duranceau, 526

France, Safety Pins, Paul Poiret, 529

France, Textile, 538

France, Midnight Sun, Herman A. Elsberg, 561

France, Printed paper, 568

France, Textile, Herman A. Elsberg, 576

France, Wallpaper, 577

France, Dress fabric, Chanel, 608

France, "Daguet" Camo, French camouflage pattern, 615

France, Kaléidoscope (Kaleidoscope), Maurice-Pillard Verneuil, 622

France, Furnishing fabric, France, 625

France, untitled, Pierre Chareau, 628

France, Pochoir print, Serge Gladky, 628

France, Lampas, Émile-Jacques Ruhlmann, 641

France, Textile, Émile-Jacques Ruhlmann, 644

France/UK, Shawl, 169

Germany, Textile, Richard Riemerschmid, 61

Germany, Wallpaper with repeating leaves, Richard Riemerschmid, 158

Germany, Wallpaper with heart shaped leaves, Richard Riemerschmid, 159

Germany, Wallpaper, Richard Riemerschmid, 174

Germany, Woven hanging, Anni Albers/ Gunta Stölzl, 306

Germany, Ziprian, Max Snischek, 326

Germany, Intaglio, Anni Albers, 332

Germany, Textile design, Gunta Stölzl, 351

Germany, Berry, Anni Albers, 362

Germany, Meander, Anni Albers, 363

Germany, Interlace Pattern with White Medallion, Albrecht Dürer, 435

Germany, Espace, Elsbeth Kupferoth, 601

Germany, German oak leaf pattern— Eichenlaubmuster, 615

Germany, Wall hanging, Gunta Stölzl, 626

Germany, Design for a hanging, Gunta Stölzl, 627

Greece, Embroidered linen, 367

Greece, Greek. Illustration for a Handbook of Colored Ornament, 480

Greece, Terracotta alabastron (perfume vase), 481

Ireland, Mandalay, Felix C. Gotto, 264

Ireland, Book of Kells, 436

Ireland, Gospel of St. Matthew, 436

Ireland, Tara Brooch, 437

Ireland, Carpet page, 439

Italy, Chinoiserie teapot, Doccia, **301**

Italy, Table top, Giuseppe Maggiolini, **325**

Italy, Folding Game Board, **325**

Italy, Table top, Giuseppe Maggiolini, **325**

Italy, Ensemble, Missoni, **371**

Italy, Mosaic floor panel, Roman, **480**

Italy, Ormeggio (Mooring), **586**

Italy, Casablanca sideboard, Ettore Sottsass, manufactured by Memphis, **606**

Italy, Poltrona di Proust, Alessandro Mendini, **607**

Italy, Spago, Gigi Tessari, **624**

Netherlands, (seedpods), Vlisco, **167**

Netherlands, Dress fabric, Sanne van Winden, **184**

Netherlands, Bavaria Stripe, Studio Job for Maharam, **186**

Netherlands, Nectar, Tord Boontje for Kvadrat, **196**

Netherlands, Prince, Tord Boontje for Kvadrat, **197**

Netherlands, Jumping Horse, Ankersmit, Vlisco, **215**

Netherlands, Happy Family, Hans Tisdall, for Edinburgh Weavers Ltd., **241**

Netherlands, Swan, M. C. Escher, **253**

Netherlands, Lizard, M. C. Escher, **259**

Netherlands, Lizard, M. C. Escher, **259**

Netherlands, BirdFish, M. C. Escher, **260**

Netherlands, LizardFishBat, M. C. Escher, **261**

Netherlands, Fish, M. C. Escher, **262**

Netherlands, (fish), Vlisco, **265**

Netherlands, (shrimp), Vlisco, **267**

Netherlands, Dress fabric, Jan Mollemans, **268**

Netherlands, Shells and Starfish, M. C. Escher, **270**

Netherlands, Beetle, M. C. Escher, **280**

Netherlands, Dress fabric, Francesca Franceschi, **296**

Netherlands, Dress fabric, (Haarlemsche Katoenmaatschappij), **297**

Netherlands, Unicorn, M. C. Escher, **303**

Netherlands, Greek No. 1, Owen Jones, **361**

Netherlands, (arrows), Vlisco, **364**

Netherlands, Dress fabric, Erwin Thomasse, **371**

Netherlands, Change Your Life, Antoon van Duppen, **400**

Netherlands, Dress fabric, **409**

Netherlands, Dress fabric, Francesca Franceschi, **487**

Netherlands, Tile (figure), **510**

Netherlands, Tile (house), **510**

Netherlands, Wall tile, **510**

Netherlands, Delft tile (drawbridge over a canal), Dutch School, **511**

Netherlands, Dress fabric, Simone Post, **532**

Netherlands, Dress fabric, Cole & Son, **537**

Netherlands, Dress fabric, Tomi Oladipo for Vlisco, **542**

Netherlands, Dress fabric, Cor van den Boogaard, **545**

Netherlands, Love Boat, Gabriela Sanchez y Sanchez de la Barquera; Vlisco, **569**

Netherlands, Dress fabric, Vlisco, **632**

Netherlands, Dress fabric, Michiel Schuurman, **635**

Netherlands/USA, Borders, Hella Jongerius for Maharam, **365**

Netherlands/USA, Reef, Hella Jongerius for Maharam, **369**

Netherlands/USA, Repeat Dot Ring, Hella Jongerius for Maharam, **385**

Portugal, Azulejo tiles, **452**

Portugal, Azulejo tiles, **453**

Russia, Wallpaper, Natalia Goncharova, **235**

Russia, Gouache on paper, Nina Shirokova, **290**

Russia, Textile design, Sergei Vashkov, **312**

Russia, no title, Varvara Stepanova, **378**

Russia, Circle Motif, Varvara Stepanova, **379**

Russia, Textile design, Alexander Rodchenko, **382**

Russia, Textile, Nina Shirokova, **397**

Russia, Textile design, Nina Shirokova, **398**

Russia, Textile design, Nina Shirokova, **475**

Russia, Town of Zagorsk, Nina Shirokova, **475**

Russia, Tractor, Sergei Burylin, **516**

Russia, Textile, not known, **517**

Russia, Fabric, not known, **521**

Russia, International Women's Day, Darya Preobrazhenskaya, **546**

Russia, Textile, Sergei Burylin, **547**

Russia, Reaping Women, L. Sillich, **547**

Russia, Industrial, Darya Preobrazhenskaya, **547**

Russia, Transport, Darya Preobrazhenskaya, **547**

Russia, Textile, **551**

Russia, Textile, Nina Shirokova, **622**

Spain, Tiles, Antoni Gaudí, **47**

Spain, Vase with cover, Real Fabrica de Buen Retiro, **357**

Spain, Ceramic tiles, **444**

Spain, Ceramic tiles, **445**

Spain, Mosaic, Court of the Lions, Alhambra, **446**

Spain, Tiles, **448**

Spain, Tiles, **449**

Spain, Mosaic, **449**

Spain, Tiles, Antoni Gaudi, **467**

Sweden, Krysantemer (Chrysanthemums), Josef Frank, **21**

Sweden, Stjärnmattan (Star Canvas), Josef Frank, **40**

Sweden, Klöverblad (Cloverleaf), Josef Frank, **73**

Sweden, Söndagsmorgon, Josef Frank, **81**

Sweden, Primavera, Josef Frank, **93**

Sweden, Eldblomman, Josef Frank, **93**

Sweden, Botanica, Maria Astrom, Ljungbergs, **97**

Sweden, Paradiset (Paradise), Josef Frank, **125**

Sweden, Fruktlåda (Fruitbox), Stig Lindberg, **179**

Sweden, Fiki (Fig), Maria Astrom, Ljungbergs, **179**

Sweden, Tallyho (orange), Stig Lindberg, Ljungbergs, **182**

Sweden, Vegetable Tree, Josef Frank, **185**

Sweden, Sagoträdet, Josef Frank, **188**

Sweden, Gräs (Grass), Birgitta Liedgren, **205**

Sweden, Elefant (Elephant), Estrid Ericson, **220**

Sweden, Butterfly, Josef Frank, **276**

Sweden, Prisma, Sven Markelius Ljungbergs, **330**

Sweden, Oomph, Viola Gråsten, Ljungbergs, **332**

Sweden, Zebra, Sven Fristedt, **367**

Sweden, Cello, Stig Lindberg, **429**

Sweden, Lustgärden (The Garden of Eden), Stig Lindberg, **474**

Sweden, Tablecloth, Stig Lindberg, **530**

Sweden, A textile pottery, Stig Lindberg, **531**

Sweden, Three Gustavsberg leaf-shaped dishes, Stig Lindberg, **643**

Switzerland, Lippen ("Lips"), Verner Panton, **476**

Switzerland, Camo, Swiss camouflage, **614**

UK, Rose, Neisha Crosland, **16**

UK, Trellis, William Morris, **16**

UK, Happy, Tord Boontje, **17**

UK, Rosetta Glory, Sam Pickard, **17**

UK, Rose and Teardrop, Charles Rennie Mackintosh, **18**

UK, Secret Garden, English Eccentrics, **18**

UK, Rosa, Imogen Heath, **18**

UK, Briar, C. F. A. Voysey, **18**

UK, Ramblas, Designers Guild, **18**

UK, Dandy (Lemony), Jocelyn Warner, **19**

UK, Mini Mean Roses, Eley Kishimoto, **19**

UK, Rose, Constance Irving, **19**

UK, Wallpaper, Charlotte Horne Spiers, **22**

UK, Chrysanthemum, William Morris, **23**

UK, Daisy, Harrison William Weir, **24**

UK, Daisy, William Morris, **24**

UK, Buttercup and Daisy, C. F. A. Voysey, **24**

UK, Dress fabric, not known, **25**

UK, Dress fabric, Calico Printers' Association, **25**

UK, Water Lily, Cole & Son, **26**

UK, Day Lily, Walter Crane, **27**

UK, Dress fabric, not known, **27**

UK, Golden Lily, John Henry Dearle, **28**

UK, Lily, William Morris, **28**

UK, Summer Lily, Cole & Son, **28**

UK, The Lily, Arthur Wilcock, **29**

UK, Lily (Blue), Jocelyn Warner, **29**

UK, Tulip, William Morris, **30**

UK, Printed cotton/rayon, Calico Printers' Association, **31**

UK, Queuing Tulips, Eley Kishimoto, **31**

UK, Furnishing fabric, Minnie McLeish, **31**

UK, Tulip and Lattice, Charles Rennie Mackintosh, **31**

UK, Dress fabric, Calico Printers' Association, **31**

UK, Pansy Stripe, Designers Guild, **32**

UK, Furnishing fabric, Sidney Haward, **32**

UK, Pansy, Enid Marx, **32**

UK, Sunflower, William De Morgan, **34**

UK, Sunflower, William Morris, **35**

UK, Kennet, William Morris, Morris & Co., **35**

Europe cont.

UK, Cestrefeld, C. F. A. Voysey, 35
UK, Fleur de Lotus, Designers Guild, 36
UK, Ceramic tile, 37
UK, Baudard, Designers Guild, 37
UK, Lotus, Owen Jones, 37
UK, Wall stencil, Alexander "Greek" Thomson, 38
UK, Anemone, William Morris, 41
UK, Bird and Anemone, William Morris, 41
UK, Anemone, Neisha Crosland, 41
UK, Iris, John Henry Dearle, 42
UK, Antoinette, Designers Guild, 43
UK, Irises, Eugène Grasset, 43
UK, Iris and Kingfisher, Walter Crane, 44
UK, Pallida, Mary Harper, 44
UK, Marigold, William Morris, 46
UK, Textile, 47
UK, African Marigold, William Morris, 47
UK, Peony, Charlotte Horne Spiers, 48
UK, Red House, Claud Lovat Fraser, 48
UK, The Oswin, C. F. A. Voysey, 49
UK, Shanghai Garden, Designers Guild, 50
UK, Peony tile, Kate Faulkner, 50
UK, Peony, Kate Faulkner, 51
UK, Sakura Flower, Jenny Frean, First Eleven Studio for Sandersons, 53
UK, Stafford, Bruce J. Talbert, 53
UK, Honeysuckle, William Morris, 54
UK, Pillow cover, 54
UK, Honeysuckle, 54
UK, Fabric sample, Arthur Wilcock, 55
UK, Furnishing fabric, Lindsay P. Butterfield, 56
UK, Hydrangea, John Drummond, 56
UK, Wallflower, William Morris, 56
UK, Crocus, George Haité, 57
UK, Fabric sample, Arthur Wilcock, 57
UK, Wallflower Stripe, Sam Pickard, 57
UK, Snakeshead, William Morris, 58
UK, Strawberry Thief, William Morris, 59
UK, Hyacinth, John Henry Dearle, 60
UK, Clematis, Neisha Crosland, 61
UK, Clematis, Mary A. Harper, 61
UK, Batchelor's Button, William Morris, 62
UK, The Iolanthe, C. F. A. Voysey, 63
UK, Larkspur, C. F. A. Voysey, 63
UK, Textile design, William Morris, 63
UK, Poppy, May Morris, 64
UK, Poppies, Lindsay P. Butterfield, 64
UK, Poppy, William Morris, 64

UK, Fabric sample, Calico Printers' Association, 65
UK, Dandelion Two, Angie Lewin for St. Jude's, 68
UK, Dandelion One, Angie Lewin for St. Jude's, 68
UK, Dandelion Clock, Lucienne Day, 69
UK, Daffodil, John Henry Dearle, 71
UK, Clover, 72
UK, Wallpaper, Owen Jones, 72
UK, Clover, 72
UK, Thistle, Eugène Grasset, 74
UK, Teazle, Walter Crane, 74
UK, Thistle, William Morris, 75
UK, Tile design, William De Morgan, 75
UK, Grand Thistle, Timorous Beasties, 75
UK, Blackberry, J. H. Dearle, 76
UK, Hedgerow, Angie Lewin for St. Jude's, 76
UK, Fool's Parsley, C. F. A. Voysey, 76
UK, Cow Parsley, Cole & Son, 77
UK, Dress fabric, Calico Printers' Association, 78
UK, French Meadow, Imogen Heath, 79
UK, Field, Tord Boontje, 79
UK, Meadow Flowers, Walter Crane, 79
UK, Bluebell, Imogen Heath, 80
UK, Bluebell, William Morris, 80
UK, Corncockle, William Morris, 80
UK, Fritillaria, Designers Guild, 80
UK, Nure, C. F. A. Voysey, 81
UK, Snowdrops, Jenny Frean, 81
UK, Pimpernel, William Morris, 81
UK, Woodland Weeds, John Henry Dearle, 81
UK, Marigold, William Morris, 82
UK, The Well at the World's End, William Morris, 82
UK, Plate, William De Morgan, 83
UK, Cray, William Morris, 84
UK, Arcadia, May Morris, 84
UK, Textile, 84
UK, Furnishing fabric, 85
UK, Dress fabric, Calico Printers' Association, 85
UK, Kentish Rose, Cath Kidston, 85
UK, The Furrow, C. F. A. Voysey for Alexander Morton & Co., 86
UK, Galahad, C. F. A. Voysey for Alexander Morton & Co., 87
UK, Seaweed, John Henry Dearle, 88
UK, Wilderness, Tord Boontje, 89
UK, Seaflower, Sam Pickard, 89
UK, Meadow Day, Imogen Heath, 90
UK, Masson, Designers Guild, 90
UK, Elizabeth, Claire de Quénetain, 91

UK, Dress fabric, 92
UK, Pink and Rose, William Morris, 92
UK, Textile, not known, 92
UK, Dress fabric, not known, 93
UK, Wallpaper, not known, 93
UK, Millom, Marianne Straub, 94
UK, Adelaide, Marianne Straub, 95
UK, Dress fabric, The Calico Printers Association. England,, 96
UK, Multifloral, Vanessa Bell, 96
UK, Columbine, Allan Vigers, 96
UK, Austria, Sidney Haward, 96
UK, Pattern design, not known, 97
UK, Delft Flower, Designers Guild, 97
UK, Lodden, William Morris, 97
UK, A New Language, Claire de Quénetain, 100
UK, Checkered flower, Neisha Crosland, 100
UK, Bloomsbury, Eley Kishimoto, 101
UK, Chairs, Hill House chairs, Charles Rennie Mackintosh, 102
UK, Untitled, Charles Rennie Mackintosh, 103
UK, Verdure, Peter Hall, 104
UK, Furnishing fabric, Minnie McLeish, 104
UK, Majella, Designers Guild, 104
UK, Requena, Designers Guild, 105
UK, Wallpaper, C. F. A. Voysey, 105
UK, Happy Flowers, Javier Mariscal for Christopher Farr, 105
UK, Tulip, Orla Kiely, 106
UK, Striped Petal, Orla Kiely, 107
UK, Shadow, Tord Boontje, 108
UK, Provence, Lucienne Day, 108
UK, Cockpen, C. F. A. Voysey, 108
UK, Wallpaper, Owen Jones, 109
UK, A. W. N. Pugin, 111
UK, Marble Damask, Timorous Beasties, 112
UK, The Lerena, C. F. A. Voysey, 113
UK, Balabina, Cole & Son, 113
UK, Cellini, Designers Guild, 113
UK, Damsel Damask, Timorous Beasties, 115
UK, Autumn Flowers, William Morris, 116
UK, La La Lyon, Eley Kishimoto, 116
UK, Birdcage, Timorous Beasties, 116
UK, Furnishing fabric, William Morris or John Henry Dearle, 117
UK, Aldwych, Cole & Son, 117
UK, Briar, Eley Kishimoto, 120
UK, Annabelle, Claire de Quénetain, 122
UK, Cottage Garden, Collier Campbell, 122

UK, The Rainbow, Claire de Quénetain, 122
UK, Minto, C. F. A. Voysey, 123
UK, Royal Garden, Cole & Son, 123
UK, Furnishing fabric, 124
UK, Flower Show, Lucienne Day, 124
UK, Furnishing fabric, 124
UK, Bloomsbury Garden, Timorous Beasties, 124
UK, untitled, Tony Trickey, First Eleven Studio, 126
UK, Mughal Garden, Matthew Williamson at Osborne & Little, 127
UK, Culpeper, Neisha Crosland, 127
UK, Garden, Tord Boontje, 127
UK, Textile design, William Kilburn, 128
UK, Corsage, Designers Guild, 129
UK, Dress fabric, Calico Printers' Association, 129
UK, Trailing rose, Cath Kidston, 129
UK, Textile design, William Kilburn, 130
UK, Galaxy Bouquet, Eley Kishimoto, 130
UK, Furnishing fabric, 130
UK, Wallpaper, 130
UK, Windflower Bunch, Cath Kidston, 131
UK, Feather Pattern, Phyllis Barron & Dorothy Larcher, 132
UK, Bouquet, Phyllis Barron & Dorothy Larcher, 133
UK, Wreath, William Morris, 134
UK, Textile design, William Kilburn, 135
UK, Heaven Scent, Tord Boontje, 135
UK, Christchurch, William Morris, 136
UK, Furnishing fabric, C. F. A. Voysey, 136
UK, Rhododendron, Orla Kiely, 137
UK, Amapola, Javier Mariscal for Christopher Farr, 137
UK, Itsy Bitsy, Eley Kishimoto, 137
UK, Textile, 138
UK, Textile, 138
UK, Attica, Marian Mahler, 140
UK, unknown, 140
UK, Sudbury, Cole & Son, 140
UK, Flowerpot, William Morris, 140
UK, unknown, poss. Owen Jones, 141
UK, The Formal Garden, Walter Crane, 141
UK, Charleston Flowers, Jenny Muncaster, 142
UK, Tuscany, John Minton, 142
UK, Art Room, Mini Moderns, 143
UK, Evergreen, Imogen Heath, 144
UK, Arbutus, Kathleen Kersey, 144

UK, Versailles Garden, Designers Guild, 145

UK, Bramble, Bruce James Talbert, 145

UK, Stylized leaf and flower design, 146

UK, Rustic, André Bicât, 146

UK, Odhni, Designers Guild, 147

UK, Palm Jungle, Cole & Son, 147

UK, Kolkata Fern, Sam Pickard 150

UK, Sans Souci, 150

UK, Leaf Pattern, Lewis Foreman Day, 150

UK, Wallpaper, Owen Jones, 151

UK, Jardin Exo'chic, Christian Lacroix for Designers Guild, 151

UK, Bottle and vases, William De Morgan. 152

UK, William de Morgan, 153

UK, Kayin, Osborne & Little, 154

UK, Foliage, 154

UK, Wallpaper (Hedera), unknown, 154

UK, Ivy Block, Sam Pickard, 155

UK, Bramble, Kate Faulkner, 156

UK, Banana Leaf, Neisha Crosland, 157

UK, Multi Acorn Spot, Orla Kiely, 157

UK, Leaf (Black/Gold), Jocelyn Warner, 157

UK, Woodland, Osborne & Little, 160

UK, Tribe, Kate Blee for Christopher Farr, 160

UK, Jindai, Designers Guild, 160

UK, Zaffera, Designers Guild, 161

UK, Athenian, Lewis Foreman Day, 161

UK, Hawthorn Rusts, Sam Pickard, 161

UK, Caterpillar Leaf, Neisha Crosland, 162

UK, Chrysler, Osborne & Little, 163

UK, Tropicana, Matthew Williamson at Osborne & Little, 163

UK, Granville, John Henry Dearle, 164

UK, Wallpaper, Walter Crane, 164

UK, Tile panel, William Morris and William De Morgan, 164

UK, Acanthus, William Morris, 165

UK, Rajapur, Cole &Son, 168

UK, Textile pattern, George Haité, 169

UK, Indian, George Gilbert Scott, 169

UK, Paisley design, George Haité, 170

UK, Montracy, Designers Guild, 171

UK, Birch Wood, Timorous Beasties, 172

UK, Forest, Lucienne Day, 172

UK, Mandara, Matthew Williamson at Osborne & Little, 173

UK, Lochwood, Nina Campbell, distributed by Osborne & Little, 174

UK, The Fairyland Design, C. F. A. Voysey, 175

UK, Oak Tree, John Henrey Dearle, 176

UK, Royal Oak and Ivy, 176

UK, Birch Tree Sun, Angie Lewin for St. Jude's, 177

UK, Tulip Tree, Lewis Foreman Day, 177

UK, Tree of Life, Timorous Beasties, 177

UK, Hollywood Grape, Neisha Crosland, 178

UK, Apple, William Morris, 178

UK, Still Life, Eley Kishimoto, 178

UK, Furnishing fabric, Pat Albeck, 179

UK, The Orange Tree, Walter Crane, 180

UK, Wild Strawberry, Cath Kidston, 180

UK, Kier, Robert Stewart, 180

UK, Bird and Pomegranate, John Henry Dearle, 181

UK, Parati, Christian Lacroix for Designers Guild, 182

UK, no title [pear], Bruce James Talbert, 182

UK, no title (pear), Sarah Battle, First Eleven Studio, 183

UK, Habanera [pineapple], Matthew Williamson at Osborne & Little, 183

UK, Apple Tree, Ryoko Sugiura, 184

UK, Woods & Pears, not known, 185

UK, Pomegranate, William Morris, 185

UK, A Discreet Revival, Claire de Quénetain, 188

UK, Pepper Trail, Neisha Crosland, 188

UK, Wild Olive, C. F. A. Voysey, 189

UK, Bird Branch Stripe, Timorous Beasties, 189

UK, Cascade (Ivory Black), Jocelyn Warner, 189

UK, Boomerang, Neisha Crosland, 190

UK, Birdtree, Neisha Crosland, 191

UK, Ludlow, 192

UK, Wallpaper, William Kilburn, 193

UK, Blossom, Kate Faulkner, 193

UK, Until Dawn, Tord Boontje, 194

UK, A Forest, Mini Moderns, 194

UK, Willow, William Morris, 194

UK, Ruskin Floral, Timorous Beasties, 195

UK, Twine, Sam Pickard, 198

UK, Great Vine, 199

UK, Vine, William Morris, 199

UK, Wisteria (Lilac Rose), Jocelyn Warner, 199

UK, Cellini, Designers Guild, 200

UK, Japoneries, Designers Guild, 201

UK, Blossom (Renaissance Gold), Jocelyn Warner, 202

UK, Isabella, Jacqueline Groag, 202

UK, Multi Stem, Orla Kiely, 203

UK, Viper Grass, Arthur Wilcock, 204

UK, Bamboo, Timorous Beasties, 204

UK, Bamboo, Sam Pickard, 205

UK, Pedigree Entourage, Eley Kishimoto, 208

UK, Sausage Dogs, Cath Kidston, 209

UK, George and Rufus, Ben Nicholson, 209

UK, Saluki design, 209

UK, Fabric sample, 209

UK, Dogs, Tony Trickey, First Eleven Studio, 209

UK, Antique Rose Blossom, Cath Kidston, 210

UK, Billie, Cath Kidston, 211

UK, Brer Rabbit, William Morris, 212

UK, Rabbit, Aki Ueda Castellani, 212

UK, Printed design, Liza Saunders, 212

UK, Bunny Dance, Eley Kishimoto, 213

UK, Horses Head, not known, 214

UK, Horses, Eley Kishimoto, 214

UK, Altamira, Christine Clegg, 215

UK, Jockeys, Calico Printers' Association, 215

UK, Enara, Karen Willinger, 217

UK, Fighting Stags, not known, 217

UK, The Duleek, C. F. A. Voysey, 217

UK, Rambo Blacks, Liza Saunders, 218

UK, Wallpaper, 219

UK, Buffalo, Diana Armfield, 219

UK, Small Elephants, Neil Bradburn, 220

UK, Safari Dance, Cole & Son collaboration with Ardmore Ceramic Art, 221

UK, Leopard Walk, Cole & Son collaboration with Ardmore Ceramic Art, 222

UK, Leopards, Varpu Kronholm, 222

UK, Tyger Tyger, Matthew Williamson at Osborne & Little, 222

UK, Almond Blossom and Swallow, Walter Crane, 224

UK, Birds, Aki Ueda Castellani, 225

UK, Purple Bird, C. F. A. Voysey, 226

UK, Dove and Rose, William Morris, 226

UK, Doveflight, Mark Hearld for St. Jude's, 226

UK, Doves, Calico Printers' Association, 227

UK, Wallpaper, 230

UK, Wallpaper, Silver Studio, 230

UK, Pair of round, flat bodied bottles, Christopher Dresser, 232

UK, Tile, Christopher Dresser, 233

UK, Textile design, not known, 234

UK, Cockatoo, Walter Crane, 234

UK, Textile, 234

UK, Macaw, Walter Crane, 235

UK, no title, Tony Trickey, First Eleven Studio, 236

UK, Chinese Magpie, William Turner, 236

UK, Arini, Matthew Williamson at Osborne & Little, 237

UK, Chickens, Sarah Battle, First Eleven Studio, 240

UK, Furnishing fabric, Hans Tisdall, 241

UK, Furnishing fabric, Margaret Cooper, 241

UK, Silk fragment, not known, 242

UK, Furnishing fabric, 242

UK, Peacock, Grapevine and Vases, William De Morgan, 242

UK, Cedar Tree, Louis Stahl, 243

UK, Byron, 243

UK, The Peacock, not known, 244

UK, Printed design, R. Silver, 244

UK, Textile, 244

UK, The Peacock Garden, Walter Crane, 245

UK, Peacock Feathers, Arthur Silver, 246

UK, Scarf, 247

UK, Leopardo, Matthew Williamson at Osborne & Little, 247

UK, Quill, Designers Guild, 248

UK, Narina, Cole & Son collaboration with Ardmore Ceramic Art, 248

UK, Starling, Imogen Heath, 249

UK, Feathers, Mini Moderns in collaboration with Matt Sewell, 249

UK, Brown Birds Perched on Holly, C. F. A. Voysey, 250

UK, Bird Garden, Mark Hearld for St. Jude's, 250

UK, Birds of America, John James Audubon, 250

UK, Strawberries and Birds, C. F. A. Voysey, 250

UK, The Fruit Looters, Timorous Beasties, 251

UK, Tropical Birds, 252

UK, Birds on Branch, Aki Ueda Castellani, 253

UK, Ascension, Eley Kishimoto, 253

UK, Flock, Jenny Frean, First Eleven Studio for Sandersons, 254

UK, Little Birds, Cath Kidston, 254

UK, Star-ling, Mini Moderns, 254

UK, Aviary, Osborne & Little, 255

UK, Gulls, Mini Moderns, 256

Europe cont.

UK, Gulls, Eley Kishimoto, **256**
UK, Aircraft, Marion Dorn, **256**
UK, The Owl, C. F. A. Voysey, **257**
UK, Iguana, Timorous Beasties, **258**
UK, Amazon, Jacqueline Colley, **258**
UK, Textile Design, Christopher Dresser, **258**
UK, Les Jardins Majorelle, Jacqueline Colley, **258**
UK, Nicaragua, Jacqueline Colley, **259**
UK, Tropical Fish Stripe, Robyn Parker, **262**
UK, Block print, Doris Carter, **263**
UK, Aquaria, Vincent Malta and Richard Munsell, **263**
UK, Billow, Walter Crane, **264**
UK, Nautilus, **265**
UK, Sea Bed, Jacqueline Colley, **266**
UK, Dress fabric, Martin Battersby, **266**
UK, Wallpaper, Walter Crane, **271**
UK, Sea Horses, Calico Printers' Association, **271**
UK, Wild Honey Bee Allover, Timorous Beasties, **272**
UK, Imperial Apiary, Timorous Beasties, **273**
UK, Charonda, Designers Guild, **274**
UK, Furnishing fabric, Minnie McLeish, **275**
UK, Papillon, Sarah Hough, **275**
UK, Butterflies, John Dilnot, **276**
UK, Camberwell Beauty, Mini Moderns, **276**
UK, Butterflies, Timorous Beasties, **277**
UK, Zig Zag Moth, Timorous Beasties, **278**
UK, White Moth Circle, Timorous Beasties, **279**
UK, Inky Insects, Varpu Kronholm, **279**
UK, Moths, John Dilnot, **279**
UK, Caterpillars, John Dilnot, **280**
UK, Dragonfly Dance, Matthew Williamson at Osborne & Little, **280**
UK, Bird Zoo, Joe Martin, **283**
UK, Zoo, Tony Trickey, First Eleven Studio, **283**
UK, Moo, Mini Moderns, **284**
UK, Sheep, Doris Scull or Joyce Clissold, **284**
UK, Harvest Hare, Mark Hearld for St. Jude's, **285**
UK, Fantasque, Osborne & Little, **286**
UK, Savuti, Cole & Son collaboration with Ardmore Ceramic Art, **286**
UK, Zambezi, Cole & Son collaboration with Ardmore Ceramic Art, **287**

UK, Merian Palm, Timorous Beasties, **287**
UK, Dress fabric, Zika Ascher, **288**
UK, Jungle, Feliks Toploski for Ascher Ltd, **289**
UK, Wallpaper, **290**
UK, Scarf, Sarah Campbell, **291**
UK, Furnishing fabric, Dorothy Hutton, **291**
UK, Graphic Croc, Eley Kishimoto, **294**
UK, Zulu Border, Cole & Son collaboration with Ardmore Ceramic Art, **295**
UK, Pardus (Leopard), Osborne & Little, **295**
UK, Giraffe, Anna Hayman, **295**
UK, Monster Skin, Eley Kishimoto, **296**
UK, Chinese Dragon, Anthony Little, **298**
UK, Tile panel, William De Morgan, **298**
UK, Celestial Dragon, Matthew Williamson at Osborne & Little, **298**
UK, Peacock and Dragon, William Morris, **299**
UK, Six tin-glazed earthenware tiles, with Chinoiserie scenes, probably Bristol, **300**
UK, Chinoiserie wallpaper, Marble Hill House, Twickenham, Richmond, Middlesex, UK, **300**
UK, Panpipes, Harry Napper, **303**
UK, Vista, Imogen Heath, **307**
UK, Homework, Mini Moderns, **307**
UK, Bar Line, Emma Jeffs/ N&N Wares, **311**
UK, Wallpaper design, Jacqueline Groag, **311**
UK, Thisbe, Enid Marx, **311**
UK, Toccata, Peter Shuttleworth, **312**
UK, Textile, Sonia Delaunay, **313**
UK, Optical, Sam Pickard, **313**
UK, Checkerboard, Rebecca Hoyes, First Eleven Studio, **314**
UK, Checkerboard, Eley Kishimoto, **314**
UK, Frith, Designers Guild, **314**
UK, Misty Ikat, Ptolemy Mann, **315**
UK, Printed design, Sally Lloyd-Thomas, **315**
UK, Reflections: 1, Marianne Straub, **315**
UK, Essex Check Dark Navy, Ian Mankin, **316**
UK, 32:64, Studio Houndstooth, **318**
UK, Ripon Dark Navy, Ian Mankin, **318**
UK, Dogtooth, Eley Kishimoto, **318**
UK, Tartan textile sample, Asher Ltd, **320**

UK, Allegro, Imogen Heath, **322**
UK, Puzzle, **322**
UK, Textile, **322**
UK, Cuteboy, Eley Kishimoto, **323**
UK, Detail of black marquetry surface, Winter and Kurth, UK, **324**
UK, Parterre, Neisha Crosland, **326**
UK, Geometric design, Rebecca Hoyes, First Eleven Studio, **328**
UK, Cube Star (Coral), Jocelyn Warner, **329**
UK, Lithograph, Owen Jones, **329**
UK, Textile, not known, **330**
UK, no title, Rebecca Hoyes, First Eleven Studio, **330**
UK, Zirconia, Osborne & Little, **331**
UK, Printed design, Sally Lloyd-Thomas, **332**
UK, Mera, Imogen Heath, **333**
UK, Wallpaper, Owen Jones, **333**
UK, Geotaxis, Sam Pickard, **335**
UK, Circus, **336**
UK, Veren, Designers Guild, **336**
UK, Kites, Kangan Arora, **336**
UK, Normandie, Osborne & Little, **337**
UK, Totley, Marianne Straub, **337**
UK, Jali, Kangan Arora, **340**
UK, Samoa, Lorca, distributed by Osborne & Little, **340**
UK, Fez, Neisha Crosland, **340**
UK, Hicks' Grand, Cole & Son collaboration with David Hicks, **342**
UK, Wallpaper, Owen Jones, **343**
UK, Scaffold, Kate Blee for Christopher Farr, **346**
UK, Blotch Stripe, Timorous Beasties, **346**
UK, Lindfield, Marianne Straub, **348**
UK, Jodphur Blue, Ptolemy Mann, **348**
UK, Skate, Phyllis Barron and Dorothy Larcher, **349**
UK, Pointed Pip, Phyllis Barron, **350**
UK, V Stripe, Sam Pickard, **350**
UK, Causeway, Lucienne Day, **351**
UK, Vintage Stripe 2 Dark Navy, Ian Mankin, **352**
UK, Vertical, Christopher Farr, **353**
UK, Textile, **354**
UK, Empire 1 Navy, Ian Mankin, **354**
UK, Tapestry Room from Croome Court, Room after a design by Robert Adam, **356**
UK, Shuttle and Shaft, Eley Kishimoto, **358**
UK, Luxor, **360**
UK, Bakst, Osborne & Little, **361**
UK, Lucknow, Kangan Arora, **364**

UK, Shaded Chevron, Eley Kishimoto, **366**
UK, Memphis, El Ultimo Grito for Christopher Farr, **366**
UK, Jagged Edge, Neisha Crosland, **367**
UK, Chevron, Enid Marx, **367**
UK, Nevis, Matthew Williamson at Osborne & Little, **367**
UK, Peacock, Phyllis Barron and Dorothy Larcher, **368**
UK, Small Way, Kit Kemp for Christopher Farr, **369**
UK, Catseye utility furnishing fabric, Enid Marx, **370**
UK, Zebra, Neisha Crosland, **371**
UK, Sun Loving Bollards, Eley Kishimoto, **372**
UK, Flash, Eley Kishimoto, **373**
UK, Vortex, Ptolemy Mann, **374**
UK, Ikat Damask, Timorous Beasties, **375**
UK, Parure, Osborne & Little, **376**
UK, Geo Star Floral, Rebecca Hoyes, First Eleven Studio, **377**
UK, Watermark, Neisha Crosland, **377**
UK, Recurrence, Barbara Brown, **380**
UK, Chains, Eley Kishimoto, **380**
UK, Helmsley, Marianne Straub, **380**
UK, Bokhen, Emma Jeffs/ N&N Wares, **381**
UK, Circles, Rebecca Hoyes, First Eleven Studio, **381**
UK, Great 8 (Gold), Jocelyn Warner, **381**
UK, Textile, Arthur Sanderson & Sons, **383**
UK, Spiral Spot, Sam Pickard, **383**
UK, Pollen, Kate Blee for Christopher Farr, **384**
UK, Amlapura, Designers Guild, **384**
UK, Textile, not known, **384**
UK, Diagonal Beaded Stripe, Neisha Crosland, **386**
UK, Dorothy, Imogen Heath, **386**
UK, Printed design, Sally Lloyd-Thomas, **387**
UK, Small Ovals, Neisha Crosland, **388**
UK, Sgt Pepper, Anna Hayman, **389**
UK, Florence, **389**
UK, Textile, Susan Bosence, **390**
UK, Bibana, Anna Hayman, **390**
UK, Carpet design, **393**
UK, Moresque, Owen Jones, **393**
UK, Color lithograph, Edward Bawden, **393**
UK, Dianne, Anna Hayman, **393**
UK, Spiral, Barbara Brown, **396**

UK, Spiral, Sam Pickard, **396**
UK, Aztec, Eley Kishimoto, **399**
UK, Textile, Calico Printers' Association, **400**
UK, Dress fabric, Charles Rennie Mackintosh, **400**
UK, Maroon, Eileen Hunter, **400**
UK, Hedgehog, Neisha Crosland, **404**
UK, Furnishing fabric, Gregory Brown, **405**
UK, Pirouette, Tord Boontje, **406**
UK, Waves, Jenny Frean, **407**
UK, Shimmy, Natalie Gibson, **407**
UK, Jali Trellis, Matthew Williamson at Osborne & Little, **408**
UK, Aladdin, Neisha Crosland, **408**
UK, Palmprint, Anna Hayman, **412**
UK, Feather Fan, **413**
UK, Pollen, Neisha Crosland, **413**
UK, Viaduct, Imogen Heath, **414**
UK, Furnishing fabric, O. R. Plaistow, **415**
UK, Lempicka, Osborne & Little, **415**
UK, Swans, Eileen Hunter, **417**
UK, Furnishing fabric, Augustus Pugin, **417**
UK, Color lithograph, Owen Jones, **417**
UK, Sultan, Owen Jones, **417**
UK, Ardmore Cameos, Cole & Son with Ardmore Ceramic Art, **418**
UK, Fabric, not known, **419**
UK, Quatrefoil, Edward Bawden, **421**
UK, Wallpaper, Owen Jones, **421**
UK, Margot, Anna Hayman, **422**
UK, Ropey Heritage, Eley Kishimoto, **422**
UK, Weave, **423**
UK, Kelburn, Nina Campbell, distributed by Osborne & Little, **423**
UK, Barbade, Christian Lacroix for Designers Guild, **423**
UK, Sloyd, Enid Marx, **424**
UK, Aleppo, Marianne Straub, **424**
UK, Lattice, Emma Jeffs/N & N Wares, **424**
UK, Penton Villas, Old Town for St. Jude's, **424**
UK, Light on Lattice, Eley Kishimoto, **425**
UK, Pyramids, Neisha Crosland, **426**
UK, Petipa, Osborne & Little, **426**
UK, Pompeian, Cole & Son, **426**
UK, Porto, Kate Blee for Christopher Farr, **427**
UK, Gridlock, Neisha Crosland, **428**

UK, Porden, Designers Guild, **429**
UK, Window Ikat, Ptolemy Mann, **429**
UK, Laguna, **432**
UK, Ropey, Eley Kishimoto, **434**
UK, Book illustration, Christopher Dresser, **434**
UK, Chainmail, Eley Kishimoto, **438**
UK, Equinox, Mini Moderns, **439**
UK, Lithograph, **439**
UK, Wallpaper, Owen Jones, **440**
UK, Crace Diaper, Augustus Pugin, **441**
UK, Lee Priory, **441**
UK, Maize, Neisha Crosland, **441**
UK, Portrait, Enid Marx, **442**
UK, Picture Quiz, Enid Marx, **442**
UK, Spot and Stripe, Enid Marx, **443**
UK, Alcazar, **444**
UK, Oriel, not known, **445**
UK, Fair Isle Scotland, **458**
UK, Fair Isle Scotland, **459**
UK, Victorian Military Quilt, **463**
UK, Victorian Military Quilt, **464**
UK, Piccadilly, not known, **466**
UK, Darjeeling, Mini Moderns, **467**
UK, Moorish Circles, Neisha Crosland, **467**
UK, Piscatore, John Drummond, **470**
UK, Dancing Naked Figures, Frank and Mary Dobson, **471**
UK, Statues, Frank Dobson, **471**
UK, Dress fabric, Feliks Topolski, **472**
UK, Transport, Feliks Topolski, **472**
UK, Family Groups, Henry Moore, **472**
UK, Dress fabric, Henry Moore, **473**
UK, Furnishing fabric, Henry Moore, **473**
UK, Festival, not known, **474**
UK, Masks, Robert Stewart, **476**
UK, Legs, Jane Wealleans, **476**
UK, True Romance, Mini Moderns, **482**
UK, Raspberry Lips, Jane Wealleans, **483**
UK, Macrahanish, Robert Stewart, **484**
UK, Hands, Helen David, **484**
UK, Textile, **484**
UK, London, Cath Kidston, **486**
UK, Gaudi, Helen David, **486**
UK, NYC, Chloe Geary-Smith, **488**
UK, Do You Live In a Town?, Mini Moderns, **488**
UK, Prefab Stripe, Sharon Elphick, **489**
UK, Watercolor, not known, **489**
UK, Village Church, Hilda Durkin, **489**
UK, Billie Goes to Town, Cath Kidston, **491**
UK, Urban Chaos, Timorous Beasties, **491**
UK, NYC, Chloe Geary-Smith, **492**

UK, Welwyn Garden City, Doris Gregg, **492**
UK, Metroland, Mini Moderns, **492**
UK, Miami, not known, **493**
UK, New York City Toile, Timorous Beasties, **494**
UK, London Toile, Cath Kidston, **495**
UK, New York Toile 2, Timorous Beasties, **495**
UK, Textile, not known, **496**
UK, Dungeness, Mini Moderns, **496**
UK, Deep Sea, Emily Sutton for St. Jude's, **496**
UK, Great Wave, not known, **497**
UK, Marmara, Osborne & Little, **497**
UK, Brighten Up Your Day, Cath Kidston, **498**
UK, Ocean View, Eley Kishimoto, **498**
UK, Nautical, Calico Printers' Association, **499**
UK, Sea Shanties, Calico Printers' Association, **499**
UK, Lifeboats, Calico Printers' Association, **499**
UK, Porto Fino, Mary Oliver, **499**
UK, Havana, Collier Campbell, **500**
UK, Côte d'Azur, Collier Campbell, **501**
UK, Aerial View, Calico Printers' Association, **502**
UK, Carnac, Phyllis Barron and Dorothy Larcher, **502**
UK, Cowboy, Cath Kidston, **503**
UK, Textile, Julian Trevelyan, **504**
UK, Sussex Downs, Jenny Frean, First Eleven Studio for Sandersons, **504**
UK, Cornish Farm, Alec Walker, **504**
UK, Moordale, Mini Moderns, **505**
UK, Orcades, Edward Bawden, **506**
UK, Sahara, Edward Bawden, **507**
UK, Japanese Garden, Osborne & Little, **509**
UK, Exotisme, Christian Lacroix for Designers Guild, **509**
UK, Hunting Toile, Timorous Beasties, **512**
UK, Versailles Grand, Cole & Son, **513**
UK, Motor Bike, Sholto Drumlanrig, **516**
UK, Bicycles, Sholto Drumlanrig, **517**
UK, Sailing Boats, Doris Carter, **518**
UK, Baraka, **518**
UK, Whitby, Mini Moderns, **519**
UK, Textile, **519**
UK, Yacht, **519**
UK, Swoop, Sholto Drumlanrig, **520**
UK, Space Walk, Sue Thatcher Palmer, **522**

UK, Lunar Rocket, Eddie Squires, **523**
UK, Locomotion, F. Schumacher & Co, **525**
UK, Hold Tight, Mini Moderns, **525**
UK, Flags, Jane Edgar, **525**
UK, Ceramica, Matthew Williamson at Osborne & Little, **526**
UK, Matrinah, Cole & Son collaboration with Ardmore Ceramic Art, **526**
UK, Malaga, **527**
UK, Wallpaper, **528**
UK, Ribbon and Lace, John Aldridge, **533**
UK, Khulu Vases, Cole & Son collaboration with Ardmore Ceramic Art, **533**
UK, Dress fabric, Henry Moore, **535**
UK, Cocarde, Christian Lacroix for Designers Guild, **538**
UK, Textile, Alastair Morton, **539**
UK, Shoes, Sholto Drumlanrig, **539**
UK, Curio, Osborne & Little, **542**
UK, Sitting Comfortably, Mini Moderns, **543**
UK, Textile, Jacqueline Groag, **544**
UK, Penguin Library, Osborne & Little, **544**
UK, Beauty Parlour, Sholto Drumlanrig, **545**
UK, Keys, A. Richard Allen, **545**
UK, Backgammon, Mini Moderns, **548**
UK, Marbles, Eley Kishimoto, **549**
UK, Fun and Games, Calico Printers' Association, **549**
UK, Maison de Jeu (Gambling House), Christian Lacroix for Designers Guild, **549**
UK, C60, Mini Moderns, **552**
UK, The Angel with the Trumpet, Herbert Horne, **552**
UK, Keyboard, Henry Moore, **553**
UK, Pet Sounds, Mini Moderns, **553**
UK, Opera, Joyce Clissold, **554**
UK, Last Waltz, **554**
UK, Block print, K. McDonald, **555**
UK, Fayres Fair, Mini Moderns, **555**
UK, Fisherman's Tale, Hilda Durkin, **555**
UK, Gala Night, Jacqueline Groag, **556**
UK, Birthday Party, Cath Kidston, **556**
UK, Dress fabric, not known, **557**
UK, Paints and Palettes, Rae Spencer-Cullen, **557**
UK, Sunset, Sholto Drumlanrig, **558**
UK, Sunburst, Neisha Crosland, **558**
UK, Solar Flare, Catherine Worsley, **558**

Europe cont.

UK, Sunrise, Lucienne Day, 559
UK, Pyramid Sunrise, Sholto Drumlanrig, 560
UK, Birds, Cloud, Sun, Rain, Frank Dobson, 561
UK, Clouds, Cath Kidston, 562
UK, Cloud Toile, Timorous Beasties, 563
UK, Air Rave, Eley Kishimoto, 566
UK, Ceiling pattern, Christopher Dresser, 566
UK, Star Ikat, Ptolemy Mann, 567
UK, Star and Stripe, Enid Marx, 567
UK, Love Field, Eley Kishimoto, 568
UK, Happy Dreams, Natalie Gibson, 569
UK, Knock Knock, Mini Moderns, 570
UK, Letter (Boutique), Jocelyn Warner, 571
UK, Tudor Rose and Fleur-de-lis, Augustus Pugin, 576
UK, The Fleur-de-lis, not known, 576
UK, Apparel for an Alb, Augustus Pugin, 577
UK, Breakwater, Christopher Farr, 580
UK, Impasto, Designers Guild, 580
UK, Tracks, Kate Blee for Christopher Farr, 581
UK, Salvage, 581
UK, Kaleido Splatt Allover, Timorous Beasties, 584
UK, Furnishing fabric, Calico Printers' Association, 585
UK, Printed design, Rebecca Hoyes, First Eleven Studio, 585
UK, Raindrop Flowers, Jenny Frean, First Eleven Studio for Sandersons, 585
UK, Watermarks, Catherine Worsley, 586
UK, Paint Blobs, Marni Stuart, 586
UK, Sea Glass, Catherine Worsley, 587
UK, Paper, not known, 587
UK, Design for fabric, Vanessa Bell and Duncan Grant, 588
UK, White, Vanessa Bell and Duncan Grant, 588
UK, Decorative end paper, 590
UK, Marbled end paper, 590
UK, Decorative end paper, 591
UK, Marbled end paper, 591
UK, Tracey, Emma Jeffs/N & N Wares, 592
UK, Springboard, Lucienne Day, 598
UK, Raimoult, Robert Stewart, 599
UK, Flotilla, Lucienne Day, 599

UK, Treehouse, Alice Stevenson for St. Jude's, 600
UK, Rig, Lucienne Day, 600
UK, Acres, Lucienne Day, 602
UK, Perpetua, Lucienne Day, 603
UK, Scribble, Orla Kiely, 608
UK, Strand, 609
UK, Mirage, Robert Stewart, 609
UK, Scribble (Grey), Jocelyn Warner, 610
UK, Basuto, not known, 610
UK, Furnishing fabric, Henry Moore, 612
UK, Dress fabric, Paule Vézelay, 612
UK, Tarentel, Tord Boontje, 613
UK, Palisade, Lucienne Day, 613
UK, DPM Camo, British Disruptive Pattern, 614
UK, Wallpaper, 616
UK, Grand Blotch Damask, Timorous Beasties, 617
UK, Galeria, Barbara Brown, 618
UK, Dolores, Eddie Squires, 618
UK, Woodstock, 618
UK, Shape, Shirley Craven for Hull Traders, 620
UK, Kaplan furnishing fabric, Shirley Craven for Hull Traders, 621
UK, Simple Solar, Shirley Craven, 622
UK, furnishing fabric, Vanessa Bell, 623
UK, Trios, Lucienne Day, 624
UK, Petrus, Peter Hall, 624
UK, Brazil, Eileen Hunter, 624
UK, Fabric design, Vanessa Bell, 625
UK, Foreshore, Lucienne Day, 625
UK, Textile, Christopher Dresser, 625
UK, Textile, E. Geggs, 628
UK, Applecross, Robert Stewart, 629
UK, Textile, F. Gregory Brown, 629
UK, Portrait, Jacqueline Groag, 630
UK, Kiddies Town, Jacqueline Groag for John Line & Son Ltd, 630
UK, Melody, Jacqueline Groag for Edinburgh Weavers, 631
UK, Compendium, Rosemary Newson, 632
UK, Extension, Haydon William, 633
UK, Kernoo, Victor Vasareley, 633
UK, P.L.U.T.O. (Pipeline Laid Under The Ocean), Mini Moderns, 634
UK, Mosaic, 634
UK, Indigo Blur, Ptolemy Mann, 634
UK, Haze, Emma Jeffs/ N&N Wares, 635
UK, Textile, Claud Lovat Fraser, 635
UK, Decor, Barbara Brown, 636

UK, Moonlight Daisy, Eley Kishimoto, 637
UK, Riley, Neisha Crosland, 637
UK, Ruhlman, Osborne & Little, 637
UK, Braided, Neisha Crosland, 637
UK, Unnamed, Barbara Brown for Heals Fabrics Ltd, 638
UK, Frequency, Barbara Brown for Heals Fabrics Ltd, 639
UK, Ebru, Osborne & Little, 640
UK, Quartz, 641
UK, Festival of Britain style furnishing fabric, English, 642
UK, Strata, Lucienne Day, 644
UK, Abstract Malachite, Christian Lacroix for Designers Guild, 645
UK, Haemoglobin, not known, 646
UK, Textile, Bernard Rowland, 646
UK, Haemoglobin 8.26, Bernard Rowland, 646
UK, Kairi, Matthew Williamson at Osborne & Little, 647
UK, Cells, Eley Kishimoto, 647
UK, Afwillite 8.45, S. M. Slade, 647
UK, Tiger Moon, Neisha Crosland, 648
UK, Pluto, Neisha Crosland, 648
UK (possibly), Furnishing fabric, 600
UK/France, Armature Feuille, Raoul Dufy/Christopher Farr, 146
UK/France, Pantigre, Christian Lacroix for Designers Guild, 297
UK/France, Reveries, Christian Lacroix for Designers Guild, 302
UK/France, Crochet, Raoul Dufy/ Christopher Farr, 349
UK/Nigeria, Dress fabric, Tomi Oladipo, 361
UK/Spain, Mosaic, Javier Mariscal for Christopher Farr, 467
UK/USA, Wallpaper, not known, 184
UK/USA, Assembled Check, Paul Smith, 310
UK/USA, Houndstooth, Paul Smith for Maharam, 319

North America

Mexico, Sarape, 358
USA, Wallpaper, not known, 23
USA, Quilt, not known, 31
USA, Wallpaper, William Justema, 33
USA, Sunflower Stalks, Carrie Carpenter, 34
USA, Wallpaper, not known, 42
USA, Wallpaper, not known, 45
USA, Wallpaper, not known, 49
USA, Frieze, not known, 64

USA, Wallpaper, 64
USA, Wallpaper, 69
USA, Fabric sample, not known, 71
USA, Fabric sample, Candace Wheeler, 71
USA, Wallpaper, not known, 88
USA, Wallpaper, not known, 90
USA, A "Cherry Blossom" table lamp, Tiffany Studios, 99
USA, Mikado, Alexander Girard, 120
USA, Whig Rose quilt, not known, 121
USA, Quilt, Mary Hergenroder Simon, 139
USA, Eden, Hella Jongerius for Maharam, 145
USA, Leaves, Alexander Girard, 145
USA, Eden, Alexander Girard, 147
USA, Quilt, not known, 163
USA, Wood's Edge, Elenhank, 173
USA, Textile, Herman A. Elsberg, 175
USA, Dress fabric, not known, 180
USA, Summer Stock, not known, 187
USA, Spencerian Horses, Marguerite Mergentime, 214
USA, Falcon Hunt, Herman A. Elsberg, 216
USA, Fabric design, Lilli Meissinger, 217
USA, Three Poppies, Four Wheat Sheaves, Marion Dorn, 228
USA, Avis, Marion Dorn for Edinburgh Weavers, 229
USA, Parrot with Pineapple, Yoko Honda, 236
USA, Feathers, Alexander Girard, 248
USA, Feathers, Tirzah Dunn, 249
USA, Turtle, Tommi Parzinger, 259
USA, A Fish is a Fish, Ken Scott, 262
USA, Poisson (Fish), Pablo Picasso, 265
USA, Crabs, Andre Durenceau, 266
USA, Sea Shells, not known, 268
USA, Coral and Shells, Kimberly McSparran, 269
USA, Shells & Sand, William Justema, 269
USA, Sea Things, Charles & Ray Eames, 270
USA, Bees with Honeycomb, Candace Wheeler, 272
USA, Girafters, Ben Rose, 282
USA, Animal Kingdom, Edgar Miller, 283
USA, Bavaria, Studio Job for Maharam, 284
USA, Parade, John Rombola, 291
USA, Tenayuca, Ben Rose, 306

USA, Zambezie, Ben Rose, **307**

USA, Chair, A DAR (Dining and Desk Chair), Charles Eames **308**

USA, Crosspatch, Ray Eames, **309**

USA, Matrix, Jack Lenor Larsen, **315**

USA, Drag Box Plaid, D. D. Tillett and Leslie Tillett, **320**

USA, Exaggerated Plaid, Paul Smith for Maharam, **321**

USA, Lorenzo, Jonathan Adler, **322**

USA, Multi Triangles, Alexander Girard, **330**

USA, Trapeze, not known, **330**

USA, Textile, Marianne Strengell, **334**

USA, On Point, Michelle Engel Bencsko, **334**

USA, Design 706, Frank Lloyd Wright, **335**

USA, Textile, not known, **341**

USA, Quilt, Anne Record, **343**

USA, Walpole, not known, **344**

USA, Color Dance, **344**

USA, Quilt, not known, **344**

USA, Nairobi, Ben Rose, **345**

USA, Meteoric, Ben Rose, **346**

USA, Repeat Classic Stripe, Hella Jongerius for Maharam, **347**

USA, Treads, Alexander Girard, **349**

USA, Ottoman Stripe, Paul Smith for Maharam, **350**

USA, Mexicotton Stripe, Alexander Girard, **351**

USA, Triangulated, Anni Albers, **361**

USA, Textile, not known, **364**

USA, Arrowhead, Alexander Girard, **364**

USA, Leaded glass, Frank Lloyd Wright, **366**

USA, Kinetics, Ben Rose, **370**

USA, Textile, not known, **377**

USA, Bola, Eleanor Grosch, **382**

USA, Circles, Charles and Ray Eames, **382**

USA, Disguise, Sarah Watson, **383**

USA, Pompoms, Ben Rose, **387**

USA, Wallpaper, not known, **390**

USA, Border, not known, **391**

USA, Wallpaper, not known, **392**

USA, Leather cloth, Jack Lenor Larsen, **402**

USA, Happiness, Jack Lenor Larsen, **403**

USA, Wallpaper, not known, **408**

USA, Broadway, Boym Partners, **414**

USA, Cutout (Arabesque), Alexander Girard, **416**

USA, Textile fragment, not known, **418**

USA, Textile, not known, **418**

USA, Wallpaper, not known, **418**

USA, Wallpaper, not known, **419**

USA, Textile, not known, **419**

USA, Quatrefoil, Alexander Girard, **420**

USA, Wallpaper, not known, **421**

USA, Ceiling paper, **421**

USA, Wicker, Tommi Parzinger, **422**

USA, Triangle, Alexander Girard, **427**

USA, Crosses, Alexander Girard, **433**

USA, Richard Nixon, Jonathan Adler, **433**

USA, Wallpaper, not known, **438**

USA, Wallpaper, not known, **440**

USA, Amish Quilt, **462**

USA, American Quilt, **462**

USA, American Quilt, **463**

USA, Kaleidoscope Quilt, **463**

USA, Touching Stars Quilt, **463**

USA, Quilt, **463**

USA, Textile, Ruth Reeves, **474**

USA, Bachelor's Wallpaper, Charles Dana Gibson, **477**

USA, Love Comic, Nicky Zann, **482**

USA, Faces, not known, **483**

USA, Wallpaper, not known, **485**

USA, Aftermath, Studio Job, **490**

USA, Metropolis, Elenhank, **492**

USA, High Seas, Michéle Brummer Everett, **498**

USA, Fabric, L. Kahn, **502**

USA, Fabric, Rose Taibbi, **519**

USA, Wallpaper, not known, **522**

USA, Astronauts and Spaceships, **522**

USA, Wallpaper, not known, **523**

USA, Flying Colors, Michéle Brummer Everett, **524**

USA, Bon Voyage, not known, **524**

USA, Wallpaper, not known, **527**

USA, Batterie de Cuisine (Cookware), Piazza Prints, **527**

USA, Heirlooms, Albert John Pucci, **528**

USA, Peggy, Michelle Engel Bencsko, **528**

USA, Wound Up, not known, **532**

USA, Vases, Hella Jongerius for Maharam, **534**

USA, Bottle and Jar Bouquets, Emily Isabella, **535**

USA, Penny Candy, Ben Rose, **535**

USA, Magic Pearls, William Ward Beecher, **537**

USA, Fan Fantasy, Schier and Doggett, **540**

USA, Textile design, Tommi Parzinger, **541**

USA, Pocket Change, Jack Denst, **542**

USA, Library, Rob Bancroft, **544**

USA, Open Sesame, Anton Refregier, **545**

USA, Golf Magic, Brian Connelly, **550**

USA, Stadium, René Clarke, **550**

USA, Play Ball Two, Joe Martin, **551**

USA, Treasure Trove, William Ward Beecher, **553**

USA, Kites and Mites, Paul McCobb, **557**

USA, Morn's Rays, Michelle Engel Bencsko, **558**

USA, Solar, Elenhank, **561**

USA, The Fool, Marijke Koger, **562**

USA, Big Sky, Elenhank, **563**

USA, April, Clayton Knight, **563**

USA, Textile, Educational Alliance, **564**

USA, Textile design, Tommi Parzinger, **564**

USA, Wallpaper, not known, **565**

USA, Snowflakes, Charlotte Sternberg, **565**

USA, Crystals, Janice Hart White, **565**

USA, Dress fabric, Helen Wills Moody, **567**

USA, Evenstar, Wendy Klein, **567**

USA, Alphabet Stripe, Alexander Girard, **570**

USA, Pause, 2x4, **570**

USA, Names, Alexander Girard, **570**

USA, Alpha Omega, Joe Martin, **571**

USA, Ceiling paper, not known, **577**

USA, Wallpaper, **577**

USA, Speckled, Holly DeGroot, **585**

USA, Hand made tie-dyed cotton fabric, **594**

USA, Fishnet, Ben Rose, **609**

USA, Ripple, Anna Graham, **610**

USA, The Dance, Hans Moller, **612**

USA, Bird IN-A Box, Angelo Testa, **612**

USA, US Army desert camouflage, **615**

USA, Round Tower, Larsen Design Studio, **616**

USA, Cotton fabric, **617**

USA, Bojangles, Larsen Design Studio, **619**

USA, Get Lost, Jessica Jones, **622**

USA, Arches, Rob Bancroft, **629**

USA, Earthforms, Ben Rose, **640**

USA, Time Capsule, Ben Rose, **647**

USA, Aurora, Larsen Design Studio, **648**

USA, Borealis, Elenhank, **649**

USA/France, Wallpaper, not known, **139**

USA/Native American, Sarape, American, **359**

USA/Native American, Sarape, Navajo Wearing Blanket, **359**

USA/Netherlands, Inlay, Hella Jongerius for Maharam, **428**

Oceania

Australia, Folded Geometric, Marni Stuart, **334**

Australia, Orange Orchard, Marni Stuart, **334**

Bali, Plangi tie-dye silk fabric, **596**

Bali, Plangi tie-dye silk fabric, **597**

Fiji, Bark cloth, **457**

Polynesia, (Niue), Hiapo, **456**

Polynesia, Hiapo, or Tapa cloth, **457**

Samoa, Bark cloth, **456**

Samoa, Bark cloth, **457**

Picture Credits

Cooper-Hewitt, Smithsonian Design Museum/Scala, Florence **139** **3** © Victoria & Albert Museum, London **4** © Met Museum/Mary Evans Picture Library **5** © 2018 Cooper-Hewitt, Smithsonian Design Museum/Scala, Florence **140** **1**© Victoria & Albert Museum, London **2** © Victoria & Albert Museum, London **3** © Cole & Son **4** © Victoria & Albert Museum, London **141** **5** © Victoria & Albert Museum, London **6** © Victoria & Albert Museum, London **142** **7** © Medici/Mary Evans Picture Library **8** © Victoria & Albert Museum, London **9** © 2018 Cooper-Hewitt, Smithsonian Design Museum/Scala, Florence **143** **10** © Mini Moderns **144** **1** © Imogen Heath **2** © Victoria & Albert Museum, London **145** **3** © Designers Guild **4** © Maharam/ Hella Jongerius **5** ©2018 Girard Studio, LLC. All rights reserved. Alexander Girard™ **6** © 2018 Bridgeman Images **146** **7** © Christopher Farr Cloth (© ADAGP, Paris and DACS, London 2018)/Bianchini-Férier**8** © Mary Evans Picture Library/Retrograph Collection **9** © Victoria & Albert Museum, London **147** **10** © Designers Guild **11** ©2018 Girard Studio, LLC. All rights reserved. Alexander Girard™**12** © Cole & Son **148** **1** © Getty Images **2** © Alamy (© ADAGP, Paris and DACS, London 2018)/Bianchini-Férier **149** **3** © Victoria & Albert Museum, London (© ADAGP, Paris and DACS, London 2018)/Bianchini-Férier **150** **13** © Victoria & Albert Museum, London **14** © Victoria & Albert Museum, London (© ADAGP, Paris and DACS, London 2018)/Bianchini-Férier **15** © Victoria & Albert Museum, London **16** © Victoria & Albert Museum, London **151** **17** © Victoria & Albert Museum, London **18** © Designers Guild **152** **1** © Alamy **2** © Alamy 153 © Victoria & Albert Museum, London **154** **19** © Osborne & Little **20** © Victoria & Albert Museum, London **21** © 2018 Cooper-Hewitt, Smithsonian Design Museum/Scala, Florence **155** **22** Sam Pickard **156** **23** © Victoria & Albert Museum, London **157** **24** © Neisha Crosland **25** © Orla Kiely **26** © 2018 Bridgeman Images **27** © Jocelyn Warner **158** **1** © Mary Evans Picture Library/SZ Photo/Scherl **2** © 2018 Bridgeman Images (© DACS 2018) 159 © 2018 Bridgeman Images (© DACS 2018) **160** **28** © Osborne & Little **29** © Christopher Farr Cloth **30** © Designers Guild **161** **31** © Designers Guild **32** © Victoria & Albert Museum, London **33** © Sam Pickard 2018 **162** **34** © Neisha Crosland **35** © Nuno **36** © Nuno **163** **37** © Osborne & Little **38** © Osborne & Little **39** © Metropolitan Museum of Art **164** **1** © Victoria & Albert Museum, London **2** © Victoria & Albert Museum, London **3** © Victoria & Albert Museum, London **165** **4** © Victoria & Albert Museum, London **166** **1** © 2018 Cooper-Hewitt, Smithsonian Design Museum/Scala, Florence **2** © 2018 Marimekko **3** © 2018 Cooper-Hewitt, Smithsonian Design Museum/Scala, Florence **167** **4** © Victoria & Albert Museum, London **5** design © Vlisco B.V., www.vlisco.com **168** **1** © Cole & Son **169** **2** © Victoria & Albert Museum, London **3** © Metropolitan Museum of Art **4** © Mary Evans Picture Library/The National Archives, London. England. **5** © Victoria & Albert Museum, London **170** **1** © Victoria & Albert Museum, London **2** © Victoria & Albert Museum, London **3** © Victoria & Albert Museum, London **4** © Victoria & Albert Museum, London **171** **5** © Designers Guild **172** **1** © Timorous Beasties **2** Image ©Victoria & Albert Museum, Design © The Robin and Lucienne Day Foundation **173** **3** © Osborne & Little/ Nina Campbell **4** © 2018 Marimekko **5** © 2018 Cooper-Hewitt, Smithsonian Design Museum/ Scala, Florence **6** © 2018 Cooper-Hewitt, Smithsonian Design Museum/Scala, Florence **174** **7** © 2018 Marimekko **8** © 2018 Bridgeman Images (© DACS 2018) **9** © Osborne & Little **175** **10** © 2018 Cooper-Hewitt, Smithsonian Design Museum/Scala, Florence **11** © Victoria & Albert Museum, London **176** **1** © Victoria & Albert Museum, London**2** © Victoria & Albert Museum, London **3** © Victoria & Albert Museum, London **177** **4** © Simon Lewin/St Jude's **5** © Victoria & Albert Museum, London **6** © Timorous Beasties **178** **1** © Neisha Crosland **2** © Victoria & Albert Museum, London **3** © Eley Kishimoto **179** **4** ©Ljungbergs Textile (© Stig Lindberg/DACS 2018) **5** ©Ljungbergs Textile **6** © Victoria & Albert Museum, London/© Estate of Pat Albeck/Matthew Rice **180** **7** © Victoria & Albert Museum, London **8** © Cath Kidston **9** © 2018 Cooper-Hewitt, Smithsonian Design Museum/Scala, Florence **10** © Victoria & Albert Museum, London **181** **11** © Victoria & Albert Museum, London **182** **12** © Designers Guild **13** ©Ljungbergs Textile (© Stig Lindberg/DACS 2018) **14** © Victoria & Albert Museum, London **183** **15** design © Sarah Battle, First Eleven Studio. Image thanks to Rebecca Hoyes **16** © Osborne & Little **184** **1** design © Vlisco B.V. www.vlisco.com **2** © Nuno **3** © 2018 Cooper-Hewitt, Smithsonian Design Museum/Scala, Florence **185** **4** design © Cole & Son **5** © 2018 Cooper-Hewitt, Smithsonian Design Museum/ Scala, Florence **6** © Victoria & Albert Museum, London **186** **1** ©Studio Job **2** © 2018 Marimekko **187** **3** © 2018 Cooper-Hewitt, Smithsonian Design Museum/Scala, Florence **188** **1** © Claire de Quénetain **2** © Svenskt Tenn **3** © Neisha Crosland **189** **4** © Victoria & Albert Museum, London **5** © Timorous Beasties **6** © Jocelyn Warner **190** **1** © Neisha Crosland **2** © Neisha Crosland 191 © Neisha Crosland **192** **7** © Cole & Son **193** **8** © Victoria & Albert Museum, London **9** © Victoria & Albert Museum, London **10** © 2018 Marimekko **194** **11** © StudioTord Boontje(STB) **12** © Mini Moderns **13** © 2018 Cooper-Hewitt, Smithsonian Design Museum/Scala, Florence **195** **14** © Timorous Beasties **196** **1** © Alamy **2** © StudioTord Boontje(STB) 197 © StudioTord Boontje(STB) **198** **1** © Sam Pickard 2018 **199** **2** © Cole & Son **3** © 2018 Cooper-Hewitt, Smithsonian Design Museum/Scala, Florence **4** © Jocelyn Warner **200** **1** © Getty Images **2** © Designers Guild 201 © Designers Guild **202** **1** © 2018 Marimekko **2** © Jocelyn Warner **3** © Victoria & Albert Museum, London **4** © Nuno **203** **5** © Orla Kiely **204** **6** © 2018 Cooper-Hewitt, Smithsonian Design Museum/ Scala, Florence **7** © Victoria & Albert Museum, London **8** © Timorous Beasties **205** **9** © 2018 Marimekko **10** ©Ljungbergs Textile **11** © Sam Pickard 2018 206 Josef Frank © Svenskt Tenn **208** **1** © Eley Kishimoto **209** **2** © Cath Kidston **3** © Victoria & Albert Museum, London **4** © Mary Evans Picture Library **5** © 2018 Cooper-Hewitt, Smithsonian Design Museum/Scala, Florence **6** Tony Trickey/First Eleven Studio **210** **1** © Cath Kidston **2** © Cath Kidston **211** © Cath Kidston **212** **1** © 2018 Bridgeman Images **2** ©Aki Ueda **3** GM Syntex/First Eleven Studio **213** **4** © Eley Kishimoto **214** **1** © Victoria & Albert Museum, London **2** © Eley Kishimoto **3** © 2018 Cooper-Hewitt, Smithsonian Design Museum/Scala, Florence **215** **4** © Victoria & Albert Museum, London **5** © Victoria & Albert Museum, London **6** design © Vlisco B.V., www.vlisco.com **216** **1** © 2018 Cooper-Hewitt, Smithsonian Design Museum/Scala, Florence **217** **2** © Victoria & Albert Museum, London **3** © 2018 Cooper-Hewitt, Smithsonian Design Museum/Scala, Florence **4** © Victoria & Albert Museum, London **5** © Victoria & Albert Museum, London **218** **1** © Tony Trickey/First Eleven Studio **219** **2** © 2018 Cooper-Hewitt, Smithsonian Design Museum/Scala, Florence **3** © Mary Evans Picture Library/John Maclellan **4** © Victoria & Albert Museum, London **5** © Victoria & Albert Museum, London. Reproduced by permission of Diana Armfield **6** © Metropolitan Museum of Art **220** **1** © Victoria & Albert Museum, London **2** © Svenskt Tenn **221** **3** design © Cole & Son with Ardmore Ceramic Art **222** **1** design © Cole & Son with Ardmore Ceramic Art **2** © Varpu Kronholm **3** © Osborne & Little/ Matthew Williamson **223** **4** © 2018 Bridgeman Images **224** **1** © Victoria & Albert Museum, London **225** **2** ©Aki Ueda Castellani **3** © 2018 Cooper-Hewitt, Smithsonian Design Museum/Scala, Florence **4** © 2018 Cooper-Hewitt, Smithsonian Design Museum/Scala, Florence **226** **1** © Victoria & Albert Museum, London **2** © Victoria & Albert Museum, London **3** © Simon Lewin/St Jude's **227** **4** © Victoria & Albert Museum, London **228** **1** © Getty Images **2** © Victoria & Albert Museum, London 229 © Victoria & Albert Museum, London **230** **1** © 2018 Cooper-Hewitt, Smithsonian Design Museum/Scala, Florence **2** © 2018 Bridgeman Images **3** © 2018 Bridgeman Images **231** **4** © 2018 Bridgeman Images **5** © 2018 Bridgeman Images **232** **1** © Metropolitan Museum of Art **2** © Metropolitan Museum of Art 233 © Metropolitan Museum of Art **234** **1** © Mary Evans Picture Library/TAH Collection **2** © Victoria & Albert Museum, London **3** © 2018 Cooper-Hewitt, Smithsonian Design Museum/Scala, Florence **235** **4** © 2018 Cooper-Hewitt, Smithsonian Design Museum/Scala, Florence **5** © 2018 Bridgeman Images (© ADAGP, Paris and DACS, London 2018) **236** **6** Parrot with Pineapple, 2015 (digital illustration) © Honda, Yoko/Private Collection/Bridgeman Images **7** © Tony Trickey/First Eleven Studio **8** © Victoria & Albert Museum, London **237** **9** © Osborne & Little **238** **1** © Getty Images **2** © Svenskt Tenn 239 © Svenskt Tenn **240** **1** © Sarah Battle, First Eleven Studio **241** **2** design © Vlisco B.V., www.vlisco.com **3** © Victoria & Albert Museum, London **4** © Victoria & Albert Museum, London **242** **1** © 2018 Cooper-Hewitt, Smithsonian Design Museum/Scala, Florence **2** © Victoria & Albert Museum, London **3** © Victoria & Albert Museum, London **243** **4** © 2018 Cooper-Hewitt, Smithsonian Design Museum/Scala, Florence **5** © Cole & Son **244** **6** © 2018 Cooper-Hewitt, Smithsonian Design Museum/Scala, Florence **7** © Mary Evans Picture Library/TAH Collection **8** © 2018 Cooper-Hewitt, Smithsonian Design Museum/Scala, Florence **245** **9** © 2018 Cooper-Hewitt, Smithsonian Design Museum/Scala, Florence **246** **1** © Victoria & Albert Museum, London **247** **2** © Victoria & Albert Museum, London **3** © 2018 Cooper-Hewitt, Smithsonian Design Museum/ Scala, Florence **4** © Osborne & Little **248** **1** © Designers Guild **2** © Cole & Son with Ardmore Ceramic Art **3** ©2018 Girard Studio, LLC. All rights reserved. Alexander Girard™ **4** © 2018 Bridgeman Images **249** **5** © Imogen Heath **6** © 2018 Cooper-Hewitt, Smithsonian Design Museum/ Scala, Florence **7** © 2018 Cooper-Hewitt, Smithsonian Design Museum/Scala, Florence **8** © Mini Moderns **250** **1** © Victoria & Albert Museum, London **2** © Simon Lewin/St Jude's **3** © Victoria & Albert Museum, London **4** © Victoria & Albert Museum, London **251** **5** © Timorous Beasties **252** **1** low res images until agreed **253** **2** © Aki Ueda **3** M.C. Escher's 'Swan' © 2018 The M.C. Escher Company-The Netherlands. All rights reserved. www.mcescher.com **4** © Eley Kishimoto **254** **5** © Jenny Frean/First Eleven Studio **6** © Cath Kidston **7** © Mini Moderns **255** **9** © Osborne & Little **256** **10** © Mini Moderns **11** © Eley Kishimoto **12** © Victoria & Albert Museum, London **257** **13** © Victoria & Albert Museum, London **14** © 2018 Cooper-Hewitt, Smithsonian Design Museum/ Scala, Florence **258** **1** © Timorous Beasties **2** Amazon © Colley, Jacqueline/Private Collection/ Bridgeman Images **3** © Mary Evans Picture Library/The National Archives, London. England **4** Les Jardins Majorelle - Succulents © Colley, Jacqueline/Private Collection/Bridgeman Images **259** **5** Nicaragua © Colley, Jacqueline/Private Collection/Bridgeman Images **6** M.C. Escher's 'Lizard' © 2018 The M.C. Escher Company-The Netherlands. All rights reserved. www.mcescher.com **7** M.C. Escher's 'Lizard' © 2018 The M.C. Escher Company-The Netherlands. All rights reserved. www.mcescher.com **8** © 2018 Cooper-Hewitt, Smithsonian Design Museum/Scala, Florence 260 M. C. Escher M.C. Escher's 'Birdfish' © 2018 The M.C. Escher Company-The Netherlands. All rights reserved. www.mcescher.com 261 M.C. Escher's 'LizardFishBat' © 2018 The M.C. Escher Company-The Netherlands. All rights reserved. www.mcescher.com **262** **1** © Victoria & Albert Museum, London **2** Tropical Fish Stripe © Parker, Robyn/Private Collection/ Bridgeman Images **3** © 2018 Cooper-Hewitt, Smithsonian Design Museum/Scala, Florence **263** **4** © 2018 Bridgeman Images **5** © 2018 Cooper-Hewitt, Smithsonian Design Museum/Scala, Florence **264** **6** Silk Textile © 2018 The M.C. Escher Company-The Netherlands. All rights reserved. www.mcescher.com **7** © Victoria & Albert Museum, London **8** © Victoria & Albert Museum, London **265** **9** Cole & Son **10** © 2018 Cooper-Hewitt, Smithsonian Design Museum/Scala, Florence (© Succession Picasso/DACS, London 2018) **11** design © Vlisco B.V., www.vlisco.com **266** **1** © Bridgeman Images **2** Sea Bed Repeat Pattern © Colley, Jacqueline/Private Collection/Bridgeman Images **3** © Victoria & Albert Museum, London **267** **4** design © Vlisco B.V., www.vlisco.com **268** **1** © Victoria & Albert Museum, London (© ADAGP, Paris and DACS, London 2018)/Bianchini-Férier **2** © 2018 Cooper-Hewitt, Smithsonian Design Museum/Scala, Florence **3** design © Vlisco B.V., www.vlisco.com **269** **4** © 2018 Cooper-Hewitt, Smithsonian Design Museum/Scala, Florence **5** Coral and Shells 45.72allover textile-surface design, 2012, digital file © McSparran, Kimberly/ Private Collection/Bridgeman Images **6** © 2018 Cooper-Hewitt, Smithsonian Design Museum/ Scala, Florence **270** **1** M.C. Escher's 'Shells and Starfish' © 2018 The M.C. Escher Company-The Netherlands. All rights reserved. www.mcescher.com **2** © 1950, 2018 Eames Office LLC (eamesoffice.com) **271** **3** © 2018 Cooper-Hewitt, Smithsonian Design Museum/Scala, Florence **4** © Victoria & Albert Museum, London **5** © 2018 Cooper-Hewitt, Smithsonian Design Museum/ Scala, Florence **6** © Victoria & Albert Museum, London **272** **1** © Metropolitan Museum of Art/ Mary Evans Picture Library **2** © Timorous Beasties **3** © Bridgeman Images **273** **4** © Timorous Beasties **274** **1** Designers Guild **275** **2** © 2018 Bridgeman Images **3** © Victoria & Albert Museum, London **4** Papillon, 2008 (digital) © Hough, Sarah/Private Collection/Bridgeman Images **5** © 2018 Bridgeman Images **276** **6** © Svenskt Tenn **7** Butterflies, 2013, (screen print) © Dilnot, John/ Bridgeman Images **8** © Mini Moderns **9** © Victoria & Albert Museum, London **277** **10** © Timorous

© Osborne & Little 7 © Cloud9 545 8 Beauty Parlour © Drumlanrig, Sholto/Private Collection/Bridgeman Images 9 Keys, 2010, (mixed media) © Allen, A.Richard/Private Collection/Bridgeman Images 10 design © Vlisco B.V., www.vlisco.com 11 © 2018 Cooper-Hewitt, Smithsonian Design Museum/Scala, Florence 546 1 © 2018 Bridgeman Images 547 2 © 2018 Bridgeman Images 3 © 2018 Bridgeman Images 4 © 2018 Bridgeman Images 5 © 2018 Bridgeman Images 548 1 © Mini Moderns 549 2 © Victoria & Albert Museum, London 3 © 2018 Cooper-Hewitt, Smithsonian Design Museum/Scala, Florence 4 © Victoria & Albert Museum, London 5 © Designers Guild 550 1 © 2018 Cooper-Hewitt, Smithsonian Design Museum/Scala, Florence 2 © Victoria & Albert Museum, London 551 3 © 2018 Cooper-Hewitt, Smithsonian Design Museum/Scala, Florence 4 © 2018. Photo Scala, Florence 552 1 © Mini Moderns 2 © Victoria & Albert Museum, London 553 2 © 2018 Cooper-Hewitt, Smithsonian Design Museum/Scala, Florence 4 © Victoria & Albert Museum, London (© The Henry Moore Foundation. All Rights Reserved, DACS/www.henry-moore.org 2018)/Reproduced by permission of The Henry Moore Foundation 5 © Mini Moderns 554 1 © 2018 Bridgeman Images/Central Saint Martins College of Art & Design 2 © Victoria & Albert Museum, London 555 3 © 2018 Bridgeman Images (© Kukula McDonald/Copyright Agency. Licensed by DACS 2018) 4 © 2018 Cooper-Hewitt, Smithsonian Design Museum/Scala, Florence 5 © Mini Moderns 6 © Victoria & Albert Museum, London 556 7 © Victoria & Albert Museum, London 8 © Cath Kidston 557 9 © Victoria & Albert Museum, London (© FORM portfolios/Paul McCobb) 10 © Victoria & Albert Museum, London 11 © Victoria & Albert Museum, London 558 1 Sunset © Drumlanrig, Sholto/Private Collection/Bridgeman Images 2 © Neisha Crosland 3 Solar Flare, 2017, (mixed media) © Worsley, Catherine/Private Collection/Bridgeman Images 4 © Cloud9 559 5 Image Copyright Victoria & Albert Museum, Design Copyright The Robin and Lucienne Day Foundation. 560 6 Pyramid Sunrise © Drumlanrig, Sholto/Private Collection/Bridgeman Images 561 7 © Victoria & Albert Museum, London/© Estate of Frank Dobson 8 © 2018 Cooper-Hewitt, Smithsonian Design Museum/Scala, Florence 9 © 2018 Cooper-Hewitt, Smithsonian Design Museum/Scala, Florence 562 1 © Cath Kidston 2 © Victoria & Albert Museum, London/© Marijke Koger of The Fool; www.maryke.com 563 3 © 2018 Cooper-Hewitt, Smithsonian Design Museum/Scala, Florence 4 © Victoria & Albert Museum, London (© Clayton Knight Estate) 5 © Timorous Beasties 564 1 © 2018 Cooper-Hewitt, Smithsonian Design Museum/Scala, Florence 2 © 2018 Cooper-Hewitt, Smithsonian Design Museum/Scala, Florence 3 © 2018 Bridgeman Images 565 4 © 2018 Cooper-Hewitt, Smithsonian Design Museum/Scala, Florence 5 © 2018 Cooper-Hewitt, Smithsonian Design Museum/Scala, Florence 6 © 2018 Cooper-Hewitt, Smithsonian Design Museum/Scala, Florence 566 1 © Eley Kishimoto 2 © 2018 Cooper-Hewitt, Smithsonian Design Museum/Scala, Florence 3 © 2018 Bridgeman Images 567 4 ©Ptolemy Mann 5 © Victoria & Albert Museum, London 6 © Victoria & Albert Museum, London/© Estate of Enid Marx/Dr E Breuning 7 © 2018 Cooper-Hewitt, Smithsonian Design Museum/Scala, Florence 568 1 © Eley Kishimoto 2 © 2018 Cooper-Hewitt, Smithsonian Design Museum/Scala, Florence 569 3 © Victoria & Albert Museum, London. Reproduced by permission of Natalie Gibson 4 design © Vlisco B.V., www.vlisco.com 570 1 ©2018 Girard Studio, LLC. All rights reserved. Alexander Girard™2 © Mini Moderns 3 ©2018 Girard Studio, LLC. All rights reserved. Alexander Girard™ 4 ©2018 Girard Studio, LLC. All rights reserved. Alexander Girard™ 571 5 © Maharam/Gunnar Aagaard Andersen 6 © 2018 Cooper-Hewitt, Smithsonian Design Museum/Scala, Florence 7 © Jocelyn Warner 572 Alexander Girard © Getty Images 573 ©2018 Girard Studio, LLC. All rights reserved. Alexander Girard™ 574 1 © Getty Images 2 © Alamy 3 © Alamy 575 4 © Alamy 576 1 © 2018 Cooper-Hewitt, Smithsonian Design Museum/Scala, Florence 2 © 2018 Cooper-Hewitt, Smithsonian Design Museum/Scala, Florence 3 © 2018 Cooper-Hewitt, Smithsonian Design Museum/Scala, Florence 577 4 © 2018 Cooper-Hewitt, Smithsonian Design Museum/Scala, Florence 5 © 2018 Cooper-Hewitt, Smithsonian Design Museum/Scala, Florence 6 © 2018 Cooper-Hewitt, Smithsonian Design Museum/Scala, Florence 7 © Victoria & Albert Museum, London 578 © The Robin and Lucienne Day Foundation 580 1 © Christopher Farr Cloth 2 © Designers Guild 581 3 © Christopher Farr Cloth 4 © Cole & Son 582 1 © 2018 Bridgeman Images/VG Bild-Kunst Bonn (© DACS 2018) 2 © 2018 Bridgeman Images/VG Bild-Kunst Bonn (© DACS 2018) 583 © 2018 Bridgeman Images 584 5 © Timorous Beasties 585 6 © Victoria & Albert Museum, London 7 © Rebecca Hoyes, First Eleven Studio 8 © Holly DeGroot, Cloud9 9 Jenny Frean, First Eleven Studio for Sandersons 586 10 Watermarks, 2016 (watercolor), ©Worsley, Catherine/Private Collection/Bridgeman Images 11 © Victoria & Albert Museum, London 12 Orange Orchard, 2017, (digital print) ©Stuart, Marni/Private Collection/Bridgeman Images 13 Paint Blobs, 2017, (digital print) © Stuart, Marni/Private Collection/Bridgeman Images 587 14 Sea Glass, 2016 (mixed media) © Worsley, Catherine/Private Collection/Bridgeman Images 15 © Victoria & Albert Museum, London 588 1 © Alamy 2 © 2018 Bridgeman Images/© Estate of Vanessa Bell, courtesy Henrietta Garnett 589 © Victoria & Albert Museum, London/© Estate of Vanessa Bell, courtesy Henrietta Garnett 590 1 © 2018 Bridgeman Images 2 © 2018 Bridgeman Images 591 3 © 2018 Bridgeman Images 4 © 2018 Bridgeman Images 5 © 2018 Bridgeman Images 6 © 2018 Bridgeman Images 592 1 © Alamy 2 © Emma Jeffs/ N&N Wares 593 3 © 2018 Bridgeman Images 594 1 © Alamy 2 © Alamy 3 © Alamy 595 4 © Alamy 5 © Alamy 6 ©

Victoria & Albert Museum, London and Trustees of the Crafts Study Centre, University for the Creative Arts/© Susan Bosence Estate/Professor Daniel Bosence 596 1 © Alamy 2 © Alamy 597 3 © Alamy 598 1 Image Copyright Victoria & Albert Museum, Design Copyright The Robin and Lucienne Day Foundation. 599 2 © Victoria & Albert Museum, London 3 © Simon Lewin/St. Jude's 600 4 © 2018 Bridgeman Images 5 © Alice Stevenson/St Jude's 6 Image ©Victoria & Albert Museum, Design © The Robin and Lucienne Day Foundation. 601 7 © Victoria & Albert Museum, London 602 1 © Alamy 2 Image ©Victoria & Albert Museum, Design ©The Robin and Lucienne Day Foundation. 603 Image ©Victoria & Albert Museum, Design © The Robin and Lucienne Day Foundation 604 1 © 2018 Cooper-Hewitt, Smithsonian Design Museum/Scala, Florence (© ADAGP, Paris and DACS, London 2018) 2 © 2018 Cooper-Hewitt, Smithsonian Design Museum/Scala, Florence 605 3 © 2018 Cooper-Hewitt, Smithsonian Design Museum/Scala, Florence 4 © 2018 Cooper-Hewitt, Smithsonian Design Museum/Scala, Florence 606 1 Memphis Pattern, 2015 (digital illustration) © Honda, Yoko/Private Collection/Bridgeman Images 2 © Victoria & Albert Museum, London (© ADAGP, Paris and DACS, London 2018) 607 © 2018 Bridgeman Images 608 1 © Victoria & Albert Museum, London 2 © Orla Kiely 3 © Nuno 609 4 © Robin and Lucienne Day Foundation 5 © Cole & Son 6 © 2018 Cooper-Hewitt, Smithsonian Design Museum/Scala, Florence 7 © Victoria & Albert Museum, London 610 8 © Jocelyn Warner 9 Anna Graham/Cloud9 10 © Victoria & Albert Museum, London 611 11 © 2018 Marimekko 612 1 © Victoria & Albert Museum, London (© The Henry Moore Foundation. All Rights Reserved, DACS/www.henry-moore.org 2018)/Reproduced by permission of The Henry Moore Foundation 2 © 2018 Cooper-Hewitt, Smithsonian Design Museum/Scala, Florence 3 © 2018 Cooper-Hewitt, Smithsonian Design Museum/Scala, Florence 4 © Victoria & Albert Museum, London 613 5 © StudioTord Boontje(STB) 6 © 2018 Marimekko 614 1 © 2018 Bridgeman Images 2 © 2018 Bridgeman Images 615 4 © 2018 Bridgeman Images 5 © 2018 Bridgeman Images 6 © 2018 Bridgeman Images 7 © 2018 Bridgeman Images 616 1 © 2018 Cooper-Hewitt, Smithsonian Design Museum/Scala, Florence 2 © 2018 Cooper-Hewitt, Smithsonian Design Museum/Scala, Florence 617 3 © Timorous Beasties 4 © 2018 Cooper-Hewitt, Smithsonian Design Museum/Scala, Florence 618 5 © Victoria & Albert Museum, London 6 © Victoria & Albert Museum, London 7 © Cole & Son 619 8 © 2018 Cooper-Hewitt, Smithsonian Design Museum/Scala, Florence 620 1 © Rex images 2 © Victoria & Albert Museum, London. Reproduced by permission of Shirley Craven 621 © Victoria & Albert Museum, London. Reproduced by permission of Shirley Craven 622 1 © Mary Evans Picture Library/Retrograph Collection 2 ©Jessica Jones/Cloud9 3 © Victoria & Albert Museum, London. Reproduced by permission of Shirley Craven 4 Textile Design, 1973 (gouache on paper) © Shirokova, Nina (b.1934)/Gamborg Collection/Bridgeman Images 623 5 © Victoria & Albert Museum, London/© Estate of Vanessa Bell, courtesy Henrietta Garnett 624 6 © Victoria & Albert Museum, London 7 © Victoria & Albert Museum, London 8 © Victoria & Albert Museum, London 9 © Victoria & Albert Museum, London 625 10 © 2018 Bridgeman Images/© Estate of Vanessa Bell, courtesy Henrietta Garnett 11 © 2018 Cooper-Hewitt, Smithsonian Design Museum/Scala, Florence 12 © Victoria & Albert Museum, London 13 © Victoria & Albert Museum, London 626 1 © AKG Images 2 © Victoria & Albert Museum, London (© DACS 2018) 627 © Victoria & Albert Museum, London (© DACS 2018) 628 14 © Victoria & Albert Museum, London 15 © 2018 Bridgeman Images 16 © 2018 Bridgeman Images 629 17 © Victoria & Albert Museum, London 630 1 © Brighton Design Archives 2 © Victoria & Albert Museum, London 631 © Victoria & Albert Museum, London 632 1 © 2018 Cooper-Hewitt, Smithsonian Design Museum/Scala, Florence 2 design © Vlisco B.V., www.vlisco.com 633 3 © Victoria & Albert Museum, London 4 © Victoria & Albert Museum, London (© ADAGP, Paris and DACS, London 2018) 5 © 2018 Cooper-Hewitt, Smithsonian Design Museum/Scala, Florence 634 6 © Mini Moderns 7 © Cole & Son 8 © Ptolemy Mann 635 9 © Emma Jeffs, N&N Wares 10 © Victoria & Albert Museum, London 11 design © Vlisco B.V., www.vlisco.com 636 12 © Victoria & Albert Museum, London 637 13 © Eley Kishimoto 14 © Neisha Crosland 15 © Osborne & Little 16 © Neisha Crosland 638 1 © Brighton Design Archives 2 © Victoria & Albert Museum, London 639 © Victoria & Albert Museum, London 640 1 © Osborne & Little 2 © 2018 Cooper-Hewitt, Smithsonian Design Museum/Scala, Florence 3 © 2018 Bridgeman Images 4 © Cole & Son 642 1 © 2018 Bridgeman Images 2 © 2018 Bridgeman Images 643 © 2018 Bridgeman Images (© Stig Lindberg/DACS 2018) 644 5 © 2018 Bridgeman Images 6 Image ©Victoria & Albert Museum, Design © The Robin and Lucienne Day Foundation. 7 © Designers Guild 646 1 © Victoria & Albert Museum, London 2 © Victoria & Albert Museum, London 3 Personal collection of Rebecca Hoyes 4 © Victoria & Albert Museum, London 647 5 © 2018 Cooper-Hewitt, Smithsonian Design Museum/Scala, Florence 6 © Osborne & Little 7 © Eley Kishimoto 8 © Victoria & Albert Museum, London 648 1 © Neisha Crosland 2 © 2018 Cooper-Hewitt, Smithsonian Design Museum/Scala, Florence 3 © Neisha Crosland 649 4 © 2018 Cooper-Hewitt, Smithsonian Design Museum/Scala, Florence

Every effort has been made to trace copyright owners but if any have been overlooked or wrongly credited, the publishers will make the necessary arrangements at the first opportunity.

Acknowledgments

Rebecca Hoyes generously provided images of her private collection of vintage fabrics.

The Publishers would like to thank the following for their commitment to this book:
Claire Brooker and Sarah Smithies
The Robin and Lucienne Day Foundation

Olivia Stroud at the Victoria & Albert Museum, London
Jack Weaver at Cath Kidston Limited
Nina Luminati at Christopher Farr Cloth
Karen Cheung at Studio Tord Boontje
Gabriela Sanchez y Sanchez de la Barquera and Anke Joosten at Vlisco